What If There Were
No Significance Tests?

MULTIVARIATE APPLICATIONS BOOK SERIES

The Multivariate Applications book series was developed to encourage the use of rigorous methodology in the study of meaningful scientific issues, and to describe the applications in easy to understand language. The series is sponsored by the Society of Multivariate Experimental Psychology and welcomes methodological applications from a variety of disciplines, such as psychology, public health, sociology, education, and business. Books can be single authored, multiple authored, or edited volumes. The ideal book for this series would take on one of several approaches: (1) demonstrate the application of a variety of multivariate methods to a single, major area of research; (2) describe a methodological procedure or framework that could be applied to a variety of research areas; or (3) present a variety of perspectives on a controversial topic of interest to applied researchers. The premiere volume in the series uses the latter format in a book titled: "What if there were no significance tests?" The edited volume includes an initial overview chapter and 13 contributed chapters from well-known methodologists and applied researchers. Various viewpoints and suggestions are presented to help researchers assess the importance of their findings.

Interested persons should contact the editor, Lisa Harlow, at the following address:

Professor Lisa Harlow
Department of Psychology
University of Rhode Island
10 Chafee Rd.
Suite 8
Kingston, RI, U.S.A. 02881-0808

Phone: 401-874-4242
FAX: 401-874-5562
E- Mail: LHarlow@uriacc.uri.edu

Information can also be obtained from one of the advisory board members: Leona Aiken (Arizona State University), Gwyneth Boodoo (Educational Testing Service), Susan Embretson (University of Kansas), Michael Neale (Virginia Commonwealth University), Bill Revelle (Northwestern University), and Steve West (Arizona State University).

What If There Were No Significance Tests?

Edited by

Lisa L. Harlow
University of Rhode Island

Stanley A. Mulaik
Georgia Institute of Technology

James H. Steiger
University of British Columbia

LAWRENCE ERLBAUM ASSOCIATES, PUBLISHERS
1997   Mahwah, New Jersey   London

Lawrence Erlbaum Associates, Inc., Publishers
10 Industrial Avenue
Mahwah, New Jersey 07430

Library of Congress Cataloging-in-Publication Data

What if there were no significance tests? / edited by Lisa L. Harlow,
Stanley A. Mulaik, and James H. Steiger.
 p. cm. -- (Multivariate applications)
 Includes bibliographical references and index.
 ISBN 0-8058-2634-3 (alk. paper)
 1. Statistical hypothesis testing. I. Harlow, Lisa Lavoie, 1951-
. II. Mulaik, Stanley A., 1935- . III. Steiger, James H. IV. Series.
QA277.W48 1997
519.5'6--dc21   97-20339

•

Books published by Lawrence Erlbaum Associates are printed
on acid-free paper, and their bindings are chosen
for strength and durability.

Printed in the United States of America

10 9 8 7 6 5 4 3 2

In Memory of:

Maurice M. Tatsuoka

Contents

Overview

The Debate: Against and For Significance Testing

Suggested Alternatives to Significance Testing

A Bayesian Perspective on Hypothesis Testing

Philosophy of Science Issues

Contributors

Robert P. Abelson, Yale University
Jacob Cohen, New York University
Rachel T. Fouladi, University of Texas at Austin
Harry F. Gollob, University of Denver
Lisa L. Harlow, University of Rhode Island
Richard J. Harris, University of New Mexico
Richard A. Harshman, University of Western Ontario
John E. Hunter, Michigan State University
Roderick P. McDonald, University of Illinois at Urbana-Champaign
Paul E. Meehl, University of Minnesota
Stanley A. Mulaik, Georgia Institute of Technology
Robert M. Pruzek, State University of New York at Albany
Nambury S. Raju, Illinois Institute of Technology
Charles S. Reichardt, University of Denver
David M. Rindskopf, City University of New York
Joseph S. Rossi, University of Rhode Island
William W. Rozeboom, University of Alberta, Canada
Frank L. Schmidt, University of Iowa
James H. Steiger, University of British Columbia, Canada

Reviewers

Robert Abelson, Yale University
Leona Aiken, Arizona State University
Michael Browne, The Ohio State University
Barbara Byrne, University of Ottawa
Norman Cliff, University of Southern California
Jose Cortina, Tulane University
Robert Cudeck ,University of Minnesota
Lin Ding, University of Rhode Island
David Faust, University of Rhode Island
Joseph Fava, University of Rhode Island
Harry Gollob, University of Denver
Nick Huggett, University of Illinois at Chicago
Keith Markus, City University of New York
Roderick McDonald, University of Illinois at Urbana-Champaign
Paul Meehl, University of Minnesota
William Meredith, University of California at Berkeley
Michael Neale, Virginia Commonwealth University
Robert Pruzek, State University of New York at Albany
Colleen Redding, University of Rhode Island
Charles Reichardt, University of Denver
William Revelle, Northwestern University
David Rindskopf, City University of New York
Jennifer Rose, Indiana University
Joseph Rossi, University of Rhode Island
James Steiger, University of British Columbia, Canada
Wayne Velicer, University of Rhode Island
Stephen West, Arizona State University
Leslie Yonce, University of Minnesota

Acknowledgments

We are very grateful to Robert Sternberg for planting the idea for this book series at the 1994 meeting of the Society of Multivariate Experimental Psychology (SMEP) in Princeton, New Jersey. Bob's suggestion was that we offer books that would describe how to apply rigorous multivariate methodology to meaningful research, and to do so in very understandable writing. Everyone present agreed that this was a worthwhile goal, and the series was launched.

For their encouragement and direction, thanks are extended to the SMEP board, particularly Norman Cliff, Linda Collins, Robert Cudeck, John Horn, and Abigail Panter. They all helped get the process rolling. The editorial board for the book series (Leona Aiken, Gwyneth Boodoo, Susan Embretson, Michael Neale, William Revelle, and Steve West) provided a wealth of enthusiasm and ideas. In particular, we thank Susan Embretson for suggesting the topic for this first book. Larry Erlbaum, Judi Amsel, and Art Lizza, all from LEA, deserve our hearty thanks for making the process as easy and enjoyable as possible.

Many hours of their time were generously offered by a number of reviewers (see above), as well as production assistants, Kimberly Mitchell and Robert Schnoll. Even more hours were painstakingly offered by each of our contributors (see above). To each of you, we cannot thank you enough.

Jim Steiger deserves special commendation for his expertise and endless hours assisting with preparing this volume in camera-ready format. His patience and willingness in readily sharing his technical acumen were above and beyond the call of duty. Andree Steiger provided valuable assistance, both in the typographic design of the book, and in editing and indexing the volume.

Appreciation is extended to Grant #MH47233 from the National Institute of Mental Health for partial funding and to the other major colleagues on this grant.

We'd also like to thank our families for their understanding and support during the writing and editing of this book.

Finally, we thank Maurice Tatsuoka, to whom this book is dedicated, for his inspiration and many contributions to the field of multivariate applications. For over forty years, he quietly and unassumingly shared his wisdom with all of us. We are deeply grateful.

Preface

This series[1] was developed to encourage the use of rigorous methodology in the study of meaningful scientific issues, and to describe the applications in easy to understand language. The first book in the series was initially conceived at the 1995 meeting of the Society of Multivariate Experimental Psychology after a presentation by Frank Schmidt. Frank's main thesis, extending the views of Jacob Cohen, was that significance testing should be banned. Richard Harris and Stan Mulaik quickly countered Frank's position in a series of electronic-mail messages that stimulated several months of spirited debate from many individuals, too countless to list. To all of us involved, it became increasingly clear that this topic deserved careful thought and consideration. Hence, this book was born.

The viewpoints span a range of perspectives, though the overriding theme that emerges is that significance testing may still be useful if supplemented with some or all of (alphabetically listed): Bayesian logic, caution, confidence intervals, effect sizes and power, other goodness of approximation measures, replication and meta-analysis, sound reasoning, and theory appraisal and corroboration.

The book is organized into five general areas. First, chapter 1 (by Harlow) presents an overview of significance testing issues, synthesizing the highlights of the remainder of the book.

Second, we present the debate in which significance testing is either rejected very eloquently by Cohen in chapter 2, in favor of the use of: effect sizes, confidence intervals, graphic methods, replication, meta-analysis, and correct thinking; and quite soundly by Schmidt and Hunter in chapter 3, who quite forcefully present counter-arguments to eight common objections to banning significance tests; or retained by Mulaik, Raju, and Harshman, if used correctly, in chapter 4 where they present history on this issue and a rebuttal to Schmidt & Hunter that clarifies 11 misconceptions surrounding significance testing; and by Abelson in a witty and utterly readable chapter 5 that hypothesizes that significance testing would be re-invented if it ever were banned.

Third, the next five chapters (6–10) outline some methods that could supplement current significance testing procedures. Suggestions include: advocating a more specific, three-option hypothesis testing approach (in chapter 6, by Harris); attending to upper bounds on effect sizes and power, as well as to confidence intervals and meta analysis (in chapter 7, in which Rossi very pointedly de-

---

[1] Information on this series can be obtained by contacting Lisa Harlow, preferably by: E-mail at: Lharlow@uriacc.uri.edu; or at: Department of Psychology, University of Rhode Island, 10 Chafee Rd., Suite 8, Kingston, RI 02881-0808, Phone: 401-874-4242; FAX: 401-874-5562.

scribes a case study showing the demise of a research area that doesn't attend to these guidelines); global measures of goodness of approximation to support, not substitute for, scientific judgment (in a beautifully stated chapter 8, by McDonald); innovative and technologically rigorous methodology for estimating noncentral confidence intervals (in a very clearly written chapter 9, by Steiger & Fouladi); and a well-articulated delineation of situations in which it is preferred to use confidence intervals versus significance tests (by Reichardt & Gollob, in chapter 10).

Fourth, chapters 11 and 12 discuss a Bayesian approach to hypothesis testing, with an excellent introduction and applications (by Pruzek in chapter 11); and exposition on how Bayesian methods can more directly assess probabilities of specific effects in any direction, than classical significance testing (in chapter 12, by Rindskopf).

Finally, we close with two chapters (13–14) that present philosophy of science perspectives. In chapter 13, Rozeboom persuasively argues for an abductive or explanatory inductive approach to scientific endeavors, as opposed to the long–standing convention of deducing truths based on the dichotomous outcome of unimaginative and vague hypothesis tests. In chapter 14, Meehl advocates strong tests on very specific, highly refutable theories, offering an index for assessing how closely our data corroborate such theories.

Rather than giving you definitive prescriptions, the chapters are largely suggestive of central issues, concerns, and application guidelines. We leave it up to you to decide on the best way to conduct hypothesis testing in your field. Hopefully, your reading of these presentations, as well as any discussions they generate, will help move science toward the development of a useful and rigorous set of methods for developing and testing strong theories that are corroborated in divergent disciplines. Only then can we have confidence that our findings will produce significant and meaningful effects, thereby promoting and furthering a replicable, accruing body of knowledge.

About The Authors

Robert P. Abelson is Emeritus Eugene Higgins Professor of Psychology at Yale University, where he was on the faculty for 42 years. He was a 1953 Ph.D. in Psychology at Princeton, and was much influenced by John Tukey. Professor Abelson is a Fellow of the American Statistical Association, and is presently co-chair of the Task Force on Statistical Inference of the American Psychological Association. In 1986, he received a Distinguished Contribution Award from the American Psychological Association. His most recent book is "Statistics as Principled Argument," published in 1995, distilling his long experience as a statistics teacher and consultant.

Jacob Cohen is a Professor of Psychology Emeritus at New York University. His research focuses on social science research methodology, particularly the study of multiple regression, statistical power, and effect sizes. His work, including numerous scholarly articles and books, is widely recognized for its clarity and wisdom.

Rachel T. Fouladi received her Ph.D. from the University of British Columbia in 1996, and is currently Assistant Professor of Educational Psychology at the University of Texas at Austin. Her interests include issues of pedagogy and use of elementary and multivariate statistical procedures, in particular covariance and correlation structure analysis techniques, under a variety of distributional conditions, assumption violations, and reduced sample sizes.

Harry F. Gollob died of a heart attack on November 28, 1996 at the age of 57. He was a Professor of Psychology at the University of Denver. His research focused on social judgment, dyadic interaction, employment discrimination, and statistical analysis. Harry was unassuming both in his personality and in his science. He was loved by students, colleagues, and staff for his endless patience and caring. His intellectual counsel was valued for its insightfulness, diligence, and creativity. His quiet but trusted leadership was empowered by his unfailing truthfulness and morality. It was highly rewarding to work with him. His death is a great loss.

Lisa L. Harlow obtained her Ph.D. in 1985 from UCLA. She is currently a Professor of Psychology at the University of Rhode Island, where she teaches courses in basic and multivariate statistics, structural equation modeling, and research facilitation. Her research focuses on women's health, psychosocial, and methodological issues. She is also editor of the Multivariate Application book series published by Lawrence Erlbaum Associates.

Richard J. Harris received his Ph.D. in 1968 from Stanford University. He is currently a Professor of Psychology at the University of New Mexico. He divides his teaching research between formal models of social phenomena and social psychological analyses of statistical practice, the latter including *A Primer of Multivariate Statistics* and *An Analysis of Variance Primer.*

Richard A. Harshman obtained a Ph.D. in 1976 in Psychology from UCLA and is now an Associate Professor of Psychology at the University of Western Ontario where he teaches graduate classes in factor analysis, multidimensional scaling, linear algebra, and basic statistics and does research on new data analysis models/methods for detecting patterns. The latter includes parallel factor analysis for three-way data, and decomposition into directional components for analysis of nonsymmetrical relationships.

John E. Hunter received his Ph.D. from the University of Illinois in 1964 and is a Professor of Psychology at Michigan State University. He has published numerous quantitative and methodological articles and has co-authored two books on meta-analysis. He has received the Distinguished Scientific Contributions Award (with Frank Schmidt) from both the American Psychological Association and the Society for Industrial/Organizational Psychology.

Roderick P. McDonald received his Ph.D. in 1965 from the University of New England, Australia, and is now a Professor of Psychology, University of Illinois at Urbana-Champaign. His research has mainly focused on structural models for multivariate data.

Paul E. Meehl obtained his Ph.D. in 1945 from the University of Minnesota, where he is now Regents' Professor of Psychology Emeritus. His research has been in learning, personality testing, psychometric theory, clinical and statistical prediction, interview assessment, theory of schizophrenia, and, currently, new taxometric procedures for classification and genetic analysis in psychopathology.

Stanley A. Mulaik, Professor of Psychology at the Georgia Institute of Technology, received his Ph.D. in 1963 from the University of Utah. He is known for a text on factor analysis and articles on confirmatory factor analysis, factor indeterminacy, structural equation modeling, and philosophy of causality. He teaches elementary and multivariate statistics, and personality theory, and does research in methodology and philosophy of science. He is the exiting editor of *Multivariate Behavioral Research* and a Fellow of the American Psychological Association.

Robert M. Pruzek obtained his Ph.D. from the University of Wisconsin in 1967 and is a professor at the University of Albany, State University of New York. He is jointly appointed in the Departments of Educational Psychology and Statistics, and Biometry and Statistics. His publications focus on methods for structural analysis and prediction for social and behavioral science applications. Recent work combined psychometric and statistical principles to construct a broad class of adaptive regression methods which hold promise for improving generalizability and interpretability where there are many variables of differential reliability, and when sample sizes may be limited.

Nambury S. Raju received his Ph.D. in 1974 from the Illinois Institute of Technology, where he is now a Professor of Psychology. He is known for his work in psychometric theory and industrial/organizational psychology, with emphasis on differential item functioning, validity generalization/meta–analysis, and utility analysis. He is a Fellow of the American Psychological Association.

Charles S. Reichardt received his Ph.D. in 1979 from Northwestern University, and is currently a Professor of Psychology at the University of Denver. His research focuses on research methodology and statistics in general, and the logic and practice of causal inference in particular.

David M. Rindskopf received his Ph.D. from Iowa State University in 1976, and is now a Professor of Educational Psychology and Psychology, City University of New York Graduate School and University Center. His principal research interests are latent variable models, categorical data analysis, quasi-experimental design, and missing data methods.

Joseph S. Rossi obtained his Ph.D. in 1984 from the University of Rhode Island where he is now a Professor and Director of Research at the Cancer Prevention Research Center. His areas of interest include research methodology and measurement, health promotion and disease prevention, the transtheoretical model of behavior change, and expert systems development.

William W. Rozeboom received his Ph.D. from the University of Chicago in 1956, and is a University of Alberta Professor Emeritus of Psychology. He was a founding co-editor of the *Canadian Journal of Philosophy*; and the most recurrent theme in his writings, which range widely on both sides of the increasingly porous border between psychology and philosophy, is practicing and proseletizing for the craft of concept engineering.

Frank L. Schmidt received his Ph.D. from Purdue University in 1970, and is now the Ralph L. Sheets Professor of Human Resources at the University of Iowa. He has published numerous articles on quantitative methodology and personnel selection and is co-author (with John Hunter) of a 1990 text on meta-analysis. He is a Fellow of the American Psychological Association and a member of the Editorial Board of the Journal of Applied Psychology.

James H. Steiger received his Ph.D. from Purdue University in 1976, and is a Professor of Psychology at the University of British Columbia. His primary research interests are in factor analysis, covariance structure analysis, correlational testing, and the design aspects of software for microcomputer data analysis. Winner of the Raymond B. Cattell Award and the Killam Research Prize for his work in multivariate statistics, Steiger is a former Editor of *Multivariate Behavioral Research*, and has authored a number of commercial and academic computer programs for multivariate analysis, including the SEPATH (Structural Equations and PATH modeling) module in *Statistica*.

Overview

Chapter 1

Significance Testing Introduction and Overview

Lisa L. Harlow
University of Rhode Island

This chapter presents a brief overview of the use of significance testing. Then, the main views and suggestions from the remaining chapters are outlined as eight recommendations for conducting scientific inference. The perspectives of each chapter on these recommendations are summarized in tabular form. Finally, the recommendations are ordered in terms of their degree of endorsement by the chapter contributors, as follows: (a) earnest encouragement to investigate strong theories with critical thinking and sound judgment, as well as to calculate confidence intervals, effect sizes, and power; (b) suggestions for using goodness of approximation measures, as well as specifying several realistic hypotheses; (c) endorsement of the use of replication, meta-analysis, and Bayesian methods; and (d) acknowledgment, though not strong approval, of using the traditional dichotomous decision rule of the null hypothesis significance test, especially when it poses zero effects for the null hypothesis, a situation in which most contributors agree is almost always false. Readers are encouraged to examine each of the chapters for greater detail on the suggested methods and then decide for themselves whether our conclusions are replicated by their analysis, or whether there is too much error, too little power, or very little goodness of approximation to this set of views, as opposed to those of other scientific researchers.

What if there were no significance testing? This was the question faced by early researchers at the turn of the 20th century, and it has revisited us several times over the years (see chapter 5 of this volume by Mulaik, Raju, & Harshman, as well as Cowles & Davis, 1982; Huberty, 1993; and Keren & Lewis, 1993, for more on the history of significance testing). As early as 1901, Karl Pearson laid the preliminary groundwork for assessing a scientific hypothesis with sample data. Later, Ronald Fisher (1925/1941) formally proposed a set of methods that, with formulation from Jerzy Neyman and Egon Pearson (1928) on power, Type I, and Type II errors, evolved into the practice of null hypothesis significance testing (NHST). NHST was intended to provide a procedure for deciding whether the probability of getting sample results as extreme or more so than the null hypothesized value was small enough that it was less likely that it could be attributed to mere chance. Then, through the replication of such findings, along with the practice of parameter estimation, recognizing the presence of sampling error (Fisher, 1925/1941), as well as the need to quantify the effect with a correlation ratio or *eta* (Fisher, 1925/1941; see also Kirk, 1996), greater trust could be placed on the practical significance (see Kirk, 1996, for an excellent delineation of statistical vs. practical significance) of the scientific hypothesis. NHST was intended to provide a method for ruling out chance, thus helping to build strong evidence in favor of one or more alternative hypotheses, rather than provide an indication of the proof or probability of these hypotheses (see chapters 11–12 by Pruzek and Rindskopf for discussion on how Bayesian methods can address these probabilities). Neyman and Pearson's work helped to fine tune the NHST method, recognizing the possibility of errors that could be made, depending on whether the null hypothesis was rejected or retained. They also introduced the concept of power, the probability of correctly rejecting the null hypothesis, foreseeing the need for quality control in the NHST procedure (see chapter 2, by Cohen, and chapter 7, by Rossi, for more discussion on the importance of attending to the power of our studies).

Thus, the concepts of NHST, replication, parameter estimation and sampling error (i.e., confidence intervals), effect size, power, and Type I and II errors have been with us for about 70 years, answering the question from early researchers as to how to test scientific hypotheses.

The practice of NHST, however, has not been without controversy. Beginning with Berkson (1938, 1942), scientists have periodically engaged in anything from suggestions on how to improve NHST (see chapters 2–10 in the current volume), to advocating a Bayesian approach (see chapters 11–12 in the current volume), to revolutionizing the way we think about scientific inference (see chapters 13 and 14, from Rozeboom and Meehl, respectively), to doing away with NHST all together (see chapters 2 and 3, from Cohen, and Schmidt & Hunter, respectively). (See also: Jones' [1955] criticism of NHST, Morrison & Henkel's [1970] edited volume on significance testing, Carver's [1978a, 1978b] strenuous opposition to NHST, and a recent 1993 volume of the *Journal of Experimental Education* devoted to NHST issues.) The main target of these lively interchanges is the practice of focusing (almost exclusively) on the probability values (*p* values) from NHST and incorrectly using them to make dichotomous decisions as to the truth of a null hypothesis (e.g., that a parameter equals zero in the population) that is almost certainly false, or an alternative hypothesis, the verisimilitude (in the words of Meehl, chapter 14) of which has not actually been evaluated. Tukey (1969) aptly denoted this as the narrow and moralistic practice of "sanctification," as opposed to the broader scientific "detective work" of building evidence, the latter being similar to endorsing the "cognitive evaluation of propositions" discussed by Rozeboom (1960, p. 428; and chapter 13, current volume). Thus, authors of journal articles that are plagued with space restrictions and the pressures of dichotomous publication decisions, have seemingly placed greater emphasis on the size of their p value(s) than the importance, magnitude, or precision of any scientific inferences that can be drawn from their findings.

In this chapter, the practice of scientific inference is examined in an effort to evaluate the merit of current use, and to suggest several approaches. Eight main practices of scientific inference emerge from the 13 remaining chapters. The incorrect practice of only attending to, or misinterpreting, a p value is not even considered here as a viable option, though it is purportedly engaged in quite often in the literature (e.g., see Meehl, 1967, 1978, & chapter 14 in this volume; see also Falk & Greenbaum, 1995; Rosenthal, 1990; Rosenthal & Gaito, 1963, 1964; Shaver, 1993). The chapter closes with a summary of the main conclusions that can be drawn concerning the eight recommendations. Then, it is up to the reader to become familiar with all of the details presented very convincingly by each of the chapter authors. We recognize that our views and suggestions are only a portion of the larger body of meta-thinking and analysis on this topic, currently underway in various disciplines. We leave it up to you to either replicate and validate our findings, or show us the errors in our thinking.

A summary of the practices that we are presenting on various ways to engage in scientific inference is given at the end of the chapter in Table 1.1.

EVALUATION OF EIGHT SUGGESTED PRACTICES
OF SCIENTIFIC INFERENCE

Assess Strong Theories With Careful Thinking and Sound Judgment

Most researchers recognize that any method of assessing theories or specific hypotheses cannot be exclusively mechanized and must involve an element of mindful judgment. In a critique of Fisher's work, Yates (1951) argued that "the emphasis given to formal tests of significance . . . resulted in what seems to me to be an undue concentration . . . on investigations of tests of significance applicable to problems which are of little or no practical importance" (p. 32). Bakan (1966) continued Yates' sentiment several years later, stating that "the argument is . . . that the test of significance has been carrying too much of the burden of scientific inference. Wise and ingenious investigators can find their way to reasonable conclusions from data because and in spite of their procedures" (p. 423); "when we reach a point where our statistical procedures are substitutes instead of aids to thought . . . then we must return to the common sense basis" (p. 436). Further, Tukey (1969) cited an anonymous letter writer as saying that we should "stimulate intelligent problem formulation, without being able to say quite how this is done. Demand high standards of statistical reasoning, but without specifying a single model of statistics which might serve as a criterion for quality of reasoning" (p. 90). These statements would be undisputed by philosophers of science, such as Rozeboom (1960) who argued that "As scientists, it is our professional obligation to reason from available data to explanations and generalities," (p. 420), and Meehl, who emphasizes "the methodological and epistemological questions as being more important than the purely 'statistical' ones that are conventionally stressed" (chapter 14 in this volume). Mathematical statisticians (e.g., McDonald, chapter 8) are also quick to concur to both the veracity and need for judicious reasoning, especially when sifting through a table of quantitative indices. Kirk (1996) highlighted the irony, stating that "it is a curious anomaly that researchers are trusted to make a variety of complex decisions in the design and execution of an experiment, but in the name of objectivity, they are not expected nor even encouraged to decide whether data are practically significant" (p. 755). Kirk further cautioned that "if practical significance is to be a useful concept, its determination must not be ritualized" (p. 756). Finally, Thompson (1996) captured the essence of this by stating simply that "too many researchers wish to employ the mathematical calculation of probabilities only as a purely atavistic escape . . . from the existential human responsibility for making value judgments . . .[however,] empirical science is inescapably a subjective business" (p. 28). Human insight and wisdom need to be incorporated into the scientific process. From the current set of chapters, there is universal support for the use of strong theories, critical thinking, and sound judgment.

All of the authors endorse this view. This can be seen from the following excerpts: Cohen (1994; reprinted in chapter 2) reminded us that "as researchers, we have a considerable array of statistical techniques that can help us find our way to theories of some depth, but they must be used sensibly and be heavily informed by informed judgment" (1994, p. 1002). Schmidt and Hunter state that "resignation and conformity [to significance testing] produces an intellectual cynicism that is corrosive of scientific values. It undermines the intellectual honesty and idealistic motivation to search for truth that are the driving engines of science" (chapter 3 of this volume). Abelson (chapter 5 of this volume) warns us "that automatic entry of all results into a meta-analytic record is impossible, [whereas] the alternative of selective, theory-guided entry of results requires human judgment, undercutting the ideal of a totally objective knowledge accretion system." McDonald epitomizes the main chapter perspectives on this, arguing that "I do not believe . . . that global indices of approximation can or should be used as the sole basis for a decision . . . The investigator should use judgment as to the acceptability of an approximating model . . . and should give the grounds of the judgment in any report of the work . . . Appropriate indices will help support judgment but will not substitute for it" (chapter 8 of this volume).

Evaluation. Chapter contributors unquestionably call for the use of strong theories, accompanied by critical thinking and sound judgment. This yields a convincing case for accompanying quantitative indices of statistical appropriateness with the sturdy foundation of clearly delineated and theoretically based hypotheses, along with the wisdom of conscious and judicious reasoning.

Focus on Estimation and the Width of an Appropriate Confidence Interval

Estimating the value of a parameter, and providing a band of confidence with upper and lower limits, is well practiced in the sciences (see chapter 3 by Schmidt & Hunter in this volume). An added benefit of computing confidence (or "credible," see chapter 12 by Rindskopf) intervals (CIs) is that it readily provides significance–testing information, along with a range of plausible population values for a parameter. If the null-hypothesized value of the parameter (often, zero) does not fall within the calculated CI, the null hypothesis can be rejected at the specified alpha level. Thus, CIs provide more information than the conventional NHST procedure posed earlier, and have been viewed with much more favor. A review of the current chapters highlights this positive appraisal of CIs, with: unanimous support of their use, particularly from: Schmidt and Hunter (chapter 3), who are strong advocates of such practice; Steiger and Fouladi (chapter 9), who develop and make available procedures for calculating computationally demanding noncentral confidence intervals; and Reichardt and Gollob (chapter 10) who very clearly delineate the situations in which confidence intervals are preferred to conventional significance tests. Similarly, Meehl (chapter 14) readily endorses the use of CIs, particularly for what he calls "theory appraisal."

Evaluation. Chapter contributors decidedly agree with this, presenting a persuasive case for widespread use of confidence interval estimation in our research. Interested readers can turn to chapters 9 and 10 (by Steiger & Fouladi, and Reichardt & Gollob, respectively) in the current volume, for clear guidelines on how and when to use confidence intervals.

Effect Sizes and Power Should Be Calculated

Effect sizes include the magnitude of difference between hypothesized and sample values (e.g., of means, proportions, etc.), as well as squared measures of the strength of association (e.g., r^2, η^2, ω^2 , etc.: see Kirk, 1996, for an excellent

summary of commonly used effect size measures). Power, most notably discussed by Cohen (1962, 1988), Rossi (1990), and Sedlmeier and Gigerenzer
(1989), refers to the probability of correctly rejecting the null hypothesis. It is
positively linked to the size of alpha and the sample size, and is inversely related
to the amount of within-group variability. Some computer programs now provide
measures of effect size and power, making them readily available for research
reports and funding agency proposals, alike. Several published studies (e.g., Cohen, 1962; Cooper & Findley, 1982; Rossi, 1990; Rossi, chapter 7, current volume) demonstrate that for social science research, medium effect sizes (e.g., .5
for mean differences, and .30 for r), as well as medium levels of power (.50–
.60), are the norm. Whereas this does not speak well for the precision of our
findings and procedures, it is helpful to at least be aware of this, and effect size
and power calculations provide us with this awareness.

Reviewing the chapters in this volume, the following views emerge:

1. The large majority (11 chapter contributors) were very much in favor of
   reporting effect sizes and levels of power for our research. Most notable in
   this endorsement are Cohen, and Rossi, the latter aptly stating that "a general disregard or even ignorance of the roles of effect size and statistical
   power [can be] the asteroids that kill [a research area]" (chapter 7 of this
   volume). Further, Steiger and Fouladi (chapter 9 of this volume) present
   techniques for calculating exact confidence intervals on effects size and
   power. They thus provide a synthesis of two of the key recommendations
   in this volume. Using such confidence intervals, researchers using
   ANOVA techniques can not only estimate effect size, but can also determine the precision of such estimates, and can perform standard significance tests by simply observing whether the confidence interval includes
   zero.
2. The remaining contributors (Pruzek, and Rozeboom) at least mildly endorsed such use.

Evaluation. Support for the use of effect size and power calculations was
unanimous with our chapter contributors, arguing very convincingly for their
regular practice in social science research, and (in the case of Steiger and Fouladi) providing new techniques for enhancing their applicability.

Evaluate How Well a Model Approximates the Data, Without Necessarily Attending to Issues of Statistical Significance

Goodness of approximation entails an assessment of how well a hypothesized model fits the data at hand, and does not focus attention on significance tests. This practice has become very acceptable in recent years, particularly for the methods of structural equation modeling (SEM). With SEM, much more focus has been placed on the closeness of a hypothesized theoretical model to the actual data, than to significance tests. This is because in SEM we are essentially trying to retain the null hypothesis that our model offers a good fit to the data. Steiger and Fouladi's chapter presents an excellent discussion on the distinction between a procedure such as SEM and the majority of other methods that try to reject the null hypothesis. A central issue is that with very large sample sizes, an arguably good quality in any scientific effort, there is too much power to detect even trivial differences between the hypothesized model and the data. Thus, a potentially good model may be disregarded due to large sample size and high power to notice minor differences. Hence, the concept of goodness of approximation has offered SEM users an alternate method for evaluating how closely their data corroborate a theoretical model. Goodness of approximation is extended to other methods, such as the analysis of variance (ANOVA) model in McDonald's chapter. Reviewing all of the chapters in this volume reveals that:

1. The majority of the chapters (Cohen; Schmidt & Hunter; McDonald; Steiger & Fouladi; Reichardt & Gollob; Pruzek; Rozeboom; and Meehl) appear to favor the practice of reporting how well our data approximate a well specified theoretical model.
2. Four of the chapters (Mulaik et al.; Abelson; Harris; and Rossi) would probably endorse such practice.
3. Only one of the chapters (Rindskopf) appeared indifferent to this.

Evaluation. Support for the use of goodness of approximation measures was fairly strong, with only one of the chapters appearing neutral and thus not counted as a supporter. This suggests that goodness of approximation measures could benefit researchers, especially when there are large sample sizes and high power to detect significant differences that may well not be meaningful.

Null and/or Alternative Hypotheses Should Be Very Specific (i.e., A Particular Nonzero Value) and Realistic

Though hypotheses can be very specific, current use, which is supported by most computer programs, is to have a null hypothesis of no effects and a non-specific alternative hypothesis posing nonzero effects. Recent authors have argued for more emphasis to be placed on creating very specific, defeatable hypotheses (e.g., Harris, chapter 6; Kaiser, 1960; Mulaik et al., chapter 4). Meehl's chapter presents an understandable example concerning the prediction of weather patterns, comparing a vague, low-risk hypothesis (e.g., it will rain sometime in April) to a very specific, risky hypothesis (e.g., it will rain 10 of the days during the first half of April), the latter being much more easily refutable. If the data are close to the risky hypothesis (i.e., it actually rains 9 or 10 days in early April), we have strong corroboration. A survey of our chapters for support on the use of very specific hypotheses reveals that:

1. they are encouraged in chapters 2, 4, and 5, by Cohen; Mulaik and his colleagues; and Abelson, respectively; especially Harris (who proposes having at least three hypotheses: see chapter 6); three chapters by: Reichardt and Gollob; Pruzek; and Rindskopf, who advocate analyzing several specific hypotheses; Rozeboom (chapter 13), who argues for several well-stated propositions; and particularly Meehl who is a strong proponent of assessing how closely we corroborate very risky, specific hypotheses and theories (see chapter 14).

2. they are acceptable to both Rossi (chapter 7) and McDonald (chapter 8).

3. they are not addressed by Steiger and Fouladi (chapter 9) .

4. Schmidt and Hunter (chapter 3) appear to fiercely oppose any significance testing.

Evaluation. Taking note of the chapters that endorse specific, strong hypothesis testing (11 chapters from sets 1 and 2), as well as those less inclined to endorse this practice (i.e., two chapters from sets 3 and 4), it appears that the practice of advocating the use of specific, risky hypotheses received strong support by most of our chapter contributors.

Replicate Results in Independent Studies and/or Quantitatively Summarize Using Meta-Analysis

Replication in science refers to repeating a research study to discern the reliability and validity of a set of findings. Lykken (1968) offered three kinds of replication: literal replication, in which a study is repeated exactly as in the original;

operational replication, which attempts to reconstruct the main procedures in a study; and constructive replication, which strives to conduct another study of *the same constructs*, possibly using different sampling, procedures, and measures. This latter type of replication would provide strong evidence of the validity and generalizability of a set of findings under dissimilar conditions, should the main findings reoccur.

The value of replication was eloquently stated by Fisher (1925/1941) in his classic treatise, *Statistical Methods for Research Workers*:

> The salutary habit of repeating important experiments, or of carrying out original observations in replicate, shows a tacit appreciation of the fact that the object of our study is not the individual result, but the population of possibilities of which we do our best to make our experiments representative (p. 3).

More than 50 years later, this sentiment persists as confirmed by Meehl, who states that "the most important property of an empirical finding is inter-subjective replicability, that other investigators, relying on the description of what was done, will (almost always) make the same (or closely similar) observations" (Meehl, chapter 14 of this volume).

Similarly, meta-analysis allows us to examine a set of findings for a phenomenon, gathered from a number of studies, and synthesize the overriding effects. Schmidt and Hunter (chapter 3 of the current volume) emphasize the usefulness of this procedure, saying, "Meta-analysis can and has revealed (and calibrated with precision) underlying population effects that have been undetected in the majority of the studies going into the meta-analysis." Thus, the most salient and noteworthy effects of a study are revealed quite readily in the replication and meta-analysis of worthwhile studies. Reviewing the chapters in this volume suggests that replication and meta-analysis are:

1. recommended in chapters 2 through 7 (by: Cohen; Schmidt & Hunter; Mulaik, Raju, & Harshman; Abelson; Harris; and Rossi, respectively), as well as in chapter 14, by Meehl.

2. tacitly approved of by both McDonald (chapter 8) and Rozeboom (chapter 13).

3. not mentioned in four of the chapters (by: Steiger & Fouladi; Reichardt & Gollob; Pruzek; and Rindskopf).

Evaluation. Based on the aforementioned perspectives, 9 of the 13 remaining chapters offer support for the use of replication and meta-analysis, suggesting a moderately worthwhile practice to adopt in scientific research.

Use Bayesian Methods of Inference

Bayesian methods are useful in calculating the probability that a small or null effect is indeed trivial, as well as the probability that sample effects are worthy of further attention. According to Pruzek (chapter 11 of this volume), "Bayesian statistical methods support inferences . . . [by] use of prior information and empirical data to generate posterior distributions, which in turn serve as the basis for statistical inferences." These methods are often referred to as subjective, taking into account the researcher's previous experience or beliefs to help inform the current analysis. From our chapters, Bayesian methods have:

1. strong support from three chapters that subscribe to this approach (chapters 10–12, by Reichardt & Gollob; Pruzek; and Rindskopf, respectively);

2. what could be considered mild support from: Cohen (1994, reprinted in chapter 2), where he stated: "The very reason the statistical test is done is to be able to reject H_0 because of its unlikelihood! But that is the posterior probability, available only through Bayes' theorem, for which one needs to know $P(H_0)$, the probability of the null hypothesis before the experiment, the 'prior' probability" (1994, p. 998); Abelson (chapter 5 of this volume, with at least implicit support for what he calls "neo-Bayesian alternatives to significance tests"), Steiger and Fouladi (chapter 9, by their focus on a noncentral distribution when the null hypothesis is false), McDonald (chapter 8, with his focus on the goodness of approximation between a model in which a researcher has high belief [e.g., prior distribution], the sample likelihood, and the ability to make inferences based on an assessment of the model and the data), and Rozeboom (chapter 13 of this volume, when he states that: "we can . . . allow our thinking to be influenced by metabelieving that our opinions should generally try to approximate Bayesian ideals");

3. a reaction of indifference from: Schmidt and Hunter (chapter 3), Harris (chapter 6), Rossi (chapter 7), and Meehl (chapter 14), the latter of whom is less in favor of subjective methods than in: "the existence of objective [not subjective] probabilities, whether they are physical frequencies or 'rational, inductive logic' epistemic supports" (Meehl, chapter 14 of this volume); and

4. are opposed by Mulaik, Raju, and Harshman who state that: "Bayesian inference . . . has long been controversial, particularly when it has been invoked in connection with the use of subjective probabilities . . . Subjective opinions and descriptions of subjective states or psychological states are not relevant . . ." (chapter 4 of this volume).

Evaluation. Based on the preceding perspectives, 8 of 13 chapters advocate at least some use of Bayesian methods. This indicates that although there is a lack of full support for a Bayesian approach, it does offer some potentially useful practices, such as taking into account prior information.

Make Dichotomous Decisions With Null Hypothesis Significance Tests

The practice of null hypothesis significance testing—making a dichotomous decision to either reject or retain H_0— has a long history. From Fisher to the present day, it has offered researchers a quantitative measure of the probability of getting sample results as different or more so than what is hypothesized in H_0. When used with well-reasoned and specific hypotheses, and when supplemented with other scientific input, such as effect sizes, power, confidence intervals, and sound judgment, it can be very effective in highlighting hypotheses that are worthy of further investigation, as well as those that do not merit such efforts. A survey of our chapters reveals that:

1. NHST is acceptable to both Mulaik and his colleagues, and Abelson, when used and interpreted correctly.

2. It is tolerated by: Reichardt and Gollob in those cases when confidence intervals are not as useful; Pruzek, who espouses the use of NHST within a Bayesian approach; Rindskopf who believes that the predominant small samples and low power of most research will not encourage Type I errors and will probably pick up large effect sizes; and by Meehl for technological studies in which a decision is needed between two or more treatments.

3. Three chapters (Harris; Steiger & Fouladi; McDonald) are not in favor of the dichotomous nature of NHST, preferring the use of several alternative hypotheses, noncentral confidence intervals, and goodness of approximation assessments, respectively.

4. Four of them (Cohen; Rossi; Schmidt & Hunter; Rozeboom) are clearly opposed to using NHST, each offering alternative methods such as effect sizes and power (Cohen; Rossi), confidence intervals and meta-analysis (Schmidt & Hunter), and cognitive evaluation of well-reasoned propositions (Rozeboom).

Evaluation. Taking the views from the first two sets of chapter views (1 and 2) as indicating evidence for supporting the use of NHST and the last two sets (3 and 4) as opposition, the authors are about equally split. Compared to the other 7 recommendations for the practice of scientific inference, NHST is less endorsed by our chapter contributors. This method of focusing on a dichotomous decision: would contribute little to the development of strong theories or sound judgment; lacks the precision of either confidence intervals, effect sizes, or power calculations; is less informative than goodness of approximation assessment or the use of specific, realistic, and nonzero hypotheses; and is less thorough than either replication, meta-analysis, or Bayesian inference. Rozeboom, with the wisdom of a mystic and the prose of a witticist, denounces the all or nothing logic of traditional NHST, claiming it "is intellectually at par with a dictator's executing all his [or her] senior advisors in response to evidence that one of them is a traitor" (chapter 13 of this volume). In sum, the overriding view on this issue is that NHST may be overused and unproductive, particularly when used as simply a dichotomous decision rule.

CONCLUSIONS AND APPLICATIONS

This chapter attempted to summarize the main issues in the current significance-testing debate by presenting a set of eight recommendations for the practice of scientific inference, along with the amount of endorsement for each from the 13 remaining chapters. It is recognized that the qualitative summaries in this chapter could be oversimplifying the richness and complexity of the ideas presented in the remaining chapters. However, given the overriding goal of methodological clarity for this new Multivariate Application book series, I was willing to err on the side of simplicity instead of complexity. Hopefully, this served to both introduce the reader to the content of the remainder of the book, as well as to provide a structure for evaluating the main suggestions. From my reading of the chapters, along with the summary presented in Table 1.1, it appears that:

1. There is strong concurrence that statistical inference should include the calculation of effect sizes and power, estimation of appropriate confidence intervals, goodness of approximation indices, and the evaluation of strong theories with critical thinking and sound judgment. The chapter contributors were unanimous in their support of all of these except goodness of approximation, and nearly so for the latter. Thus, researchers should be encouraged to incorporate these methods into their programs of scientific research.

2. There is good support in favor of using specific, realistic hypothesis tests, as opposed to the more conventional, dichotomous form that poses no effects for the null hypothesis. The large majority of our chapters advocate

using the stronger, more risky specification of clearly stated hypotheses, a practice we soundly encourage.

3. There is moderate approval for emphasizing replication and the use of meta-analysis to highlight the most salient, and valid findings. Nine of the 13 remaining chapters would endorse this practice. We recognize that hesitancy to explicitly call for more replication and meta-analytic studies is probably due to the labor-intensive nature of such studies. Lykken (1968, reprinted in Morrison & Henkel, 1970, p. 279) stated categorically that "ideally, all experiments would be replicated before publication but this goal is impractical." Thompson (1996) agreed, noting that "most researchers lack the stamina to conduct all their studies at least twice" (p. 29). Thus, we believe that replication and meta-analysis of research studies is a highly positive practice, and one for which greater participation should be encouraged.

4. There is moderate encouragement for using Bayesian methods of inference, with 8 of the 13 chapters advocating such procedures. It is recognized that some lack of enthusiasm for this approach may be attributed to the greater difficulty of these methods over the classical hypothesis–testing procedures. Pruzek (chapter 11 of this volume), who advocates the use of Bayesian methods, openly acknowledges that "despite their virtues, . . . Bayesian methods are often much harder to implement [than classical methods]." Perhaps the two chapters (11–12) in the current volume that present very clear descriptions of Bayesian inference will assist researchers in considering greater use of these methods, or, at the very least, in a greater understanding of what they entail.

5. Compared to the other recommended practices of scientific inference, there is less enthusiasm for focusing on the traditional dichotomous form of null hypothesis significance testing, and thus this method should probably not be used exclusively.

In closing this chapter, we encourage you to decide for yourself which methods appear most appropriate for your work. The chapters following should help you in making informed choices in your particular practice of scientific inference, and help you to answer the question posed at the onset: "What if there were no significance tests?"

TABLE 1.1

Suggested Practices of Scientific Inference Endorsed[1] by One or More Chapters[2]

Suggestions	Chapter												
	2	3	4	5	6	7	8	9	10	11	12	13	14
1. Strong theories/sound judgment	++	++	++	++	++	++	++	++	++	++	++	++	++
2. Confidence intervals	++	++	++	++	++	++	++	++	++	++	++	++	++
3. Effect sizes and power	++	++	++	+	+	+	++	++	++	+	–	+	++
4. Goodness of approximation	++	––	+	+	++	+	++	+	+	++	++	++	++
5. Specific, non-zero hypotheses	++	++	++	++	++	++	+	–	–	++	–	+	++
6. Replication/meta-analysis	+	–	––	+	–	–	+	–	–	–	++	+	––
7. Bayesian inference	+	–	++	+	–	–	+	+	+	+	+	+	+
8. NHST dichotomous decisions	––	–	++	++	–	––	–	–	+	+	+	––	+

[1] Note: ++ Endorsed, + Somewhat endorsed, – Probably not endorsed, –– Not endorsed.

[2] Chapters: 2 = Cohen, 3 = Schmidt & Hunter, 4 = Mulaik, Raju, & Harshman, 5 = Abelson, 6 = Harris, 7 = Rossi, 8 = McDonald, 9 = Steiger & Fouladi, 10 = Reichardt & Gollob, 11 = Pruzek, 12 = Rindskopf, 13 = Rozeboom, 14 = Meehl.

REFERENCES

Bakan, D. (1966). The test of significance in psychological research. *Psychological Bulletin, 66*, 423–437.

Berkson, J. (1938). Some difficulties of interpretation encountered in the application of the chi-square test. *Journal of the American Statistical Association, 33*, 526–542.

Berkson, J. (1942). Tests of significance considered as evidence. *Journal of the American Statistical Association, 37*, 325–335.

Carver, R. P. (1978a). The case against statistical significance testing. *Harvard Educational Review, 48*, 378–399.

Carver, R. P. (1978b). The case against statistical significance testing, revisited. *Journal of Experimental Education, 61*, 287–292.

Cohen, J. (1962). The statistical power of abnormal-social psychological research: A review. *Journal of Abnormal and Social Psychology, 69*, 145–153.

Cohen, J. (1988). *Statistical power analysis for the behavioral sciences* (2nd ed.). Hillsdale, NJ: Lawrence Erlbaum Associates.

Cohen, J. (1994). The earth is round (p < .05). *American Psychologist, 49*, 997–1003.

Cooper, H. M., & Findley, M. (1982). Expected effect sizes: Estimates for statistical power analysis in social psychology. *Personality and Social Psychology Bulletin, 8*, 168–173.

Cowles, M. P., & Davis, C. (1982). On the origins of the .05 level of significance. *American Psychologist, 37*, 553–558.

Falk, R., & Greenbaum, C. W. (1995). Significance tests die hard: The amazing persistence of a probabilistic misconception. *Theory and Psychology, 5*, 75–98.

Fisher, R. A. (1941). *Statistical methods for research workers* (84th ed.). Edinburgh, Scotland: Oliver & Boyd. (Original work published 1925)

Huberty, C. J. (1993). Historical origins of statistical testing practices. *Journal of Experimental Education, 61*, 317–333.

Jones, L. V. (1955). Statistics and research design. *Annual Review of Psychology, 6*, 405–430.

Kaiser, H. F. (1960). Directional statistical decisions. *Psychological Review, 67*, 160–167.

Keren, G. & Lewis, C. (Eds.). (1993). *A handbook for data analysis in the behavioral sciences: Methodological issues* (pp. 311–339). Hillsdale, NJ: Lawrence Erlbaum Associates.

Kirk, R. E. (1996). Practical significance: A concept whose time has come. *Educational and Psychological Measurement, 56,* 746–759.

Lykken, D. E. (1968). Statistical significance in psychological research. *Psychological Bulletin, 70,* 151–159.

Meehl, P. E. (1967). Theory testing in psychology and physics: A methodological paradox. *Philosophy of Science, 34,* 103–115.

Meehl, P. E. (1978). Theoretical risks and tabular asterisks: Sir Karl, Sir Ronald, and the slow progress of soft psychology. *Journal of Consulting and Clinical Psychology, 46,* 806–834.

Morrison, D. E., & Henkel, R. E. (1969). Significance tests reconsidered. *American Psychologist, 4,* 131–140.

Morrison, D. E., & Henkel, R. E. (Eds.) (1970). *The significance test controversy.* Chicago: Aldine.

Neyman, J., & Pearson, E. S. (1928). On the use and interpretation of certain test criteria for purposes of statistical inference. *Biometrika, 29A,* Part I: 175–240; Part II 263–294.

Pearson, K. (1901). On the correlation of characters not quantitatively measurable. *Philosophical Transactions of the Royal Society of London, 195,* 1–47.

Rosenthal, R. (1990). How are we doing in soft psychology? *American Psychologist, 45,* 775–777.

Rosenthal, R., & Gaito, J. (1963). The interpretation of levels of significance by psychological researchers. *Journal of Psychology, 55,* 33–38.

Rosenthal, R., & Gaito, J. (1964). Further evidence for the cliff effect in the interpretation of levels of significance. *Psychological Reports, 15,* 570.

Rossi, J. S. (1990). Statistical power of psychological research: What have we gained in 20 years? *Journal of Consulting and Clinical Psychology, 58,* 646–656.

Rozeboom, W. W. (1960). The fallacy of the null hypothesis significance test. *Psychological Bulletin, 57,* 416–428.

Sedlmeier, P., & Gigerenzer, G. (1989). Do studies of statistical power have an effect on the power of studies? *Psychological Bulletin, 105,* 309–316.

Shaver, J. P. (1993). What statistical significance testing is, and what it is not. *Journal of Experimental Education, 61,* 293–316.

Thompson, B. (1996). AERA editorial policies regarding statistical significance testing: Three suggested reforms. *Educational Researcher, 25,* 26–30.

Tukey, J. W. (1969). Analyzing data: Sanctification or detective work? *American Psychologist, 24,* 83–91.

Yates, F. (1951). The influences of statistical methods for research workers on the development of the science of statistics. *Journal of the American Statistical Association, 46*, 19–34.

The Debate:
Against and For Significance Testing

Chapter 2

The Earth Is Round ($p < .05$)[1]
Jacob Cohen

After 4 decades of severe criticism, the ritual of null hypothesis significance testing—mechanical dichotomous decisions around a sacred .05 criterion—still persists. This article reviews the problems with this practice, including its near-universal misinterpretation of p as the probability that H_0 is true, the misinterpretation that its complement is the probability of successful replication, and the mistaken assumption that if one rejects H_0 one thereby affirms the theory that led to the test. Exploratory data analysis and the use of graphic methods, a steady improvement in and a movement toward standardization in measurement, an emphasis on estimating effect sizes using confidence intervals, and the informed use of available statistical methods is suggested. For generalization, psychologists must finally rely, as has been done in all the older sciences, on replication.

I make no pretense of the originality of my remarks in this article. One of the few things we, as psychologists, have learned from over a century of scientific study is that at age three score and 10, originality is not to be expected. David Bakan said back in 1966 that his claim that "a great deal of mischief has been associated" with the test of significance "is hardly original," that it is "what 'everybody knows,' " and that "to say it 'out loud' is . . . to assume the role of the child who pointed out that the emperor was really outfitted in his underwear" (p. 423). If it was hardly original in 1966, it can hardly be original now. Yet this naked emperor has been shamelessly running around for a long time.

Like many men my age, I mostly grouse. My harangue today is on testing for statistical significance, about which Bill Rozeboom (1960) wrote 33 years ago, "The statistical folkways of a more primitive past continue to dominate the local scene" (p. 417).

And today, they continue to continue. And we, as teachers, consultants, authors, and otherwise perpetrators of quantitative methods, are responsible for the ritualization of null hypothesis significance testing (NHST; I resisted the

---

[1] This article was published originally in *American Psychologist*, Vol. 49, No. 12, pp. 997-1003.

temptation to call it statistical hypothesis inference testing) to the point of meaninglessness and beyond. I argue herein that NHST has not only failed to support the advance of psychology as a science but also has seriously impeded it.

Consider the following: A colleague approaches me with a statistical problem. He believes that a generally rare disease does not exist at all in a given population, hence H_0: $P = 0$. He draws a more or less random sample of 30 cases from this population and finds that one of the cases has the disease, hence $P_s = 1/30 = .033$. He is not sure how to test H_0, chi-square with Yates's (1951) correction or the Fisher exact test, and wonders whether he has enough power. Would you believe it? And would you believe that if he tried to publish this result without a significance test, one or more reviewers might complain? It could happen.

Almost a quarter of a century ago, a couple of sociologists, D. E. Morrison and R. E. Henkel (1970), edited a book entitled *The Significance Test Controversy.* Among the contributors were Bill Rozeboom (1960), Paul Meehl (1967), David Bakan (1966), and David Lykken (1968). Without exception, they damned NHST. For example, Meehl described NHST as "a potent but sterile intellectual rake who leaves in his merry path a long train of ravished maidens but no viable scientific offspring" (p. 265). They were, however, by no means the first to do so. Joseph Berkson attacked NHST in 1938, even before it sank its deep roots in psychology. Lancelot Hogben's book-length critique appeared in 1957. When I read it then, I was appalled by its rank apostasy. I was at that time well trained in the current Fisherian dogma and had not yet heard of Neyman-Pearson (try to find a reference to them in the statistics texts of that day—McNemar, Edwards, Guilford, Walker). Indeed, I had already had some dizzying success as a purveyor of plain and fancy NHST to my fellow clinicians in the Veterans Administration.

What's wrong with NHST? Well, among many other things, it does not tell us what we want to know, and we so much want to know what we want to know that, out of desperation, we nevertheless believe that it does! What we want to know is "Given these data, what is the probability that H_0 is true?" But as most of us know, what it tells us is "Given that H_0 is true, what is the probability of these (or more extreme) data?" These are not the same, as has been pointed out many times over the years by the contributors to the Morrison-Henkel (1970), book, among others, and, more recently and emphatically, by Meehl (1978, 1986, 1990a, 1990b), Gigerenzer (1993), Falk and Greenbaum (1995), and yours truly (Cohen, 1990).

The Permanent Illusion

One problem arises from a misapplication of deductive syllogistic reasoning. Falk and Greenbaum (1995) called this the "illusion of probabilistic proof by contradiction" or the "illusion of attaining probability." Gigerenzer (1993) called it the "permanent illusion" and the "Bayesian Id's wishful thinking," part of the "hybrid logic" of contemporary statistical inference—a mishmash of Fisher and Neyman-Pearson, with invalid Bayesian interpretation. It is the widespread belief that the level of significance at which H_0 is rejected, say .05, is the probability that it is correct, or at the very least, that it is of low probability.

The following is almost but not quite the reasoning of null hypothesis rejection:

If the null hypothesis is correct, then this datum (D) can not occur.
    It has, however, occurred.
    Therefore, the null hypothesis is false.

If this were the reasoning of H_0 testing, then it would be formally correct. It would be what Aristotle called the modus tollens, denying the antecedent by denying the consequent. But this is not the reasoning of NHST. Instead, it makes this reasoning probabilistic, as follows:

If the null hypothesis is correct, then these data are highly unlikely.
    These data have occurred.
    Therefore, the null hypothesis is highly unlikely.

By making it probabilistic, it becomes invalid. Why? Well, consider this: The following syllogism is sensible and also the formally correct modus tollens:

If a person is a Martian, then he is not a member of Congress.
    This person is a member of Congress.
    Therefore, he is not a Martian.

Sounds reasonable, no? This next syllogism is not sensible because the major premise is wrong, but the reasoning is as before and still a formally correct modus tollens:

If a person is an American, then he is not a member of Congress. (WRONG!)
    This person is a member of Congress.
    Therefore, he is not an American.

If the major premise is made sensible by making it probabilistic, not absolute, the syllogism becomes formally incorrect and leads to a conclusion that is not sensible:

If a person is an American, then he is probably not a member of Congress (TRUE, RIGHT?)
This person is a member of Congress.
Therefore, he is probably not an American. (Pollard & Richardson, 1987)

This is formally exactly the same as

If H_0 is true, then this result (statistical significance) would probably not occur.
This result has occurred.
Then H_0 is probably not true and therefore formally invalid.

This formulation appears at least implicitly in article after article in psychological journals and explicitly in some statistics textbooks—"the illusion of attaining improbability."

Why $p(D|H_0) \neq p(H_0|D)$

When one tests H_0, one is finding the probability that the data (D) could have arisen if H_0 were true, $P(D \mid H_0)$. If that probability is small, then it can be concluded that if H_0 is true, then D is unlikely. Now, what really is at issue, what is always the real issue, is the probability that H_0 is true, given the data, $P(H_0 \mid D)$, the inverse probability. When one rejects H_0, one wants to conclude that H_0 is unlikely, say, $p < .01$. The very reason the statistical test is done is to be able to reject H_0 because of its unlikelihood! But that is the posterior probability, available only through Bayes's theorem, for which one needs to know $P(H_0)$, the probability of the null hypothesis before the experiment, the "prior" probability.

Now, one does not normally know the probability of H_0. Bayesian statisticians cope with this problem by positing a prior probability or distribution of probabilities. But an example from psychiatric diagnosis in which one knows $P(H_0)$ is illuminating.

The incidence of schizophrenia in adults is about 2%. A proposed screening test is estimated to have at least 95% accuracy in making the positive diagnosis (sensitivity) and about 97% accuracy in declaring normality (specificity). Formally stated, $P(\text{normal} \mid H_0) \approx .97$, $P(\text{schizophrenia} \mid H_1) > .95$. So, let

H_0 = The case is normal, so that
H_1 = The case is schizophrenic, and
D = The test result (the data) is positive for schizophrenia.

With a positive test for schizophrenia at hand, given the more than .95 assumed accuracy of the test, $P(D \mid H_0)$—the probability of a positive test given that the case is normal—is less than .05, that is, significant at $p < .05$. One would reject the hypothesis that the case is normal and conclude that the case has schizophrenia, as it happens mistakenly, but within the .05 alpha error. But that's not the point.

The probability of the case being normal, $P(H_0)$, given a positive test (D), *that is,* $P(H_0 \mid D)$, is not what has just been discovered however much it sounds like it and however much it is wished to be. It is not true that the probability that the case is normal is less than .05, nor is it even unlikely that it is a normal case. By a Bayesian maneuver, this inverse probability, the probability that the case is normal, given a positive test for schizophrenia, is about .60! The arithmetic follows:

$$P(H_0 \mid D) = \frac{P(H_0) * P(\text{test wrong} \mid H_0)}{P(H_0) * P(\text{test wrong} \mid H_0) + P(H_1) * P(\text{test correct} \mid H_1)}$$

$$= \frac{(.98)(.03)}{(.98)(.03) + (.02)(.95)} = \frac{.0294}{.0294 + .0190} = .607$$

The situation may be made clearer by expressing it approximately as a 2×2 table for 1,000 cases. The case is shown in Table 2.1. As the table shows, the conditional probability of a normal case for those testing as schizophrenic is not small—of the 50 cases testing as schizophrenics, 30 are false positives, actually normal, 60% of them!

This extreme result occurs because of the low base rate for schizophrenia, but it demonstrates how wrong one can be by considering the p value from a typical significance test as bearing on the truth of the null hypothesis for a set of data.

It should not be inferred from this example that all null hypothesis testing requires a Bayesian prior. There is a form of H_0 testing that has been used in astronomy and physics for centuries, what Meehl (1967) called the "strong" form, as advocated by Karl Popper (1959). Popper proposed that a scientific theory be

TABLE 2.1

Test Results for Schizophrenics and Normals

Result	Normal	Schiz	Total
Negative test (Normal)	949	1	950
Positive test (Schiz)	30	20	50
Total	979	21	1,000

tested by attempts to falsify it. In null hypothesis testing terms, one takes a central prediction of the theory, say, a point value of some crucial variable, sets it up as the H_0, and challenges the theory by attempting to reject it. This is certainly a valid procedure, potentially even more useful when used in confidence interval form. What I and my ilk decry is the "weak" form in which theories are "confirmed" by rejecting null hypotheses.

The inverse probability error in interpreting H_0 is not reserved for the great unwashed, but appears many times in statistical textbooks (although frequently together with the correct interpretation, whose authors apparently think they are interchangeable). Among the distinguished authors making this error are Guilford, Nunnally, Anastasi, Ferguson, and Lindquist. Many examples of this error are given by Robyn Dawes (1988, pp. 70–75); Falk and Greenbaum (1995); Gigerenzer (1993, pp. 316–329), who also nailed R. A. Fisher (who emphatically rejected Bayesian theory of inverse probability but slipped into invalid Bayesian interpretations of NHST (p. 318)); and Oakes (1986, pp. 17–20), who also nailed me for this error (p. 20).

The illusion of attaining improbability or the Bayesian Id's wishful thinking error in using NHST is very easy to make. It was made by 68 out of 70 academic psychologists studied by Oakes (1986, pp. 79–82). Oakes incidentally offered an explanation of the neglect of power analysis because of the near universality of this inverse probability error:

> After all, why worry about the probability of obtaining data that will lead to the rejection of the null hypothesis if it is false when your analysis gives you the actual probability of the null hypothesis being false? (p. 83)

A problem that follows readily from the Bayesian ID's wishful thinking error is the belief that after a successful rejection of H_0, it is highly probable that replications of the research will also result in H_0 rejection. In their classic article "The Belief in the Law of Small Numbers," Tversky and Kahneman (1971) showed that because people's intuitions that data drawn randomly from a population are highly representative, most members of the audience at an American Psychological Association meeting and at a mathematical psychology conference believed that a study with a significant result would replicate with a significant result in a small sample (p. 105). Of Oakes's (1986) academic psychologists 42 out of 70 believed that a t of 2.7, with $df = 18$ and $p = .01$, meant that if the experiment were repeated many times, a significant result would be obtained 99% of the time. Rosenthal (1993) said with regard to this replication fallacy that "Nothing could be further from the truth" (p. 542f) and pointed out that given the typical .50 level of power for medium effect sizes at which most behavioral scientists work (Cohen, 1962), the chances are that in three replications only one in eight would result in significant results, in all three replications, and in five replications, the chance of as many as three of them being significant is only 50:50.

An error in elementary logic made frequently by NHST proponents and pointed out by its critics is the thoughtless, usually implicit, conclusion that if H_0 is rejected, then the theory is established: If A then B; B therefore A. But even the valid form of the syllogism (if A then B; not B therefore not A) can be misinterpreted. Meehl (1990a, 1990b) pointed out that in addition to the theory that led to the test, there are usually several auxiliary theories or assumptions and ceteris paribus clauses and that it is the logical product of these that is counterpoised against H_0. Thus, when H_0 is rejected, it can be because of the falsity of any of the auxiliary theories about instrumentation or the nature of the psyche or of the ceteris paribus clauses, and not of the substantive theory that precipitated the research.

So even when used and interpreted "properly," with a significance criterion (almost always $p < .05$) set a priori (or more frequently understood), H_0 has little to commend it in the testing of psychological theories in its usual reject-H_0-confirm-the-theory form. The ritual dichotomous reject-accept decision, however objective and administratively convenient, is not the way any science is done. As Bill Rozeboom wrote in 1960, "The primary aim of a scientific experiment is not to precipitate decisions, but to make an appropriate adjustment in the degree to which one . . . believes the hypothesis . . . being tested" (p. 420).

The Nil Hypothesis

Thus far, I have been considering H_0s in their most general sense—as propositions about the state of affairs in a population, more particularly, as some specified value of a population parameter. Thus, "the population mean difference is 4" may be an H_0, as may be "the proportion of males in this population is .75" and "the correlation in this population is .20." But as almost universally used, the null in H_0 is taken to mean nil, zero. For Fisher, the null hypothesis was the hypothesis to be nullified. As if things were not bad enough in the interpretation, or misinterpretation, of NHST in this general sense, things get downright ridiculous when H_0 is to the effect that the effect size (ES) is 0—that the population mean difference is 0, that the correlation is 0, that the proportion of males is .50, that the raters' reliability is 0 (an H_0 that can almost always be rejected, even with a small sample—Heaven help us!). Most of the criticism of NHST in the literature has been for this special case where its use may be valid only for true experiments involving randomization (e.g., controlled clinical trials) or when any departure from pure chance is meaningful (as in laboratory experiments or clairvoyance), but even in these cases, confidence intervals provide more information. I henceforth refer to the H_0 that an ES = 0 as the "nil hypothesis."

My work in power analysis led me to realize that the nil hypothesis is always false. If I may unblushingly quote myself,

> It can only be true in the bowels of a computer processor running a Monte Carlo study (and even then a stray electron may make it false). If it is false, even to a tiny degree, it must be the case that a large enough sample will produce a significant result and lead to its rejection. So if the null hypothesis is always false, what's the big deal about rejecting it? (p. 1308)

I wrote that in 1990. More recently I discovered that in 1938, Berkson wrote

> It would be agreed by statisticians that a large sample is always better than a small sample. If, then, we know in advance the p that will result from an application of the Chi-square test to a large sample, there would seem to be no use in doing it on a smaller one. But since the result of the former test is known, it is no test at all. (p. 526f)

Tukey (1991) wrote that "It is foolish to ask 'Are the effects of A and B different?' They are always different—for some decimal place" (p. 100).

The point is made piercingly by Thompson (1992):

> Statistical significance testing can involve a tautological logic in which tired researchers, having collected data on hundreds of subjects, then conduct a statistical test to evaluate whether there were a lot of subjects, which the researchers already know, because they collected the data and know they are tired. This tautology has created considerable damage as regards the cumulation of knowledge. (p. 436)

In an unpublished study, Meehl and Lykken cross-tabulated 15 items for a sample of 57,000 Minnesota high school students, including father's occupation, father's education, mother's education, number of siblings, sex, birth order, educational plans, family attitudes toward college, whether they liked school, college choice, occupational plan in 10 years, religious preference, leisure time activities, and high school organizations. All of the 105 chi-squares that these 15 items produced by the cross-tabulations were statistically significant, and 96% of them at $p < .000001$ (Meehl, 1990b).

One might say, "With 57,000 cases, relationships as small as a Cramer ϕ of .02–.03 will be significant at $p < .000001$, so what's the big deal?" Well, the big deal is that many of the relationships were much larger than .03. Enter the Meehl "crud factor," more genteelly called by Lykken "the ambient correlation noise." In soft psychology, "Everything is related to everything else." Meehl acknowledged (1990b) that neither he nor anyone else has accurate knowledge about the size of the crud factor in a given research domain, *"but the notion that the correlation between arbitrarily paired trait variables will be, while not literally zero, of such minuscule size as to be of no importance, is surely wrong"* (p. 212, italics in original).

Meehl (1986) considered a typical review article on the evidence for some theory based on nil hypothesis testing that reports a 16:4 box score in favor of the theory. After taking into account the operation of the crud factor, the bias against reporting and publishing "negative" results (Rosenthal's, 1979, "file drawer" problem), and assuming power of .75, he estimated the likelihood ratio of the theory against the crud factor as 1:1. Then, assuming that the prior probability of theories in soft psychology is ≤ .10, he concluded that the Bayesian posterior probability is also ≤ .10 (p. 327f). So a 16:4 box score for a theory becomes, more realistically, a 9:1 odds ratio against it.

Meta-analysis, with its emphasis on effect sizes, is a bright spot in the contemporary scene. One of its major contributors and proponents, Frank Schmidt (1992), provided an interesting perspective on the consequences of current NHST-driven research in the behavioral sciences. He reminded researchers that, given the fact that the nil hypothesis is always false, the rate of Type I errors is 0%, not 5%, and that only Type II errors can be made, which run typically at about 50% (Cohen, 1962; Sedlmeier & Gigerenzer, 1989). He showed that typically, the sample effect size necessary for significance is notably larger than the actual population effect size and that the average of the statistically significant effect sizes is much larger than the actual effect size. The result is that people who do focus on effect sizes end up with a substantial positive bias in their effect size estimation. Furthermore, there is the irony that the "sophisticates" who use procedures to adjust their alpha error for multiple tests (using Bonferroni, Newman-Keuls, etc.) are adjusting for a nonexistent alpha error, thus reduce their power, and, if lucky enough to get a significant result, only end up grossly overestimating the population effect size!

Because NHST *p* values have become the coin of the realm in much of psychology, they have served to inhibit its development as a science. Go build a quantitative science with *p* values! All psychologists know that *statistically significant* does not mean plain-English significant, but if one reads the literature, one often discovers that a finding reported in the Results section studded with asterisks implicitly becomes in the Discussion section highly significant or very highly significant, important, big!

Even a correct interpretation of *p* values does not achieve very much, and has not for a long time. Tukey (1991) warned that if researchers fail to reject a nil hypothesis about the difference between A and B, all they can say is that the direction of the difference is "uncertain." If researchers reject the nil hypothesis then they can say they can be pretty sure of the direction, for example, "A is larger than B." But if all we, as psychologists, learn from a research is that A is larger than B ($p < .01$), we have not learned very much. And this is typically all we learn. Confidence intervals are rarely to be seen in our publications. In another article (Tukey, 1969), he chided psychologists and other life and behavior scientists with the admonition "Amount, as well as direction is vital" and went on to say the following:

> The physical scientists have learned much by storing up amounts, not just directions. If, for example, elasticity had been confined to "When you pull on it, it gets longer!," Hooke's law, the elastic limit, plasticity, and many other important topics could not have appeared (p. 86). . . . Measuring the right things on a communicable scale lets us stockpile information about amounts. Such information can be useful, whether or not the chosen scale is an interval scale. Before the second law of thermodynamics—and there were many decades of progress in physics and chemistry before it appeared—the scale of temperature was not, in any nontrivial sense, an interval scale. Yet these decades of progress would have been impossible had physicists and chemists refused either to record temperatures or to calculate with them. (p. 80)

In the same vein, Tukey (1969) complained about correlation coefficients, quoting his teacher, Charles Winsor, as saying that they are a dangerous symptom. Unlike regression coefficients, correlations are subject to vary with selection as researchers change populations. He attributed researchers' preference for correlations to their avoidance of thinking about the units with which they measure.

> Given two perfectly meaningless variables, one is reminded of their meaninglessness when a regression coefficient is given, since one wonders how to interpret its value. . . . Being so uninterested in our variables that we do not care about their units can hardly be desirable. (p. 89)

The major problem with correlations applied to research data is that they can not provide useful information on causal strength because they change with the degree of variability of the variables they relate. Causality operates on single instances, not on populations whose members vary. The effect of A on B for me can hardly depend on whether I'm in a group that varies greatly in A or another that does not vary at all. It is not an accident that causal modeling proceeds with regression and not correlation coefficients. In the same vein, I should note that standardized effect size measures, such as d and f, developed in power analysis (Cohen, 1988) are, like correlations, also dependent on population variability of the dependent variable and are properly used only when that fact is kept in mind.

To work constructively with "raw" regression coefficients and confidence intervals, psychologists have to start respecting the units they work with, or develop measurement units they can respect enough so that researchers in a given field or subfield can agree to use them. In this way, there can be hope that researchers' knowledge can be cumulative. There are few such in soft psychology. A beginning in this direction comes from meta-analysis, which, whatever else it may accomplish, has at least focused attention on effect sizes. But imagine how much more fruitful the typical meta-analysis would be if the research covered used the same measures for the constructs they studied. Researchers could get beyond using a mass of studies to demonstrate convincingly that "if you pull on it, it gets longer."

Recall my example of the highly significant correlation between height and intelligence in 14,000 school children that translated into a regression coefficient that meant that to raise a child's IQ from 100 to 130 would require giving enough growth hormone to raise his or her height by 14 feet (Cohen, 1990).

What to Do?

First, don't look for a magic alternative to NHST, some other objective mechanical ritual to replace it. It doesn't exist.

Second, even before we, as psychologists, seek to generalize from our data, we must seek to understand and improve them. A major breakthrough to the approach to data, emphasizing "detective work" rather than "sanctification" was heralded by John Tukey in his article "The Future of Data Analysis" (1962) and detailed in his seminal book *Exploratory Data Analysis* (EDA; 1977). EDA seeks not to vault to generalization to the population but by simple, flexible, informal, and largely graphic techniques aims for understanding the set of data in hand. Important contributions to graphic data analysis have since been made by Tufte (1983, 1990), Cleveland (1993; Cleveland & McGill, 1988), and others. An excellent chapter-length treatment by Wainer and Thissen (1981), recently updated (Wainer & Thissen, 1993), provides many useful references, and statistical program packages provide the necessary software (see, for an example, Lee Wilkinson's [1990] SYGRAPH, which is presently being updated).

Forty-two years ago, Frank Yates, a close colleague and friend of R. A. Fisher, wrote about Fisher's "Statistical Methods for Research Workers" (1925/1951),

> It has caused scientific research workers to pay undue attention to the results of the tests of significance they perform on their data . . . and too little to the estimates of the magnitude of the effects they are estimating (p. 32).

Thus, my third recommendation is that, as researchers, we routinely report effect sizes in the form of confidence limits. "Everyone knows" that confidence intervals contain all the information to be found in significance tests and much more. They not only reveal the status of the trivial nil hypothesis but also about the status of non-nil null hypotheses and thus help remind researchers about the possible operation of the crud factor. Yet they are rarely to be found in the literature. I suspect that the main reason they are not reported is that they are so embarrassingly large! But their sheer size should move us toward improving our measurement by seeking to reduce the unreliable and invalid part of the variance in our measures (as Student himself recommended almost a century ago). Also, their width provides us with the analogue of power analysis in significance testing—larger sample sizes reduce the size of confidence intervals as they increase the statistical power of NHST. A new program covers confidence intervals for mean differences, correlation, cross-tabulations (including odds ratios and relative risks), and survival analysis (Borenstein, Cohen, & Rothstein, in press). It also produces Birnbaum's (1961) "confidence curves," from which can be read all confidence intervals from 50% to 100%, thus obviating the necessity of choosing a specific confidence level for presentation.

As researchers, we have a considerable array of statistical techniques that can help us find our way to theories of some depth, but they must be used sensibly and be heavily informed by informed judgment. Even null hypothesis testing complete with power analysis can be useful if we abandon the rejection of point nil hypotheses and use instead "good-enough" range null hypotheses (e.g., the effect size is no larger than 8 raw score units, or $d = .5$), as Serlin and Lapsley (1993) have described in detail. As our measurement and theories improve, we can begin to achieve the Popperian principle of representing our theories as null hypotheses and subjecting them to challenge, as Meehl (1967) argued many years ago. With more evolved psychological theories, we can also find use for likelihood ratios and Bayesian methods (Goodman, 1993; Greenwald, 1975). We quantitative behavioral scientists need not go out of business.

Induction has long been a problem in the philosophy of science. Meehl (1990a) attributed to the distinguished philosopher Morris Raphael Cohen the saying "All logic texts are divided into two parts. In the first part, on deductible logic, the fallacies are explained; in the second part, on inductive logic, they are committed" (p. 110). We appeal to inductive logic to move from the particular results in hand to a theoretically useful generalization. As I have noted, we have a body of statistical techniques, that, used intelligently, can facilitate our efforts. But given the problems of statistical induction, we must finally rely, as have the older sciences, on replication.

ACKNOWLEDGMENTS

This article was originally an address given for the Saul B. Sells Memorial Lifetime Achievement Award, Society of Multivariate Experimental Psychology, San Pedro, California, October 29, 1993.

I have made good use of the comments made on a preliminary draft of this article by Patricia Cohen and other colleagues: Robert P. Abelson, David Bakan, Michael Borenstein, Robyn M. Dawes, Ruma Falk, Gerd Gigerenzer, Charles Greenbaum, Raymond A. Katzell, Donald F. Klein, Robert S. Lee, Paul E. Meehl, Stanley A. Mulaik, Robert Rosenthal, William W. Rozeboom, Elia Sinaiko, Judith D. Singer, and Bruce Thompson. I also acknowledge the help I received from reviewers David Lykken, Matt McGue, and Paul Slovic.

REFERENCES

Bakan, D. (1966). The test of significance in psychological research. *Psychological Bulletin, 66,* 1–29.

Berkson, J. (1938). Some difficulties of interpretation encountered in the application of the chi-square test. *Journal of the American Statistical Association, 33,* 526–542.

Birnbaum, A. (1961). Confidence curves: An omnibus technique for estimation and testing statistical hypotheses. *Journal of the American Statistical Association, 56,* 246–249.

Borenstein, M., Cohen, J., & Rothstein, H. (in press). *Confidence intervals, effect size, and power* [Computer program]. Hillsdale, NJ: Erlbaum.

Cleveland, W. S. (1993). *Visualizing data.* Summit, NJ: Hobart.

Cleveland, W. S., & McGill, M. E. (Eds.). (1988). *Dynamic graphics for statistics.* Belmont, CA: Wadsworth.

Cohen, J. (1962). The statistical power of abnormal-social psychological research: A review. *Journal of Abnormal and Social Psychology, 69,* 145–153.

Cohen, J. (1988). *Statistical power analysis for the behavioral sciences* (2nd ed.). Hillsdale, NJ: Erlbaum.

Cohen, J. (1990). Things I have learned (so far). *American Psychologist, 45,* 1304–1312.

Dawes, R. M. (1988). *Rational choice in an uncertain world.* San Diego, CA: Harcourt Brace Jovanovich.

Falk, R., & Greenbaum, C. W. (1995). Significance tests die hard: The amazing persistence of a probabilistic misconception. *Theory and Psychology, 5,* 75–98.

Fisher, R. A. (1951). *Statistical methods for research workers.* Edinburgh, Scotland: Oliver & Boyd. (Original work published 1925)

Gigerenzer, G. (1993). The superego, the ego, and the id in statistical reasoning. In G. Keren & C. Lewis (Ed.), *A handbook for data analysis in the behavioral sciences: Methodological issues* (pp. 311–339). Hillsdale, NJ: Erlbaum.

Goodman, S. N. (1993). P values, hypothesis tests, and likelihood implications for epidemiology: Implications of a neglected historical debate. *American Journal of Epidemiology, 137,* 485–496.

Greenwald, A. G. (1975). Consequences of prejudice against the null hypothesis. *Psychological Bulletin, 82,* 1–20.

Hogben, L. (1957). *Statistical theory.* London: Allen & Unwin.

Lykken, D. E. (1968). Statistical significance in psychological research. *Psychological Bulletin, 70,* 151–159.

Meehl, P. E. (1967). Theory testing in psychology and physics: A methodological paradox. *Philosophy of Science, 34,* 103–115.

Meehl, P. E. (1978). Theoretical risks and tabular asterisks: Sir Karl, Sir Ronald, and the slow progress of soft psychology. *Journal of Consulting and Clinical Psychology, 46,* 806–834.

Meehl, P. E. (1986). What social scientists don't understand. In D. W. Fiske & R. A. Shweder (Eds.), *Metatheory in social science: Pluralisms and subjectivities* (pp. 315–338). Chicago: University of Chicago Press.

Meehl, P. E. (1990a). Appraising and amending theories: The strategy of Lakatosian defense and two principles that warrant it. *Psychological Inquiry, 1,* 108–141.

Meehl, P. E. (1990b). Why summaries of research on psychological theories are often uninterpretable. *Psychological Reports, 66* (Monograph Suppl. 1–V66), 195–244.

Morrison, D. E., & Henkel, R. E. (Eds.). (1970). *The significance test controversy.* Chicago: Aldine.

Oakes, M. (1986). *Statistical inference: A commentary for the social and behavioral sciences.* New York: Wiley.

Pollard, P., & Richardson, J. T. E. (1987). On the probability of making Type I errors. *Psychological Bulletin, 102,* 159–163.

Popper, K. R. (1959). *The logic of scientific discovery.* London: Hutchinson.

Rosenthal, R. (1979). The "file drawer problem" and tolerance for null results. *Psychological Bulletin, 86,* 638–641.

Rosenthal, R. (1993). Cumulating evidence. In G. Keren & C. Lewis (Ed.), *A handbook for data analysis in the behavioral sciences: Methodological issues* (pp. 519–559). Hillsdale, NJ: Erlbaum.

Rozeboom, W. W. (1960). The fallacy of the null hypothesis significance test. *Psychological Bulletin, 57,* 416–428.

Schmidt, F. L. (1992). What do data really mean? Research findings, meta-analysis, and cumulative knowledge in psychology. *American Psychologist, 47,* 1173–1181.

Sedlmeier, P., & Gigerenzer, G. (1989). Do studies of statistical power have an effect on the power of studies? *Psychological Bulletin, 105,* 309–316.

Serlin, R. C., & Lapsley, D. K. (1993). Rational appraisal of psychological research and the good-enough principle. In G. Keren & C. Lewis (Eds.), *A handbook for data analysis in the behavioral sciences: Methodological issues* (pp. 199–228). Hillsdale, NJ: Erlbaum.

Thompson, B. (1992). Two and one-half decades of leadership in measurement and evaluation. *Journal of Counseling and Development, 70,* 434–438.

Tufte, E. R. (1983). *The visual display of quantitative information.* Cheshire, CT: Graphics Press.

Tufte, E. R. (1990). *Envisioning information.* Cheshire, CT: Graphics Press.

Tukey, J. W. (1962). The future of data analysis. *Annals of Mathematical Statistics, 33,* 1–67.

Tukey, J. W. (1969). Analyzing data: Sanctification or detective work? *American Psychologist, 24,* 83–91.

Tukey, J. W. (1977). *Exploratory data analysis.* Reading, MA: Addison-Wesley.

Tukey, J. W. (1991). The philosophy of multiple comparisons. *Statistical Science, 6,* 100–116.

Tversky, A., & Kahneman, D. (1971). Belief in the law of small numbers. *Psychological Bulletin, 76,* 105–110.

Wainer, H., & Thissen, D. (1981). Graphical data analysis. In M. R. Rosenzweig & L. W. Porter (Eds.), *Annual review of psychology* (pp. 191–241). Palo Alto, CA: Annual Reviews.

Wainer, H., & Thissen, D. (1993). Graphical data analysis. In G. Keren & C. Lewis (Eds.), *A handbook for data analysis in the behavioral sciences: Statistical issues* (pp. 391–457). Hillsdale, NJ: Erlbaum.

Wilkinson, L. (1990). *SYGRAPH: The system for graphics.* Evanston, IL: SYSTAT.

Yates, F. (1951). The influence of statistical methods for research workers on the development of the science of statistics. *Journal of the American Statistical Association, 46,* 19–34.

Chapter 3

Eight Common But False Objections to the Discontinuation of Significance Testing in the Analysis of Research Data

Frank L. Schmidt
University of Iowa

John E. Hunter
Michigan State University

Logically and conceptually, the use of statistical significance testing in the analysis of research data has been thoroughly discredited. However, reliance on significance testing is strongly embedded in the minds and habits of researchers, and therefore proposals to replace significance testing with point estimates and confidence intervals often encounter strong resistance. This chapter examines eight of the most commonly voiced objections to reform of data analysis practices and shows each of them to be erroneous. The objections are: (a) Without significance tests we would not know whether a finding is real or just due to chance; (b) hypothesis testing would not be possible without significance tests; (c) the problem is not significance tests but failure to develop a tradition of replicating studies; (d) when studies have a large number of relationships, we need significance tests to identify those that are real and not just due to chance; (e) confidence intervals are themselves significance tests; (f) significance testing ensures objectivity in the interpretation of research data; (g) it is the misuse, not the use, of significance testing that is the problem; and (h) it is futile to try to reform data analysis methods, so why try? Each of these objections is intuitively appealing and plausible but is easily shown to be logically and intellectually bankrupt. The same is true of the almost 80 other objections we have collected. Statistical significance testing retards the growth of scientific knowledge; it never makes a positive contribution. After decades of unsuccessful efforts, it now appears possible that reform of data analysis procedures will finally succeed. If so, a major impediment to the advance of scientific knowledge will have been removed.

Although the use of statistical significance testing in the analysis of research data is still almost universal, it has now become a controversial practice. Two recent articles (Cohen, 1994; Schmidt, 1996) have argued strongly that the long-standing practice of reliance on significance testing is logically indefensible and retards the research enterprise by making it difficult to develop cumulative knowledge. These articles call for replacing significance tests with point estimates and confidence intervals. Articles of this sort have appeared from time to time since the mid-1950s, but the present situation appears to be different in two important respects. For the first time, the American Psychological Association (APA) Board of Scientific Affairs is looking into the possibility of taking the lead in the effort to reform data analysis procedures. In March of 1996, the Board appointed a task force to study the issue and make recommendations, recommendations that presumably will influence journal editors and reviewers. This development has the potential to effect major changes in data analysis practices.

A second development that makes the current situation different concerns meta-analysis. Over the last 20 years, the use of meta-analysis methods to integrate the findings of research literatures has become increasingly common (Schmidt, 1992). Meta-analysis methods also can be used to present dramatic demonstrations of how reliance on significance testing in data analysis makes it virtually impossible to discern the real meaning of research literatures. Previous arguments against significance testing have been based mostly on logical deficiencies in significance-testing procedures; these abstract logic-based arguments seem to have had only a limited impact. Meta-analysis-based demonstrations seem to be more effective in driving home the concrete distortions created by reliance on significance testing.

Significance testing has been the dominant mode of data analysis in psychology and many other disciplines since the 1930s (Cohen, 1994; Schmidt, 1996). As a result, no practice is more firmly embedded in the minds and habits of researchers than the practice of reliance on significance testing. Not surprisingly, then, the current proposals to replace significance testing with point estimates and confidence intervals have been met with reactions of surprise and shock from some researchers. For some, this proposal seems too radical to be acceptable, and they have advanced specific objections stating why it should not be implemented. For over 2 years, we have been systematically soliciting and collecting such objections. The purpose of this chapter is to present and examine some of these objections. However, only a small number of such objections can be examined here. We have collected more than 80 such objections; those presented in this chapter are only a selected subset of these.

All of the objections examined here are logically deficient and can be shown to be false for that reason. However, it is not possible or desirable to fully explicate all of their deficiencies in this chapter. This chapter is meant to be read in conjunction with Cohen (1994), Schmidt (1996), Carver (1978), Guttman (1985), Rozeboom (1960) and other articles that have critiqued significance testing.

OBJECTION 1

Perhaps the most common objection—and the most deeply rooted psychologically—is the one that states that significance tests are essential because without them we would not know whether a finding is real or just due to chance. The following are three statements of this objection:

> To my way of thinking, statistical significance should precede any discussion of effect size. To talk of effect sizes in the face of results that are not statistically significant does not make sense. In a nutshell, if it is not real, call it zero.

> Null hypothesis significance testing *does* serve a useful purpose. In conducting experiments, the first hypothesis we need to rule out is that the difference or effect is zero. That is, we must, as the first step, rule out the possibility that the result is something that could commonly occur by chance when the null hypothesis that the difference is zero is true.

> We need to be able to separate findings that are real from those that are just chance events. How can a researcher know whether two means are (or two correlations) are really different if he or she does not test to see if they are significantly different?

ANSWER TO OBJECTION 1

Of all the objections against discontinuing significance testing that we have collected, this one is the most fascinating to us. It is fascinating not for any technical statistical reasons, but because of what it reveals about the psychology of researchers. Of special significance here is the fact that we have seen this objection raised by researchers who had read (and seemingly understood) Cohen (1994), Schmidt (1996), and other similar articles. The content of these papers demonstrates that significance tests cannot separate real findings from chance findings in research studies. Yet because this objection, worded specifically as it is here, is not explicitly addressed in those articles, this point apparently escapes many readers. We attribute this psychologically interesting fact to the virtual brainwashing in significance testing that all of us have undergone, beginning with our first undergraduate course in psychological statistics.

It would indeed be desirable to have a simple data analysis technique that could reveal whether observed differences or relations in a data set are real or "just due to chance." This objection assumes that null hypothesis significance testing can perform that feat. Unfortunately, no such method exists—or is even possible. Certainly, the null hypothesis statistical significance test cannot achieve this purpose.

The facts that have long been known about statistical power make this abundantly clear. The average power of null hypothesis significance tests in typical studies and research literatures is in the .40 to .60 range (Cohen, 1962, 1965, 1988, 1992; Schmidt, 1996; Schmidt, Hunter, & Urry, 1976; Sedlmeier & Gigerenzer, 1989). Suppose we take .50 as a rough average. With a power of .50, half of all tests in a research literature will be nonsignificant. The objection under consideration here assumes that if it is not significant, it is zero. (E.g., "In a nutshell, if it is not real, call it zero.") This assumption is not an aberration; it reflects the nearly universal decision rule among researchers that a nonsignificant result is probably just due to chance and should be considered to be zero (Oakes, 1986; Schmidt, 1996). So the conclusion in half of all studies will be that there is no relationship. Every one of these conclusions will be false. That is, in a research area in which there really is a difference or relation, when the significance test is used to determine whether findings are real or just chance events, the null hypothesis significance test will provide an erroneous answer about 50% of the time. This level of accuracy is so low that it could be achieved just by flipping a (unbiased) coin!

In fact, coin flipping would in many cases provide a higher level of accuracy than the significance test. With coin flipping, the expected error rate is never less than 50%. But in many research domains, the average statistical power is *less* than .50. One example is the literature on the relation between job satisfaction and absenteeism; there the power is approximately .15. Another example is the literature on the relation between job performance and job satisfaction, which has an average power of about .20. A third example is the literature on the relation between the personality trait of conscientiousness and job performance (Barrick & Mount, 1991), where mean power is less than .30. In these and other research areas, meta-analysis has shown that the relation was indeed always present and was never zero. In all such research areas, significance tests have an error rate (in distinguishing between real effects and chance effects) than is greater than that of a coin flip.

But, one might object, this is not a defect of the significance test per se. This is just a problem of low statistical power. The problem of low power could be solved by requiring all researchers to use large enough sample sizes to ensure high power. Schmidt (1996) showed that this "solution" will not solve the problem. Such a requirement will make it impossible for most studies ever to be conducted. The effect sizes and relations examined in most research are small enough that power of even .80 (which still produces an error rate of 20%) requires more subjects than are often feasible to obtain. They may be unavailable at any cost or be beyond the resources of the researcher to obtain. Furthermore, as the theories tested and compared become more sophisticated over time, the effects sizes studied tend to become smaller (Schmidt, 1996), making the problem worse. So with this requirement, most of the studies in our current research literatures could never have been conducted. Would this be a loss? It certainly would. Such studies contain valuable information when combined with others like them in a meta-analysis. Precise meta-analysis results can be obtained based on studies that *all* have low statistical power individually. In fact, many of the meta-analyses in our current literature—meta-analyses that are the foundation of our accepted research conclusions—are of this type. All valuable information of this sort would be needlessly lost if a statistical power requirement were imposed on researchers in an ill-advised attempt to salvage the current practice of reliance on significance testing. So imposing a statistical power requirement on researchers will not work as a solution.

The preceding analysis of errors made by the significance test applies only when there really is an effect or relation. What about the case in which the population effect really is zero? If the population effect is zero, then the error rate of the significance test is always the alpha level (typically 5% or 1%). For example, if the true difference between two means in a study using analysis of variance (ANOVA) is zero, and we use an alpha level of .05, the error rate is only 5%. The problem with this objection is that it is rarely if ever the case that the population effect is zero (Carver, 1978; Cohen, 1994; Rozeboom, 1960; Schmidt, 1996). First, there is the fact that, even in the absence of substantive considerations, it is virtually impossible for the null hypothesis to be exactly true (Carver, 1978; Cohen, 1994; Rozeboom, 1960). Hence, it is virtually never true that the error rate is equal to the alpha level. Instead, it is equal to one minus the statistical power to detect the existing deviation of the population effect size from zero.

But there are more substantive considerations that are important here, too. In fact, they are more important. In most research areas, as researchers gain more experience with the phenomenon they are studying, they become more sophisticated in the hypotheses they advance. When research in a given area is first begun, hypotheses may be advanced that are truly false (or as nearly false as they can be)—for example, the hypothesis that raising self-esteem raises IQ. In these cases, the actual population effect is in fact zero—or very nearly so. But as time goes by the hypotheses proposed become more likely to be correct, and hence the corresponding null hypotheses become more and more likely to be false. After a time, virtually all null hypotheses tested are false—not only in a philosophical or logical sense, but (more importantly) in a substantive sense. When the null hypothesis is in fact false, the overall error rate is not the alpha level, but the Type II error rate. That is, when the null is false, the alpha level becomes irrelevant to the error rate of the significance test; it is impossible to falsely conclude that there is a relation when in fact there is a relation. The overall error rate is then one minus the statistical power. There is reason to believe that most research areas today have reached this point (Schmidt, 1996). Hence, it is typically the case that the error rate of the significance test is not 5% but somewhere in the 40% to 60% range, and often higher.

So in light of these considerations, let us reconsider Objection 1. Psychologically, it is easy to understand the desire for a technique that would perform the desirable function of distinguishing in our data sets between relations, differences, and effects that are real and those that are just chance fluctuations. This objection, we believe, is motivated psychologically by precisely this strong desire. But wanting to believe something is true does not make it true. Significance testing cannot perform this function.

OBJECTION 2

This objection holds that without significance testing, researchers would no longer be able to test hypotheses, and we would therefore no longer have a science. This objection has been phrased as follows:

> Discontinuing significance testing means the elimination of hypothesis testing. After all, the purpose of significance testing is to test scientific hypotheses. Nothing is more basic and fundamental to science than the testing of hypotheses; this is the process by which useful theories are developed. You cannot have a science without hypothesis testing. So it makes no sense to call for the discontinuation of significance testing.

ANSWER TO OBJECTION 2

The first aspect of this objection that should be noted is that it equates hypothesis tests based on significance tests with *scientific hypothesis testing in general.* It assumes that there are no other ways to test hypotheses. If these two are one and the same thing, then it follows that discontinuing significance testing means the elimination of hypothesis testing. The fact that many researchers believe that null hypothesis significance testing and hypothesis testing in science in general are one and the same thing is a tribute to the persuasive impact of Fisher's writings (Fisher, 1932, 1935, 1959, 1973). In his writings, Fisher equated null hypothesis significance testing with scientific hypothesis testing.

Let us explore this objection. The physical sciences, such as physics and chemistry, do not use statistical significance testing to test hypotheses or interpret data. In fact, most researchers in the physical sciences regard reliance on significance testing as unscientific. So it is ironic that some psychologists and other behavioral scientists defend the use of significance tests on grounds that such tests are necessary for rigorous tests of scientific hypotheses!

How do researchers in the physical sciences analyze data and test hypotheses? Hedges (1987) found that in individual studies they use procedures that are equivalent to point estimates and confidence intervals. That is, in each individual study an estimate of the quantity of theoretical interest is computed and an "error band" (confidence interval) is placed around this estimate. Hypotheses are tested by comparing the estimated value to the theoretically predicted value; this comparison is *not* based on a significance test. Hedges also found that in combining findings across studies, researchers in the physical sciences employ methods that are "essentially identical" to meta-analysis. The tests of hypotheses and theories that are considered the most credible are those conducted based on data combined across studies. Estimates from the different studies are averaged, and the standard error of the mean is computed and used to place a confidence interval around the mean estimate. (The confidence interval is *not* interpreted as a significance test.) These are essentially the procedures advocated by Hunter and Schmidt (1990) and Schmidt (1992, 1996). Hence, it is no accident that the physical sciences have not experienced the debilitating problems described, for example, in Schmidt (1996) that are the inevitable consequence of reliance on significance tests.

Let's consider a couple of examples from physics. Einstein's general theory of relativity produced the hypothesis that as light passes a massive body, it would be bent—and it predicted the amount by which it would be bent. That hypothesis was tested in a famous study that measured the amount of bending in light produced by its passing the sun by comparing the apparent position of stars at the edge of the disk of the sun during an eclipse with their apparent positions when not near the sun. Several different observatories made these measurements and the measurements were averaged. The measured amount of bending corresponded to the figure predicted by Einstein's general theory, and so the hypothesis was confirmed and hence the more general theory from which it was derived was supported. In this important study, *no significance tests were used.*

Consider a second example. Einstein's special theory of relativity predicts that a clock (of any kind—mechanical, electrical, or atomic) that is in an airplane traveling around the world at a certain speed (say, 500 miles per hour) will run slower than exactly the same clock on the ground. Studies were conducted to test this hypothesis derived from the theory, using various kinds of clocks and airplanes. Measurements were averaged across studies. The hypothesis was confirmed. The amount by which the clocks in the airplanes ran slower corresponded to the amount predicted by the theory. Again, *no significance tests were used.*

The objection we are evaluating here would hold that these studies—and countless others in physics, chemistry, and the other physical sciences—are not really scientific because no significance tests were run on the data. For example, no significance test was run to see if the amount of bending was significantly greater than zero (test of the null hypothesis) or to see if the observed amount of bending was significantly different from the amount predicted by the theory (a significance test preferred by some). Most people do not find it credible that these studies in physics are not scientific.

Null hypothesis significance testing was popularized by Fisher in the 1930s (e.g., Fisher, 1932). The Neyman-Pearson approach to significance testing was introduced about 10 years later (Neyman, 1962). Hence, this objection implies that prior to the 1930s, no legitimate scientific research was possible. If hypothesis testing is essential to science, and if the only way to test scientific hypotheses is by means of statistical significance tests, then all the physics and chemistry of the 19th century and earlier—including the work of Newton and the development of the periodic table of the elements—was pseudo science, not real science. How credible is such a position?

OBJECTION 3

This objection holds that the problems that researchers have experienced in developing cumulative knowledge stem not from reliance on significance tests, but from failure to develop a tradition of replication of findings:

> Cohen (1994) and Schmidt (1996) have called for abandonment of null hypothesis significance testing, as advanced by R. A. Fisher. But they have both very much misunderstood Fisher's position. Fisher's standard for establishing firm knowledge was not one of statistical significance in a single study but the ability to repeatedly produce results significant at (at least) the .05 level. Fisher held that replication is essential to confidence in the reliability (reproducibility) of a result, as well as to generalizability (external validity). The problems that Cohen and Schmidt point to result not from use of significance testing, but from our failure to develop a tradition of replication of findings. Our problem is that we have placed little value on replication studies.

ANSWER TO OBJECTION 3

Of all the objections considered in this chapter, this one is perhaps the most ironic. It is not that this objection misstates Fisher's position. Fisher *did* hold that a single statistically significant rejection of the null hypothesis was not adequate to establish a scientific fact. And Fisher *did* state that the appropriate foundation for scientific knowledge was replication, specifically the ability to repeatedly produce statistically significant results (Oakes, 1986).

The irony is this. Reproducibility requires high statistical power. Even if all other aspects of a study are carried out in a scientifically impeccable manner, the finding of statistical significance in the original study will not replicate consistently if statistical power is low. As discussed elsewhere in this chapter, statistical power in most psychology literatures averages about .50. Under these circumstances, only 50% of all replications will be successful according to Fisher's criterion of success—rejection of the null hypothesis at the .05 level or less.

Furthermore, the probability of a successful *series* of replications is the product of statistical power across studies. For example, suppose the requirement is that any statistically significant finding must be replicated in two additional studies before it is accepted as real. Then, if power in each study is .50, the probability of meeting this replication requirement is $(.50)(.50) = .25$. So the error rate is now 75%, instead of 50%. Suppose the requirement is five replications. Then the probability of successful replication in all five studies is .50 raised to the 5th power, which is .03. So there is only a 3% chance that an effect that really exists would be concluded to be real, given this replication requirement. And the error rate is 97%; that is, 97% of the time when this replication rule is applied, it will lead to the false conclusion that no effect exits! So much for the value of requiring replication.

We note in passing a curious thing about this objection: It contains a double standard for statistically significant and statistically nonsignificant findings. It requires significant findings to be replicated, but does not require this of nonsignificant findings. That is, in the case of nonsignificant findings, it implicitly holds that we can accept these without need for replication. It assumes that nonsignificant finding will replicate perfectly. But in fact in most real literatures nonsignificant findings do not replicate any better than significant findings. The probability of replication of a nonsignificant finding in a new study is one minus the statistical power in that study. If the statistical power assumes the typical value of .50, then one minus the power is also .50. So the probability of replicating a nonsignificant finding in a second study is .50. The probability of replicating in each of two new studies is $(.50)(.50) = .25$. And the probability of successful replication of each of five new studies is .03. So in the typical research literature, nonsignificant findings do not replicate any better than significant findings.

Three factors combine to determine statistical power: the size of the underlying population effect, the sample size, and the alpha level. Sample size and alpha level may sometimes be subject to control by the researcher; the population effect usually is not. But long before these factors are considered there is another requirement: One must acknowledge the fact that statistical power is a critical determinant of the success of any effort at replication. Fisher did not take this essential first step. In fact, Fisher rejected the very concept of statistical power and tried to discredit both the concept and the methods for its analysis when these were introduced by Neyman and Pearson in the 1930s and 1940s (Neyman & Pearson, 1933; Oakes, 1986). Fisher based his approach to statistical significance testing solely on the null hypothesis and its rejection. He rejected the concept of any alternative hypothesis that could be the basis for computing power. Hence in Fisherian statistics, there is no concept of statistical power. Therefore, there is no method for determining whether statistical power is high or low, either in a single study or in a series of replication studies. So there is nothing in Fisherian statistics and research methodology to hold power to adequate levels or to prevent statistical power from being quite low. As a result, there is nothing to prevent failures of replication due solely to low statistical power. For example, if replication fails in, say, 50% of the replication attempts, there is no way to discern whether this failure is due to low statistical power or to some other problem.

Hence the irony is that although Fisher made replication the foundation of scientific knowledge, his methods made it impossible to determine whether it was statistically logical or not to *expect* research findings to replicate. Remember that this objection is specifically a defense of Fisher against Cohen (1994) and Schmidt (1996). Problems of statistical power exist also, of course, with the Neyman-Pearson approach to significance testing. But with that approach, the researcher can at least estimate levels of statistical power. These estimates then allow one to determine whether it is logical from a statistical standpoint to expect the findings to replicate.

Internal contradictions aside, what would be the practical result of accepting this objection at face value? This objection holds that findings that do not repeatedly and consistently replicate must be rejected as not demonstrating any scientific knowledge. Looking at typical research literatures in psychology and other social sciences, we see significance rates for individual hypotheses of around 50%. That is, after the appearance of the first study obtaining significant results, about half of the subsequent replication attempts fail to get significant results. According to the rule advanced in this objection, all such research literatures are completely inconclusive. They demonstrate nothing and establish no scientifically reliable findings.

Is this really the case? Is this conclusion realistic? First, a 50% significance rate is much higher than the 5% rate one would expect if the null hypothesis were true. This fact would appear to cast serious doubt on the Fisherian conclusion. But more revealing are the results of two other analyses that can be performed on such research literatures. A statistical power analysis would reveal an average power of 50% and therefore indicate that, if the effect or relation were present in every study, we should nevertheless expect only 50% of these studies to attain statistical significance—just what we in fact observe. Second, meta-analysis applied to this literature would likely indicate a substantial effect size (or relation) underlying the research literature—and perhaps little real variation around this mean value after controlling for variation produced by sampling error and other artifacts. This is in fact what many meta-analyses to date of such literatures have shown to be the case (Hunter & Schmidt, 1990; Schmidt, 1992).

So we can now contrast the two conclusions. The Fisherian conclusion is that this research literature is inconclusive; it can support no scientific conclusions. The meta-analysis-based conclusion is that the hypothesis tested in the studies making up this literature is strongly supported, and the best estimate of this effect size is, say, $d = .65$ (that is, the treatment effect is 65% of a standard deviation). The Fisherian conclusion is false; the meta-analysis conclusion is correct.

So in conclusion, this attempted defense of Fisherian null hypothesis significance testing fails on all counts.

OBJECTION 4

This position holds that significance testing has the practical value of making it easier to interpret research findings—one's own and others. It does this by allowing one to eliminate from further consideration all findings that are not statistically significant. The following are three statements of this objection:

> I work in survey research. In that area, there are often hundreds of relationships that can be examined between the various responses and scales. Significance testing is very useful in sifting through these and separating those that are real from those that are just due to chance. Being able to do this has important practical value to me as a researcher. For one thing, it saves a tremendous amount of time.

> I am a great fan of confidence intervals, but for some purposes significance tests are quite useful from a practical point of view. For example, suppose you are doing an ANOVA on a full 2 by 8 by 4 factorial design with all the interactions. While it might be virtuous to look at all the confidence intervals, using significance tests (p values) to pick out the interesting effects saves you a lot of time.

> Significance tests are needed to eliminate whole classes of variables that have no effect on, or relation to, dependent variables. Otherwise, it becomes impossible to see what is important and what is not, and interpretation of the data becomes an almost impossibly complex task. I know that when I read research reports in journals, I just look for the variables that are significant. If I had to think about *all* the relationships that were considered, significant or not, I would be driven to distraction.

ANSWER TO OBJECTION 4

We suspect that this objection is one that all of us can identify with. How many of us, when faced in our reading of a research study with several regression equations each containing 20 or more independent variables, have not yielded to the temptation to simplify the task by just singling out for our attention only those variables that are significant? Most of us do this, yet it is not a valid argument for the significance test.

Although it is perhaps not readily apparent, Objection 4 is essentially Objection 1 with a practical, rather than a scientific, rationale. Objection 1 holds that we need to use significance tests to distinguish between chance findings and real findings *for scientific reasons*. Objection 4 holds that we need to do the same thing, *but for practical reasons*. That is, Objection 4 holds that significance testing should be used to separate real from chance findings because doing so reduces the amount of time and effort required in interpreting data, both in one's own studies and in studies that one reads in the research literature.

Both objections falsely assume that significance testing can separate real from chance findings. And in both cases, this assumption is based on the further false assumption that findings that are nonsignificant are zero, whereas findings that are significant are real. These false assumptions are explored and refuted in the response to Objection 1; there is no need to repeat this material here. Instead, we want to point out certain features unique to this objection.

First, the "convenience rationale" underlying Objection 4 is the product of an undesirably atheoretical, rawly empirical approach to science; that is, the approach that empirically "mines" scientific data rather than focusing on the testing of specific hypothesis and theories. The practice of scanning a large number of relationships looking for those with low p values has never been successful in contributing to the development of cumulative knowledge. Successful science requires the hard work of theory development followed by focused empirical tests.

But one might object that, although this is true, researchers are sometimes going to use this rawly empirical approach anyway, if for no other reason than the fact that they are often not going to be willing to supply the needed theoretical framework if the author of the study did not provide it to begin with. This leads to our second point: Even under these circumstances, use of significance test results is an inferior way to proceed. That is, even if one deliberately decides to "scan" data in this unprofitable rawly empirical manner, this can better be accomplished by focusing not on p values, but on point estimates of effect sizes. Even under these circumstances, it is better to pick out for more detailed attention the largest effect sizes (largest d values, correlations, or etas) than the smallest p values. It is true that the same problems of capitalization on chance exist in both cases. It is also true that when sample sizes are the same, there is a perfect relation between any index of effect size and its p value. However, sample sizes are not always the same, even within the same study; so the largest effect sizes may not be the relations with the smallest p values. And in comparing across studies, sample sizes are virtually never the same. But more importantly, focusing on the effect size keeps the actual magnitude of the effects and relations foremost in one's mind. This is important. To the extent that this empirical data-mining procedure ever works at all, it works by singling out unexpected large effects or relations—which can perhaps provide the basis for subsequent hypothesis construction. On the other hand, findings with very low p values can reflect underlying effects that are so small as to be of no theoretical or practical interest. If so, this fact is concealed by the p value.

So in conclusion, there is never a legitimate role for significance testing, not even in data-mining.

Finally, we would like to use Objections 1 and 4 to point out another fascinating aspect of the psychology of addiction to significance testing. As noted earlier, Objections 1 and 4 are conceptually identical; they are objectively and logically the same objection. Yet to most researchers they do not appear to be identical; in fact, to most researchers in our experience they appear to be not only different objections, but *unrelated* ones as well. We have found this to be a general phenomenon: If they appear under different guises, defenses of significance testing that are conceptually identical appear to most researchers to be different arguments. Thus a researcher who has accepted a telling refutation of one defense will continue to cling to another that is conceptually identical. This creates the apparent necessity on the part of proponents of data analysis reform to address separately each and every possible wording in which defenses of significance testing appear—an impossible task, because the number of different wordings is seemingly limitless. For example, for every objection quoted in this chapter, we have alternative wordings of the same objection that have not been included because of space limitations. (In addition to the space required to list them, it requires space to explain why they are conceptually identical to others already listed and discussed.) Although fully addressed in this chapter, many of these alternately worded statements would probably appear plausible to researchers who have read and accepted the contents of this chapter.

Psychologically, why is this the case? We suspect that the explanation is something like the following. Accepting the proposition that significance testing should be discontinued and replaced by point estimates and confidence intervals entails the difficult effort of changing the beliefs and practices of a lifetime. Naturally such a prospect provokes resistance. Researchers would like to believe it is not so; they would like to believe there is a legitimate rationale for refusing to make such a change. This desire makes it hard for them to see that new defenses of significance testing are conceptually identical to those they have already acknowledged are vacuous. So they accept these arguments as new challenges that have not yet been met by the critics of significance testing. In the meantime, they are relieved of the feeling of any obligation to make changes in their data analysis practices. We and others promoting reform of data analysis methods can only hope that at some point this process will come to an end.

OBJECTION 5

This objection holds that replacing significance testing with point estimates and confidence intervals will *not* mean discontinuation of significance testing:

> There is less than meets the eye to the change that you are advocating. You and others call for discontinuing use of significance testing, but the confidence intervals that you say should replace the significance test are in fact significance tests! If the lower bound of the confidence interval does not include zero, then the result is statistically significant. If it does, then the result is not significant. So the confidence interval *is* a significance test. You are throwing significance tests out the front door and then sneaking them back in through the back door!

ANSWER TO OBJECTION 5

This objection is incorrect, but we want to first point out that even if it were true, replacing significance tests with point estimates and confidence intervals would still be an improvement—although a limited one. That is, even if researchers *interpreted* confidence intervals as significance tests, there would still be benefits from using confidence intervals to conduct the significance tests, because the confidence intervals would reveal to researchers useful facts that are completely concealed by the significance test. First, researchers would see a point estimate of the effect size or relation, so the researcher would have knowledge of the magnitude of the effect. The researcher does not see this information when using only a significance test. Second, the confidence interval would reveal to the researcher the extent of uncertainty in his or her study. For typical studies, the confidence interval would be quite large, revealing that the study contains only very limited information, an important fact concealed by the significance test. Likewise, the researcher would see that a wide range of estimates of the effect size are plausible—many of which if realized in a study would be statistically significant. Finally, consideration of this information revealed by the confidence interval would likely temper and reduce the emphasis placed by the researcher on the outcome of the significance test. That is, researchers might learn to take the significance test less seriously. So there would be benefits even if researchers interpreted confidence intervals as significance tests. But they need not and should not.

The assumption underlying this objection is that because confidence intervals *can* be interpreted as significance tests, they *must* be so interpreted. But this is a false assumption. Long before the significance test was ever proposed, confidence intervals were being used and were interpreted as "error bands" around point estimates. In fact, confidence intervals have a very long history, much longer than that of significance tests. Significance tests were advanced (mostly by Ronald Fisher) in the 1930s, but confidence intervals were advanced, advocated, and applied by some of the earliest contributors to statistics, including Bernoulli, Poisson, and others in the 1700s. In the 20th century, prior to the appearance of Fisher's 1932 and 1935 texts, data analysis in individual studies typically was conducted using point estimates and confidence intervals (Oakes, 1986). The confidence interval that was usually presented along with the point estimate was the "probable error"—the 50% confidence interval. Significance testing generally was not employed, and the confidence intervals presented were not interpreted as significance tests.

In fact, the probable error confidence interval is perhaps the best reply to the proposition that confidence intervals must be interpreted as significance tests. Individuals maintaining that confidence intervals must be interpreted as significance tests have in mind 95% or 99% confidence intervals. These are indeed the two most frequently used confidence intervals today. But confidence intervals of any width can be used. For example, many statistics books today still discuss and present the 68% confidence interval—which extends one standard error above and below the point estimate. The 68% confidence interval is just as correct and legitimate as the 99% confidence interval. So is the 50% probable error confidence interval. It seems clear that those who advance Objection 5 would not be willing to interpret these confidence intervals as significance tests. Perhaps they would revise their objection to say that not *all* confidence intervals must be interpreted as significance tests, but only 95% and wider confidence intervals. Obviously, this is a purely arbitrary position and could not salvage the original objection. Hence it seems clear that no confidence interval *must* be interpreted as a significance test.

In responding to this objection, it is also revealing to look at the use of confidence intervals in the physical sciences, such as physics and chemistry. In the physical sciences, confidence intervals are used but not significance tests. (See the discussion in the response to Objection 2.) So the physical sciences provide us with a model of successful research endeavors that have employed confidence intervals but have not interpreted those confidence intervals as significance tests. Would those who advance Objection 5 maintain that data analysis practices in the physical sciences are erroneous and unscientific? To be logically consistent, they would have to.

Although it is clear that confidence intervals need not (and, we argue, should not) be interpreted as significance tests, it does seem to be the case that many feel a strong compulsion to so interpret them. What is the basis for this compulsion? We believe it is a strongly felt need for an objective, mechanical procedure for making a dichotomous decision in analyzing study data. That is, it is based on the belief that the researcher must make a dichotomous decision; the researcher must conclude either that the study results support the hypothesis or that they do not. The traditional use of significance testing provides a procedure for doing this. Because this dichotomous decision must be made, this belief holds, an objective procedure for doing this is essential and must be retained—even if confidence intervals are used in place of significance tests.

But in fact no such dichotomous decision need be made in any individual study. Indeed, it is futile to do so, because no single individual study contains sufficient information to support a final conclusion about the truth or value of an hypothesis. Only by combining findings across multiple studies using meta-analysis can dependable scientific conclusions be reached (Hunter & Schmidt, 1990; Schmidt, 1992, 1996). From the point of view of the goal of optimally advancing the cumulation of scientific knowledge, it is best for individual researchers to present point estimates and confidence intervals and refrain from attempting to draw final conclusions about research hypotheses. These will emerge from later meta-analyses.

However, although this is the situation objectively, it is not one that many researchers feel comfortable with. In many cases, the motivation that moves the primary researcher to undertake and complete an arduous and time-consuming primary study is the belief that his or her study will answer the relevant scientific question. We suspect that it is usually not the case that the motivation is to contribute a study to a large group of studies that will be included in a meta-analysis. This feeling on the part of primary researchers is understandable (and we have experienced it ourselves), but the belief that one's individual study will answer a scientific question will not make it true, no matter how understandable the belief.

Objectively, this belief has never been true; and even in the routine practice of the research enterprise, it has never been accepted as true. Long before the advent and acceptance of meta-analysis, research literatures accumulated on many research hypotheses. When these literatures were interpreted using traditional narrative review methods, no single study was ever viewed by the reviewer as having itself alone resolved the scientific question. Hence it is not the case, as maintained by some, that the ascendance of meta-analysis has reduced the status and probative value of the individual primary study. That process took place much earlier; in every research area it occurred as soon as a substantial research literature accumulated on a particular scientific question.

One last note: Some have interpreted our position that single studies cannot be the basis for final conclusions as forbidding researchers from discussing and interpreting the findings in their individual studies. This is not our position. Results in individual studies—and in particular the results in the first study on a question—can be and should be taken as preliminary findings and can be considered and discussed as such and even used in preliminary and tentative evaluations of theories. In fact, one advantage of replacing significance testing with point estimates and confidence intervals is that these more desirable data analysis methods allow researchers to see that the findings in individual studies are clearly tentative and preliminary. Reform of data analysis procedures does not mean that researchers will no longer be allowed to discuss and interpret their findings in individual studies. In fact, it means they will be able to do so better.

OBJECTION 6

This objection states that significance testing serves the invaluable purpose of ensuring objectivity in the interpretation of research data:

> One of the important distinguishing features of science as a human activity is *objectivity*. Unlike art or literature, science strives for objectivity. Its conclusions are to be independent of the subjective judgments of any one individual. A major reason why significance testing has become dominant in data analysis is the need to have an objective procedure that does not depend on subjective judgments made by individual researchers. Significance testing provides this objectivity better than alternative procedures. Significance testing is objective in the important sense that the results obtained are (or should be) the same no matter who conducts the test.

ANSWER TO OBJECTION 6

There is an implicit assumption in this objection that significance testing is objective but that confidence intervals are not. In fact, point estimates and confidence intervals are just as objective as significance tests. There is nothing less objective about the computation of confidence interval or the properties of the final confidence interval. Hence objectivity is a non-issue.

Implicit in this objection is the assumption that objectivity requires in each study a dichotomous decision as to whether the hypothesis being studied is confirmed (supported) or disconfirmed (not supported). This objection views significance testing as providing an objective, mechanical set of rules for making the necessary binary decision whether to accept or reject the research hypothesis. Point estimates and confidence intervals, on the other hand, do not necessarily produce a dichotomous decision. They provide instead a point estimate and an error band around that estimate. But there is no scientific reason to have or want a binary decision to accept or reject an hypothesis in an individual study—because the final decision on whether to accept or reject an hypothesis cannot depend on the results of one study. Instead, decisions to accept or reject an hypothesis must be based on results integrated across all the studies that have tested that hypothesis. The usual way of doing this is through meta-analysis. (There may be several meta-analyses, because different clusters of studies may have tested the hypothesis in different ways or tested different aspects of the hypothesis.)

This objection appears to be based on a desire for something that is not possible: a procedure that will provide the answer to whether the hypothesis is correct or incorrect from a single study. We know from statistical power analyses that the significance tests cannot do this. The fact that power in typical research is usually between .30 and .60 shows that the individual study does not contain enough information to allow a conclusion about the truth or falseness of the hypothesis tested. The confidence interval reveals this lack of information more clearly and directly: Confidence intervals are typically quite wide. The significance test conceals the lack of information; only those rare researchers who go beyond computing the significance test itself and compute the statistical power of their study ever actually see how little information there is in their study. This concealment is very convenient for users of significance tests: It allows them to feel good about making accept-reject decisions about hypotheses even when the error rate is 50% or more.

To adopt a procedure because it has the virtue of being objective when it has typical error rates of 50%, 60%, or 70% is to make a fetish of objectivity. This is especially so given that an equally objective procedure is available that will hold the total error rate to 5%, 1%, or whatever we want it to be. That procedure is the confidence interval (Schmidt, 1996).

Flipping a coin to decide whether to accept or reject an hypotheses would also be objective. Furthermore, from a statistical power point of view, it would guarantee that the average error rate would not go above 50%—a guarantee the significance test cannot provide. And, of course, it would be more efficient: No study would have to be done. So from the perspective of objectivity as the overriding value, flipping a coin is often a better choice than the significance test.

But aren't there at least some studies with either large enough Ns, large enough effect sizes, or both to produce very high statistical power? If so, can't such a single study answer a scientific question (i.e., provide a sound basis for accepting or rejecting an hypothesis)? And in the case of such studies, why not use significance tests, because power is not a problem?

Taking the last question first: Low statistical power in typical research studies is only one of the severe problems associated with significance testing. There are many other reasons for not using significance testing (see Carver, 1978; Cohen, 1994; Rozeboom, 1960; Schmidt, 1996; and others; see also the responses to Objections 3 and 7 in this chapter).

Second, there are reasons beyond inadequate power why a single study is not adequate to settle a scientific question. That is, there are additional reasons why multiple studies are necessary in science. There may be, for example, measurement differences between studies (e.g., the dependent variable may be measured differently), treatment operationalization differences, study design differences, instructional differences, sample composition differences, and other differences. Once a body of studies has accumulated, meta-analysis can be used to determine whether any of these differences make any difference in research outcomes; a finding that they do not greatly strengthens the final conclusion. For example, the mean effect sizes can be compared for the cluster of studies that used operationalization A and the cluster using operationalization B. In this way, possible methodological moderators of results can be disconfirmed or identified.

In addition to methodological moderators, substantive moderator hypotheses can also be tested in meta-analysis. For example, a researcher may hypothesize that the increased use of computers over time will reduce the correlation between constructs X and Y among high school students. If multiple studies are available across time and are examined in a meta-analysis, this hypothesis can be evaluated. A single study, no matter how large, is unlikely to permit such an analysis. Hence even if statistical power is very high, a single study still cannot answer a scientific question. And it is clear that there is potentially much more useful information in a large number of smaller studies than in a single large study with the same total sample size.

Many primary researchers do not like these facts. They strongly want to believe that their individual primary study can answer an important scientific question. But wanting something to be true does not make it true.

OBJECTION 7

This objection holds that the problem is not use but *misuse* of significance testing:

> The problem is not the use of significance testing per se, but the *misuse*. It is true that misuse—and even abuse—of significance testing is quite common in our research literatures. This occurs when researchers give significance tests erroneous interpretations and when significance tests are used despite violations of their underlying assumptions. But the solution is to educate researchers to end their misuses, not to discontinue significance testing. Significance testing is just a tool. We just need to teach researchers to use that tool properly.

ANSWER TO OBJECTION 7

The response to this objection must address two questions. First, is it possible to educate researchers so that they will no longer misinterpret the meaning of significance tests and no longer use them inappropriately? Second, if we could successfully do this, would significance testing then be a useful research tool?

The evidence indicates that the answer to the first question is no. Significance testing has been the dominant mode of data analysis in psychology and many other disciplines for approximately 50 years. During that long period, there has been no apparent decrease in the prevalence of misinterpretation of the meaning of significance tests, despite the efforts of many methodologists. This is in part because some teachers of statistics courses implicitly and explicitly accept and endorse some of these misinterpretations and even incorporate them into their textbooks (Carver, 1978; Schmidt, 1996). Of all these misinterpretations, the one most devastating to the research enterprise is the belief that if a difference or relation is not statistically significant, then it is zero. This is the false belief underlying Objection 1; it was discussed in detail there. Another frequent misinterpretation is the belief that level of statistical significance (p value) indicates the importance or size of a difference or relation. A third is the false belief that statistical significance indicates that a finding is reliable and will replicate if a new study is conducted. These misinterpretations are discussed in some detail in Schmidt (1996) and Oakes (1986); these and still others are discussed by Carver (1978), in what is probably the most thorough published exploration of the misinterpretations researchers place on significance tests. Recently, Carver (1993) stated that there is no indication that his 1978 article has had any noticeable impact on the practices and interpretations of researchers. Perhaps a reasonable conclusion would be that it is unlikely that it will be possible to wean researchers away from their attachment to erroneous beliefs about, and interpretations of, significance tests.

By contrast, the story with respect to point estimates and confidence intervals is very different. Point estimates of effect sizes and their associated confidence intervals are much easier for students and researchers to understand and, as a result, are much less frequently misinterpreted. Any teacher of statistics knows it is much easier for students to understand point estimates and confidence intervals than significance testing with its strangely inverted logic. This is another plus for point estimation and confidence intervals.

But suppose it were possible to eliminate "misuse" of significance tests. Suppose researchers were somehow all educated to avoid misinterpretations of significance tests. Would use of significance tests then be a useful research tool? The answer is no. Even if misinterpretations were eliminated, it still remains that statistical significance testing is singularly unsuited to the task of advancing the development of cumulative scientific knowledge. This is true in interpreting both individual studies and research literatures. In individual studies, significance testing conceals rather than reveals the important information researchers need. Unlike point estimates, it provides no estimate of the *size* of the effect or relation; so there is no information to indicate whether the effect is minuscule or quite large. Unlike confidence intervals, significance testing provides no information on the degree of uncertainty in the study. Confidence intervals correctly reveal that individual small-sample studies contain very little information about the hypothesis being tested; this is revealed by the fact that the confidence interval is surprisingly wide. The significance test conceals this important piece of evidence from researchers, allowing them to continue to harbor false beliefs about the evidential value of their individual studies.

Another important fact is that even in the absence of misinterpretations of significance tests, the problem of low statistical power would remain. What would change is that in the absence of misinterpretations, researchers would no longer falsely conclude that nonsignificant differences are in fact zero. Instead, they would conclude that they are merely inconclusive, the correct conclusion according to Fisher (1932). However, this "proper" interpretation of significance tests would create major errors in the interpretation of research literatures. A typical research literature, with approximately 50% of studies finding significance and 50% not, would be incorrectly interpreted as inconclusive. Meta-analysis shows that such research literatures do provide the foundation for research conclusions, as explained in the response to Objection 3. In fact, the conclusions that can be reached are often precise conclusions about the magnitudes and variation of effects and relations in the relevant population.

Finally, in addressing the question of whether significance tests would be a useful research tool if only researchers did not misinterpret them, it is useful to remember the function that researchers feel significance tests perform: they provide an objective, mechanical procedure for making a dichotomous, yes–no decision about whether the hypothesis is confirmed or not. But as explained in more detail in the response to Objection 5, there is in fact no need in individual studies for such a binary decision, and it is futile to even attempt such a decision. Findings in any individual study are (at best) preliminary and tentative. Thus the primary purpose for which significance testing has been used is a purpose for which there is no need.

In conclusion, even if there were no misinterpretations of the meaning of significant and nonsignificant findings, significance testing would still not be a useful research tool. On the contrary, its use would still be strongly counterproductive in the interpretation of research literatures. Its use also would mean that significance testing would be displacing procedures that *are* useful in the research enterprise: point estimates and confidence intervals. This means that *any* use of significance tests, even in the complete absence of misinterpretations, is a *misuse* of significance tests.

Significance testing never makes a useful contribution to the development of cumulative knowledge.

OBJECTION 8

This position holds that the effort to reform data analysis methods should be dropped because it is futile. The following statement, from an older researcher, is the purest formulation we have found of this objection:

> The controversy over significance testing is an old debate which crops up repeatedly every 10 years or so. I remember discussing these same issues in a graduate class in the 1950s and reading articles in *Psychological Bulletin* on this debate in the 1950s and 1960s. This debate keeps repeating itself but never leads to any definitive conclusions or changes in practices. So it is basically just a waste of time. As researchers in the trenches, we must collect data and make decisions. Our tools and methods are imperfect and there are many philosophical problems with them. However, despite this we must work. That is the nature of the game. As a result of these problems and imperfections of our methods, we undoubtedly make errors in our conclusions, but science is an open enterprise, so someone will eventually point out and correct these errors. As research accumulates, it will become apparent what the truth is. So in the long run, our present system probably does work.

ANSWER TO OBJECTION 8

Not everything in this statement is false. It is true that telling critiques of reliance on significance testing have appeared periodically and stimulated widespread debate and discussion. Schmidt (1996) reviewed the history of this process. The earliest such critique we have been able to find in the psychology literature was published in 1955, over 40 years ago. Jones (1955) pointed out the logical deficiencies of significance testing and called for replacing significance tests with point estimates and confidence intervals. The last such episode prior to the current debate appears to have been in the late 1970s (Carver, 1978; Hunter, 1979). It is also true that none of these attempts to reform data analysis procedures has produced any real change in data analysis practices. In fact, Hubbard (1996) and Hubbard, Parsa, and Luthy (1996) have shown that over the period from the 1950s to the present, the use of significance tests in published research has actually *increased*. This increase has been continuous and steady and has continued up to 1995.

However, at the beginning of this chapter, we pointed out two reasons why the present situation may be different. For the first time, the APA Board of Scientific Affairs is looking into the possibility of taking the lead in the reform effort. The Board has appointed a task force to study the question and make recommendations. The report produced by this group and its recommendations will for the first time give *institutional support* to the effort to reform data analysis procedures. We can expect this report to be read by, and to have influence on, journal editors and journal reviewers. We can also expect it to be cited by researchers in their research reports as justification for data analysis procedures that do not include significance tests. In the past, there has been no such "top-down" support for reform; instead, each episode of debate over significance testing has been stimulated by a lone individual who publishes a single critical article, usually without even a follow-up article by that same author, and with no support from prestigious centers within institutional science.

The second development that makes the current situation different is the impact of meta-analysis. Meta-analysis can be used to present dramatic demonstrations of how reliance on significance testing makes it virtually impossible to discern the true meaning of research literatures. Schmidt (1996) presented two such demonstrations; others are presented in Hunter and Schmidt (1990) and Hunter, Schmidt, and Jackson (1982). Most previous critiques of significance testing have focused on logical and philosophical deficiencies and contradictions in reliance on significance testing. These are the issues referred to in Objection 8 as "philosophical problems." An example is the fact that in testing and rejecting the null hypothesis researchers are focusing not on the actual scientific hypothesis of interest, but on a scientifically irrelevant hypothesis. Another is the fact that we always know in advance that the null hypothesis must be false to some degree, so that a finding of statistical significance is merely a reflection of whether the sample size was large or not. Criticisms of this sort *should* be compelling to researchers but often are not; they are apparently too abstract and seemingly removed from the actual experiences of researchers in doing data analysis to have much impact. On the other hand, the demonstrations that can be produced using meta-analysis are more concrete; they are based on the kinds of data analysis that researchers actually carry out. In our experience, they have a greater impact on audiences and readers.

So for both these reasons we believe there is a basis for the hope that this time the reform effort will actually bear fruit.

Objection 8 states that, because science is an open system, errors in data interpretation resulting from reliance on significance testing eventually will be corrected as more research is conducted on a given question. This statement is erroneous. The average statistical power in many research areas is less than .50. And the predominant interpretational rule is that if a difference or relation is not significant, then it is just a chance finding and can be considered to be zero. That is, the predominant decision rule is: If it is significant, it is a real effect; if it is nonsignificant, it is zero. Under these circumstances, as more and more research studies are conducted the probability of an erroneous conclusion about the meaning of the research literature *increases* (Hedges & Olkin, 1980; Schmidt, 1996). That is, as more and more studies become available, it becomes increasingly clear that the majority of studies found "no relationship," strengthening the false conclusion that no relationship exists. So it is clear that we cannot rely on the accumulation of additional significance test-based research studies to eliminate erroneous conclusions.

Suppose, on the other hand, that average statistical power is approximately .50. Then as more and more studies are conducted, researchers become increasingly likely to conclude that the research literature is conflicting and inconclusive. So it is again clear that we cannot rely on the accumulation of additional significance test-based research studies to lead us to correct conclusions.

In the last 15 years, application of meta-analysis to such research literatures *has* corrected such errors resulting from reliance on significance testing (Hunter & Schmidt, 1990; Hunter, Schmidt & Jackson, 1982; Schmidt, 1992, 1996). Meta-analysis can and has revealed (and calibrated with precision) underlying population effects that have been undetected in the majority of the studies going into the meta-analysis. So it is true that at the level of research *literatures* meta-analysis can detect and correct the errors resulting from reliance on significance testing in individual studies. However, two points are important here. First, this is not the correction process that this objection has in mind; this objection postulates that the accumulation of individual studies per se will correct such errors, a proposition that we see here is patently untrue.

Second, the use of meta-analysis to synthesize research literatures represents the elimination of significance tests at that level of analysis. The effort to reform data analysis procedures has two aspects or prescriptions. The first is that in data analysis *in individual studies*, point estimates and confidence intervals should replace significance testing. The second is that in analyzing and interpreting research *literatures*, meta-analysis should replace traditional narrative reviews. This second objective of the reform effort has now largely been realized in many research areas and disciplines. The first objective—reforming data analysis in individual studies—is really an extension downward to individual studies of the second reform. This objective has *not* been attained. It is the subject of the current reform effort.

The objection that attempts to reform data analysis methods are futile is sometimes expressed in forms that are more cynical than the statement quoted earlier. The following statement from a younger researcher (in his 30s) is an example of this more cynical version of this objection:

> You have ignored an important reason why researchers are *not* going to give up significance testing. It is easier to use significance testing because it is what reviewers expect and require and some researchers (myself included, I must reluctantly admit) feel they have more important things to do than educate reviewers and editors about significance testing. Such efforts are probably futile anyway; they have been in the past. So we just comply and use significance tests. To be sure, from an ethical standpoint, this response is problematic–we are complicators in an illegitimate process that impairs scientific progress. But most researchers

comply with all sorts of illegitimate processes (e.g., worrying more about getting something published than about whether it really advances knowledge in the field, data mining, etc.). I have my moments of weakness like most, but at least I am willing to admit it!

This statement reflects the often expressed feeling that it is futile to fight against a powerful conventional establishment supporting significance tests. This established conventional wisdom may be obviously erroneous, but it cannot be successfully opposed. So one has no choice but to conform. We have heard this feeling expressed by many researchers, particularly younger researchers concerned about publication, tenure, and promotion. This resignation and conformity to error produces an intellectual cynicism that is corrosive of scientific values. It undermines the intellectual honesty and idealistic motivation to search for truth that are the driving engines of science. One important benefit that successful reform of data analysis procedures will bring is the reduction, and perhaps elimination, of such cynicism. This is not a minor benefit.

APPLICATIONS

Each chapter in this book is supposed to contain a section stating how the content of the chapter is to be applied by readers. The most important application of this chapter is this: Do not use significance testing in data analysis; instead, use confidence intervals and point estimates in individual studies and meta-analysis in integrating findings across multiple studies. In doing so, you will be helping to advance cumulative scientific knowledge. However, these applications are contained in earlier articles (e.g., Cohen, 1994; Schmidt, 1996) and are not new to this chapter. The main lesson specific to this chapter is this: Beware of plausible and intuitively appealing objections to discontinuing the use of significance testing. They are always false, no matter how convincing they may seem. Finally, try to show enough intellectual courage and honesty to reject the use of significance tests despite the pressures of social convention to the contrary. Scientists must have integrity.

CONCLUSION

In this chapter, we have examined eight objections to discontinuing significance testing and using instead point estimates and confidence intervals to analyze research data. We have seen that each of these objections, although appearing plausible and even convincing to many researchers, is logically and intellectually bankrupt. What has been shown for these 8 objections can also be shown for each of the additional 79 that we have collected but could not include in this chapter. It could also be shown for any "new" objections yet to be collected by us. Significance testing never makes a positive contribution.

For almost 3 years, we have challenged researchers to describe even one legitimate contribution that significance testing makes or has made to the research enterprise (i.e., to the development of cumulative research knowledge). This challenge has resulted in the large collection of objections from which the eight presented in this chapter are sampled. But it has produced no examples of contributions significance testing has made to research. The fight to reform data analysis methods so that those methods contribute to the development of knowledge, rather than detract from this effort, has been long and hard. It has been resisted at every turn by rock-hard psychological defenses. But there is now reason to hope that reform is finally a realistic possibility.

REFERENCES

Barrick, M. R., & Mount, M. K. (1991). The big five personality dimensions and job performance: A meta-analysis. *Personnel Psychology, 41,* 1–26.

Carver, R. P. (1978). The case against statistical significance testing. *Harvard Educational Review, 48,* 378–399.

Carver, R. P. (1993). The case against statistical significance testing, revisited. *Journal of Experimental Education, 61,* 287–292.

Cohen, J. (1962). The statistical power of abnormal-social psychological research: A review. *Journal of Abnormal and Social Psychology, 65,* 145–153.

Cohen, J. (1965). Some statistical issues in psychological research. In B. B. Wolman (Ed.), *Handbook of clinical psychology* (pp. 95–121), New York: McGraw-Hill.

Cohen, J. (1988). *Statistical power analysis for the behavioral sciences* (2nd ed.) Hillsdale, NJ: Lawrence Erlbaum Associates.

Cohen, J. (1990). Things I have learned (so far). *American Psychologist, 45,* 1304–1312.

Cohen, J. (1992). Statistical power analysis. *Current Directions in Psychological Science, 1,* 98–101.

Cohen, J. (1994). The earth is round (r < .05). *American Psychologist, 49,* 997–1003.

Fisher, R. A. (1932). *Statistical methods for research workers* (4th ed.). Edinburgh, Scotland: Oliver and Boyd.

Fisher, R. A. (1935). *The design of experiments* (subsequent editions 1937, 1942, 1947, 1949, 1951, 1966). London: Oliver and Boyd.

Fisher, R. A. (1959). *Statistical methods and scientific inference* (2nd ed.). Edinburgh, Scotland: Oliver and Boyd.

Fisher, R. A. (1973). *Statistical methods and scientific inference* (3rd ed.). Edinburgh, Scotland: Oliver and Boyd.

Guttman, L. B. (1985). The illogic of statistical inference for cumulative science. *Applied Stochastic Models and Data Analysis, 1*, 3–10.

Hedges, L. V. (1987). How hard is hard science, how soft is soft science: The empirical cumulativeness of research. *American Psychologist, 42*, 443–455.

Hedges, L. V., & Olkin, I. (1980). Vote counting methods in research synthesis. *Psychological Bulletin, 88*, 359–369.

Hubbard, R. (1996). *Sanctifying significance and relegating replication: A misplaced emphasis.* Manuscript under review.

Hubbard, R., Parsa, A. R., & Luthy, M. R. (1996). *The diffusion of statistical significance testing in psychology: The case of the Journal of Applied Psychology.* Manuscript under review.

Hunter, J. E. (1979, September). *Cumulating results across studies: A critique of factor analysis, canonical correlation, MANOVA, and statistical significance testing.* Invited address presented at the 86th Annual Convention of the American Psychological Association, New York.

Hunter, J. E., & Schmidt, F. L. (1990). *Methods of meta-analysis: Correcting error and bias in research findings.* Newbury Park, CA: Sage.

Hunter, J. E., Schmidt, F. L., & Jackson, G. B. (1982). *Meta-analysis: Cumulating research findings across studies.* Beverly Hills, CA: Sage.

Jones, L. V. (1955). Statistics and research design. *Annual Review of Psychology, 6*, 405–430. Stanford, CA: Annual Reviews, Inc.

Neyman, J. (1962). Two breakthroughs in the theory of statistical decision making. *Review of the International Statistical Institute, 25*, 11–27.

Neyman, J., & Pearson, E. S. (1933). On the problem of the most efficient tests of statistical hypotheses. *Philosophical Transactions of the Royal Society of London, Series A, 231*, 289–337.

Oakes, M. (1986*). Statistical inference: A commentary for the social and behavioral sciences.* New York: Wiley.

Rozeboom, W. W. (1960). The fallacy of the null hypothesis significance test. *Psychological Bulletin, 57*, 416–428.

Schmidt, F. L. (1992). What do data really mean? Research findings, meta-analysis, and cumulative knowledge in psychology. *American Psychologist, 47*, 1173–1181.

Schmidt, F. L. (1996). Statistical significance testing and cumulative knowledge in psychology: Implications for the training of researchers. *Psychological Methods, 1,* 115–129.

Schmidt, F. L., Hunter, J. E., & Urry, V. E. (1976). Statistical power in criterion-related validation studies. *Journal of Applied Psychology, 61,* 473–485.

Sedlmeier, P., & Gigerenzer, G. (1989). Do studies of statistical power have an effect on the power of studies? *Psychological Bulletin, 105,* 309–316.

Chapter 4

There Is a Time and a Place for Significance Testing

Stanley A. Mulaik
Georgia Institute of Technology

Nambury S. Raju
Illinois Institute of Technology

Richard A. Harshman
University of Western Ontario

We expose fallacies in the arguments of critics of null hypothesis significance testing who go too far in arguing that we should abandon significance tests altogether. Beginning with statistics containing sampling or measurement error, significance tests provide prima facie evidence for the validity of statistical hypotheses, which may be overturned by further evidence in practical forms of reasoning involving defeasible or dialogical logics. For example, low power may defeat acceptance of the null hypothesis. On the other hand, we support recommendations to report point estimates and confidence intervals of parameters, and believe that the null hypothesis to be tested should be the value of the parameter given by a theory or prior knowledge. We also use a Wittgensteinian argument to question the coherence of concepts of subjective degree of belief underlying subjective Bayesian alternatives to significance testing.

INTRODUCTION

An accumulating literature (Bakan, 1966; Carver, 1978; Cohen, 1994; Gigerenzer, 1993; Guttman, 1977, 1985; Meehl, 1967, 1978; Oaks, 1986; Pollard, 1993; Rozeboom, 1960; Serlin and Lapsley, 1993; Schmidt, 1992, 1996) has called for a critical reexamination of the common use of "null hypothesis significance testing" (NHST) in psychological and social science research. Most of these articles expose misconceptions about significance testing common among researchers and writers of psychological textbooks on statistics and measurement. But the criticisms do not stop with misconceptions about significance testing. Others like Meehl (1967) expose the limitations of a statistical practice that focuses only on testing for zero differences between means and zero correlations instead of testing predictions about specific nonzero values for parameters derived from theory or prior experience, as is done in the physical sciences. Still others emphasize that significance tests do not alone convey the information needed to properly evaluate research findings and perform accumulative research. For example, reporting that results are significant at some pre-specified significance level (as in the early Fisher, 1935 or Neyman-Pearson, 1933, significance testing paradigms) or the p level of significance (late Fisher, 1955, 1959) do not indicate the effect size (Glass, 1976; Hays 1963; Hedges, 1981), nor the power of the test (Cohen, 1969, 1977, 1988), nor the crucial parameter estimates that other researchers may use in meta-analytic studies (Rosenthal, 1993; Schmidt, 1996). A common recommendation in these critiques is to report confidence interval estimates of the parameters and effect sizes. This provides data usable in meta-analyses. The confidence interval also provides a rough and easily computed index of power, with narrow intervals indicative of high power and wide intervals of low power (Cohen, 1994). A confidence interval corresponding to a commonly accepted level of significance (e.g. .05) would also provide the information needed to perform a significance test of pre-specified parameter values.

Other than emphasizing a need to properly understand the interpretation of confidence intervals, we have no disagreements with these criticisms and proposals.

But a few of the critics go even further. In this chapter we will look at arguments made by Carver (1978), Cohen (1994), Rozeboom (1960), Schmidt (1992, 1996), and Schmidt and Hunter (chapter 3 of this volume), in favor of not merely recommending the reporting of point estimates of effect sizes and confidence intervals based on them, but of abandoning altogether the use of significance tests in research. Our focus will be principally on Schmidt's (1992, 1996) papers, because they incorporate arguments from earlier papers, especially Carver's (1978), and also carry the argument to its most extreme conclusions. Where appropriate, we will also comment on Schmidt and Hunter's (chapter 3 of this volume) rebuttal of arguments against their position.

Our position with respect to Schmidt (1992, 1996), Schmidt and Hunter (chapter 3 of this volume), and Carver (1978) is that their opposition to significance testing arises out of confusion regarding a number of things: (a) that significance testing is the same as misconceptions held by many researchers about significance testing, (b) that a null hypothesis is necessarily a statistical hypothesis of zero difference, zero effect, or zero correlation, (c) that significance testing is principally concerned with testing a null hypothesis of zero difference, zero effect, or zero correlation, (d) that proponents of significance testing believe significance tests are supposed to yield absolute and final determinations of the truth or falsity of a statistical hypothesis, (d) that meta-analysis not only replaces significance testing, but has no need ever of significance tests, (f) that because in small samples significance tests have very little power to detect small effects, they are useless, (g) that because in large samples significance tests have very large power to detect small effects, they will always do so, and thus are useless, (h) that significance tests per se are, or should be, concerned with the accumulation of knowledge, (i) that knowing the power of a test implies that one knows the probability that the hypothesis will be rejected, (j) that confidence intervals around point estimates of parameters should be reported and are not or should not be used for significance testing, (k) that the physical sciences do not use significance tests but instead compute confidence intervals and perform meta-analyses. We answer these criticisms. We place significance testing in the context of seeking to make objective judgments about the world. We also defend significance testing against criticisms raised by others based on the idea that while significance tests concern making a dichotomous decision, that is, the statistical hypothesis is either true or false, we should instead focus on determining how our degrees of belief in the hypothesis are affected by the evidence. We follow-up this essay with a brief appendix on some of the historical controversies in the area of significance testing, for this history has bearing on the current controversy involving significance testing.

PRELIMINARY ARGUMENTS AGAINST SIGNIFICANCE TESTING

Schmidt (1992, 1996) draws heavily on Carver (1978) in focusing his attack on significance testing from the perspective that it "has systematically retarded the growth of cumulative knowledge in psychology" (Schmidt, 1996, p. 115). Schmidt (1996) believed that authors like Carver have "carefully considered all … arguments [for retaining significance testing] and shown them to be logically flawed and hence false" (p. 116). Our own reading of Carver suggests that "significance testing" for him refers primarily to testing a statistical "null hypothesis" of zero differences between means, zero effect sizes, or zero correlations. He did not consider point hypotheses involving possibly nonzero values for parameters, which is the more general case considered by mathematical statisticians for "significance testing." In fact, most statisticians who do significance testing, regard the "null hypothesis" as simply the hypothesis to be tested or "nullified" (Gigerenzer, 1993). Much of Carver's argument also involved exposing what are actually misconceptions about significance testing, for example, interpreting the p value of the significance level as an unconditioned probability that you would be wrong in accepting the null hypothesis. Criticisms of these misconceptions are not actually arguments against significance testing properly conceived and are somewhat tangential to the issue of significance testing. (We discuss some of these arguments further on).

Corrupt Scientific Method

Carver (1978) also described how significance testing of the null hypothesis involves a "corrupt scientific method" (p. 387). According to Carver, researchers begin with a research hypothesis about the efficacy of some experimental treatment. Proponents of the "corrupt scientific method" recommend that researchers perform experiments in which differences between experimental and control treatments are compared to differences one would expect under a hypothesis of random measurement and sampling error. A statistical "null hypothesis" is then proposed of no difference between experimental treatments. The null hypothesis is to be rejected and results regarded as "significant" only if a difference as large or larger than some specified amount occurs that would occur only rarely under a hypothesis of chance. "If the null hypothesis can be rejected, empirical support can automatically be claimed for the research hypothesis. If the null hypothesis cannot be rejected, the research hypothesis receives no support" (Carver, 1978, p. 387). Carver did not oppose conducting experiments, but giving emphasis to the null hypothesis as opposed to one's research hypothesis. He was troubled by the fact that in small samples one might fail to detect a large, real difference, and yet in very large samples one would almost always reject the null hypothesis, but the effects detected as merely significant might be small or theoretically negligible, so the outcome depends on the sample size. Furthermore, one is almost always guaranteed, Carver felt, of rejecting the null hypothesis with very large samples and he cited Bakan (1966) as indicating that it is unlikely that two groups represent *exactly* the same population with respect to the variable being measured. But Bakan's example seems to concern natural groups being compared rather than groups of experimental units assigned by randomization to experimental treatments, where there are reasonable grounds to expect no differences unless there are effects, either experimental effects or systematic error. Nevertheless, Carver did put his finger on problems in the logic of "null hypothesis significance testing". But his analysis of these problems leaves many issues confounded, especially the issue of significance testing per se versus the issue of the kinds of hypotheses to test and the inferences to be drawn from tests of them.

Criticism of the "Nil" Hypothesis.

One of the problems of "null hypothesis significance testing" is with the null hypothesis of zero difference between means or zero correlation (known as the "nil hypothesis" (Cohen, 1994)). Meehl (1967) incisively showed how routine and exclusive use of this hypothesis in research prevents progress by inhibiting researchers from formulating and testing hypotheses about specific nonzero values for parameters based on theory, prior knowledge and/or estimates of parameters based on accumulated data, in situations where they have such knowledge and theory to go on. And the logic of "nil hypothesis testing" seems askew, because if a researcher has a theory that a certain treatment has an effect, his theory is supported by rejecting another hypothesis (that there is no effect) rather than by making a successful specific prediction that is within the bounds of measurement error of the observed value. It seems unreasonable to regard as support for a theory that some other hypothesis is rejected in favor of an alternative hypothesis that is so vague in its content ("there is a difference") that it would be compatible with almost any substantive hypothesis predicting almost any size of difference. At best a test of the hypothesis of no difference can provide evidence against the null hypothesis of no difference, no effect, or no correlations. But it provides little evidence for any particular alternative hypothesis.

Meehl (1967) contrasted the "nil hypothesis" approach in the behavioral sciences to hypothesis testing in physics where proponents of theories are required to make specific predictions about a parameter based on theories, and the theories are provisionally accepted only if the outcomes are within measurement error of the predicted value, and no other theories make predictions that also fall within the range of measurement error around the estimate of the parameter. Furthermore, in physics as more and more data accumulate and standard errors of parameter estimates get smaller and smaller, tests of a theory become more and more stringent, because to retain support, predicted values must stay within an increasingly narrower range of measurement error around the estimated parameter as gauged by the standard error. But in "nil hypothesis significance testing" almost any theory that predicts an unspecified nonzero effect will have greater possibilities of being "supported" as measurement precision and sample sizes increase, because the range of measurement and/or sampling error around the zero value of the null hypothesis will get narrower and narrower and the power to detect any small effect increases.

So, one issue concerns the hypotheses to test statistically and whether there are ways to formulate a statistical hypothesis so that it takes into account what is currently known or theorized. There may be times when the no-difference and no-relation hypothesis is appropriate to test, and others when it is not. But, as we shortly argue, the issue of what hypothesis to test is distinct from the issue of significance testing itself, and criticisms of the testing of improper hypotheses should not be taken as criticisms of the concept of significance testing.

Building on Previous Studies in Hypothesis Testing.

It seems that the most appropriate time to test the null hypothesis of no-effect or no-correlation is when one has no prior knowledge or theory of what value to expect and subjects have been assigned at random to experimental treatment conditions so that the expectation would be, failing an experimental effect or systematic error, of no effect. However, once previous studies have been conducted, and the no-effect/no-correlation hypothesis rejected, then there will be estimates of the parameter based on the prior data and these can be used as the hypothesized value for the parameter in a significance test with a new set of data. (Or a hypothesis formulated on the basis of examining a number of prior estimates may be used.) The hypothesis to test concerns the value of the parameter—not that previous samples and a new sample come from populations having equal (but unspecified) population values for the parameter, which is a less informative result, when confirmed.

For example, suppose the estimate of a population mean based on prior data is 50.1. We now construct a confidence interval estimate of the mean in a new sample. Let $\overline{X}$ designate a sample mean based on the new data. Let $\sigma_{\overline{X}}$ designate the standard error of the sample mean. Then assuming further that $\overline{X}$ is normally distributed, a random interval

$$\left[\overline{X} - 1.96\sigma_{\overline{X}}, \overline{X} + 1.96\sigma_{\overline{X}}\right]$$

may be constructed round the sample mean for which

$$P\left(\overline{X} - 1.96\sigma_{\overline{X}} \leq \mu \leq \overline{X} + 1.96\sigma_{\overline{X}}\right) = .95.$$

In other words, the lower and upper limits of this interval are *random variables*, based on the random sample mean plus or minus 1.96 times the standard error (which we presume is known, to simplify our illustration). Such *random intervals* based on the sample means will contain the true population mean in 95% of all samples. Now, if $\overline{X}$ computed from the new data is 49 and $\sigma_{\overline{X}} = 2$, then a 95% level confidence interval is given by

$$\left[49 - 1.96(2), 49 + 1.96(2)\right],$$

which in this case is [45.08, 52.92]. Because 50.1 is contained within this random interval, we provisionally accept the hypothesis that the mean equals 50.1 in the population from which we have drawn the new data. If 50.1 fell outside the sample-based interval, we would provisionally reject the hypothesis that the population mean is 50.1. This illustrates a use of a confidence interval to perform a significance test of a hypothesis based on previously collected data.

We need to add that instead of using for one's hypothesis previous estimates for the parameter, one may also develop a theory of what the "true" value is and test this theoretical value in new studies. Sometimes there may be several theories and more than one theoretical value to test (as we illustrate later with a case in physics that illustrates significance testing with confidence intervals in choosing between theories.) In some cases, when one theoretical value falls within the confidence interval and the other outside it, one can readily take support for the theory whose value falls within the confidence interval and reject the theory whose value falls without. But sometimes both theories may hypothesize values that fall within the confidence interval. In that case, the proper course may be to suspend judgment, collect more data with tighter standard errors so as to be able to exclude one or the other or both hypothesized values.

Proper Interpretation of a Confidence Interval

It is important to note that it is improper to interpret a specific confidence interval constructed around a sample estimate of a parameter as itself containing the population parameter with the specified probability (Kendall & Stuart, 1979; Neyman, 1941). The specific interval either contains the population parameter or it does not, so it contains the population parameter with a probability of unity or of zero. The probability associated with a confidence interval concerns the class of random intervals so constructed around the sample estimates of the parameter and not any specific interval. In contrast, assuming normality and a known standard error, an interval, constructed to have endpoints at 1.96 standard errors above and below a hypothesized value for the population parameter can be said to have a probability of approximately .95 of containing the sample estimate of the parameter, *if* the hypothesized value is correct. (Kendall & Stuart, 1979; Neyman, 1941).

If theory dictates a specific value for a parameter, then all available data that are independent of the formulation of the theoretical value can be used to estimate the parameter with a confidence interval estimate. If the theoretical value is contained within the confidence interval, that is provisional support for the theory. If not, that is provisional evidence against the theory.

The Purpose of a Significance Test

It is important to realize that in contrast to the issue of what hypothesis to test, significance testing arises because of the presumption that statistical estimates of parameters contain random errors of measurement and/or sampling error. Error in our parameter estimates introduces an element of uncertainty in inferences about the parameter values from those estimates. A significance test is a way of applying a rational criterion of what values of a test statistic are to be regarded provisionally and defeasibly as inconsistent with and unsupportive of a hypothesized value (or range of values) because they would be too extremely different from the hypothesized value and too improbable under a hypothesis of random error combined with the hypothesized parameter's value. Thus a frequent use for significance testing is distinguishing (provisionally) whether a difference between observed and hypothesized values results from effects of random errors of measurement and/or sampling error. This is what significance testing is principally about. The "statistical significance" of a deviation is a problem that has to be resolved in some way and at some point in a research program, especially if one seeks to evaluate theoretical predictions against data in an efficient and economical way.

The Argument that Meta-Analysis Should Replace Significance Testing

Nevertheless, Schmidt (1992, 1996) built on Carver's (1978) arguments. Being an advocate of the use of meta-analytic procedures, he and his collaborator, John Hunter, ". . . have used meta-analysis methods to show that these traditional data analysis methods [significance testing] militate against the discovery of the underlying regularities and relationships that are a foundation for scientific progress (Hunter & Schmidt, 1990)" (Schmidt, 1996, pp. 115–116). Schmidt (1996) argued that "we must abandon the statistical significance test. In our graduate programs we must teach that for analysis of data from individual studies, the appropriate statistics are point estimates of effect sizes and confidence intervals around these point estimates. And we must teach that for analysis of data from multiple studies, the appropriate method is meta-analysis" (p. 116). Schmidt believed that the development and widespread use of meta-analysis methods "reveals more clearly than ever before the extent to which reliance on significance testing has retarded the growth of cumulative knowledge in psychology" (p. 116).

Schmidt claims that even ". . . these few defenders of significance testing (e.g., Winch and Campbell, 1969) agree that the dominant usages of such tests in data analysis in psychology are misuses and they hold that the role of significance tests in data analysis should be greatly reduced" (Schmidt, 1996, p. 116). (Misuses, however dominant they may be in practice, are nevertheless not evidence against the proper use of significance tests. Whether significance tests will be deemed to have a more limited application than now believed by rank-and-file researchers is certainly a legitimate question we would be willing to entertain. At the same time we think there is a legitimate role to be played by significance testing). Schmidt issued the following challenge to statisticians who still believe in significance tests: "Can you articulate even one legitimate contribution that significance testing has made (or makes) to the research enterprise (i.e., any way in which it contributes to the development of cumulative scientific knowledge)? I believe you will not be able to do so" (p. 116).

We feel this challenge stacks the deck against significance testing, because it asks one to cite a contribution for significance testing that significance testing per se is not designed to make and for which it is not directly relevant. Significance testing is not directly concerned with accumulating scientific knowledge. We feel that function is served by the formulation of hypotheses to be tested, which, to lead to accumulating knowledge, should incorporate prior knowledge and theory into the formulation of the hypothesis. In contrast, significance testing per se concerns drawing defeasible inferences from data at hand as to the validity of a statistical hypothesis. A defeasible inference is an inference that ". . . is subject to defeat (nullification, termination, or substantial revision) by further considerations (e.g., later facts or evidence)" (Finnis 1995, p. 181). Significance testing concerns a framework for deciding (provisionally or defeasibly) whether observed results (under presumptions of randomness, sampling, and error of measurement) that differ from hypothesized values are to be treated as consistent with chance error outcomes under the assumption that the hypothesis is true, or to be regarded as so divergent and different as well as improbable under the assumption of the truth of the hypothesis as to provide little or no support for the hypothesis (Fisher, 1959). That's all a significance test provides, no more, no less. It doesn't accumulate anything. That is not its function. There are no accumulative operations intrinsic to a significance test.

On the other hand, significance testing contributes to the cumulative research enterprise in allowing one to assess whether differences from predicted values under an integrative hypothesis are more reasonably regarded as due to random measurement errors and sampling errors or not. For example, suppose you are seeking to accumulate knowledge by synthesizing findings from various studies. At some point the data "at hand" shifts from the data found in individual studies to the data across numerous studies, as in a meta-analysis, where one presumes that outcomes of each study are random and independent of one another along with whatever other assumptions needed to make the meta-analytic inferences. Significance testing comes back into play in deciding whether the data at hand across the studies are consistent with and hypothetically probable under a pre-specified statistical hypothesis of interest to the researcher, or so different and so hypothetically improbable under that hypothesis as to cast doubt on the hypothesis by being possibly not a chance result at all. In other words, in statistical studies with probabilistic outcomes there will always be criteria for deciding (defeasibly) whether differences from expectations are to be treated as real differences or as due to chance error, and those criteria will represent significance tests. But we do not claim that significance tests encompass all that is important in evaluating statistical hypotheses. We certainly support journals requiring the reporting of confidence interval estimates of parameters and effect sizes because these convey more of the crucial information about the results that may be joined with other findings in developing hypotheses and conducting meta-analyses.

Misconceptions About the Misconceptions About Significance Testing

Our concerns with these essays critical of hypothesis testing is that a major portion of their arguments to do away with significance testing are based on criticisms of abusive misconceptions of the use and interpretation of significance testing by researchers. They can hardly be regarded as criticisms of significance testing properly understood and applied. It is important to note that these critical essays rarely quote critically and accurately Fisher or Neyman and Pearson, the founding fathers of the major schools of significance testing, or mathematical statisticians well trained in their methods. But if one reads these eminent statisticians' writings, he or she often will come across passages in which they are critical of the very same abuses and misconceptions of significance testing that the current crop of critics of significance testing cite as evidence against significance testing. So, if we are to clear the air and get to the heart of their criticisms of significance testing, we need to stipulate what these misconceptions about significance testing are and show how irrelevant they are to the issue of whether to abandon or retain significance tests in our research.

Misconceptions About Significance Testing

Carver (1978), Cohen (1994) and Schmidt (1996) all cite critically variants of the following fallacious misinterpretations of significance testing. We add one or two of our own:

1. *The p value of a significant test statistic is the probability that the research results are due to chance* (Carver 1978). It is hard to imagine how someone would arrive at this conclusion. Perhaps, because the statistic is significant, one wonders how this might occur by chance and then thinks of the statistical hypothesis tested, H_0, as the hypothesis of chance. One reasons that if H_0 is true, a result D as extreme or more extreme than the critical value could occur by chance only with a conditional probability $P(D \mid H_0)$ equal to the significance level. That is, the significance level is always the *conditional* probability of getting a result D as extreme or more

extreme than some critical value *given* the hypothesis H_0 is true. Of course, we never know for certain that it is true, but only reason to this probability hypothetically. But the fallacy is that the statement asserts a different kind of conditional probability. What is the probability that the null hypothesis generated this data, given that we have observed a significant result, that is what is $P(H_0 | D)$? But without knowledge of the prior probability for H_0 and each of the various alternative hypotheses, we cannot work this out (using Bayes' theorem). No mathematical statistician would be so naive as to confuse these kinds of probabilities.

2. *The probability of rejecting H_0 is α*. Again the fallacy is to confuse an unconditioned statement of probability with a conditioned statement of probability. α is the conditional probability of rejecting the hypothesis H_0 given H_0 is true—regarded hypothetically. In contrast, without further prior knowledge, we have no idea what the actual probability is of rejecting the null hypothesis at a given significance level. It all depends upon what is the case in the world, and we would not perform a significance test if we knew what the true effect was. Schmidt (1992, 1996) makes a similar error when he imagined scenarios in which the true effect size is .50 and then declared that the probability of making a Type I error is not .05 but zero because, he says, in this scenario the null hypothesis is always false and so there is no error to be made in rejecting the null hypothesis. The only error to be made, he said, is a Type II error, accepting the null hypothesis when it is false. In this scenario Schmidt further computed the probability of rejecting the null hypothesis of no effect to be .37 and not .05. Furthermore, he said the true error rate in making decisions from tests of a hypothesis of no effect in studies against an effect size of .50 is $1-.37=.63$, not .05, as he claimed many researchers believe. Within Schmidt's scenario the actual error rates he considered are correct, but Schmidt failed to see that Type I and Type II error rates are never actual probabilities of making these errors. Having no knowledge about the true effects when setting out to perform a significance test, we have no way of knowing what the true error rates will be. So these error rates are hypothetical probabilities considered conditionally under the case where the null hypothesis is true and under a case where the null hypothesis is false, respectively. These hypothetical error rates are used, for example, in reasoning hypothetically to set a critical value of a significance test and to evaluate the power of the significance test against hypothetical alternatives in establishing what will represent prima facie evidence for or against a null hypothesis. Type I and Type II error rates should never be thought of as unconditional probabilities.

3. *Replicability fallacy: A hypothesis accepted as significant at the α level of significance has the probability of $1 - \alpha$ of being found significant in future replications of the experiment.* Carver (1978) cited Nunnally (1975, p. 195) as asserting this fallacy. The fallacy is to presume that because one has accepted the hypothesis H_0, it is therefore true, and therefore according to the conditional probability distribution of the statistic when H_0 is true, the probability of observing a value of the test statistic again within the region of acceptance will be $1 - \alpha$. But, as Fisher (1935) was careful to point out, accepting the null hypothesis (H_0 for Neyman and Pearson) does not determine that the hypothesis is true. It still might be false. Consequently the rest of the inference fails.

4. *Validity fallacy: A hypothesis accepted as significant at the α level of significance has a probability of $1 - \alpha$ of being true.* This is a gross misinterpretation. As Cohen (1994) points out, a statement about the conditional probability $P(D \mid H_0)$ that a result will fall in the region of rejection (D) given one assumes the hypothesis H_0 is true is not the same as a statement about the probability $P(H_0 \mid D)$ of the hypothesis being true given the result has fallen in the region of rejection D, nor even unconditional probabilities about the truth of the hypothesis $P(H_0)$. As Fisher (1959) stated, the significance level tells nothing about probabilities in the real world. All the significance level tells us is a hypothetical probability that D will occur given the hypothesis H_0 is true, and that is not sufficient to allow us to infer the actual probability of the truth of the hypothesis in a real-world setting.

5. *The size p of the significance level of a result is an index of the importance or size of a difference or relation.* Schmidt (1996) cited this fallacy. An example would be to regard a finding significant at the .05 level to be not as important as a finding significant at the .001 level. The fallacy is to confuse size or magnitude of an effect with the improbability of an effect under the null hypothesis. The p value does not tell you the size or magnitude of an effect. In large samples a p value of .001 may represent a small magnitude effect, which practically speaking may be of negligible importance. On the other hand, it is true that a result significant at the .05 level is not as deviant from the hypothesized value as a result significant at the .001 level, although the p values alone tell you nothing about the difference in magnitude between them. There is also a danger of interpreting the p value as a measure of the improbability of the truth of the null hypothesis and then inferring that results with smaller p values indicate that the null hypothesis is even more improbable. Remember that the p value is the conditional probability of observing a result as deviant or more deviant from

the hypothesized value given that the hypothesized value is the true value. It is not a measure of the probability of the hypothesized value. It is, however, a measure of the plausibility of the hypothesis, because a very small value for p indicates an observed value for the statistic that would be very improbable were the hypothesized value the true value of the parameter. Some of the confusion resides in confusing the logical "improbability" of a hypothesis when evidence quite inconsistent with or improbable according to it is observed—which may have no clear quantitative value— with the "probability" of probability theory that the p value under the null hypothesis represents. In this regard this is the same as the fallacy given in case 1 above.

6. *A statistically significant result is a scientifically significant result.* This fallacy plays on the ambiguity of the word "significant." Knowledgeable statisticians recognize that regarding a result as statistically significant does not imply its size or importance scientifically. It is well known that the standard error of a test statistic varies inversely as the square root of the size of the sample so that in larger and larger samples the power to detect smaller and smaller differences from the hypothesized parameter as "significant" increases. Thus in very large samples a difference significant at the .001 level may still be very small in both absolute terms and in relative terms with respect to the initial variance of the variable. Thus no inference may be drawn as to the size or importance of a result from a knowledge that it is a significant result.

7. *If a result of a test of a hypothesis about a parameter is not significant, then the parameter equals the hypothesized value.* This fallacy is a variant of the fallacy of presuming that if a result is not significant then this means the null hypothesis is true. Schmidt (1996) believed this assumption is the most devastating to the research enterprise. He claimed it prevents researchers who get nonsignificant results with small samples from reporting and pooling their data with data from other studies in meta-analytic studies, which may be able to detect small effects with greater power that were overlooked in the individual studies because of lack of power. We agree that it is reasonable to suggest people should suspend judgment from small-sample studies because they lack power to detect meaningful differences. We agree that it is reasonable to criticize them for presuming without warrant they have made an indefeasible and final judgment in order to get them to seek additional evidence. However, again, none of the original proponents of significance tests, neither Fisher nor Neyman and Pearson would interpret significance tests as determining absolutely the validity of the hypothesized parameter, Fisher least of all. So, again, it is a misinter-

pretation of the results of a significance test. As Fisher (1935) put it, not rejecting the null hypothesis does not mean one has proven the null hypothesis to be true.

8. *The fallacy that a statistical hypothesis is the same as one's theoretical hypothesis.* Frequently, a theoretical prediction will state that a parameter has a certain value. This value is then made the value of a statistical hypothesis to be tested with a significance test. If we observe results that would be too different from the hypothesized value and too improbable according to sampling and/or measurement error under the tested hypothesis, we may be led to reject that hypothesis. But this need not imply that the theoretical hypothesis on which the statistical hypothesis is based is necessarily to be rejected. There may be in the experimental setting experimental artifacts that produce effects different from those anticipated by the theory. So, rejecting the statistical hypothesis may lead to a search for experimental artifacts instead of rejection of the theory.

9. *The argument that nothing is concluded from a significance test.* Schmidt (1996) stated "If the null hypothesis is not rejected, Fisher's position was that nothing could be concluded. But researchers find it hard to go to all the trouble of conducting a study only to conclude that nothing can be concluded" (p. 126). We think this is an unfair reading of Fisher. The issue is what inference is reasonable, although defeasible, to draw from the empirical findings of a study.

A major difference between Fisher and Neyman and Pearson was over the idea that significance testing involves an automated decision-making procedure forcing a researcher to choose one of several predetermined alternative choices. Fisher did not want to lose the freedom to exercise his own judgment as a scientist in whether or not to accept (provisionally) a tested hypothesis on the basis of a significance test. "A test of significance contains no criterion for 'accepting' a hypothesis. According to circumstances it may or may not influence its acceptability" (Fisher, 1959, p. 42). Fisher's attitude seems to reflect, furthermore, many physicists' suspicions of the Neyman-Pearson approach to significance testing, that a decision to accept or reject a theory or hypothesis can be completely encapsulated in the automated significance test. For example, a significant result that runs counter to well-established theory, may not be regarded as evidence against the theory but possibly evidence for an experimental artifact, which the researcher must then isolate. An option for Fisher was to suspend judgment.

A bitter debate between Fisher and Neyman and Pearson followed their (1933) alluding to the relevance of their paradigm to sampling inspection problems in mass-production industry. In discussing the difference between acceptance decisions in manufacturing and opinions and judgments based on significance tests formed in scientific settings, Fisher (1959) held, "An important difference is that [Acceptance] Decisions are final, while the state of opinion derived from a test of significance is provisional, and capable, not only of confirmation, but of revision" (p. 100). Fisher's belief that Acceptance Decisions might be final seems reasonable, because a decision to return goods to the manufacturer or to stop the assembly line, once implemented, is final. But the point is that from Fisher's point of view a provisional scientific opinion can be formed about the null hypothesis from the results of a significance test, and one may even seek to confirm it with additional evidence, or revise one's opinion on the basis of that additional evidence. What Fisher seemed to sense is that such concepts as "truth" and "falsity" and "logical inference," that work very well in geometry and other areas of mathematics where one presumes one has in the axioms all one needs to arrive at a final decision regarding the truth or falsity of some proposition, do not work very well in science when one is making generalizations or inferences from experience. Our information is incomplete, so our opinions formed from experience will be provisional and defeasible by additional experience. This is different from saying that one forms no conclusions, no opinions at all if a test is not significant. The conclusions, opinions, "decisions" are not final, only provisional. (See Mulaik & James, 1995; Pollock, 1986).

THE NULL HYPOTHESIS IS ALWAYS FALSE?

Cohen (1994), influenced by Meehl (1978), argued that "the nil hypothesis is always false" (p. 1000). Get a large enough sample and you will always reject the null hypothesis. He cites a number of eminent statisticians in support of this view. He quotes Tukey (1991, p. 100) to the effect that there are always differences between experimental treatments—for some decimal places. Cohen cites an unpublished study by Meehl and Lykken in which cross tabulations for 15 Minnesota Multiphasic Personality Inventory (MMPI) items for a sample of 57,000 subjects yielded 105 chi-square tests of association and every one of them was significant, and 96% of them were significant at $p < .000001$ (Cohen, 1994, p. 1000). Cohen cites Meehl (1990) as suggesting that this reflects a "crud factor" in nature. "Everything is related to everything else" to some degree. So, the question is, why do a significance test if you know it will always be significant if the sample is large enough? But if this is an empirical hypothesis, is it not one that is established using significance testing?

But the example may not be an apt demonstration of the principle Cohen sought to establish: It is generally expected that responses to different items responded to by the same subjects are not independently distributed across subjects, so it would not be remarkable to find significant correlations between many such items.

Much more interesting would be to demonstrate systematic and replicable significant treatment effects when subjects are assigned at random to different treatment groups but the *same* treatments are administered to each group. But in this case, small but significant effects in studies with high power that deviate from expectations of no effect when no differences in treatments are administered are routinely treated as systematic experimenter errors, and knowledge of experimental technique is improved by their detection and removal or control. Systematic error and experimental artifact must always be considered a possibility when rejecting the null hypothesis. Nevertheless, do we know a priori that a test will *always* be significant if the sample is large enough? Is the proposition "Every statistical hypothesis is false" an *axiom* that needs no testing? Actually, we believe that to regard this as an axiom would introduce an internal contradiction into statistical reasoning, comparable to arguing that all propositions and descriptions are false. You could not think and reason about the world with such an axiom. So it seems preferable to regard this as some kind of empirical generalization. But no empirical generalization is ever incorrigible and beyond testing. Nevertheless, if indeed there is a phenomenon of nature known as "the crud factor," then it is something we know to be objectively a fact only because of significance tests. Something in the background noise stands out as a signal against that noise, because we have sufficiently powerful tests using huge samples to detect it. At that point it may become a challenge to science to develop a better understanding of what produces it. However, it may turn out to reflect only experimenter artifact. But in any case the hypothesis of a crud factor is not beyond further testing.

The point is that it doesn't matter if the null hypothesis is always judged false at some sample size, as long as we regard this as an empirical phenomenon. What matters is whether *at the sample size we have* we can distinguish observed deviations from our hypothesized values to be sufficiently large and improbable under a hypothesis of chance that we can treat them reasonably but provisionally as not due to chance error. There is no a priori reason to believe that one will always reject the null hypothesis at any given sample size. On the other hand, accepting the null hypothesis does not mean the hypothesized value is true, but rather that the evidence observed is not distinguishable from what we would regard as due to chance if the null hypothesis were true and thus is not sufficient to disprove it. The remaining uncertainty regarding the truth of our null hypothesis is measured by the width of the region of acceptance or a function of the standard error. And this will be closely related to the power of the test, which also provides us with information about our uncertainty.

The fact that the width of the region of acceptance shrinks with increasing sample size, means we are able to reduce our uncertainty regarding the provisional validity of an accepted null hypothesis with larger samples. In huge samples the issue of uncertainty due to chance looms not as important as it does in small- and moderate-size samples.

THE NEED FOR SIGNIFICANCE TESTS

We cannot get rid of significance tests because they provide us with the criteria by which *provisionally* to distinguish results due to chance variation from results that represent systematic effects in data available to us. As long as we have a conception of how variation in results may be due to chance and regard it as applicable to our experience, we will have a need for significance tests in some form or another.

Schmidt and Hunter (chapter 3 of this volume) ignore the provisional way statisticians treat their decisions based on significance tests in arguing that significance tests do not reveal whether observed differences or relations in a data set are real or "just due to chance." "This objection [against doing away with significance tests] assumes," they say, "that null hypothesis significance testing can perform that feat. Unfortunately, no such method exists—or is even possible." Their argument subtly portrays significance tests as designed to determine absolutely that relations or differences are "real or due to chance." Of course, there can be no such thing. They neglect to point out that Fisher denied that the significance test yields absolute and incorrigible determinations that something is "real or due to chance." Whatever opinions one forms as to the reality or chance basis of a difference or a relation are provisional. Most statisticians, including us, interpret them in this way. So Schmidt and Hunter's argument is simply a misrepresentation of what significance tests provide. What is important to consider is that under the circumstances in which they are employed, where one has no knowledge a priori of the truth of one's statistical hypotheses, significance tests provide a reasonable way of using the data available to arrive at prima facie evidence for the truth or falsity of the statistical hypothesis. Prima facie evidence is sufficient to establish truth or falsity, but conclusions based on it may be disproved or defeated by further evidence or reasoning. Thus we may use the provisional truth or falsity of such hypotheses in forms of defeasible reasoning (Pollock, 1986, 1990), which is the way we reason from experience as opposed to the way we reason in classical logic and mathematics where truths of propositions are presumed inalterably given. In defeasible reasoning truths of propositions may change with further reasoning or evidence. Truths are provisional.

A FALLACIOUS USE OF POWER IN CRITICISM
OF SIGNIFICANCE TESTING

The Meaning of the Power of a Significance Test

Statistical power is analogous to the concept of resolving power in evaluating optical instruments. Power is the hypothetical conditional probability of rejecting the null hypothesis under some alternative hypothesis for the population parameter's value. Power is influenced by three things: (a) the size of the significance level α—increasing α increases power but also increases the probability of rejecting the null hypothesis when it is true; (b) the sample size, which with increasing sample size has the effect of reducing the size of the standard error, thereby increasing power; and (c) the difference between the value of the parameter under the null hypothesis and the value of the parameter under the alternative hypothesis—the larger the difference, the greater the power to detect it. Paradoxically one's confidence in acceptance of the null hypothesis increases with an increase in power to detect a standard difference regarded as important. On the other hand, knowing power is low to detect an effect of a size less extreme than the critical value should temper any enthusiasm for an accepted null hypothesis. We now turn to a fallacious use of the concept of power in criticizing significance testing. Schmidt and Hunter (chapter 3 of this volume) create scenarios, which they imply are realistic, that illustrate the inadequacy of significance tests. They state "The average power of null hypothesis significance tests in typical studies and research literatures is in the .40 to .60 range (Cohen, 1962; 1965, 1988, 1994; Schmidt, 1996; Schmidt, Hunter, & Ury, 1976; Sedlmeier & Gigerenzer, 1989). Suppose we take .50 as a rough average. With a power of .50, half of all tests in a research literature will be nonsignificant." They argue next that supporters of significance tests assume that if a test of a null hypothesis is not significant, it is interpreted to be a zero effect. Schmidt and Hunter then claim that this means that in half of all the studies the conclusion will be that there is no relationship. "Every one of these conclusions will be false. That is, in a research area where there really is a difference or a relation, when the significance test is used to determine whether findings are real or just chance events, the null hypothesis significance test will provide an erroneous answer about 50% of the time."

Our view is that this is fallacious reasoning. We looked up the article by Sedlmeier and Gigerenzer (1989) to see how they computed power for the studies reported in the various journal articles. They noted that they followed Cohen (1962). It is important to realize that power is one of four interrelated quantities: power, significance level, sample size N, and effect size. Determine any three of these quantities and you determine the fourth. So to determine the power of a study reported in the literature, you have to specify the sample size, the significance level, and an effect size to be detected. Sample size is reported in a journal article about the study. To standardize comparisons across studies, it suffices to pick an arbitrary fixed significance level .05 and an arbitrary hypothetical effect size. Cohen chose to use three arbitrary hypothetical effect sizes, a small, medium, and large effect size. He chose further to operationalize the three effect sizes as corresponding to the dimensionless Pearson correlations of .20, .40, and .60, respectively. He then computed the power of a study as the power to detect a specified correlation as significant at the .05 level given the sample size N of the study. It is extremely important for the reader to see that the effect size is completely hypothetical and does not represent an actual effect present to be detected by the study. No effort was made to find out what the true effect was, and even if such an effort had been made it could have only reported an estimated effect that would be subject to sampling and measurement error. Thus the only thing that varied across studies was sample size N, and this N was converted into three power figures for the study, the power to detect a small, medium and large effect, respectively, at that sample size.

Sedlmeier and Gigerenzer (1989) followed Cohen's (1962) procedure in determining power for the studies reported a decade or more later than Cohen's studies. The figures Schmidt and Hunter (chapter 3 of this volume) chose to report as typical on the basis of these studies corresponded to the powers to detect as significant a medium effect (correlation of .40) at the study's sample size. On the other hand, although citing the power values Sedlmeier and Gigerenzer (1989) reported, as illustrative of typical psychological studies, Schmidt (1996) compared those power values with the power values of an artificial scenario he constructed of normally distributed data having a true .5 standard deviation effect and a power of .37 to detect that effect against the null hypothesis of no effect at the .05 level. Because he had been discussing an artificial scenario in which the true effect was .5 standard deviations, his comparison with the Sedlmeier and Gigerenzer power figures conveyed the impression that their power figures were also powers to detect the typical true effects in the fields surveyed. By citing Schmidt (1996) and the Cohen (1962) and the Sedlmeier and Gigerenzer (1989) articles together as sources for typical effects, the same impression is created by Schmidt and Hunter (chapter 3 of this volume). And this is borne out because they then use the rough average power of .50 to conclude that in half of the studies the researcher's conclusion will be that there is no relationship, but this conclusion, they say, will be false in every case. But in our view, to suggest that, in approximately half of the psychological studies surveyed by Cohen and Sedlmeier and Gigerenzer, the null hypothesis was accepted and that in every one of these cases the decision to do so was in error, is wrong and grossly misleading.

The power figures reported by Cohen (1962) and Sedlmeier and Gigerenzer (1989) and used by Schmidt and Hunter (chapter 3 of this volume) are not powers to detect the true effect of the respective studies. Their power figures were only the hypothetical powers to detect an arbitrary medium-sized effect if there were one, given the sample sizes of the studies. We have no idea what the true effects were in those studies. They could have all been much larger than the medium effect on which the powers had been computed, in which case the true power would have been much larger than .50 and the proportion of nonsignificant results would have been lower than .50. Or they could have all been much smaller than the medium effect and the true power would have been much less than .50 and the proportion of nonsignificant results greater than .50. So any attempt to extrapolate to what the typical error rate is in using significance tests in these fields is totally unwarranted. In effect this is the same kind of error of confusing a hypothetical conditional probability with an actual probability of an event happening in the world that critics of significance tests accuse many users of significance tests of making.

On the other hand, it is legitimate to generate hypothetical scenarios in which a true effect is presumed known and then investigate the performance of a significance test as Schmidt (1996) has done. Within the framework of such hypothetical assumptions, Schmidt's conclusions are correct. But the power to detect a true effect varies with the size of the true effect, the sample size, and the significance level. For example, although a given study may have a power of only .5 to detect a medium-size effect, it may have a power greater than .8 to detect a moderately large effect. So it is misleading to generalize these scenarios with medium-size effects to all studies.

But it is important also to remember that significance testing is performed in circumstances where one does *not* have prior knowledge of the size of the true effect nor of the probability of a certain effect size's occurrence. What is important is whether a significance-testing procedure provides a reasonable way of forming a judgment about the validity of a hypothesis about a population parameter from sample data. Significance testing must be judged on those terms. Unlike in Schmidt's scenarios, a typical significance test is performed when one has no prior information about the nature of the effect. If one has such information, it must be incorporated into the hypothesis to be tested.

We urge researchers to specify the value of the parameter to be tested to a value that reflects prior knowledge about it. In experiments with randomization, one knows that there should be no differences—unless there are effects, which one does not yet know. In field studies with correlation it is somewhat problematic to say what prior knowledge dictates H_0 should be. The question then is, "Does the significance test reasonably use the information given to it to guide the researcher to a provisional judgment given one has no idea whether the hypothesis is true or not until one gets the data?"

It is not necessarily a fault of significance testing if in one of these hypothetical scenarios where the true standardized effect size is .5 one accepts the null hypothesis in 74% of the cases and rejects it in only 26%. The question is whether it was reasonable, given what one does not know other than what is given in the data, to arrive at one's decisions in this manner? After all, if the null hypothesis of a zero standardized effect were true, one would reject the null hypothesis in only 5% of the cases, which is much less than 26%. But knowing that the power to detect a small effect of .5 standardized effect units is only 26%, one might be unwilling to put too much stock in such decisions, if one is looking for effects that small. One needs to use knowledge of power to temper the confidence one has in one's decisions if one has any reason to believe the effects to be detected are at most that size.

Other indirect indices of power and corresponding uncertainty associated with an accepted null hypothesis are the standard error of the test statistic, width of the acceptance region, the standardized effect size corresponding to a critical value of the test statistic, and the confidence interval calculated around a point estimate of the effect. Prior calculations of the power to detect an expected effect size can also guide the researcher to obtain the sample sizes to reach a decision with adequate power. But in those cases where one feels one has insufficient power to resolve the issue we have no quarrel with Schmidt (1996) who argued that one can simply report point estimates of the effect size and the confidence interval estimate of the effect. One always has the option to suspend judgment while waiting to obtain sufficient evidence to reach a decision. (Editors need to evaluate articles not on the grounds of statistical significance in studies where power is low against an effect size regarded as important, but of the potential of the data's being useful in combination with data from other studies for meta-analysis). But this does not mean giving up significance testing, only postponing it.

No Need to Abandon Significance Tests

There is no need to abandon significance tests altogether as Schmidt (1996) recommended, especially in those cases where one observes significant effects that exceed in value effects detectable with high power. For example, a true effect that is four standard errors in size has approximately a power of .975 of being detected by any significance test involving a two-tailed test with a .05 level of significance. And any true effect that is 2.84 standard errors in size may be detected by any such significance test with a power of approximately .80. Of course, in contrast, the observed effect will contain error, and one's remaining uncertainty regarding its true value will be gauged by the standard error or some function of it.

Schmidt (1996) rejected the advice that researchers should calculate sample sizes needed to achieve a specified power against a specified effect. His argument is that this requirement would make it impossible for most studies to ever be conducted. As research progresses within an area sample size requirements become increasingly larger to achieve powers commensurate to detect ever smaller effects as one moves from simply detecting the presence of an effect to determining its specific value or relative size with respect to other effects. In correlational research, he cited how sample sizes may need to be quite large—often 1,000 or more. For example, with a sample of size 1,000 one has the power to detect a correlation of .089 as significantly different from zero at the .05 level with a power of .80. He believed to make these demands on researchers would be unrealistic. But many researchers with commercial and educational tests have access to large data bases today of far more than 1,000 cases. The issue is not whether or not to do a study, for small studies, as Schmidt suggests, can be integrated with other small studies by meta-analyses, but to consider the power of detecting a certain size effect with a significance test with the sample at hand. If one is looking only for large effects, then a significance test can be taken seriously with small samples.

META-ANALYSIS AND SIGNIFICANCE TESTING

Schmidt (1996) believed the issue of power is resolved if one abandons significance testing. Power, he believed, is only relevant in the context of significance testing. But this is not so. Power concerns resolving power, and this issue will remain in any meta-analysis, especially those that investigate the presence of moderator effects and interactions or hypothesizes their nonexistence. To use an analogy, one does not discard an 8× field glass just because it cannot detect objects the size of a house on the moon. One uses it to detect objects within its resolving power. The same is true of a significance test. The point is that one must decide (provisionally) whether deviations from hypothesized values are to be regarded as chance or real deviations and with sufficient power to resolve the issue.

Schmidt and Hunter (chapter 3 of this volume) believe that ". . . no single study contains sufficient information to support a conclusion about the truth or value of a hypothesis. Only by combining findings across multiple studies using meta-analysis can dependable scientific conclusions be reached . . . ." The implication is that significance testing with a single study is thus unable to reach any conclusion about the truth or value of a statistical hypothesis.

We think this argument confuses a number of complex issues. On the one hand, one may consider pooling the sample data from several studies into one large sample to achieve adequate power to test a hypothesis in question. On the other hand, there is the issue of whether one needs to show invariant results across many laboratory settings, which is an issue entirely separate from the issue that significance testing addresses. One may, for example, regard each of the studies as representing a sample from the same population (defined by comparable experimental conditions). A meta-analysis of these studies may take the form of pooling the samples from the individual studies to obtain one large sample that one uses to compute an estimate of the effect. The question will be whether the estimated effect equals some hypothesized effect. Any deviation between the estimated effect and the hypothesized effect will raise the question of whether the deviation is so large and so improbable as to be reasonably (but provisionally) regarded as not due to chance under the hypothesis. Whatever method you use to resolve this question will correspond to a significance test. So, why are we to suppose that this one large meta-analysis allows us to resolve issues about the validity of a hypothesis that no individual study can? Is it simply that individual studies have small samples and insufficient power to resolve the issue raised by the hypothesis? But suppose the individual study has a very large sample with adequate power to detect about any size effect with adequate power. Why is it we cannot reach a (provisional) judgment about the validity and value of a statistical hypothesis from such a single study, just as we do with the single meta-analytic study that has a combined sample size equal to that of the single study? What makes a meta-analysis not itself a single study?

The assertion that one cannot establish the validity and value of a hypothesis in a single study seems to be about other issues than just the issues of sample size and the pooling of samples. One of the values replication of results across many studies conveys is the objectivity of the result. Regardless of the researcher and the researcher's biases, regardless of the laboratory in which the results are observed, regardless of the research equipment used, the same results are obtained. Objectivity just is the demonstration of invariance in what is observed that is independent of the actions and properties of the observer (Mulaik, 1995).

But meta-analysis cannot establish this invariance if it simply pools studies and gets estimates of pooled effects. The resulting estimates may mask a hodge-podge of effects in the various studies. Although careful examination of the reported procedures used to perform the studies may allow one to select studies that appear effectively equivalent in their methodology and research subjects, the possibility remains that some unreported moderating variable had different effects upon the dependent variable in the studies accumulated. If plausible reasons based on prior experience for the possible existence of such a moderating variable can be given, this would undermine the assumption of invariance across the studies. The effect of moderating variables would have to be ruled out with positive evidence to allow one to proceed. Can one detect in the data themselves when a hypothesis of invariance across studies fails? The problem is analogous to an analysis of variance (ANOVA), but more complex, particularly when the parameters evaluated are not means. But even when the problem involves simply mean effects, one may not be able to presume homogeneity of variance within studies, which, with different size samples as commonly occurs in meta-analysis, will make implementation of traditional ANOVA procedures problematic. Nevertheless, an issue that will arise is the power to detect the differences between studies that would undermine the use of pooled estimates of effects across studies. The decision that there are no such differences will involve a form of significance test, if it is driven by the data at all.

Examples of Meta-Analyses

To get a better grasp of the problems of meta-analysis, let us consider the following scenario (Scenario 1) in which multiple samples are drawn from a single population. Scenario 2 will deal with samples drawn from several populations.

Scenario 1: The statistical model underlying this scenario may be written as

$$r_i = \rho + e_i \tag{4.1}$$

where r_i is a sample correlation that we may think of as the population correlation ρ to which sampling error e_i has been added. Other things being equal, if the sample size is small (e.g., $N = 68$), it is known that the statistical test associated with the null hypothesis (of $\rho = 0$) will not have adequate power for detecting nonzero, medium-size population correlations. This power can be brought to an adequate level (say, of .80) either by increasing the individual sample size or by combining data from several samples. In the example given in Schmidt (1996), the bivariate data from the 21 samples, with 68 cases per sample, can be combined in one big sample with $N = 1428$. The correlation based on the bigger sample is .22, which is also the result one would obtain using meta-analytic procedures. In this example, meta-analysis does not really provide any additional useful information. However, the same result as Schmidt's (1996) meta-analysis is obtained from this single-pooled sample using a pooled estimate of the population correlation and determining that it is significantly different from zero with a significance test. The power of this test to detect a correlation of .20 is greater than .80.

If correlations in the 21 different samples are based on *different but comparable* measures of X and Y, it would not be possible to combine different samples into one big sample for assessing the relationship between X and Y. This could happen if X and Y represent cognitive ability and grade point average (GPA), respectively, and different but comparable measures of cognitive ability are used in the 21 samples. Because different cognitive ability measures are likely to be in different metrics, combining the *raw data* from different samples to compute a single correlation coefficient between X and Y is not advisable. One, however, may be able to average the 21 correlations (as it is done in meta-analysis) to arrive at an overall strength of the relationship between X and Y, because by definition all correlations are on a common metric. Whereas correlations, like the effect sizes, offer the common or standard metric needed in most meta-analyses, Cohen (1994) noted that they "cannot provide useful information on causal strength because they change with the degree of variability of the variables they relate" (p. 1001).

Scenario 2: In this scenario, different samples are drawn from different populations and the underlying statistical model can be expressed as

$$r_{ij} = \rho_j + e_{ij}, \tag{4.2}$$

where subscript j refers to population j and i to a sample drawn from that population. In meta-analysis, or especially in validity generalization studies, the aim is to estimate the mean and variance of the ρ_j (denoted, respectively as μ_ρ and σ_ρ^2). In this scenario, one can also pool the data from different samples into a single data set and compute the correlation between X and Y. Such an analysis, although adequate in Scenario 1, is inadequate in Scenario 2 because the r_js may differ from population to population. One way to estimate the needed parameters is to first note that, under the assumption that $E(e_{ij}) = 0$,

$$\mu_r = \mu_\rho \tag{4.3}$$

and

$$\sigma_r^2 = \sigma_\rho^2 + E(\sigma_{e_j}^2) \tag{4.4}$$

These two equations can be used to estimate μ_ρ and σ_ρ^2 respectively (Hedges & Olkin, 1985; Hunter & Schmidt, 1990). Estimates of these two parameters provide useful information in practice, with estimation of σ_ρ^2 receiving more attention when one is concerned with the generalizability of the correlation between X and Y across situations or populations. In the latter application (i.e., in validity generalization studies), Equation 4.4 plays an important role. σ_r^2 on the left-hand side of Equation 4.4 can be estimated by the variance of observed correlations, and let us denote this estimate by s_r^2; the second quantity on the right-hand side of Equation 4.4 can be estimated by the average of sampling-error variances of sample-based correlations denoted by $\bar{s}_e^2$. Then the difference, $\hat{\sigma}_\rho^2 = s_r^2 - \bar{s}_e^2$, can be used as an estimate of σ_ρ^2. Two aspects of this estimate are important in the present context.

First, even when $\sigma_\rho^2 = 0$, the estimate s_r^2 generally will not equal estimate $\bar{s}_e^2$ and, therefore, $\hat{\sigma}_\rho^2$ rarely will equal zero. In explaining the benefits of meta-analysis (and there are several), Schmidt (1996) provides an example (his Figure 3) in which $s_r^2 = \bar{s}_e^2$ to claim that "meta-analysis reaches the correct conclusion" (p. 118). Here, according to Schmidt (1996), the correct conclusion is that $\sigma_\rho^2 = 0$. This illustration is misleading because with a small finite number of samples, s_r^2 rarely equals $\bar{s}_e^2$; one typically has a nonzero residual which must be assessed for its proximity to zero. As an illustration, let us consider the example given by Schmidt in his Table 2. The variance s_r^2 of the 21 observed correlations is .0109 and the average $\bar{s}_e^2$ of the 21 sampling variances is .0133. Therefore $\hat{\sigma}_\rho^2 = s_r^2 - \bar{s}_e^2 = .0109 - .0133 = -.0024$, which is close to zero but not exactly zero. Since variance can only be nonnegative, one may treat this negative difference as zero, which is sometimes done in generalizability theory (Brennan, 1983). What if this residual σ_ρ^2 is small but positive? How does one decide when an estimate is small enough to be considered zero? Would null hypothesis testing be an appropriate tool for deciding whether a residual σ_ρ^2 or an estimate of σ_ρ^2 is significantly different from zero? We think so. Now to the second point:

Second, in validity generalization studies, one is interested in finding out if σ_ρ^2 is zero. This result has important theoretical and practical implications. Therefore, one typically estimates σ_ρ^2 and then tries to determine if that estimate is significantly different from zero. Both Hunter and Schmidt (1990) and Hedges and Olkin (1985) have proposed approximate chi-square tests for this purpose. The aim of these tests is to assess whether the observed correlations or effect sizes are significantly different from each other, a pure and simple case of null hypothesis testing. Hunter and Schmidt (1990) also proposed an ad hoc procedure, which is commonly referred to as the 75% rule. Furthermore, Hunter and Schmidt recommend the use of lower credibility values in inferring the generalizability of validity. These credibility values are derived with the help of estimates of μ_ρ and σ_ρ^2. However, the estimates of μ_ρ and σ_ρ^2 by definition contain sampling error which are reflected in the lower credibility values. Hunter and Schmidt did not take into account the associated sampling errors in establishing the lower credibility values and therefore their recommended procedure raises questions about its true practical utility. It appears that the straightforward null hypothesis testing of an estimate of σ_p^2 is a more defensible route to establishing the generalizability of a validity coefficient across populations.

Along the lines of null hypothesis testing, Hedges and Olkin (1985) have recommended between and within chi-square tests (which are significance tests) for those investigators looking for moderators. Despite the fact that moderators are hard to find in practice (because they are difficult to detect with adequate power when the number of studies compared is small and sample sizes are small), these chi-square tests have been useful in identifying sub-populations in which the validity is found to be generalizable.

SIGNIFICANCE TESTS IN PHYSICS

Schmidt and Hunter (chapter 3 in this volume) argue that physicists do not perform significance tests. What they do in their studies is compute an estimate of the parameter of interest and place an error band or confidence interval around the estimate. To test a theoretical hypothesis they compare the estimated value to the theoretical value. Schmidt and Hunter say specifically ". . . this comparison is not based on a significance test." Furthermore physicists, Schmidt and Hunter say, combine results from different studies in ways that are not essentially different from meta-analyses. "The tests of hypotheses and theories that are considered the most credible are those conducted based on data combined across studies. Estimates from the different studies are averaged, and the standard error of the mean is compared and used to place a confidence interval around the mean estimate. (The confidence interval is not interpreted as a significance test)." They then offer a couple of examples from physics. Of interest to us is their first example, the test of Einstein's theory of relativity which states that gravity of a large massive body like the sun will bend light by a certain amount. They say that

> ...the hypothesis was tested in a famous study that measured the amount of bending in light produced by its passing the sun by comparing the apparent position of stars at the edge of the disk of the sun during an eclipse with their apparent positions when not near the sun. Several different observatories made these measurements and the measurements were averaged. The measured amount of bending corresponded to the figure predicted by Einstein's general theory, and so the hypothesis was confirmed and hence the more general theory from which it was derived was supported. In this important study *no significance tests were used.*

Schmidt and Hunter (chapter 3 of this volume) say further "...no significance test was run to see if the amount of bending was significantly greater than zero (test of the null hypothesis) or to see if the observed amount of bending was significantly different from the amount predicted by the theory (a significance test preferred by some.)"

Although it is true that no test of the nil hypothesis (that the parameter is zero) was performed, it is not quite true to say that no test was performed to see if the observed amount of bending was significantly different from the amount predicted by the theory. As we will see, the measured amount of bending of the light did not correspond to what was predicted by either theory (Newton's or Einstein's), and so some criterion was needed to determine whether the difference between the predicted and measured values was greater than what would be typical as a result of random error of measurement.

Moyer (1979) recounts how in 1916–1917, the British astronomer Arthur S. Eddington published an article in which he showed that Newton's theory of gravity would predict that gravitation would deflect light by one-half the amount predicted by Einstein's theory of relativity. By 1918, Eddington had derived from Einstein's general theory of relativity that a ray of light from a star passing near the edge of the sun would be bent in such a way that the star's image would be shifted outward by $1''.75\ r_0/r$, where r_0 is the radius of the sun and r the closest approach of the star's light to the center of the sun when compared to the star's image without the sun. In contrast Newtonian theory predicted a shift of $0''.87$ r_0/r. Thus a test of Einstein's and Newton's theories could be made during a total eclipse of the sun, when the disc of the moon would just cover the disc of the sun and stars next to the sun in the field of view could be observed.

In 1919 a total eclipse of the sun was predicted, and Eddington and A. C. D. Crommelin led expeditions to the island of Principe in the Gulf of Guinea, West Africa and to Sobral, northern Brazil, respectively, to observe and photograph the eclipse. In his summary of the experiment, Eddington (1920/1987) noted that Einstein's theory predicts a deflection of $1''.74$ at the edge of the sun, with the amount decreasing inversely as the distance from the sun's center. In contrast Newtonian theory predicts a deflection that is half this, $0''.87$. The final estimates of the deflection (reduced to the edge of the sun) obtained at Sobral and Principe (with their 'probable accidental errors') were: Sobral, $1''.98 \pm 0''.12$; Principe, $1''.61 \pm 0''.30$. Eddington then said, "It is usual to allow a margin of safety of about twice the probable error on either side of the mean. The evidence of the Principe plates is thus just about sufficient to rule out the possibility of the 'half-deflection,' and the Sobral plates exclude it with practical certainty" (p. 245). He then noted that because of the obscuring effects of the clouds, the value of the data obtained at Principe could not be put higher than about one-sixth of that at Sobral. Nevertheless, he felt it was difficult to criticize this confirmation of Einstein's theory because ". . . it was obtained independently with two different instruments at different places and with different kinds of checks" (p. 245).

A probable error is .67449 of a standard error in a normal distribution (Fisher, 1925). Twice the probable error equals approximately 1.35 standard errors. This corresponds in a two-tailed test to a significance level of .177. So, if Eddington was using a margin of safety of two probable errors on either side of the mean, any hypothesized value outside of the confidence band would be rejected at the .177 level. In this case Newton's prediction of $0''.87$ lies outside the two probable error confidence intervals from each site and is evidently rejected by Eddington, in favor of Einstein's prediction of $1''.74$, which falls within each band. But if Eddington's probable errors are converted to standard errors by multiplying them by $1/.67449 = 1.4826$, we get for Sobral $1.4826 \times 0''.12 = 0''.178$, and for Principe $1.4826 \times 0''.30 = 0''.44$. So a confidence interval of two standard errors for Sobral would be [1.624, 2.336], and for Principe [.73, 2.49]. The results obtained at Principe (which was partly covered by clouds during the eclipse) were fewer and of lower quality than those from Sobral, and Eddington gave the Principe results only 1/6 of the weight given the Sobral results. By current standards the results from Sobral clearly supported Einstein's hypothesized value and not Newton's, because Einstein's value of $1''.75$ is contained in the interval, and the Newtonian value of $0''.87$ is not; the Principe results were equivocal, since the predicted values of each hypothesis, $0''.87$ and $1''.75$, fell within the two standard-error confidence interval. We believe that Eddington used the confidence bands as a significance test, but by current standards his Type I error was greater than most statisticians would feel comfortable with today, although his power was likely fairly good for the small sample of 28 observations from Sobral because of the large size of the probability of a Type I error.

We have consulted physicists on the Internet regarding their use of significance tests. Evidently they get very little formal training in statistics. So, one reason why they might not perform formal significance tests is that they have not been trained to do so. But they do use confidence bands sometimes in the way many statisticians use confidence intervals as significance tests. If a hypothesized value falls within the confidence interval, that is evidence in favor of the hypothesized value. If it falls outside of the confidence interval, that is evidence against the hypothesized value. Another reason physicists often do not do significance tests is because they are not always testing hypotheses, but rather are trying to improve their estimates of physical constants. Their journals consider reporting estimates to be beneficial to the physics community, because they may be combined with results from other studies. (This supports Schmidt and Hunter's argument in chapter 3 of this volume that one does not always have to perform a significance test to have publishable results, and we concur with this aspect of their argument.) Physicists are also very suspicious of automated decision-making procedures, and Neyman-Pearson significance testing suggests that to them. They also tend to regard results that differ significantly from predicted values to be most likely due to artifacts and systematic errors. Only after exhaustive efforts to identify the source of systematic errors has failed to turn up anything will they then take seriously such significant differences as providing lack of support for established theory and in favor of some other theory that predicts such results. Finally, as Giere (1987, p. 190) notes, physicists have long realized that the typical experiment produces results with errors of only 2%. But most theories, even good ones in physics, make predictions to only within 20% of the data. Thus if one goes by significance tests alone, one would reject almost all such theories and not pursue them further. So, measures of approximation are often much more meaningful than significance tests in physics. This does not mean there are no situations where they might be used.

Hedges (1987) (cited by Schmidt and Hunter in chapter 3 of this volume as supporting their position) indicates that physicists *do* use procedures that are comparable to significance tests. Although many of their studies are equivalent to meta-analyses in the social sciences, they use a ratio known as Birge's R to evaluate the hypothesis that the population value for a parameter is the same in all studies considered for review. When this ratio is near unity, this is evidence for the consistency of the estimates across the studies; when the ratio is much greater than unity this is evidence for a lack of consistency. Birge's ratio is given as

$$R = \frac{\sum_{i=1}^{k} \omega_i (T_i - T_{\bullet})^2}{k-1}$$

where $T_1, \ldots, T_k$ are estimates of a theoretical parameter in each of k studies, $S_1, \ldots, S_k$ their respective standard errors, and $T_{\bullet}$, their weighted average

$$T_{\bullet} = \frac{\sum_{i=1}^{k} \omega_i T_i}{\sum_{i=1}^{k} \omega_i},$$

with $\omega_i = 1/S_i^2$.

Hedges (1987) notes that Birge's ratio is directly related to a chi-square statistic

$$\chi^2 = (k-1)R = \sum_{i=1}^{k} \omega_i (T_i - T_\bullet)^2$$

with $k-1$ degrees of freedom. In other words, Birge's ratio is a chi-square statistic divided by its degrees of freedom. The mean of a chi-square distribution equals the degrees of freedom of the distribution, so this ratio compares the size of the obtained chi-square to the mean of the chi-square distribution. The ratio serves to test whether differences among the estimates are greater than what would be expected on the basis of unsystematic (measurement) error.

This chi-square statistic is very similar to comparable chi-square statistics proposed for meta-analysis by Hedges (1981) and Rosenthal and Rubin (1982) in the social sciences to test whether differences in estimates of a parameter in question across studies are greater than what would be expected by sampling error. In this respect, Schmidt and Hunter (1996) are correct in saying that physicists use statistics like those used in meta-analysis. But it is clear that Hedges regards these as significance tests. Thus this is further evidence that physicists have not abandoned significance tests—nor have most meta-analysts.

Hedges (1987) also notes the availability of a comparable approximate chi-square statistic

$$\chi_k^2 = \sum_{i=1}^{k} \omega_i (T_i - \tau)^2$$

for testing whether several studies confirm a theoretically predicted value for a parameter. Instead of the estimate $T_\bullet$, the theoretical value τ of the parameter is used in the formula, and because an unknown value for the parameter is not estimated, one gains a degree of freedom so that the resulting chi-square statistic has k degrees of freedom.

These approximate chi-square statistics used in meta-analysis are appropriate only in large samples ($n_i > 30$) where estimates of the standard errors are stable and the sampling distributions of the parameter estimates are approximately normal.

THE MEANING OF OBJECTIVITY

Objectivity Derived from a Schema of Perception

We have already mentioned the objectivity of significance tests. We would like to bring out why science cannot proceed merely by estimating parameters, as suggested by Schmidt and Hunter (1996) when they recommend reporting confidence interval estimates of parameters while denying their use in significance tests. Tests of hypotheses are essential to integrating and unifying conceptually the diversity of our observations into concepts of an objective world. The issue is not the uniformity of procedures followed, of clear-cut statements of alternatives and how to decide between them, or how to calculate the results in a uniform way. Uniformity of procedure, it is true, is relevant to establishing objective findings, but the ultimate issue concerns establishing invariant features in the observations that are independent of the actions and properties of the observer.

Mulaik (1995) regarded "objectivity" as a metaphor taken from a schema of perception, the schema involved in the perception of objects. J. J. Gibson (1966, 1979) regarded visual perception of objects to take place in the context of an organism's constantly moving within and interacting with its environment. The organism's motion through the environment produces varying information to the senses about the environment, but the transformations these motions and actions produce, in what is given to the organism perceptually, occur in certain invariant ways that are correlated with those motions and actions. The organism is thus able to factor out the effects of its own actions from the optic array of information presented to it. The term for this is *proprioception*. Objects, on the other hand, for Gibson are invariants through time in the varying optic array that are distinct from invariants of transformations in the optic array produced by the organism. The detection of these objective invariants is known as *exteroception.*

This schema of object perception serves to integrate information gathered almost continuously at adjacent instants in time and points in space into information about objects and acts of the embodied self. Perception of objects and perception of self (as body-in-action) occur simultaneously together and are two aspects of the same process.

Mulaik (1995) argued that when extended conceptually beyond what is given immediately in sensory perception to information collected at widely spaced points in time and space, the schema of objectivity serves as a metaphor to integrate this information conceptually through memory and narration into our objective knowledge about the world and our place within it. It is the driving metaphor of science and even of law. It is also the metaphor that underlies the worlds of virtual reality in computer graphics.

Relevance to Hypothesis Testing

The relevance of objectivity to hypothesis testing is that hypothesis testing is a way of integrating information conceptually into objective forms, of extending them beyond a given situation or context and independent of the observer. The hypothesis is stated before the data are given. The hypothesis must be formulated independently of the data used to evaluate it. The reason for this is because whatever the data are to reveal must be regarded as independent of the one who formulates the hypothesis. Only then will the data be an objective basis for comparison to the hypothesis and thereby a way of conveying objectivity to the hypothesis, if the data conform to the hypothesis.

In contrast, a hypothesis, so-called, formulated by observing the data to be used in its evaluation and formulated in such a way as to conform to that data, cannot then be regarded as objective by its conforming to those same data. To begin with, more than one hypothesis can be constructed to conform perfectly to a given set of data. Thus any particular hypotheses formulated by a researcher to conform to a set of data may be regarded as relative to the researcher in reflecting the particular context, perspective, biases and even media of representation used by the researcher, imposed onto the data. On the other hand, hypotheses constructed to fit a given set of data logically might not fit an independent data set. Thus fit of a hypothesis to an independent data set can serve as a test of the independent and objective validity of the hypothesis. It is logically possible to fail such tests. But it is logically impossible for data to fail to fit a hypothesis tailored to fit them by the researcher. Thus a test of possible lack of fit cannot even be performed on a hypothesis using data that the hypothesis was constructed to fit, because there is no logical possibility of a lack of fit. On the other hand, most hypotheses are formulated by interacting with data, but not the data used to evaluate them.

We humans do not have to formulate our hypotheses out of nothing. We formulate them from past experience and test them as generalizations with new experience. Or we use one set of data for formulating a hypothesis and another set for testing it. Sometimes in models with many unspecified parameters we can use some aspects of a given data set to complete an incompletely specified hypothesis by estimating the unspecified parameters, and still test the prespecified aspects of the hypothesis with other aspects of the data not used in determining the unspecified parameter estimates (Mulaik, 1990). This conforms very well to the schema whereby we determine perceptually that an object and not an illusion stands before us, by getting new information from a different point of view and comparing it to what we expect to see given what we thought is there initially by hypothesis and according to how that should appear from the new point of view.

Significance testing is concerned with hypothesis testing. The hypothesis-testing aspect of significance testing does concern the integration and accumulation of knowledge, and it is for this reason why formulation of the proper hypothesis to test is crucial to whether or not the test will contribute to the accumulation and synthesis of knowledge. But the particular aspect of hypothesis testing that significance testing is concerned with is whether or not an observed difference from the hypothesized value is so different and so improbable under the presumption that chance error is combined with the true value, as to cast doubt on the truth of the hypothesized value. In this regard significance testing is blind to the relevance of the hypothesis chosen to test.

We believe that a major problem with nil hypothesis significance testing that brings on the accusation that significance tests prevent the accumulation of knowledge, is that once one has gained some knowledge that contradicts one's initial null hypothesis, one does not modify one's hypotheses to reflect that new knowledge. After rejecting the null hypothesis, a replication study proceeds again to test the same null hypothesis that one now has reason to believe is false. But a hypothesis one ought to test is that the effect is equal to the value estimated in the previous study, which one judged to be significantly different from a zero effect. Or if one does not trust the results of the first study because one believes the effect is an artifact, one should eliminate suspected sources of systematic error in a new experiment and collect new data, with a sample sufficiently large to detect any remaining meaningful effects with sufficient power.

Unfortunately in the context of traditional factorial ANOVA, it is not easy in terms of methods and computer programs for researchers to specify their hypotheses in terms of earlier found effects. It is easier to test the hypothesis that there is no difference between groups and no interaction effects. But we have learned through the development of algorithms for structural equation modeling that one can fix some parameters and free others in specifying a model. Perhaps the time has come to modernize ANOVA and the general linear model, to make it easy to specify and test models with fixed nonzero parameters for certain effects.

DEGREES OF BELIEF?

Rozeboom (1960) criticized null-hypothesis significance testing because it conceptualizes the problem as one in which a decision is to be made between two alternatives. Here his critique is directed more to Neyman-Pearson (1933) rather than Fisherian (1935, 1959) conceptions of significance testing. He argued "But the primary aim of a scientific experiment is not to precipitate decisions, but to make an appropriate adjustment in the degree to which one accepts, or believes, the hypothesis or hypotheses being tested" (Rozeboom, 1960, p. 420). Rozeboom objected to the decision-theoretic concept that a motor-act is to be determined by the evidence of an experiment. Decisions are voluntary commitments to action, that is, motor sets. But ". . . acceptance or rejection of a hypothesis," he said, "is a cognitive state which may provide the basis for rational decisions, but is not itself arrived at by such a decision . . ." (p. 420). In other words:

As scientists, it is our professional obligation to reason from available data to explanations and generalities—i.e., beliefs—which are supported by these data. But belief in
(i.e., acceptance of) a proposition is not an all-or-none affair; rather it is a matter of degree, and the extent to which a person believes or accepts a proposition translates prag-
matically into the extent to which he is willing to commit himself to the behavioral adjustments prescribed for him by the meaning of that proposition" (pp. 420–21).

Rozeboom seemed inclined to distinguish cognitive from behavioral states,
although we think he would have been hard pressed to find criteria for attribut-
ing certain cognitive states to individuals without reference to behavioral criteria.

Nevertheless, Rozeboom's (1960) critique of the Neyman-Pearson decision-
theoretic approach to significance testing (about which we also have some concerns in the context of evaluating scientific theories and hypotheses by comparing them to specific rival hypotheses) raises issues whose complexities cannot be
dealt with in detail in the short space that remains in this chapter. But we can
make the following comments: To some extent, when he wrote his critique, Rozeboom was entertaining Bayesian inference as a possible replacement for Neyman-Pearson significance testing. Bayesian inference, however, has long been
controversial, particularly when it has been invoked in connection with the use
of subjective prior probabilities. Critiques of the philosophical assumptions of
Bayesian inference may be found in Giere (1987), Pollock (1986), Glymour
(1981), Gillies (1973), and Hacking (1965), whereas a summary of the Bayesian
argument and an attempted rebuttal of many of these criticisms from a subjective
Bayesian point of view that rejects a behavioral interpretation of degrees of belief was given by Howson and Urbach (1989), which in turn has been criticized
by Chihara (1994) and Maher (1996). Another source on this debate was given
by the Bayesian Earman (1992) and a subsequent critique by non-Bayesian Forster (1995), who argued that the Bayesian philosophy of science cannot explain
the relevance of simplicity and the unification of data via theory to confirmation,
induction, and scientific inference. But in joining with the critics, we can add the
following comments to the argument, which were suggested to the first author by
reading commentaries on the works of the philosopher Ludgwig Wittgenstein
(Budd 1989; Schulte, 1992).

The focus on belief as a cognitive state that varies in degree confuses the issue of how to justify beliefs in propositions on the basis of evidence—which is a
normative issue concerned with the use of objective criteria of support for a belief—with a psychological theory concerned with describing and measuring a
problematic cognitive belief state that presumably is a causal effect of evidence
that varies as evidence accumulates, obeys Bayes' theorem, and which in turn is
a cause of subsequent behavior. Bayesians attempt to use this implicit psycho-

logical theory, which is at best a hypothesis—and one that does not fit well with the psychological facts about probabilistic beliefs either (Kahneman & Tversky, 1972)—as a normative account of how one is to modify one's degrees of belief on the basis of evidence. But a descriptive theory or hypothesis about psychological processes involving belief states is not a normative framework for justifying beliefs. We justify beliefs in a framework of norms of what constitutes supportive or disconfirming evidence for a proposition. And norms must be understood and applicable in an objective way. In fact, objectivity is a basic norm. As we evaluate the evidence in terms of these norms, our belief states take care of themselves and are not ordinarily explicitly relevant to making the evaluation itself.

The problem with arguments designed to justify beliefs by focusing on private, introspected belief states is that these arguments are based on the same pattern of reasoning used by empiricists to justify our knowledge based on experience. Empiricists sought to ground our knowledge of the world in an incorrigible foundation of inwardly experienced sense data. But the empiricist enterprise sank on the rocks of solipsism and the realization that ultimately the sense data of logically private experience involve a logically incoherent idea that is useless in the public dialogues aimed at justifying beliefs about experience. Not only are the so-called logically private sense data of one individual logically inaccessible to others for the purposes of verification, they are intractable even to the individual who would try to bring them into a kind of private language he or she would use to reason about them. Wittgenstein's (1953) famous "private-language argument" showed the incoherence of the idea of a logically private language based on logically private experience. Because the concept of language involves an activity governed by rules, and rules demand objective criteria for their application, so that one can distinguish between thinking one is following the rules and actually following them and not making them up as one goes along, language cannot be applied to that which is logically and irretrievably private. Wittgenstein's private-language argument knocked the linchpin out of the framework of arguments designed to justify one's beliefs via an incorrigible foundation in subjective, introspected experience. What remains to justify our beliefs are reasons we locate in the world, reasons that are thus public and available to everyone, and judged by rules and norms that we share.

Wittgenstein's (1953) private-language argument rules out the possibility of using language to refer to an inner, logically private "inner state" that reflects an individual's degree of belief. Historically, the concept of "degree of belief" is a metaphor based on the idea of probability that originally developed in connection with games of chance (Hacking, 1975). The concept of probability was extended from objective settings (such as games of chance) with stable well-understood causal constraints built in to the gaming apparatus and clear, objective criteria of how to assign the probabilities, along with predictive success in use of these probabilities reinforced by the stable physical conditions of the games, through settings in which a probability represented an individual's gut feel as to what might happen next in a poorly understood situation, to degrees of belief in any proposition. The metaphor of life as a series of games of chance in which one constantly assesses the odds extended the idea of probability beyond the settings in which assessing the odds and probability could be done in an objective, rule governed manner to produce numbers assigned to events that obey Kolmogorov's axioms of probability theory. To be sure, numbers can be produced that represent people's degrees of belief, and these may have many of the superficial appearances of probabilities, but they are not probabilities.

Whatever the numbers that Bayesian statisticians elicit from clients as their subjective prior probabilities, they are not under all the constraints needed to guarantee numbers satisfying Kolmogorov's axioms. To begin with, the quantities given must be numbers between zero and unity. Most people can be trained to provide those on request. We would also conjecture that people must have knowledge of the proper use of probabilities in situations where probabilities are objectively determined to use these cases as examples to guide them. This means they must recognize the constraints on the way quantities denoting probabilities are to be distributed over a redefined sample space of alternative possibilities. One is often at a loss to specify the sample space of alternative scientific hypotheses appropriate in a given context, which one needs to do to distribute numerical quantities properly over the possible alternatives to represent probabilities satisfying the axioms of probability theory. Furthermore there is no corresponding concept of some reason for there being a specific value for one's uncertainty about the truth of a scientific hypothesis, as there is a reason for the specific value for the probability of a specific outcome in a game of chance, which is based on the invariant physical properties of the gaming equipment and its configuration. So, even if one can prescribe to a person how in any given situation to define such a space of alternative possibilities, how then do you train them to pick the numbers to assign to the alternatives to represent the individual's subjective degrees of belief about them? How can the subjective Bayesian know that the individual is giving numbers that represent the individual's subjective degree of belief? How can the person him- or herself know he or she is giving the right numbers that represent true subjective degree of belief? What criterion would one use? It is not sufficient to say that whatever the person says is "right" is "right", for in that case we cannot speak of following a rule, which requires being able to distinguish between cases where persons say they are right and their actually being right (Wittgenstein, 1953). Unless there is some objective way to determine this, the task is an impossible one not only for us external to the individual, but for the individual as well, and the numbers given are thus of dubious value. Unless an individual can be taught rules whose application can be objectively verified as to how to assign degrees of belief in scientific hypotheses that satisfy the axioms of probability, there is no such thing as a subjective degree of belief that an individual can learn to express that corresponds to the probability of probability theory.

But one might argue that we ordinarily do not question the subjective reports of individuals but take them at face value. That is true, but in this case we do not treat their reports as objective truths about themselves, but, as Wittgenstein (1953) suggested, verbal substitutes for observable natural reactions, which we simply accept without judgment as their reactions. There is no requirement that we regard their subjective reactions as right or wrong or descriptive of anything, for there is nothing against which we could compare their expressions to validate them. Nor can the individual privately validate his expressions, because he is in no position to distinguish between being right and thinking he is right, which we are able to do with public phenomena and public criteria. This undermines claims that the use of subjective prior probabilities in Bayesian inference leads to optimal rational inference from experience, for even if the numbers given satisfied axioms of probability in representing some subjective phenomenon, who would be able to tell? Finally the argument fails that subjective Bayesian inference can still be used as an ideal norm prescribing optimal rational inference, as if ideally we could attain subjective prior probabilities satisfying the axioms of probability (Howson & Urbach, 1989), because it is not a norm for humans if humans cannot follow it correctly and objectively.

Recognizing these difficulties for subjective Bayesian prior probabilities, some Bayesians have sought to ground "personal" prior probabilities in behavioral criteria, such as Ramsey's (1931) or de Finetti's (1937) assumption that a degree of belief p in a hypothesis h is equivalent to a disposition to bet indifferently on or against the truth of the hypothesis h at odds $p/(1 - p)$, so long as the stakes are kept small (Howson & Urbach, 1989). Ramsey and de Finetti showed that if the degrees of belief did not satisfy the probability axioms and if the one taking your bet could dictate which side of the issue you were to take and the size of the stakes, then you could be made to lose no matter what. Supposedly then one should have degrees of belief that satisfy the probability axioms or one would lose bets in this situation. But the usual arguments against this view point out that there are many good reasons (or none at all) why you might be willing to bet at odds different than those dictated by one's degree of belief (Howson & Urbach, 1989). Behavior in betting situations is influenced by too many things other than degree of belief to serve as a univocal indicator of degree of belief. Besides, no practical Bayesian statistician uses this method to assess personal prior probabilities.

But the strongest argument against "degrees of belief" as propounded by both the subjective and behavioristic personal-probability Bayesians is that their concept of degree of belief confounds evidentiary reasons for belief with non-evidentiary (nonepistemological) reasons, such as the hope one has that one's way of conceiving a situation will turn out to be "right" (whatever that means), which may have no prior evidence to support it. What a theory of justified knowledge requires is evidentiary reasons for one's belief, no more and no less. Subjective and/or personal probabilities are determined by more than what the person knows to be true, and it is impossible to separate in these subjective/personal probabilities what is known from what is hoped for or purely conjectured. And different individuals will have different "subjective," non-evidentiary reasons for their belief; as a consequence, Bayesians believe Bayesian inference will yield different inferences for different individuals, although accumulating data will eventually overwhelm the subjective/personalistic element in these inferences and converge to common solutions. The personal/subjective element enters in primarily at the outset of a series of updated Bayesian inferences. Nevertheless, at the outset, subjective/personal Bayesian inference based on these subjective/personal probabilities does not give what is just the evidentiary reasons to believe in something and is unable to separate in its inference what is subjective from what is objective and evidentiary (Pollock, 1986).

These criticisms of subjective Bayesian inference are not designed to refute the legitimate uses of Bayes' theorem with objectively determinable prior probabilities defined on explicitly defined sample spaces. But the proponents of objective Bayesian inference have not been inclined to regard their method as a universal prescription for inference, but rather as a method limited to situations where objectively determinable prior probabilities are possible. In the meantime that leaves significance testing as another route to probabilistic inference where knowledge of prior probabilities is not available or an incoherent idea.

The point to be made with respect to significance testing, is that significance testing is a procedure contributing to the (provisional) prima facie judgment about the objective, evidentiary validity of a substantive proposition. Subjective opinions and descriptions of subjective states or psychological states are not relevant to such judgments.

APPENDIX

There have been two major schools of thought advocating forms of significance testing, and the distinctions between these schools have not always been recognized. In fact, because of similarities in some of their positions and methods, they generally have been confused by textbook writers on psychological statistics and in the teaching of psychological and social statistics (Gigerenzer, 1989, 1993; Gigerenzer & Murray, 1987). The first, and older of these two schools is due to the eminent statistician R. A. Fisher. The other is due to a successor generation of statisticians, Jerzy Neyman and Egon S. Pearson (the son of Karl Pearson who worked out the formula for the product-moment correlation coefficient that bears his name). Although there are similarities between these two schools, and the later school is in part a logical development from the earlier, a bitter debate between them lasted from the mid-1930's until Fisher died in 1962. Cowles (1989) provided an excellent summary of the development of these two schools and how the debate reflected conflicts between strong-willed, defensive personalities, although there are meaningful differences in emphasis.

Fisherian Significance Testing. R. A. Fisher, known both as a geneticist and a statistician, thought of himself as a research scientist first and statistician second. Yet his mathematical skills were formidable and these allowed him to make numerous major contributions to the mathematics of modern statistics during its formative years. Fisher's approach to significance testing grew out of his rejection of inductive inference based on the concept of inverse probability using prior probabilities (subjective Bayesian inference), an approach advocated by Laplace over 100 years before and still popular. On the one hand, Fisher regarded judgments of prior probabilities for scientific hypotheses to be either too subjective or impossible to formulate to the rigor required of a scientific method, while on the other hand he found the Bayesian argument—that in the absence of any prior knowledge, all hypotheses are to be regarded as being equally probable—to be unconvincing or to lead to mathematical contradictions. Furthermore he did not regard the mathematically well-defined concept of probability to be appropriate for expressing all forms of uncertainty or degrees of belief, which are often based on vague and uncircumscribed grounds. Thus he regarded mathematical probabilities as best limited to objective quantities that could be measured by observed frequencies. Consequently, he sought methods of inductive inference that dealt only with objective quantities and phenomena. In his first position as an agricultural statistician he formulated a system of how to design and draw inferences from experiments (Fisher, 1935). He argued that researchers should always include control conditions among their experimental treatments and should assign experimental treatments at random to experimental units. This would allow one to treat extraneous variable influences on the dependent variable, introduced via the experimental units, as randomized and unrelated to the experimental treatments. The effects of randomized extraneous variation would then in theory cancel one another in deriving expected mean outcomes.

Now a natural hypothesis to be tested, Fisher (1935) held, was that there is no effect from the experimental treatments. This would imply no difference between the expected means of any of the experimental treatments. This value reflects what you know you have put into the experiment by the process of randomization. You do not know whether there will be an effect or not. Fisher called this natural hypothesis the *null hypothesis*. To those who wondered why one did not test the opposite hypothesis, that there is an effect, he argued *that* is not an exact hypothesis, because no specific value for the effect is set forth by simply saying there will be an effect. By implication it would seem that for Fisher, if one had some specific value for the expected effect, one could use that as one's null hypothesis. But in most experimental situations where the researcher has no specific expected effect in mind, and is uncertain whether there will be an effect at all, the natural exact hypothesis to test is that there is no effect because that is what you would expect from randomization alone.

Fisher (1935) then held that grounds for not believing the null hypothesis would consist in experimental results in the form of statistical values so improbable and so extreme from expected values according to the hypothesized distribution for the statistic under the presumption of the truth of the null hypothesis that to believe these results are consistent with the null hypothesis would strain belief. This gives rise to a significance test. He noted that researchers frequently regard as "significant" extreme results that under the hypothetical distribution of the null hypothesis would be that extreme or more in only 5% of cases. But deciding in this way that a result is significant, implying a lack of support for the null hypothesis is not an irreversible decision. "If we use the term rejection for our attitude to such a hypothesis," he said, it should be clearly understood that no irreversible decision has been taken; that as rational beings, we are prepared to be convinced by future evidence that appearances were deceptive, and that in fact a very remarkable and exceptional coincidence had taken place" (Fisher 1959, p. 35). On the other hand, Fisher held that if one does not obtain a significant result this does not mean the null hypothesis is necessarily true. As he put it, ". . . it should be noted that the null hypothesis is never proved or established, but is possibly disproved, in the course of the experimentation. Every experiment may be said to exist only in order to give the facts a chance of disproving the null hypothesis" (Fisher, 1935, p. 19) .

In some respects Fisher's views on hypothesis testing anticipated the views of Karl Popper (1959/1935), the Viennese philosopher of science who argued that science cannot prove hypotheses from evidence but only falsify them. Popper argued that science may proceed with logic and deductive reasoning only insofar as it deduces hypotheses from certain premises and seeks to falsify them (see Mulaik and James, 1995). Fisher's approach to hypothesis testing with significance tests followed this recommendation, but with the realization that Popper overlooked, that even finding a deduced consequence to be false is not sufficient to prove a scientific hypothesis to be false. In this respect Fisher even anticipated more recent views in epistemology that all inferences from experience are defeasible and reversible with additional evidence. His attitude that there are no final decisions or irreversible conclusions reached in science explains his often negative reactions to other approaches to statistical inference that he perceived (sometimes wrongly) to automate the process of reasoning from evidence and thereby to force the researcher to abide by some final decision imposed by the algorithm.

The other important point about Fisher's views of significance testing was that the significance test does not provide an actual probability for the truth of the hypothesis. As he put it: "In general, tests of significance are based on *hypothetical* probabilities calculated from their null hypothesis. They do not generally lead to any probability statements about the real world, but to a rational and well-defined measure of reluctance to the acceptance of the hypotheses they test" (Fisher, 1959, p. 44). In other words, one can imagine what the probability distribution would be like for a test statistic if the null hypothesis were true. One can then imagine in connection with this hypothetical distribution what the probability would be of obtaining a deviation from the distribution's mean as extreme or more extreme than a certain value. If one selects first a small value for this probability and then finds the corresponding value of the test statistic that would be this extreme or more with this probability, then this value could serve as the critical value of the test statistic for rejecting the null hypothesis. The probabilities involved have nothing to do with real-world probabilities. They are all probabilities in an argument involving counterfactual or subjunctive conditionals (as the logicians would say) as to what sort of things should count in a researcher's mind as evidence against a hypothesis. This point is important, because a frequent criticism of significance testing is that researchers usually believe the probabilities described in connection with a significance test are about *actual* probabilities of making an error when one regards something to be significant. What is criticized in these cases is not Fisher's view of hypothesis testing, but some researchers' misconceptions about it.

It is also important to realize that Fisher's view was that ". . . a significance test of a null hypothesis is only a 'weak' argument. That is, it is applicable only in those cases where we have very little knowledge or none at all. For Fisher significance testing was the most primitive type of argument in a hierarchy of possible statistical analyses and inferences (see Gigerenzer et al., 1989, chapter 3)" (Gigerenzer, 1993, p. 314).

Neyman-Pearson Decision-Theoretic Significance Testing. The other school of significance testing grew out of what its authors initially believed was simply an extension of Fisher's ideas. Beginning in 1928 Jerzy Neyman, a young Polish statistician studying at the University of London, and Egon Pearson, Karl Pearson's son, published a series of articles (Neyman & Pearson 1928, 1933) that had a major impact on hypothesis testing in the years afterward (Cowles, 1989; Kendall & Stuart, 1979). In their articles Neyman and Pearson argued that the outcome of a significance test should be behavioral, *accepting* or *rejecting* some hypothesis and acting accordingly. Hypotheses, furthermore, are of two kinds, simple and composite. Simple hypotheses specify a unique point in the sample space of the statistic, which represents the set of all possible values that the statistic can take. Composite hypotheses specify a region of points of the sample space. The hypothesis you are to test has to be a well-defined hypothesis. It may be a point hypothesis or a composite hypothesis. To test any hypothesis one first has to divide the sample space into two regions. If the test statistic z falls in one of these regions, one accepts the hypothesis. If it falls in the other region, one rejects the hypothesis. (*Acceptance* and *rejection* of the hypothesis are only provisional actions the researcher takes and do not imply final, irreversible decisions nor determinations that the hypothesis is incorrigibly true or false [Kendall & Stuart 1979, p. 177].)

But to get the best critical region of rejection, you first have to specify a probability α—determined hypothetically according to the distribution you presume the test statistic will have if the hypothesis is true—that you will reject the hypothesis if the test statistic z falls in the critical region of rejection. To determine this critical region, you will also need to specify further what alternative hypothesis is to be considered. This too can be either a simple or a composite hypothesis. Neyman and Pearson in the works cited referred to the initial hypothesis as H_0 and the alternative hypothesis as H_1. (They did not call H_0 the "null hypothesis", but because of the "null" subscript on H_0 and its correspondence to the null hypothesis of Fisherian significance testing, most statisticians continue to call it that. But it is important to realize that "null hypothesis" in this context does not mean the hypothesized parameter value is zero. It can be *any* specific value. It is the hypothesis to be "nullified" (Gigerenzer 1993)). Once the alternative hypothesis has been specified, one can then seek the best critical region (BCR) for a test of the hypothesis. The best critical region is that region of rejection with size α that also would have the largest possible *power* of rejecting the hypothesis if the alternative hypothesis is true.

Power was a new concept introduced by Neyman and Pearson. It refers to the probability that one would accept the alternative hypothesis if it were true given the critical region for rejecting the null hypothesis. Again this is not an actual probability that one will accept the alternative hypothesis, but a hypothetical probability referred to a hypothetical probability distribution set up under the assumption that the alternative hypothesis is true. Power is related to the probability of making one of the two kinds of errors when testing a hypothesis:

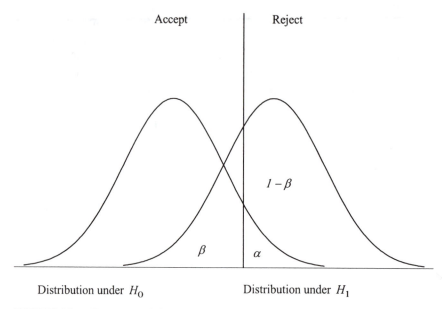

FIGURE 4.1   Power as probability under alternative hypothesis H_1 of rejecting H_0

1. *Type I Error.* Rejecting the null hypothesis when it is true.
2. *Type II Error.* Accepting the null hypothesis when the alternative hypothesis is true.

The conditional probability of making a Type I error when hypothesis H_0 is true is given by α and refers in the case of continuous statistics to the conditional probability of the test statistic's taking a value in the critical region of the statistic calculated according to the sampling distribution of the test statistic under the presumption that the hypothesis H_0 is true. This is also known as the a priori significance level of the test. The value of α is also regarded by Neyman and Pearson as a long-run relative frequency by which you would make a Type I error in repeated samples from the same population under the same significance-testing setup when H_0 is true.

The conditional probability of making a Type II error when the alternative hypothesis H_1 is true is given by β and is the hypothetical probability of the test statistic's falling in the region of acceptance derived from the hypothetical sampling distribution of the test statistic under the assumption that the alternative hypothesis H_1 is true.

Power is the conditional probability of accepting the alternative hypothesis when it is true. Power is given by $1 - \beta$, and refers to the area in the region of re-

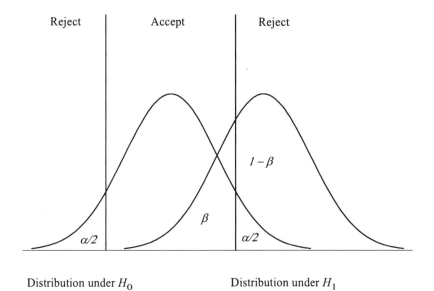

Reject | Accept | Reject

$1-\beta$

β

$\alpha/2$ | $\alpha/2$

Distribution under H_0 Distribution under H_1

FIGURE 4.2   Power under a two-tailed test.

jection under the hypothetical curve of the distribution of the test statistic considered as if the alternative hypothesis is true.

Finding best critical regions for a given α when both the hypothesis H_0 and H_1 are simple hypotheses is relatively straightforward. The situation is illustrated in Figure 4.1, where H_0 is that the population mean $\mu = \mu_0$ and the alternative hypothesis H_1 is that $\mu = \mu_1$. The test statistic is $z = (\bar{x} - \mu_0)/\sigma$. In this case a one-tailed test is appropriate.

On the other hand, when one tests a simple hypothesis against a composite hypothesis as in the case where one hypothesizes $H_0: \mu = \mu_0$ against a composite, $H_1: \mu \neq \mu_0$, finding the region that maximizes power varies with the specific value of the parameter of the composite set chosen to consider. If one searches for a unique best critical region which is the best in the sense of optimizing power for all values of the parameter under H_1, then one will not find such a region. But a reasonable compromise is to split the value of α in half and locate the region of rejection in the two tails of the distribution, that is, to perform a two-tailed test. This is illustrated in Figure 4.2.

Neyman and Pearson's approach to significance testing focused on what affects power and how the researcher could optimize it when testing a hypothesis against specific alternatives. They noted that power depends on α, and power can be increased by increasing α, or by increasing sample size, or by redefining the critical region of rejection.

Conflicts Between Fisher and Neyman and Pearson

Fisher's (1959) rejection of the Neyman-Pearson approach to significance testing grew out of his perception that the method prescribed a mechanical, automated decision to accept or reject the null hypothesis in a final, irreversible way. Neyman and Pearson used language that equated significance testing with testing for acceptance in manufacturing. This comparison was not appropriate, Fisher held, for significance testing in science. To behave toward a scientific hypothesis the way you behave toward acceptance or rejection of manufactured goods would take away from the researcher the obligation to use his/her independent judgment in making scientific inferences. Acceptance testing involves finite, well-defined populations from which samples can be repeatedly drawn. Acceptance testing also takes into account cost functions. Finally acceptance testing involves making final and irrevocable decisions. One decides irrevocably and finally to accept or reject a lot of manufactured goods on the basis of a sample of them. In science the hypothesized populations have no objective reality but are simply the products of a statistician's imagination. There is no well-defined population from which repeated samples can be drawn. There are also no well-defined cost functions. And no decision about a hypothesis is irrevocable or final.

The one-tailed test of a simple hypothesis against a simple alternative also leads to paradoxes when an observed value of the statistic falls very far to the extreme in the tail opposite the tail where the critical region is located. It seems to strain credibility that something is not wrong with the initial hypothesis H_0, but the observed value does not fall in a region of rejection. Furthermore, in any given application, H_0 may be rejected for some other reason than that H_1 is true. Being forced to chose between two alternatives is unrealistic.

Fisher, it would also seem, regarded a test of a hypothesis to be based on the ordinary view of what in experience invalidates a hypothesis about the value of a parameter in cases where random error of measurement is absent and one has perfect precision of measurement: the observed value differs from the hypothesized value. This difference can either be positive or negative. Furthermore, the larger the difference in absolute magnitude, the more incredible the hypothesis. That random error is added to a true value in obtaining an observed value only changes things insofar as one then has uncertainty as to the true value of the observed parameter. One's uncertainty is less as the observed value becomes more extreme in differing from the hypothesized value, and values that or more extreme when the hypothesized value is correct have quite low probability. This reasoning implies that a two-tailed test of a point hypothesis is the only appropriate test to apply in theoretical scientific work. It corresponds to a test of a hypothesis of the form $H_0: \theta = \theta_0$ against the composite alternative $H_1: \theta \neq \theta_0$. Thus

Fisher could regard Neyman and Pearson's focus on alternate hypotheses and power, to determine an optimal critical region, as irrelevant.

Perhaps Fisher's greatest error was that he refused to consider the import of other uses for the concept of power than determining a region of rejection, even though he had recognized the rudiments of such a concept in his discussion of the effects of sample size on the sensitivity of a test of a person's ability to detect how a batch of tea has been formed when illustrating significance testing (Fisher, 1935, pp. 17–18). Power analysis, after all, is simply an extension of the conditional reasoning implicit in the reasoning used to choose a significance level for a significance test, which Fisher indulged in every time he considered a significance test. If one uses subjunctive reasoning to establish a critical region of acceptance of the null hypothesis with respect to a probability distribution of the test statistic under the assumption that the null hypothesis is true, one uses counterfactual reasoning to consider the probability distribution of the test statistic under the assumption that the true value of the parameter is some other value. Power is the conditional probability of rejecting the null hypothesis given that the population parameter is some specific value other than the value under the null hypothesis. Fisher seems to have been prejudiced against considering the concept of power because it was framed in terms of a decision to be made between two hypotheses, and he was only concerned with evaluating a given statistical hypothesis in terms of the support given to it by data. But the value of the parameter considered counterfactually when evaluating power, need not be a "hypothesis" one is forced to consider along with the value of the null hypothesis and to accept when the original hypothesis is not supported by the data. The alternative value for the parameter merely represents a possible reality against which one evaluates the capacity of the significance test to detect the difference between that value and the value of the null hypothesis. When one obtains data so different from the hypothesized value and improbable under the distribution given the hypothesized value, it may be for any of an infinite number of possible values for the true value of the parameter. One is not thereby able to infer what specific value this is. All one can infer is that the hypothesis is likely not true. Power concerns the resolving power of a significance test. So the concept of power can be incorporated into the framework of Fisherian significance testing, while one rejects the paradigm of choosing between alternative point *hypotheses*.

We have set forth this discussion of these two schools of significance testing so that the reader can compare what is asserted by the critics of significance testing with the positions of those who developed these methods.

REFERENCES

Bakan, D. (1966). The test of significance in psychological research. *Psychological Bulletin, 66,* 423–437.

Brennan, R. L. (1983). *Elements of generalizability theory.* Iowa City, IA: American College Testing Program.

Budd, M. (1992). *Wittgenstein's philosophy of psychology.* London: Routledge.

Carver, R. P. (1978). The case against statistical significance testing. *Harvard Educational Review, 48,* 378–399.

Chihara, C. S. (1994). The Howson-Urbach proofs of Bayesian principles. In E. Eells & B. Skyrms (Eds.) *Probability and conditionals,* pp. 179–199.

Cohen, J. (1962). The statistical power of abnormal-social psychological research: A review. *Journal of Abnormal and Social Psychology, 65,* 145–153.

Cohen, J. (1965). Some statistical issues in psychological research. In B. B. Wolman (ed.), *Handbook of clinical psychology,* (pp. 95–121). New York: McGraw-Hill.

Cohen, J. (1977). *Statistical power analysis for the behavioral sciences* (2nd ed.). New York: Academic Press.

Cohen, J. (1988). *Statistical power analysis for the behavioral sciences* (2nd ed.). Hillsdale, NJ: Lawrence Erlbaum Associates.

Cohen, J. (1994). The earth is round ($p < .05$). *American Psychologist, 49,* 997–1003.

Cowles, M. P. (1989). *Statistics in psychology: a historical perspective.* Hillsdale, NJ: Lawrence Erlbaum Associates.

Earman, J. (1992). *Bayes or bust?* Cambridge, MA: MIT Press.

Eddington, A. S. (1920/1987). The new law of gravitation and the old law. In J. H. Weaver (Ed. and commentator) *The world of physics. Volume II.* New York: Simon and Schuster.

Finnis, J. M. (1995). "defeasible". In T. Honderich (ed.) *The Oxford companion to philosophy* (p. 181). Oxford: Oxford University Press.

Fisher, R. A. (1925). *Statistical methods for research workers.* Edinburgh: Oliver and Boyd.

Fisher, R. A. (1935). *The design of experiments.* Edinburgh: Oliver and Boyd.

Fisher, R. A. (1955). Statistical methods and scientific induction. *Journal of the Royal Statistical Society, B, 17,* 69–78.

Fisher, R. A. (1959). *Statistical methods and scientific inference.* Edinburgh: Oliver and Boyd.

Forster, M. R. (1995). Bayes and bust: Simplicity as a problem for a probabilistic approach to confirmation. *British Journal for the Philosophy of Science, 46,* 399–424.

Funk & Wagnalls New Encyclopedia. (1994/1995). *Infopedia.* San Diego, CA: Future Vision Multimedia, Inc.

Gibson, J. J. (1966). *The senses considered as perceptual systems.* London: George Allen & Unwin Ltd.

Gibson, J. J. (1979). *The ecological approach to visual perception.* Boston: Houghton Mifflin.

Giere, R. N. (1988). *Explaining Science.* Chicago: University of Chicago Press.

Gigerenzer, G. (1989). *The empire of chance.* Cambridge, England: Cambridge University Press.

Gigerenzer, G. & Murray, D. J. (1987). *Cognition as intuitive statistics.* Hillsdale, N. J.: L. Erlbaum Associates.

Gigerenzer, G. (1993). The superego, the ego, and the id in statistical reasoning. In G. Keren & C. Lewis (Eds.) *A handbook for data analysis in the behavioral sciences: methodological issues.* Hillsdale, NJ: Lawrence Erlbaum Associates, pp. 311–339.

Gillies, D. A. (1973). *An objective theory of probability.* London: Methuen.

Glass, G. V. (1976). Primary, secondary and meta-analysis of research. *Educational Researcher, 5,* 3–8.

Glymour, C. (1981). *Theory and evidence.* Chicago: University of Chicago Press.

Glymour, C. (1996). Why I am not a Bayesian. In D. Papineau (ed.) *Philosophy of Science.* Oxford: Oxford University Press pp. 290–313. (Published originally as a part of Glymour, C. (1981). *Theory and evidence.* Chicago: University of Chicago Press).

Guttman, L. B. (1977). What is not what in statistics. *The Statistician, 26,* 81–107.

Guttman, L. B. (1985). The illogic of statistical inference for cumulative science. *Applied Stochastic Models and Data Analysis, 1,,* 3–10.

Hacking, I. (1965). *Logic of statistical inference.* Cambridge, England: Cambridge University Press.

Hacking, I. (1975). *The emergence of probability.* Cambridge, England: Cambridge University Press.

Hays, W. L. (1963). *Statistics.* New York: Holt, Rinehart, and Winston.

Hedges, L. V. (1981). Distribution theory for Glass's estimator of effect size and related estimators. *Journal of Educational Statistics, 6,* 107–128.

Hedges, L. V. (1982). Estimation of effect size from a series of independent experiments. *Psychological Bulletin, 92,* 490–499.

Hedges, L. V. (1987). How hard is hard science, how soft is soft science? *American Psychologist, 42,* 443–455.

Hedges, L. V., & Olkin, I. (1985). *Statistical methods for meta-analysis.* Orlando, FL: Academic Press.

Howson, C., & Urbach, P. M. (1989). *Scientific reasoning: the Bayesian approach.* La Salle: Illinois: Open Court.

Hunter, J. E., & Schmidt, F. L. (1990). *Methods of meta-analysis: Correcting error and bias in research findings.* Newbury Park, CA: Sage.

Kendall, M. & Stuart, A. (1979). *The advanced theory of statistics. Vol. 2. Inference and relationship.* London: Charles Griffin & Co.

Kahneman, D., & Tversky, A. (1972). Subjective probability: a judgment of representativeness. *Cognitive Psychology, 3,* 430–454.

Maher, P. (1996). Subjective and objective confirmation. *Philosophy of Science, 63,* 149–174.

Meehl, P. E. (1967). Theory-testing in psychology and physics: A methodological paradox. *Philosophy of Science, XX,* 103–115.

Meehl, P. E. (1978). Theoretical risks and tabular asterisks: Sir Karl, Sir Ronald, and the Slow Progress of Soft Psychology. *Journal of Consulting and Clinical Psychology, 46,* 806–834.

Moyer, D. F. (1979). Revolution in science: the 1919 eclipse test of general relativity. In A. Perlmutter & L. F. Scott (Eds.) *On the path of Einstein.* New York: Plenum Press.

Mulaik, S. A. (1990, June). An analysis of the conditions under which the estimation of parameters inflates goodness of fit indices as measures of model validity. Paper presented at the annual meeting of the Psychometric Society, Princeton, NJ.

Mulaik, S. A. (1995). The metaphoric origins of objectivity, subjectivity, and consciousness in the direct perception of reality. *Philosophy of Science, 62,* 283–303.

Mulaik, S. A., & James, L. R. (1995). Objectivity and Reasoning in Science and Structural Equations Modeling. In R. H. Hoyle (Ed.) *Structural Equation Modeling: Issues and Applications* (pp. 118–137). Beverly Hills, CA: Sage.

Neyman, J. (1941). Fiducial argument and the theory of confidence intervals. *Biometrika, 32,* 128–150.

Neyman, J., & Pearson, E. S. (1928). On the use and interpretation of certain test criteria for purposes of statistical inference. *Biometrika, 20a,* 175–240, 263–294.

Neyman, J., & Pearson, E. S. (1933). The testing of statistical hypotheses in relation to probabilities a priori. *Proceedings of the Cambridge Philosophical Society, 29,* 492–510.

Nunnally, J. C. (1975). *Introduction to statistics for psychology and education.* New York: McGraw-Hill.

Pollard, P. (1993). How significant is "significance?" In G. Keren & C. Lewis (Eds.) *A handbook for data analysis in the behavioral sciences: methodological issues* (pp. 449–460). Hillsdale, NJ: Lawrence Erlbaum Associates.

Pollock, J. L. (1986). *Contemporary theories of knowledge.* Totowa, NJ: Rowman & Littlefield.

Pollock, J. L. (1990). *Nomic probability and the foundations of induction.* New York: Oxford University Press.

Popper, K. R. (1959/1935). *The logic of scientific discovery.*. (K. R. Popper, Trans.). London: Hutchinson & Co. Ltd. (Original work published 1935).

Rosenthal, R. (1993). Cumulating Evidence. In G. Keren & C. Lewis (Eds.), *A handbook for data analysis in the behavioral sciences: methodological issues* (pp. 519–559). Hillsdale, NJ: Lawrence Erlbaum Associates.

Rosenthal, R. & Rubin, D. B. (1982). Comparing effect sizes of independent studies. *Psychological Bulletin, 92,* 500–504.

Rozeboom, W. W. (1960). The fallacy of the null-hypothesis significance test. *Psychological Bulletin, 57,* 416–428.

Schmidt, F. L. (1992). What do data really mean? *American Psychologist, 47,* 1173–1181.

Schmidt, F. L. (1996). Statistical significance testing and cumulative knowledge in psychology: Implications for the training of researchers. *Psychological Methods, 1,* 115–129.

Schmidt, F. L. & Hunter, J. E. (1996). Measurement error in psychological research: Lessons from 26 research scenarios. *Psychological Methods, 1,* 199–223.

Schulte, J. (1992). *Wittgenstein.* W. H. Brenner & J. F. Holley, translators. Albany, NY: State University of New York Press.

Sedlmeier, P. & Gigerenzer, G. (1989). Do studies of statistical power have an effect on the power of studies? *Psychological Bulletin, 105,* 309–316.

Serlin, R. C. & Lapsley, D. K. (1993). Rational appraisal of psychological research and the good-enough principle. In G. Keren & C. Lewis (Eds.), *A handbook for data analysis in the behavioral sciences: methodological issues* (pp. 199–228). Hillsdale, NJ: Lawrence Erlbaum Associates.

Wittgenstein, L. (1953). *Philosophical Investigations.* New York: MacMillan.

Chapter 5

A Retrospective on the Significance Test Ban of 1999
(If There Were No Significance Tests,
They Would be Invented)

Robert P. Abelson
Yale University

Recognizing that hindsight often provides the clearest vision, this article examines the current significance testing controversy from a unique perspective—the future! It is the year 2006, significance tests have been banned since 1999, and already the pendulum of public opinion is swinging back in their favor. At this point, the author rediscovers a long-lost manuscript written in 1996, and finds that his views on the significance testing controversy have renewed relevance. Specifically: (1) Although bad practice certainly has characterized some significance testing, many of the critics of significance tests overstate their case by concentrating on such bad practice, rather than providing a balanced analysis; (2) Proposed alternatives to significance testing, especially meta-analysis, have flaws of their own; (3) Significance tests fill an important need in answering some key research questions, and if they did not exist they would have to be invented.

As we know, the notorious ban on significance tests was instituted in 1999 in response to a groundswell of criticism of null hypothesis tests. Passions ran high in 1997, and gave rise to protest demonstrations in 1998 by students and some faculty at many institutions. The rallying cries of the activists were, "Support the total test ban," and "Nix the Null!" There were rumors that at one point, militants had taken over the editorial offices of several journals, but this could not be confirmed. Due to the popularity of the cellular phone and the laptop, most journals are edited in airplanes, and the major airlines disclaimed any knowledge of hijackings by statistics students. You know the more recent history. There has been a gradual increase in complaints about confidence limits, hippogriff charts, and neo-Bayesian alternatives to significance tests. For some purposes, these methods produce too much information. Although it is doubtful that the pendulum of 2006 will swing all the way back to where it was in the last pre-ban years, serious consideration is being given to repeal of the ban on significance tests. In reflecting on statistical practice over the past seven years, it may be helpful to consider how matters looked before the ban, when the issue began to be seriously debated. Recently, I ran across an expanded version of a talk delivered in June of 1996 at the annual convention of the American Psychological Society. I do not remember delivering such a talk, but the written text expanding on the talk is mine. In fact an original, shorter version, which stayed extremely close to the talk, was published under my name (Abelson, 1997) in the journal *Psychological Science*, with the fanciful title, "On the surprising longevity of flogged horses: Why there is a case for the significance test." Here is the expanded version I discovered in my file, with a different title.

(BANNED SIGNIFICANCE TESTS: WILL THEY BE REINVENTED?)[1]

Of late, there has been much flogging of the horse of significance testing, with exhortations that the creature deserves to die. It is an act of kindness on my part, therefore, to urge against creating a research environment with this old bag of bones dead at our feet.

I deal with significance testing from my viewpoint of statistics as principled argument (Abelson, 1995). I confess that I resonate to the general dismay regarding significance tests. In the words of a famous empathizer, "I feel your pain." I present my candidates for the most damning criticisms, balanced by reasonable rebuttals, if any. I try to elaborate some appropriate uses of significance tests, despite the general advantages of confidence intervals and meta-analyses. The take-home message will be that, as always, we should suit statistical analyses to cases. If we do that, we will find that there still exist cases of useful null hypothesis tests.

CRITICISMS OF NULL HYPOTHESIS TESTS

Many types of significance tests are breeding grounds for silliness. The greatest potential for sophomoric, wrong-headed applications arises when we conduct atheoretical tests of mean differences[2].

The significance test has been billed as a tool for deciding between two alternatives for explaining the observation of a modest difference between the means

---

[1] (Manuscript written in 1996, recently rediscovered.)

[2] I consider only univariate situations. Multivariable analysts will, I think, be able to translate the discussion appropriately.

of two groups (say, males and females; or subjects receiving an experimental treatment vs. untreated control subjects). The skeptical explanation (the "null" hypothesis) is that there is no true difference, the appearance of a difference having been due to the randomly chosen collection of the particular individuals included in the two groups, or to other types of random variation.

The alternative explanation is that there is a true difference between the two groups (of unspecified magnitude). The test involves a seemingly precise numerical procedure for deciding whether to "accept" the null hypothesis (typically, a t test yielding a "p value" for the improbability of the observed difference if the null hypothesis were true). The investigator usually doesn't believe the null hypothesis, and hopes to reject it in favor of a claim of a "significant" mean difference.

This is the purported "bad" cholesterol—statistical practice said to be dangerous to the health of the field. The p values from null hypothesis tests are easily misinterpreted as the probability that the null hypothesis is true; worse, p values are highly sensitive to arbitrary sample size differences, and therefore cannot be regarded as an intrinsic quantitative property of the phenomenon under study. I later discuss "good" cholesterol—useful significance tests that are not nearly as vulnerable to criticism. At this point, let me confine myself to "bad" significance tests, taking tests of differences between means as the prototype.

I give my personal list of no-nos and oi, veys.

Doing Arithmetic on Words

Almost everybody has, at one time or another, engaged in a type of inappropriate reasoning from significance test results, using a strange mixture of qualitative and quantitative inference. I call the bastardized procedure "doing arithmetic on words." Let us consider the following conundrum: If a test of effect A is significant, and a test of a conceptually parallel effect A^* is not significant, does it logically follow that the differential effect $(A - A^*)$ must be statistically significant? (*No!*)

Suppose we say, "In the frombis paradigm, the experimental effect is significant for wombats but not for dingbats, confirming the hypothesized moderator role of the bats factor in the frombis environment." This claim would immediately be regarded as fishy in certain cases. If the wombat effect had achieved $p = .05$, but the dingbat effect only $p < .07$, we would obviously be making too much of the tiny difference between the two outcomes if we declared these two effects significantly different. It is harder to acknowledge that this inferential leap is also inappropriate in less obvious cases. The hypothetical researcher hoping for the outcome that the dingbat effect is strong in comparison to the weak wombat effect presumably should be testing the difference between the two effects, i.e., the interaction between the experimental treatment and the moderator ("bats") variable. Investigators are loathe, however, to test for interactions, partly because the standard error of a differential difference is bigger than the standard error for a simple effect.

An elementary derivation yields what I call the 42% Rule (Abelson, 1995). If the simple dingbat effect of size d just reaches the .05 significance level, the simple wombat effect has to be at least 42% as big as d in the opposite direction in order for the interaction to reach the .05 level. Perhaps this fact makes testing for interactions seem paradoxical, or wrong, and encourages many research psychologists to prefer the apparently straightforward strategy of the two separate simple tests, only to find that the interpretation is infelicitous if both results are of borderline significance or to throw up their hands in despair (if they haven't already), and beat up with renewed vigor on significance testing.

In this reaction, however, the significance test is an innocent scapegoat. The paradox, if any, comes from the property that the standard error of a difference is larger than the standard errors of its components. The only fault of significance tests is to offer the temptation to try to do simple addition and subtraction with words. It is not appropriate to say, "Effect A is significant; effect $A*$ is not; therefore the differential effect $(A - A*)$ is significant."[3] If a legal case were being brought against the significance test, the charge here would be that the test is an "attractive nuisance," like a neighbor's pond in which children drown. It tempts you into making inappropriate statements.

The Role of Sample Size

Another pervasive misunderstanding of significance tests is the underappreciation of the role of sample size. Consider the following quiz question: "In a well-designed study, the investigator is pleased to obtain a significant mean difference between two groups, at exactly the .05 level. Under which of two scenarios would she be more happy: (a) there had been 10 cases per group or (b) 50 cases per group, and why?" Undergraduates inevitably give the trite, incorrect response: "Fifty cases per group, because a bigger sample is more reliable." The appropriate answer is of course "Ten cases per group, because if the p values are the same, the observed effect size would be bigger with a smaller n."

---

[3] As a general rule for making a qualitative claim about a composite quantity such as $[A - B]$, $[A + B]$, $[(A - B) - (C - D)]$, $[(A1 + A2 + A3) + (B1 + B2 + B3)]$, etc., to compare different groups and/or aggregate over different measures, it is appropriate to use quantitative measures on the pieces to calculate the arithmetic composite that will be the basis of the claim. It is inappropriate to make qualitative claims about the pieces and then try to combine them. You can't do arithmetic on words.

Gratuitous Significance Tests

Another category of misuse consists of gratuitous significance testing, telling readers what they already know. Consider my candidate for the most idiotic all-time use of a significance test[4]: A researcher wants to compare high and low personality test scorers on a set of behaviors. He creates High and Low groups by dividing his personality score distribution at its median. Before going on, however, he wants to be sure that the High and Low score groups are really different—so he runs a significance test on the mean difference between the two! Pass the antacid tablets! With no score overlap, of course the test comes out significant, and he proceeds happily to his further analysis. (Those of us who ooze with human kindness may grant that in this case, no harm is actually done, other than to the digestive systems of readers.)

A pet peeve of mine is the presentation of correlation matrices thoroughly pimpled by asterisks indicating levels of significant difference from zero. Typically, mere difference from zero is totally uninteresting. And when a reliability coefficient is declared to be nonzero, that is the ultimate in stupefyingly vacuous information. What we really want to know is whether an estimated reliability is .50'ish or .80'ish.

"*p*-clutter"

A similarly painful presentation is the cluttering of research reports by listing of *F*'s and *t*'s for everything that can possibly be significance tested, as though authors fear that otherwise their research licenses will be revoked. Many editors collude in this obsession, presumably to try to avoid the appearance of having lax standards. Psychology has long suffered from an austere statistical climate in which editors consider it politically prudent to enforce law and order with automatic weapons. The criminal code says that committing a *p* value greater than .05 is a misdemeanor, but being caught capitalizing on chance to gain illegal possession of a *p* value less than .05 is a felony.

---

[4] This is a real example. However, the perpetrator of this gaffe is protected from embarrassment (as I am from the accusation of cruelty) by the simple fact that I have long since forgotten what the research was about, who wrote the manuscript, and whether or not it was published in the journal that I don't remember.

IN DEFENSE OF NULL HYPOTHESIS TESTS

The Null Hypothesis: Merely Misused, or Really Idiotic?

Are the bad examples of hypothesis testing based on correctable misuses, or is the technique unavoidably flawed? If the problems arise "merely" from misuse, we can try to improve the horse's handling, training, and regimen, rather than shooting him. Misuse is correctable, and in any case is not unique to significance testing. Human error arises for all ideas and things: Create a small list of things that people misuse—for example, oboes, band saws, skis, and college educations. Would you be inclined to ban them because people make errors with them? Will we want to ban effect sizes, too, when their misuse escalates?

Those who wield the heavy horsewhips against the null hypothesis test do not split hairs about misuse. Frank Schmidt and John Hunter are convinced that it lacks any intelligent use. Schmidt (1996), Hunter (1997), and Schmidt and Hunter, (chapter 3 of this volume), have stated that null hypothesis tests are intrinsically nonsensical, and cannot be rescued. I disagree with their "fundamental flaw" argument. Their argument is very persuasive on its face, but I find its premises weak. Let me review it in detail. The attack pivots on the typically low statistical power of significance tests, and on the claim that the null hypothesis is always false.

(The power of the test is the probability of rejecting a false null hypothesis—i.e., of success in recognizing a real difference.) Low power inflates the number of opportunities for mindless acceptance of the null hypothesis as a proof of no real mean difference. Schmidt (1996), Hunter (1997), Cohen (1994), and several others have remarked that the null hypothesis is always false to some degree (or as Tukey (1991) puts it, " . . . in some decimal place"). The very idea of a test to decide whether you will "accept" something you know to be false seems an insult to the intelligence. Indeed, those who have militantly pushed this argument against the null hypothesis usually ask for the death penalty, following a suitable period of public ridicule.

Schmidt (1996) was particularly contemptuous of the rigid two-valued decision algorithm that so often seems to compel acceptance of the null hypothesis. Staying close to Cohen's (1962) estimate of the statistical power characteristic of psychological research, he took the power to be 50%. He then asserted that because the null hypothesis is always false, and 50% power means that researchers will declare it false only half the time, it follows that the other 50% of the time, a false null hypothesis is accepted, and for all intents and purposes treated as though it were true. What makes this situation even more preposterous from Schmidt's point of view is the prospect that the particular occasions on which the null hypothesis is accepted constitute a totally random half of all occasions.

This argument is presented forcefully, with such conviction that one hardly dares raise doubts. Eventually, however, as one reviews the details, one suspects that sleight-of-hand has been used.

A Self-Destructing Argument

I share Schmidt and Hunter's aggravation over the all too common misconstrual of acceptance of the null hypothesis as proof of its truth, but their extreme accusations are untenable. The 50% power figure is an average over a collection of studies, some with power lower than 50%, some with power higher. Apart from unsystematic differences in sample n's, the cause of this variation in power is variation in true effect sizes. However, to sustain the image of totally random distinction between accepted and rejected null hypotheses, Schmidt and Hunter implicitly assumed homogeneous true effect sizes. "What's wrong with that?" Null Hypothophobes may ask. Well, it simply makes the main argument self-contradictory, a veritable Catch-22. The assumption of equal effect size parameters for all studies is itself a null hypothesis.[5] Thus Schmidt and Hunter's own premise that "all null hypotheses are false," implies that true effect sizes cannot be all equal. Their logic entails a self-destructing premise.

If my analysis on this point seems a bit too cunning, consider another consequence of the assumption of homogeneous effect sizes. The assumption that there is a single true effect size, invariant over time, place, and the methodological circumstances of each study, implies that it doesn't matter statistically which studies are randomly chosen for meta-analysis, as long as they belong to a well-defined set of relevant, competently conducted studies that have not been winnowed in a biasing manner, as for example by a decision whether or not to publish them. (If editors on the whole make publication decisions that implicitly or explicitly tend to exclude research reports with p values above .05, this creates a selection bias that typically yields a higher estimated true effect size in published than in unpublished studies. I do not doubt the reality of this particular phenomenon.)

If an entailment of the homogeneous effect size assumption were to be the use of smaller sets of studies, randomly chosen, I for one would consider this undesirable. Commonly, the broad question of the nature of the variables that moderate effect size is of more interest than is an aggregated effect size measure. The smaller study set, the lower the sensitivity of the search for moderators. Empirically, considerable heterogeneity of effect sizes is quite often found in meta-analyses. We can argue abstractly all we want, but in the end, we must at-

---

[5] A chi-square test of the null hypothesis of homogeneous effect sizes is a staple procedure in meta-analysis (Rosenthal, 1991, p. 78; Mullen, 1989, p. 81).

tend to behavior of our methods when confronted with real data. The assumption of constant true effect sizes is rarely sustainable. And when there are variable true ds, the expected true effect size in cases of rejection of the null hypothesis will be larger than it is for cases of acceptance. With all the flaws of significance tests, being totally vacuous is not one of them.

The Necessity of Categorical Statements: The Lore and the Record

An irony in all this is that despite many pitfalls, it is necessary for psychology to have a "lore" of two-valued categorical statements about the results of experiments, despite their uncertain and provisional status, and a widespread skepticism in the research community about the epistemological utility of isolated studies. (Journal policies often require that more than one study be presented.) A collective, informal summary of the state of knowledge (the "lore") in a given subfield promotes communication between researchers, stimulating creative debate that points the way toward needed research. The assertion that a single study never can stand alone, and that knowledge only advances through meta-analytic aggregation is in a formal scientific view quite true. However, even though a single study cannot strictly prove anything, it can challenge, provoke, irritate, or inspire further research to generalize, elaborate, clarify, or to debunk the claims of the single study. Meta-analysis, as currently constituted, contains no engine that generates suggested next research steps. In that aspect, the passive formal record of results in a domain is less useful than the active, informal lore.

ALTERNATIVE METHODS

Meta-Analysis Has Warts, Too

The newfound enthusiasm for reporting quantitative effect size measures is based on the perceived need to aggregate and compare results across multiple studies by the same experimenter, or more typically, across studies from different times and places. Effect sizes are intended to convey the magnitude of effect, ordinarily a much more useful datum than a simple categorical statement. Effect sizes are especially informative if they are measured on a familiar scale like milliseconds of reaction time, or proportions of respondents behaving in a given way, because this directly conveys the practical consequence of the result. I applaud the development of cumulative quantitative records of research findings. Some cautionary observations would be salutary, however, lest we abandon our critical faculties in the blush of enthusiasm for what is undeniably a positive development.

"Effect Size" is Relative to "Cause Size"

First off, there is a technical oversight a blind spot in the standard procedures recommended for meta-analysis (e.g., by Rosenthal, 1991). The heavy focus on effect size ignores variations in the strength of the independent variable. As Prentice and Miller (1992) pointed out, modest effect sizes can be quite impressive if the experimental manipulation is apparently extremely weak. In other words, we should be concerned about the "cause size," too, so that we can look at the ratio of effect size to cause size. This is akin to a regression slope, b. In principle, b is superior[6] as a measure of magnitude to the frequently recommended correlation coefficient r. There are two reasons: b has dimensional units (such as "test score points gained per week of participation in a tutoring program)", a desirable practical feature. Second, r is vulnerable to the "restricted range" artifact (Cohen & Cohen, 1983), but b is not. When the dependent variable has a true linear relation to the independent variable, estimates of b are not affected by constraints on the range of values of the independent variable. ("Linear is forever," one might say.)

However, the correlation r tends to get systematically smaller, the lower the range on the independent variable. In practical terms, this means that studies with small cause sizes will tend to yield smaller rs than studies with large cause sizes[7]. Admittedly there are problems in assessing cause size, or even in conceptualizing what it might mean in a given case. I have given some suggestions elsewhere (Abelson, 1995), and I strongly urge meta-analysts and research designers to consider this issue explicitly.

Meta-Analysis and the Lore

Core knowledge can often grow from qualitative narratives that are digested by the research community in a particular subfield. Debate about the methodology and implications of pivotal experiments often leads to ideas for follow-up stud-

---

[6] Judd, McClelland, and Culhane (1995) and Cohen (1994) have independently made essentially the same point. Hunter and Schmidt (1990) had previously recommended taking account of cause sizes, although this advice may not have been noticed in the blizzard of other procedural modifications urged by these authors.

[7] In practical terms, this phenomenon suggests that a good way to increase statistical power is to favor strong experimental manipulations, increasing the cause size. Indeed, experienced researchers often will recommend "sledgehammer manipulations" for initial studies of phenomena believed to have small effect sizes.

ies. In many cases, different researchers choose up sides, and a narrative story line develops about who is "winning," and why.

This view of narrative knowledge cumulation may remind people of the old-fashioned style of narrative reviews of the literature on particular topics, a style that virtually went out of business when meta-analysis came along. There is a difference, however. The old narrative review was commonly post hoc and/or atheoretical. By contrast, narrative communal lore is generated on-line as each successive study emerges, and the quality of the ongoing story depends on the theoretical coherence, or "signature" (Abelson, 1995) of the sequence of results. This usually requires a well-defined problem with neat (often admittedly narrow) boundaries, dominated by clearly specifiable psychological processes. Given a tractable research problem, I maintain that the lore is a legitimate, useful type of knowledge base, one that complements the formal record. A disadvantage of the lore is that it is sometimes flawed by "findings" that don't stand up. But it is qualitatively rich, may include subtle procedural details, and can cover bare spots in the meta-analytic record. If a single well-run study with surprising results makes a crucial theoretical point, it is especially likely to be widely discussed, and become part of the lore, but not the record. If a large number of studies consistently come up with weak results that are virtually all in the same direction, this glacial empirical accretion will usually not be dramatic enough to enter the lore, but the record will pick it up.

Vexing Questions for the Meta-Analyst

There are those who claim that a formal meta-analytic record is the only device for accumulating knowledge, rather than according it joint responsibility with the lore (each epistemology covering the weak features of the other). To them I would pose some vexing questions: What do we do with studies whose function is to rule out particular explanations of known effects? Example: The demonstration by Zajonc (1965) that cockroaches run faster when in the presence of other cockroaches than when alone, the implication being that social facilitation of performance, often found in studies with human subjects, is not necessarily verbally mediated. Do we put this study into the general meta-analysis for social facilitation, marking it with the feature "cockroachiness?" If not, what then? A subhuman category with an *n* of 1?

Consider other types of study relevant to the explanation of a previous research finding. Moscovici and Personnaz (1980) tried to bolster a prior finding that a minority subgroup, if consistent in claiming that a green slide was blue, would influence majority members to see it as blue. Such an outcome was obtained in an initial study, but the interpretation remained in dispute because subjects could simply say the slide was blue, without really seeing it as blue. The experimenters therefore substituted a clever new procedure: subjects were asked if the afterimage was yellow or red, after they had been exposed to the green slide falsely labeled as blue. The logic behind the afterimage measure is not difficult to figure out, but let us picture a meta-analyst who knows a lot of social psychology, but can't tell an afterimage from an aftershave. There would be two or three ways to miss the point of particular patterns of results; for example, "The minority persuasion effect was moderately strong when the alternatives were blue and green, but failed to replicate when red and yellow were the choices."

I realize that my hypothetical meta-analyst sounds like a dodo. But much more complicated experiments are not all that rare, and even non-dodos will miss the points of sophisticated experimental arrangements and response measures. Defenders of meta-analysis of course don't deny that the meta-analyst should know the area and study the details of each experiment; otherwise, it would be like a city desk editor sending the crime reporter to cover fashion shows and tennis matches. Yet I think that the need for the meta-analyst to be deeply knowledgeable in the lore of an area has been underappreciated. We have made such a to-do over meta-analysis as a method, that we seem to presuppose that because everyone should be well trained methodologically, everyone should be able to do a skilled meta-analysis on any topic. Not so. I think this problem is nontrivial.

Here's a slightly different type of challenge: How should a new finding be entered in the data bank record when it leads to a redefinition of what is being studied? Who classifies it? Example: After several years of research, it was realized that the so-called "risky shift" effect (Stoner, 1961) had no intrinsic bearing on risk at all, but was really a "group polarization effect" (Myers & Lamm, 1976). Or suppose that a flaw in an initial experiment is discovered later. Should the data bank include further experiments that naively repeat the flaw, or should we set them and all early flawed studies aside? Should past published meta-analyses be given thorough vacuum cleaning to remove studies that are not clean? I raise all these pesky queries not out of hostility to meta-analysis, but as a dash of cold water on anyone who thinks that its quantitative, formal nature makes it automatic and correct.

A Dual System for Accumulating Knowledge

The lore is laced with studies that suddenly clarify effects or redefine phenomena "paradigm shifts," if you will. This category of research has great qualitative importance in influencing the growth of a field, influence that is not easily picked up by meta-analytic procedures. We don't have a marker that says, "Hey, gang, this study is the one to pay real attention to; it signals a sea change in thinking about such-and-such."

Meta-analysis is much better at retrospective summaries of the descriptive facts on familiar, old issues than prospective tabulations on emerging issues. Consider the rather large category of studies that are potential turning points on the road to knowledge. Some researchers make claims of a paradigm shift, but the shift meets opposition, or at best a mixed reaction from the community of researchers in the field. Example: Studies by Wynn (1992) with disappearing and reappearing puppets, purporting to show that infants as young as 5 months have a conceptual understanding of $(1 + 1) = 2$; and $(2 - 1) = 1$. This is one of those issues of "is it there, or not there?", like extrasensory perception. What is the relevant meta-analytic data bank for infants doing arithmetic? While you're thinking that one over, it should be noted that a similar study was subsequently carried out on rhesus monkeys. Should it go in the same tabulation? Be sent to the cockroach file?

What about a later study by Wynn (1996), finding that 6-month-olds can distinguish a puppet who makes three jumps from one that makes two? In infants, is making distinctions that are sensitive to numerosity based on the same cognitive apparatus as sensitivity to addition and subtraction? In other words, do the two Wynn (1992, 1996) studies belong in the same meta-analysis?

I venture to say that nobody really knows. The two studies both support the point of view that infants are smarter sooner than most developmentalists had imagined, but this would be a very loose basis on which to group them together. That fruits are even more healthy for you than had previously been supposed does not tell us whether or not to put apple research in the same analytic category as kumquat research. In statistics as in politics, there is mass yearning for simple answers, and mass disillusionment when policies that seemed so promising turn out to be flawed. "The devil is in the details," some pundit has said. No statistical method is immune from misuse, even meta-analysis, the hero of the morality play with the isolated conclusion and the significance test as villains.

Unfortunately, Meta-Man sometimes also strays into evil ways. Occasionally, a meta-analysis appears in the literature that averages opposite effects over a systematic moderator variable, thereby canceling out positives and negatives in order to advance a claim of no main effect, while hiding the interaction. Lepper (1995), in a thoughtful critique of meta-analysis which has influenced my own views, cited one such case, and made the general point that meta-analysis seems not well suited to research aimed at theoretical clarification. Knight, Fabes, and Higgins (1996) expressed similar doubts.

These various dilemmas suggest that automatic entry of all results into a meta-analytic record is impossible, whereas the alternative of selective, theory-

guided entry of results requires human judgment, undercutting the ideal of a totally objective knowledge accretion system. Fortunately, the lore and the record
are systemically connected: Inconsistencies in the lore sooner or later lead to examination of the record, and robust retrospective conclusions emerging from the
record get added to the lore. The dual system of lore and record maintains its coherence by these periodic checks and balances, but in the meanwhile has greater
coverage than either one alone.

What has this got to do with significance testing? Just this: If we give up significance tests (and their equivalents, inferred from lower and upper confidence
limits), we give up categorical claims of surprising and theoretically important
results. Realistically, if the null hypothesis test did not exist, it would have to be
(re)invented. We need some categorical statements of empirical claims. There
will always be gatekeepers such as editors who will have to decide yes or no on
the basis of the quality of manuscripts. (I state that categorically.)

Other Criteria of Research Quality

By quality I mean low vulnerability to principled criticism. One common form
of criticism of a piece of research is that random effects were large enough to
preclude a sufficiently confident statement of the direction of effect, that is, the
null hypothesis could not be convincingly rejected, or what amounts to the same
thing the interior confidence bound straddled zero.

Failure to reject the null hypothesis is not the only principled criticism, and
usually not even the most important. In my recent book, *Statistics as Principled
Argument* (Abelson, 1995), I proposed five criteria for judging the persuasive
quality of a research claim. Using the acronym MAGIC, these are: Magnitude of
effect, Articulation of effect, Generality of effect, Interestingness, and Credibility. Associated with credibility are several factors, such as theoretical coherence,
plausibility of the psychological processes said to produce the results, and last
and least, the p value(s) associated with the null hypothesis test(s).

CONFIDENCE LIMITS: A GOOD BUT NOT PERFECT ALTERNATIVE

John Tukey (1991), in a clear-headed article dispelling much of the confusion
over significance tests, argued that the truth of the null hypothesis is a non-issue;
what we are really doing with t tests and the like is assessing the degree of confidence we can have in the direction of the effect. He went on to recommend
confidence intervals as the information of choice in reporting comparative differences between means. The confidence interval, demarcated by lower and upper boundaries, specifies a probable range of magnitudes for the effect size. If

zero is not included in this range, the direction of the effect is given by the sign on the lower and upper confidence limits. If, however, the lower limit falls below zero and the upper limit above (so that the interval includes zero), we cannot with high confidence specify the true direction. In hypothesis-testing terminology, the null hypothesis is not rejected. Before we pit null hypothesis tests against confidence intervals as potential analytic summary devices, what we should ask ourselves is, "Is the magnitude of the effect interesting and important, or will a simple statement of high (or low) confidence in a particular direction for the effect suffice?" If all we want to carry away from the study is the direction of the difference under consideration, and this is regarded by the research audience as of theoretical or applied importance, then a null hypothesis test is quite suitable. Sure, the directional outcome is implied by the confidence limits; but why merely imply the outcome, when you can say it?

Other implications flow from the fact that (the signs on) the boundary values of the confidence interval subsume the result of a corresponding null hypothesis test. One irritating prospect is that researchers might be tempted to play with the percentage value associated with the confidence limits. In cases that focus on whether the confidence limits include the zero point, some wise guy will note that a 93% confidence band seems no less reasonable than a 95% confidence band, and proceed to fatten his list of systematic results by using 93% confidence limits. This is equivalent to using the .07 level instead of .05. Indeed, under the Law of Diffusion of Idiocy, every foolish application of significance testing is sooner or later going to be translated into a corresponding foolish practice for confidence limits. The logical subsumption of the result of a null hypothesis test by confidence interval calculations poses a pedagogical problem in teaching the two methods. We return to this matter later.

I close this section with a puzzling question about confidence limits. My purpose is to disabuse the reader of the glib idea that the properties of confidence limits are crystal clear compared to the murky, opaque logic of hypothesis tests. The question is this: Why aren't confidence limits regressive? If the observed value of a mean or a mean difference lies toward the extreme of the range of possibilities, isn't it more likely that the true value lies on the interior side than on the exterior side? But then the limits would be asymmetrically located around the observed value, and how often does one see that?

SCHMIDT'S CHALLENGE

We ought to be able to apply the foregoing discussion of criticisms and defenses of significance testing and confidence limits to the possibility that we can distinguish good applications of hypothesis testing from bad applications. Schmidt

(1996) was so convinced of the total worthlessness of significance tests that he issued a challenge: "Can you [defenders of significance tests] articulate even one legitimate contribution that significance testing has made . . . to the development of cumulative scientific knowledge?" I believe you will not be able to do so (p. 116)."

There are two categories of significance test worth scanning to find examples meeting Schmidt's Challenge. We must either look for a pivotal experiment for which competing theories strongly predict opposite directions of, say, a mean difference, or else seek a goodness-of-fit test of a well-specified quantitative model, such that the judgment of good or bad fit has a clear interpretation and meaningful consequences.

Rival Theoretical Predictions in Opposite Directions

The first category—the pivotal experiment—propels us into confrontation with the highly skeptical view of the worth of isolated studies. With complex phenomena, it is aggravatingly frequent for a second study to yield different results from a first. Schmidt (1996) believes that aggregation of studies is the road to progress, rather than reliance on individual studies with the noxious machinery of significance testing. He stated, " . . . meta-analysis has made clear that any single study is rarely adequate by itself to answer a scientific question" (p. 124). Abelson (1995), in discussing the rhetorical use of significance test outcomes, gave the following advice: "Even in those rare cases . . . where the outcome of a simple significance test may have . . . news value, a single study is never so influential that it eliminates all argument" (p. 11). Nevertheless, the psychological literature contains a number of examples of "isolated" studies that somehow have bravely managed to have an impact despite these admonitions. Such studies do not settle arguments; rather, they initiate or channel arguments.

A Famous Example

I call your attention to one of these, a famous example of the "opposed directions" case in the social psychological literature. In the early 1960s, there was great interest in a self-persuasion effect when subjects are offered a payment for creating arguments opposed to their genuine beliefs. A hot debate emerged over the influence of the size of the payment on the degree of self-persuasion in this paradigm. Incentive theory (Janis & Gilmore, 1965) predicts that the greater the reward, the greater the self-persuasion effect, whereas dissonance theory (Festinger, 1957) predicts the opposite. There is a shaggy literature on this controversy, spilling over into secondary issues that I do not review here. By hindsight, it is fair to say that the seminal early experiment by Festinger and Carlsmith (1959) supporting dissonance theory had a definitive and permanent influence on the understanding of self-persuasion effects in this so-called counterattitudinal advocacy paradigm (Rosenberg, 1968).

The two crucial conditions in this study were a $1 payment versus a $20 payment for agreeing to misrepresent to a waiting subject the interestingness of a truly dull task for which this new subject had signed up, and that the old subject had just finished. (Without going into details, there was a cover story for this unusual request, and subjects accepted it without suspicion.) Following the subjects' insincere remarks to the "waiting subject" (actually a confederate), subjects were asked (by another person in another room who knew nothing about these goings-on) their own opinions on the Interestingness of the task they had just experienced (and misrepresented). Mean "Interestingness" scores on a scale from −3.00 (extremely boring) to +3.00 (extremely interesting) were calculated. The mean of the $1 group (+1.35) was significantly higher than the mean of the $20 group (−.05); ($t_{60}$ = 2.22, p < .03). This outcome vindicated the dissonance theory prediction, and was later repeatedly replicated. This is a good example of a crucial directional finding, with no particular interest in the magnitude of the effect. The raw mean difference of +1.40 on a rating scale of "Interestingness" does not convey much information; the scale is subjective, and the relevant research community had not developed any feel for it. The standardized effect size was d = .57, a rather large effect, though nobody bothered to comment on the magnitude of the finding. Critics were upset by the unexpected direction of the result. They raised the question of whether it might have been a statistical or procedural fluke. The former concern is addressed by the p value, and the latter by a series of replications driven by theoretical analysis of the most plausible moderators of the finding.

There were a number of criticisms of the methodology of this experiment, largely related to the extraordinary convolutions in the deception involved, but these criticisms were answered either by further explication of the fine details, or by replications using very similar procedures. There was no criticism of the significance test as such, however. I therefore submit this example to the Schmidt Challenge Judges' Panel as a proper and useful application of a significance test, and claim my $10,000 prize. The essential role of the t test here is that had the result not been statistically significant, the theorists predicting the opposite result would persistently have raised the argument that the obtained difference in the dissonance theory direction could readily have come about by chance. A glib criticism, perhaps, but one that is essentially unrebuttable. In other words, significance tests can be useful rhetorical devices in making or warding off glib appeals to the operation of random influences. Fazio, Cooper, and Zanna (1984) traced the complex later developments, with several moderators, and ultimately a coherent theoretical account of self-persuasion via counterattitudinal advocacy.

OTHER APPROPRIATE USES OF NULL HYPOTHESIS TESTING

"Goodness-of-Fit" Testing

With the exception of tests of controversial, consequential directional hypotheses, most tests of null hypotheses are rather feckless and potentially misleading. However, an additional brand of sensible significance tests arises in assessing the goodness-of-fit of substantive models to data. Log-linear models of categorical data (Wickens, 1989), and confirmatory factor analysis (Cudeck, 1989) are two types of analysis of this sort. Analysis of variance can also be used in a model-fitting style (Judd & McClelland, 1989). In goodness-of-fit tests, investigators usually hope for a small value of the test statistic, and a high p value. Such an outcome is neatly parsimonious. It embodies the ideal formulation for pithy statistical analysis: DATA = FIT + RESIDUAL (Tukey, 1977), or, MESSAGE = SIGNAL + NOISE, with the property that the residual or noise component is consistent with a well-behaved random distribution of errors.

This approach, if successful, enables us to replace irregular data in our thinking with a neat, lawful summary previously hidden by random disturbances. We have extracted the message from the signal by removing the gratuitous noise. To be more specific, the most ideal case comprises a cluster of four outcomes of maximum-likelihood chi-square tests:

1. A rudimentary model fits badly (the chi-square for deviation of data from model is highly significant);
2. When one or two new parameters are included in the model, an improvement in the fit is evident (the drop in the chi-square from the original model is significant).
3. The new model fits well (the chi-square for deviations from the model is now not significant).
4. Fitting more parameters to create a better but less parsimonious fit is not useful (the drop in chi-square from the previously fitted model is not significant).

One reason this procedure works so well, with significance tests playing a central role, is that maximum likelihood chi-squares have the property of additivity: the distribution of differences between two chi-squares is itself a chi-square, with degrees of freedom equal to the difference between the degrees of freedom of the two (Wickens, 1989).

Of course there are still ways to go wrong for example, by using small samples with low power, making it difficult to discern genuinely bad fits. (Note, however, that the ideal outcome given previously compares different chi-squares from the same data set, which lessens the gratuitous role played by sample size.)

Another caution is not to neglect step 4. There are often systematic camels hiding in tents of randomness; that is, further structure may deserve to be in the FIT (or the MESSAGE), rather than in the RESIDUAL (or NOISE). As any hard-bitten data analyst knows, data are often more complex than had been hoped. Another type of problem arises in the not uncommon case in which good-fitting models are not unique. Different models, with different conceptual implications, might be "aliases" for each other: that is, they might equally well represent a fit to the data. In techniques featuring model fitting, such as log-linear analysis (Wickens, 1989), dear to sociologists, or confirmatory (also called structural) factor analysis (McArdle, 1996), treasured by those who have the wits and the software for it, expert practitioners are repeatedly exposed to goodness-of-fit statistics, and this is often helpful in avoiding misinterpretations. For example, meta-analysts know that the chi-square test for heterogeneity of effect sizes quite often yields a very high chi-square (especially in domains involving complex experimental manipulations, which almost inevitably differ in their details from one research group to another; that is to say, the true effect sizes for studies in many domains are typically rather variable.

Goodness-of-fit tests are quite useful (and alternative procedures are hard to come by). No flogging, please. Some examples: Sensible examples of goodness-of-fit significance tests abound. Some of these address the adequacy of a specified probability model to account for an observed distribution. That is, the point of the analysis is to demonstrate that an observed distribution is consistent with a particular model of a random process, and no systematic factor need be invoked. Such cases require only the first of the chi-square tests previously given, and perhaps the fourth. This procedure is a kind of null hypothesis test, except that observed distributions are tested, rather than simply one or two means.[8]

---

[8] An unusual example occurs in Pool, Abelson, and Popkin (1964, Chapter 4). There, the formal null hypothesis was that there are no statistical interactions between demographic predictors of political attitudes: in other words, demographic factors summate in their influence on political issues; for example, 10% more opposition by women to defense spending; 5% more opposition by Northeasterners, implying 15% more opposition by Northeastern females; and so forth. This hypothesis was tested by comparing the known sampling distribution of Fs with the observed distribution of F ratios for testing interaction mean squares. The no-interaction hypothesis was accepted, supporting the summative concept.

The "Hot Hand." Models of successive random events serve as baselines in experiments on: extrasensory perception (for example, Rhine & Pratt, 1954), the Maharishi effect (Orme-Johnson, Alexander, Davies, Chandler, & Larimore, 1988), day-by-day stock prices, and other serial phenomena with extremely complex or mysterious causal dynamics. Acceptance of the random model usually supports skeptics who argue that no real phenomenon exists; if the random model is rejected, then the believers have a debating advantage over the skeptics: ("How do you explain the systematic departure from randomness?"). In the debunking of the concept of the "hot hand" in basketball, Gilovich, Tversky, and Vallone (1985) gathered a large body of data entirely consistent with the notion (incredible to sports fans) that hits and misses in sequences of scoring attempts by professional basketball players display no serial correlation whatever. These researchers claimed that it is an illusion to see a shooter as "hot" or "cold"; runs of hits and misses are no more frequent than would be expected by chance. The illusion is a consequence of widespread misunderstanding of the properties of truly random sequences: People conceptualize them as more regular than they really are, and are not prepared to accept the typical "lumpiness" of chance processes. Certain types of well-structured dependencies can be built into models for frequencies in Multiway categorizations. My favorite applications arise for frequency tables of response patterns of agreement or disagreement with conceptually related survey items: for example, four items on the application of the principle of free speech to the rights of unpopular speakers, six items on the circumstances in which abortion ought to be legal, and so on. Each respondent's pattern of answers to the set of items is categorized in the appropriate cell of a $2 \times 2 \times 2 \times 2 \ldots$ table. The object of the analysis is to fit the cell frequencies in the table by a well-structured model that will give us insight into the nature of public opinion in the given domain. Several types of models for such tables might be applicable. Guttman Scales, perhaps relaxed to allow for so-called "errors," come to mind.

Other interesting possibilities, less well known, rely on an independence model as a departure point, describable as follows:

1. *Independent response to different items*: The items are not related in the thinking of the respondents, and the probability of a pattern is simply the product of the agree/disagree probabilities of the several items.

2. *Independence Except in the "Corners."* A simple but elegant model, enthusiastically championed by sociologist O. D. Duncan, is that item independence obtains throughout the $2 \times 2 \times 2 \times 2$ table except in the "corners," that is, in cells $\{++++\}$ and $\{----\}$, where an excessive number of respondents often fall. The conception behind this is that some respondents will

answer each item on the basis of a general principle: For the pattern {+ + + +} of the "allowing a speech" items, the respondent believing in the free speech principle would endorse it for any type of person. Such ideological, rather than case-by-case responding, ought to produce extra responders in the corners, over and above what the independence model would produce. For the {− − − −} corner, it is harder to articulate an ideology opposing all types of speakers, but in any event, there exists the possibility that some number of respondents might be responding en masse to clusters of items because of an abstract principle.

This possibility is the basis for an "independence plus extra people in the corners" model. Goodman (1968), among others, has given a simple method for testing whether such a "quasi-independence" model is necessary, and if necessary, whether it adequately fits the data. In the case of this model, the idealized cluster of results (1–4) given previously would be:

1. A pure independence model fits badly.
2. The inclusion of two extra parameters for extra people in one or both corners significantly improves the fit.
3. Overall departure of the data from the more inclusive model is not significant.
4. Including extra parameters, to allow for the possibility of item intercorrelations (say, between free speech for atheists and free speech for Communists) does not yield a significant gain in goodness of fit.

Such examples have been given by Duncan, Sloane, and Brody (1982), who found that the inclusion of item intercorrelation parameters does often yield a significant gain in the fit. The "independence plus corners" model fits moderately well (with the {+ + + +} corner definitely needed), but a slightly more complex model does better. This also occurs for a set of items on gender role stereotypy (adolescent girls should be told to dust furniture and make beds, whereas boys should be assigned the jobs of shoveling walks and washing the car). This model does not quite fit the independence-plus-corners model, but the only two-way associations (correlation terms) needed are ("dust" × "beds") and ("shoveling" × "car"), which nicely fit the stereotypy interpretation. (Some respondents only stereotype girls, some only boys.) By including data from several years, the authors were able to trace the decline in traditional role-stereotypic responding, and the increase in "modern" (egalitarian) responding, separating each of these trends into an ideological and a nonideological component. The most interesting result was that within the shrinking group of traditional responders, the proportion inferred to be ideological sharply increased over time, and by the end of the 1970s, was entirely made up of hard-core ideologues.

I have wandered somewhat afield here, but the point I have tried to establish in this section is that in some types of analysis, significance tests can be used in a highly textured way, a far cry from the insipid t tests of atheoretical mean differences. I do not know whether the Schmidt Challenge has been put forward in these domains, but if it has, I look forward to increasing my $10,000 take.

THE PEDAGOGY OF CONFIDENCE LIMITS AND SIGNIFICANCE TESTS

In a conversation I had recently with Jacob Cohen, he told me with some enthusiasm of his expanded coverage of confidence intervals (CIs) for the third edition of the Cohen and Cohen (1983) book on multiple correlation and regression. But he had one problem. I had convinced him that he ought not omit significance testing (ST) altogether, so he tried covering ST after detailing CIs for means and regression slopes. The CI discussion already contained the idea that if the CI brackets zero, one cannot be confident of the true direction of the effect of interest. There therefore didn't seem to be anything left to say about STs. He asked me if I thought he was missing something. I replied that he had begged the question. If you put the more inclusive method first, then the other method will seem redundant. What if you were to do it the other way around (as is now typically done)? Then the point is that the CI calculation tells you more than what the ST did. If you are uninterested in the magnitude information, then you don't want more than the ST tells you. This will be rare, but we should keep the possibility in mind.

I think that the preference for the general over the particular derives from the scientific ideal of elegant, general laws (such as Einstein's General Theory of Relativity). But what is valued among scholars need not be copied for pedagogy. One does not teach number theory to second graders in order to set up the material on ordinary arithmetic. (The failure of the New Math initiative in the elementary schools is a cautionary episode on this point.) I certainly agree that significance testing has been overused and ill-used. Since it still can be useful, however, it should still be taught, but less obsessively; whether it is covered before or after confidence intervals does not strike me as an important issue. [9]

---

[9] (This ends the text of the original manuscript.)

LOOKING BACK

With all the hullabaloo about significance testing in the 1990s, notice was served on editors, reviewers, and authors that there was widespread misuse of null hypothesis tests, and altogether too much fixation on them, and this led to the ban in 1999. As with most revolutions, however, the incoming regime tended toward excess as much as had the old order. Psychology sustained a bullet wound in the foot when the workhorse significance test was shot and killed. It is not surprising that a born-again significance test will probably appear in 2006 or 2007.

In the years of the ban, research claims were still doubted on the basis of chance variability, and authors had to find a strategy for protecting their results against this trivializing criticism. True, confidence limits gave the rhetorical protection previously provided by the significance test, but there were unintended consequences in moving from the language of p levels to that of confidence levels. There was a motivated tendency to loosen confidence levels from 95% to (say) 93% to avoid having the confidence interval straddle zero, and the same criticisms as with hypothesis testing began to be directed at confidence intervals. Furthermore, new methods had to be concocted to replace goodness-of-fit tests, which nobody had really wanted to eliminate in the first place. (They just happened to be in the line of fire directed at t tests of mean differences.) These replacements have not been as satisfactory as the original procedures. On the plus side, meta-analytic procedures have been used in a more selective and sophisticated way than they were in the 1990s, thanks to a recognition that new or surprising lines of research needed to be given free rein for story lines to develop in research discussions and arguments before they were ready to be turned over to formal, quantitative scrutiny.

We should recognize that there are no objective procedures that guarantee correct interpretations of results. We are awash in a sea of uncertainty, caused by a flood tide of sampling and measurement errors, and the best we can do is to keep our heads above water, and paddle like crazy. In doing so, we should try to avoid research vehicles that are too narrow, too loosely designed, too unanchored by theory, or too bland to recruit interested researchers. Whatever the fate of null hypothesis tests, let us maintain the view articulated by Tukey (1969) of statistical analysis as detective work, and not as a sanctification process or a morality play.

REFERENCES

Abelson, R. P. (1995). *Statistics as principled argument.* Mahwah, NJ: Lawrence Erlbaum Associates.

Abelson, R. P. (1997). The surprising longevity of flogged horses: Why there is a case for the significance test. *Psychological Science, 8,* 12–15.

Cohen, J. (1962). The statistical power of abnormal-social psychological research: A review. *Journal of Abnormal and Social Psychology, 69,* 145–153.

Cohen, J. (1994). The earth is round (p<.05). *American Psychologist, 49,* 997–1001.

Cohen, J. & Cohen, P. (1983). *Applied multiple regression and correlation analysis for the behavioral sciences* (2nd ed.). Hillsdale, NJ: Lawrence Erlbaum Associates.

Cudeck, R. (1989). Analysis of correlation matrices using covariance structure models. *Psychological Bulletin, 109,* 317–327.

Duncan, O. D., Sloane, D. M., & Brody, C. (1982). Latent classes inferred from response consistency effects. In K.G. Jöreskog (Ed.), *Systems under indirect observation,* (Part I), Amsterdam: North-Holland.

Festinger, L. (1957). *A theory of cognitive dissonance.* Evanston, IL: Row, Peterson.

Festinger, L. & Carlsmith, J. M. (1959). Cognitive consequences of forced compliance. *Journal of Abnormal and Social Psychology, 58,* 203–210.

Gilovich, T., Vallone, R., & Tversky, A. (1985). The "hot hand" in basketball: On the misperception of random sequences. *Cognitive Psychology, 17,* 295–314.

Goodman, L. (1968). The analysis of cross-classified data: Independence, quasi-independence, and interactions in contingency tables with or without missing entries. *Journal of the American Statistical Association, 63,* 1091–1131.

Hunter, J. E. (1997). Needed: A ban on the significance test. *Psychological Science, 8,* 3–7.

Hunter, J. E., & Schmidt, F. L. (1990). *Methods of meta-analysis: Correcting error and bias in research findings.* Newbury Park, CA: Sage.

Janis, I. L., & Gilmore, J. B. (1965). The influence of incentive conditions on the success of role playing in modifying attitudes. *Journal of Personality and Social Psychology, 1,* 17–27.

Judd, C. M., McClelland, G. H., & Culhane, S. E. (1995). Continuing issues in the everyday analysis of psychological data. *Annual Review of Psychology, 46,* 433–465.

Knight, G. P., Fabes, R. A., & Higgins, D. A. (1996). Concerns about drawing causal inferences from meta-analysis: An example in the study of gender differences in aggression. *Psychological Bulletin, 119,* 410–421.

Lepper, M. (1995). Theory by the numbers? Some concerns about meta-analysis as a theoretical tool. *Applied Cognitive Psychology, 9,* 411–422.

McArdle, J. J. (1996). Current directions in structural factor analysis. *Current Directions in Psychological Science, 5,* 11–18.

Moscovici, S., & Personnaz, B. (1980). Studies in social inference: V. Minority influence and conversion behavior in a perceptual task. *Journal of Experimental Psychology, 16.* 270–282.

Mullen, B. (1989). *Advanced BASIC meta-analysis.* Hillsdale, NJ: Lawrence Erlbaum Associates.

Myers, D. G. & Lamm, H. (1976). The group polarization phenomenon. *Psychological Bulletin, 83,* 602–627.

Orme-Johnson, D. W., Alexander, C. N., Davies, J. L., Chandler, H. M., & Larimore, W. E. (1988). International peace project in the Middle East: The effects of Maharishi technology of the unified field. *Journal of Conflict Resolution, 32,* 776–812.

Pool, I. deS., Abelson, R. P., & S. L. Popkin (1964). *Candidates, issues, and strategies: A computer simulation of the 1960 presidential election.* Cambridge, MA: MIT Press.

Prentice, D. A. & Miller, D. T. (1992). When small effects are impressive. *Psychological Bulletin, 112,* 160–164.

Rhine, J. B., & Pratt, J. G. (1954). A review of the Pearce-Pratt distance series of ESP tests. *Journal of Parapsychology, 18,* 165–177.

Rosenberg, M. J. (1968). Discussion: On reducing the inconsistency between consistency theories. In R. P. Abelson, E. Aronson, W. J. McGuire, T. M. Newcomb, M. J. Rosenberg, & P. H. Tannenbaum, (Eds.). *Theories of cognitive consistency: A sourcebook.* (pp. 827–832). Chicago, IL: Rand McNally.

Rosenthal, R. (1991). *Meta-analytic procedures for social research.* (Rev. Ed.). Newbury Park, CA: Sage.

Schmidt, F. L. (1996). Statistical significance testing and cumulative knowledge in psychology: Implications for the training of researchers. *Psychological Methods, 1,* 115–129.

Schmidt, F. L. & Hunter, J. E. (1997). Eight objections to the discontinuation of significance testing in the analysis of research data. In L. Harlow, S. A. Mulaik, & J. H. Steiger (Eds.), *What if there were no significance tests?* Mahwah, NJ: Lawrence Erlbaum Associates.

Stoner, J. A. F. (1961). *A comparison of individual and group decisions involving risk.* Unpublished Master's thesis, MIT, Cambridge, MA.

Tukey, J. W. (1969). Analyzing data: Sanctification or detective work? *American Psychologist, 24,* 83–91.

Tukey, J. W. (1977). Exploratory data analysis. Reading, MA: Addison-Wesley.

Tukey, J. W. (1991). The philosophy of multiple comparisons. *Statistical Sciences, 6*, 100–116.

Wickens, T. D. (1989). *Multiway contingency table analysis for the social sciences.* Hillsdale, NJ: Lawrence Erlbaum Associates.

Wynn, K. (1992). Addition and subtraction by human infants. *Nature, 358*, 749–750.

Wynn, K. (1996). Infants' individuation and enumeration of actions. *Psychological Science, 7*, 164–169.

Zajonc, R. B. (1965). Social facilitation. *Science, 149*, 269–274.

Suggested Alternatives
to
Significance Testing

Chapter 6

Reforming Significance Testing via Three-Valued Logic

Richard J. Harris
University of New Mexico

The many and frequent misinterpretations of null hypothesis significance testing (NHST) are fostered by continuing to present NHST logic as a choice between only two hypotheses. Moreover, the proposed alternatives to NHST are just as suscepti-ble to misinterpretation as is (two-valued) NHST. Misinterpretations could, how-ever, be greatly reduced by adopting Kaiser's (1960) proposal of three-alternative hypothesis testing in place of the traditional two-alternative presentation. The real purpose of significance testing (NHST) is to establish whether we have enough evidence to be confident of the sign (direction) of the effect we're testing in the population. This is an important contribution to the cumulation of scientific knowledge and should be retained in any replacement system. Confidence inter-vals (CIs—the proposed alternative to significance tests in single studies) can provide this control, but when so used they are subject to exactly the same Type I, Type II, and Type III (statistical significance in the wrong direction) error rates as significance testing. There are still areas of research where NHST alone would be a considerable improvement over the current lack of awareness of error variance. Further, there are two pieces of information (namely, maximum probability of a Type III error and probability of a successful exact replication) provided by p val-ues that are not easily gleaned from confidence intervals. Suggestions are offered for greatly increasing attention to power considerations and for eliminating the positive bias in estimates of effect-size magnitudes induced when we make statisti-cal significance a necessary condition of publication.

Null hypothesis significance testing ($NHST$[1]) as applied by most researchers and journal editors can provide a very useful form of social control over researchers' understandable tendency to "read too much" into their data, that is, to waste their

---

[1]To avoid the ugly "NHST"ing abbreviation, I use "NHST" to refer either to "null hypothesis significance testing" or to "null hypothesis significance tests," depending on context.

readers' and their own time providing elaborate explanations of effects whose sign (direction)[2] in this sample may not match the sign of the corresponding population effect. So used, NHST becomes an essential tool in determining whether the available evidence (whether from a single study or from a meta-analysis) provides us with sufficient confidence in the sign of an effect to warrant foisting upon readers elaborate explanations of why the effect points in that particular direction. This is a valuable contribution which must be retained in any replacement system.

However, NHST can be employed for this purpose only by ignoring the way in which its logical structure is presented in almost all of our textbooks—namely, as a choice between two mutually exclusive hypotheses. For instance, the fourth edition of the *Publication Manual of the American Psychological Association* (APA, 1994) specifies that "When reporting inferential statistics (one should) include information about . . . the direction of the effect" (p. 15)—a recommendation with which very few researchers would disagree. Yet, as Kaiser (1960) (first?) pointed out, a researcher who adheres to the two-valued logic of the traditional two-tailed test can never come to any conclusion about the direction of the effect being tested, and a researcher who instead employs a one-tailed test can never come to the conclusion that the predicted sign of the effect (without which prediction a one-tailed test would of course be unjustifiable) is wrong, that is, that, under the conditions of this particular study or meta-analysis the effect goes in the direction opposite to prediction. The researcher who takes traditional NHST logic seriously is thus faced with the unpalatable choice between being unable to come to any conclusion about the sign of the effect (if a two- or split-tailed test is used) and violating the most basic tenet of scientific method (empirical data as the arbiter of our conclusions) by declaring his or her research hypothesis impervious to disconfirmation (if a one-tailed test is used).

In the remainder of this chapter I argue that:

1. The many and frequent misinterpretations of null hypothesis significance testing are fostered by continuing to present NHST logic as a choice between only two hypotheses.

---

[2]When dealing with causal hypotheses there is a need to distinguish between the *direction* of an effect ($X \rightarrow Y$ vs. $Y \rightarrow X$) and the *sign* of that effect (whether the path coefficient linking X to Y is positive or negative). Because the present chapter doesn't directly discuss causal modeling, I instead use "sign" to refer to whether the difference between a population parameter and its null-hypothesized value (for example, $\mu_1 - \mu_2 - 0$) is positive or negative, and "direction" to refer to whether the population parameter is larger or smaller than its null-hypothesized value (for example, $\mu_1 - \mu_2 > 0$ and thus $\mu_1 > \mu_2$ versus $\mu_1 - \mu_2 < 0$ and thus $\mu_1 < \mu_2$.

2. These misinterpretations could, however, be greatly reduced by adopting Kaiser's (1960) proposal of three-alternative hypothesis testing in place of the traditional two-alternative presentation.

3. What appear to be the proposed alternatives to NHST are just as susceptible to misinterpretation as is (two-valued) NHST.

4. The real purpose of significance testing (NHST) is to establish whether we have enough evidence to be confident of the (direction) of the effect we're testing in the population. H_0 is tested (in a reductio-ad-absurdum spirit) only because if we can't rule out zero as the magnitude of our population effect size, we also can't rule out small negative and small positive values, and thus don't have enough evidence to be confident of the *sign* of the population effect and shouldn't waste readers' time expounding on the processes that produce a particular direction of effect.

5. The aforementioned is an important contribution to the cumulation of scientific knowledge—essentially, providing social control over researchers' tendency to "read too much" into their sample results, and should be retained in any replacement system. Confidence intervals (CIs—the proposed alternative to significance tests in single studies) can indeed provide this control, *provided* that we put the same restrictions and caveats on interpretation of effects whose CIs include zero (or some other null-hypothesized value) as we currently do on statistically nonsignificant results.

6. When the sign-determination function of significance testing is replaced by the is-zero-included? use of CIs, the CI-based procedure becomes subject to exactly the same Type I, Type II, and Type III (statistical significance in the wrong direction) error rates as significance testing.

7. Any system of social control must be evaluated against the available alternative(s). Although NHST supplemented by reporting of CIs is clearly superior to NHST by itself, there are still areas of research (e.g., Monte Carlo simulations, some meta-analysis claims) where NHST alone would be a considerable improvement over the current lack of awareness of error variance.

8. There are two pieces of information (namely, maximum probability of a Type III error and probability of a successful exact replication) provided by p values that are not easily gleaned from confidence intervals.

9. Attention to power considerations could be greatly increased by adoption of the very simple MIDS (*M*inimally *I*mportant *D*ifference *S*ignificant) and FEDS (*F*raction of *E*xpected *D*ifference *S*ignificant) criteria (Harris

& Quade, 1992) for sample size, together with reporting of CIs as a supplement to significance tests.

10. The positive bias in estimates of effect-size magnitudes induced by making statistical significance a necessary condition of publication is an inevitable consequence of any system of social control over our pursuit of random variation. Rather than abandoning such control, we should provide mechanisms whereby the methods and results sections of studies yielding no statistically significant results can be archived (sans interpretations) for use in subsequent meta-analyses.

INCONSISTENCY BETWEEN TWO-ALTERNATIVE NHST AND SOUND RESEARCH PRACTICE

For simplicity's sake, we examine the case of a two sample independent means t test (testing the statistical significance of the difference between the means of two separate groups), and assume that we have predicted that $\mu_1 > \mu_2$. The points made here are, however, perfectly generalizable to the case where we predict that $\mu_1 < \mu_2$ and to any other single-degree-of-freedom hypothesis test, such as testing a contrast within an analysis of variance (ANOVA) or testing a 2×2 contingency table.

First, let's review two-valued (traditional) logic. In what follows I will use H_0 and H_1 to stand for the null and alternative hypotheses (to be expanded to include a second alternative hypothesis H_2 when we come to three-valued logic); μ_1, μ_2, and μ_3 to stand for the means of the populations from which the samples used to compute $\overline{Y}_1$, $\overline{Y}_2$, and $\overline{Y}_3$ (the sample means) were drawn; and "DR" as the label for the *decision rule* that maps the various possible values of our test statistic into conclusions about the sign of $\mu_1 - \mu_2$ on the basis of the observed value of our t ratio (t_{obs}), relative to its critical value, t_{crit}.

Two-Valued (Traditional) Logic

    One-Tailed Test

$$H_0: \mu_1 \leq \mu_2$$
$$H_1: \mu_1 > \mu_2$$

DR: If $\overline{Y}_1 - \overline{Y}_2 > t_{crit}\left(s_{\overline{Y}_1 - \overline{Y}_2}\right)$,

            reject H_0, conclude $\mu_1 > \mu_2$.

    If $\overline{Y}_1 - \overline{Y}_2 < t_{crit}\left(s_{\overline{Y}_1 - \overline{Y}_2}\right)$,

> don't reject H_0 (retain it as a possibility),
> conclude it's possible that $\mu_1 \leq \mu_2$
> (that is, that we don't have enough evidence to be
> sure that $\mu_1 > \mu_2$).

Note that we can not conclude that μ_1 *is* $\leq \mu_2$ because, for example, $0 < \overline{Y}_1 - \overline{Y}_2 < t_{crit}(s_{\overline{Y}_1 - \overline{Y}_2})$ is more supportive of $\mu_1 > \mu_2$ than it is of $\mu_1 < \mu_2$.

Two-Tailed Test

$$H_0: \mu_1 = \mu_2$$
$$H_1: \mu_1 \neq \mu_2$$

DR: If $\left| \overline{Y}_1 - \overline{Y}_2 \right| > t_{crit}(s_{\overline{Y}_1 - \overline{Y}_2})$,

            reject H_0, conclude $\mu_1 \neq \mu_2$,

    If $\left| \overline{Y}_1 - \overline{Y}_2 \right| < t_{crit}(s_{\overline{Y}_1 - \overline{Y}_2})$

            don't reject H_0,

            conclude it's possible that $\mu_1 = \mu_2$.

Note that we never conclude that μ_1 does equal μ_2 exactly, because our sample mean difference is almost never exactly zero and thus lends greater support to nonzero values than to a population mean difference of zero. In empirical research the null hypothesis that two population means are precisely equal is almost certainly false. (If you doubt this, consider a thought experiment involving an n of 10,000,000. Do you seriously doubt that every sample mean difference or correlation, no matter how small, will yield two-tailed statistical significance at the .01 level or beyond?)

Note, too, that the two-tailed test can be applied whether or not we have made a prediction about the direction of the population difference, whereas the one-tailed test can be carried out only if a specific prediction has been made as to whether $\mu_1 > \mu_2$ or vice versa.

Split-Tailed Test (cf. Braver, 1975)

$$H_0: \mu_1 = \mu_2$$
$$H_1: \mu_1 \neq \mu_2$$

DR: If $\left(\overline{Y}_1 - \overline{Y}_2 \right) / s_{\overline{Y}_1 - \overline{Y}_2} > t_{crit,pred}$,

           or if $\left(\overline{Y}_1 - \overline{Y}_2 \right) / s_{\overline{Y}_1 - \overline{Y}_2} < -t_{crit,opp\ pred}$, reject H_0, conclude $\mu_1 \neq \mu_2$.

$$\text{If } -t_{crit,opp.pred} < \left(\overline{Y}_1 - \overline{Y}_2\right) / s_{\overline{Y}_1 - \overline{Y}_2} < t_{crit,pred} ,$$
$$\text{don't reject } H_0,$$
$$\text{conclude it's possible that } \mu_1 = \mu_2.$$

Here $t_{crit,pred}$ is set to yield some value $> \alpha/2$ (so as to give us a better chance of declaring statistically significant a sample difference in the predicted direction), whereas $t_{crit,opp.pred}$ is set to a value that yields an α equal to our desired overall α minus the α associated with $t_{crit,\,pred}$. For example, we might set α_{pred} to .049 and $\alpha_{opp.pred}$ to .001. (This latter choice leads, for very large N, to rejecting H_0 if $t_{obs} = \left(\overline{Y}_1 - \overline{Y}_2\right) / s_{\overline{Y}_1 - \overline{Y}_2}$ is either larger than 1.6546 or smaller than -3.0903.)

Reviewing the preceding outline of two-valued NHST leads to the following conclusions:

Conclusions with Respect to Two-Valued Logic:

1. Nowhere in two-valued hypothesis-testing logic is there any provision for concluding that the data provide statistically significant evidence *against* our research hypothesis. Scanning the decision rules (DRs) for the three kinds of tests reveals that the only hypotheses to be decided among (and thus the only conclusions we can reach within this logical system) are (a) that $\mu_1 > \mu_2$ (statistically significant support for our research hypothesis), or (b) that μ_1 doesn't equal μ_2 (but with no indication of the direction of this difference), or (c) that μ_1 might or not be $\leq \mu_2$ (that is, no statistically significant support for our research hypothesis, but no statistically significant evidence that it's wrong, either), or (d) that μ_1 might or might not equal μ_2.

2. Because, under two-valued logic, neither a two-tailed test nor a split-tailed test provides for any conclusion about the direction of the difference between μ_1 and μ_2, establishing the direction of the effect requires that we use a one-tailed test—and pray that we "get it right" the first time, because there is no provision within two-valued hypothesis-testing logic (or, more generally, within one-tailed-test logic) for ever concluding that the true population difference is opposite to the predicted direction.

3. Within two-valued logic there is no difference between the properties of two-tailed and split-tailed tests if H_0 is true. However, when H_0 is false, the split-tailed test will have greater power to detect population differences in

the predicted direction and lower power to detect population differences in the opposite direction, relative to the two-tailed test.

There are other conclusions that might reasonably be drawn with respect to the deficiencies of NHST based on two-valued logic, and with respect to the affront to the canons of scientific method represented by one-tailed tests, but these are more clearly seen after considering the alternative: Kaiser's (1960) three-valued logic for NHST.

CONSISTENCY BETWEEN THREE-ALTERNATIVE NHST AND SOUND RESEARCH PRACTICE

Three-Valued (Sensible) Logic (Kaiser, 1960)[3]

One-Tailed Test

$$H_0: \mu_1 \leq \mu_2$$
$$H_1: \mu_1 > \mu_2$$

DR: If $\overline{Y}_1 - \overline{Y}_2 > t_{crit}\left(s_{\overline{Y}_1 - \overline{Y}_2}\right)$,

  reject H_0, conclude $\mu_1 > \mu_2$.

If $\overline{Y}_1 - \overline{Y}_2 < t_{crit}\left(s_{\overline{Y}_1 - \overline{Y}_2}\right)$,

---

[3] Although the following description of three-valued NHST matches that of Kaiser (1960) closely, not all of the consequences listed after that description were pointed out by Kaiser. In particular, Kaiser explicitly avoided drawing any conclusions with respect to the acceptability of one-tailed tests. Kaiser also pointed out the logical equivalence of the three-alternative two-tailed test to carrying out two simultaneous one-tailed tests making opposite directional predictions. Shaffer (1972) expressed a preference for this latter approach, primarily because it retains a more direct connection to the much better known two-valued logic of traditional NHST. Given the severe mismatch between sound research practice and traditional two-valued logic, this surface similarity would appear to be a liability, rather than an advantage. It also suffers from the illogic of requiring a priori commitment to both possible directions of the effect being tested. Finally, it makes it very easy to slip into treating a non-significant result as establishing the point null hypothesis. If for instance, our observed t ratio is $-.34$, a researcher might be tempted to conclude (a) that $\mu_1 \leq \mu_2$ (because the one-tailed test of this hypothesis didn't support the H_1 that $\mu_1 > \mu_2$) and (b) that $\mu_1 \geq \mu_2$ (because the one-tailed test in the opposite direction was also nonsignificant), which pair of conclusions jointly imply that μ_1 must exactly equal μ_2.

Harris (1964) incorporated three-alternative NHST.

> don't reject H_0 (retain it as a possibility),
> conclude that it's possible that $\mu_1 \leq \mu_2$
> (that is, we don't have enough evidence to
> to be sure that $\mu_1 > \mu_2$).

Note that there is no detectable difference between the one-tailed test under three-valued as compared to under two-valued logic. This is because use of a one-tailed test reduces the possible conclusions to only two: I have statistically significant evidence in favor of my research hypothesis, or I don't have sufficient evidence to be sure that my research hypothesis is correct.

Two-Tailed Test

$$H_0: \mu_1 = \mu_2$$
$$H_1: \mu_1 > \mu_2$$
$$H_2: \mu_1 < \mu_2$$

DR: If $\overline{Y}_1 - \overline{Y}_2 > t_{crit}\left(s_{\overline{Y}_1 - \overline{Y}_2}\right)$,

  reject H_0, conclude $\mu_1 > \mu_2$

  If $\overline{Y}_1 - \overline{Y}_2 < -t_{crit}\left(s_{\overline{Y}_1 - \overline{Y}_2}\right)$,

  reject H_0, conclude $\mu_1 < \mu_2$.

  If $\left|\overline{Y}_1 - \overline{Y}_2\right| < t_{crit}\left(s_{\overline{Y}_1 - \overline{Y}_2}\right)$,

  don't reject H_0,

  conclude that we have insufficient evidence to tell
  (with sufficient confidence) whether $\mu_1 > \mu_2$, or
  vice versa.

As was the case under two-valued logic, we can carry out a two-tailed test whether or not we have made a prediction about the direction of the difference between the two population means. If, however, we have made a specific, a priori prediction, one of our two possible alternatives to H_0 will correspond to our research hypothesis, whereas the other will correspond to the opposite of our research hypothesis.

Split-Tailed Test

$$H_0: \mu_1 = \mu_2$$
$$H_1: \mu_1 > \mu_2$$
$$H_2: \mu_1 < \mu_2$$

DR: If $\overline{Y}_1 - \overline{Y}_2 > t_{crit,pred}\left(s_{\overline{Y}_1 - \overline{Y}_2}\right)$,

               reject H_0, conclude $\mu_1 > \mu_2$.

       If $\overline{Y}_1 - \overline{Y}_2 < -t_{crit,opp\,pred}\left(s_{\overline{Y}_1 - \overline{Y}_2}\right)$,

               reject H_0, conclude $\mu_1 < \mu_2$.

       If $-t_{crit,opp\,pred} < \left(\overline{Y}_1 - \overline{Y}_2\right)/s_{\overline{Y}_1 - \overline{Y}_2} < t_{crit,pred}$,

               don't reject H_0,

               conclude that we have insufficient evidence to tell
(with sufficient confidence) whether $\mu_1 > \mu_2$, or
vice versa.

Reviewing the preceding outline of three-valued NHST leads to the following conclusions:

Conclusions with Respect to Three-Valued Logic:

1. Unlike two-valued hypothesis-testing logic, three-valued logic *does* provide for the possibility of concluding that the data provide statistically significant evidence *against* our research hypothesis—provided that we carry out a two-tailed or a split-tailed test.

2. Because, whether under two-valued or three-valued logic, a one-tailed test never permits us to conclude (admit?) that our research hypothesis is wrong, a one-tailed test should never be used in a research setting. The logic of the three-valued, split-tailed test makes it especially clear that a one-tailed test is simply that special case of the split-tailed test where we have infinite bias in favor of our research hypothesis—that is, that one-tailed testing is "never having to admit we're wrong," which might be comforting but represents totally unacceptable research ethics. This proscription against one-tailed tests holds whether or not we have made a specific a priori prediction about the direction of the population difference, because scientific method requires that we always be open to serendipitous findings and to the possibility that, under the circumstances under which the present study was run, the sign of the population difference is the opposite of what we hypothesized it to be.

3. The split-tailed test provides for the greater power to detect differences in the predicted direction that is the usual justification for carrying out a one-tailed test, but without the one-tailed test's unacceptable requirement of infinite bias in favor of that prediction. You should of course always inform your readers of the degree of bias in your favor incorporated into your split-tailed test by, for example, reporting your α_{pred} and your $\alpha_{opp.pred}$.

4. Points 2 and 3 are obscured by the traditional two-valued logic because insistence that there can be only two possible outcomes of our hypothesis test leads inexorably to a situation in which only a one-tailed test has any hope of allowing us to come to a conclusion about the direction of the difference between μ_1 and μ_2, and *no* significance test can ever lead us to conclude we're wrong.

The Importance of Saying As We Do

To their credit, most researchers and textbook authors actually follow three-valued logic. For instance, they conclude in the case of a two-tailed test that the population difference matches the sample difference in sign, even though two-valued NHST provides no basis for such a conclusion. Similarly, as an anonymous reviewer of the first draft of this chapter pointed out, the common practice among researchers who claim to be using a one-tailed test is "to conduct a one-tailed test first to test the predicted directional hypothesis—followed up, if it [is] nonsignificant, by a two-tailed test to see if you [can] conclude that the effect size (in the opposite direction) was significantly greater than chance." (See Biller, 1968, for an example where this practice was spelled out explicitly.) What is being described is, of course, a three-valued, split-tailed test with α_{pred} set to .05 and $\alpha_{opp.pred}$ set to .025 for a total alpha of .075. A DR is a mapping of all possible values of our test statistic (here, our *t* ratio) into the conclusions they lead to with respect to our population parameter(s). You can combine significance tests sequentially, but the resulting sequence of tests must be evaluated in terms of the resulting combined DR, that is, in terms of the overall mapping from observed values of the test statistic to final (at least for the duration of our discussion of this study) conclusions—and this overall mapping in the present case clearly matches that of the split-tailed test.

Yet another bit of misdescribed behavior relating to one-tailed tests should be mentioned. The ubiquitous "anonymous reviewer," in concert with an Email correspondent who shall also remain anonymous, claims that "technically, lack of significance *IS* having to admit we were wrong." Thus a nonsignificant one-tailed test of the hypothesis that $\mu_1 > \mu_2$ would require concluding we were wrong, that is, that $\mu_1 \leq \mu_2$. Now that's *really* "stacking the cards" against yourself. If we hypothesize, for example, that women can perform a given task better than men, but our *t* ratio for the sample difference in our study equals, say, 1.64 (the female mean 1.64 standard errors higher than the male mean), this interpretation of the one-tailed test would require that we conclude that in the population (unlike in our sample) women have higher mean performance on this task than men. (I didn't have the opportunity to query the reviewer as to whether he really would interpret not-quite-significant one-tailed tests in this way, but my Email correspondent insisted that he would, and that this was just an unfortunate cost of the extra power provided by one-tailed tests.) In addition to the rather perverse mapping of sample results to population conclusions entailed in this interpretation, it also leads readily to mutually contradictory conclusions when applied to multiple comparisons. If, for example, $\overline{Y_1} < \overline{Y_2} < \overline{Y_3}$ and the corresponding pairwise ts are 1.64, 1.64, and 3.28, this procedure would have us conclude that $\mu_1 > \mu_2$ and $\mu_2 > \mu_3$, but that $\mu_1 < \mu_3$. The recommended procedure is thus yet another demonstration of the mischief that comes from taking literally the common labeling of the decision attendant upon nonrejection of H_0 as "Accept H_0," rather than "Fail to reject H_0" or "Declare uncertainty as to sign of effect." But, at least, researchers who adopt it do hold their research hypotheses subject to empirical disconfirmation—though their readers will be unaware of this if the approach is described simply as "conducting a one-tailed test."

It is, of course, much better to follow a scientifically sound DR (e.g., that of the split-tailed test) while describing what you're doing in terms of an unacceptable DR (such as that of a one-tailed test) than it is to accurately describe your scientifically unacceptable research practice (e.g., to both claim to and actually follow one-tailed test logic). But inaccurate description of sound practice is not cost-free. The situation is analogous to enacting a law that wives whose husbands leave the toilet seat up may shoot them, relying for protection against mass mayhem on the common understanding that this is not socially acceptable behavior. This makes it difficult for the legal system to deal with the occasional wife who *does* shoot her seat-elevating husband. Similarly, if we present NHST to our students and describe our own research behavior in terms of two-valued logic or in terms of accepting H_0, we leave ourselves in poor position to criticize the occasional textbook that says you may not come to any conclusion about direction of effect if you do a two-tailed test, or the all too frequent text that tells its readers to use a one-tailed test (and thereby declare their research hypotheses impervious to disconfirmation) whenever they have any clue as to the likely direction of their effect, or the occasional university department (surely not our own) that requires its students to state hypotheses in introductions to theses only in null form. Moreover, the contradictions between sound research practice and two-valued hypothesis-testing logic lend credibility to the impression our students often form that statistical procedures are merely an arbitrary series of barriers to publishing one's research.

It's time we adopted a formal logic of hypothesis testing (namely, three-valued hypothesis-testing logic) that corresponds to and supports acceptable research practice. This would require no changes in the conduct of scientifically appropriate research or the reporting thereof, but only in the way in which we describe the underlying logic of NHST in textbooks, to our colleagues and consultees, and to ourselves. I believe that it would, however, make misinterpretations of NHST much less likely than under two-valued logic.

THREE-VALUED LOGIC'S LOWER SUSCEPTIBILITY TO
MISINTERPRETATION

First, the three-alternative two- or split-tailed test represents the two tails of the rejection region as corresponding to the two crucial outcomes of our significance test (confidence that $\mu_1 > \mu_2$ or confidence that $\mu_1 < \mu_2$), rather than as merely a Pakistan/East Pakistan bifurcation of the t ratios that lead us to the almost certainly correct but therefore even more certainly vacuous conclusion that μ_1 doesn't precisely equal μ_2. This correctly identifies the two- or split-tailed test as the appropriate tool for choosing between the two possible signs of the population effect, rather than forcing the logically inclined reader into using a one-tailed test with its attendant loss of disconfirmability. Moreover, the great size of this central nonrejection region, relative to the two rejection regions and their corresponding meaningful conclusions about direction of effect, should make it much clearer that this NHST is *not* an even-handed competition between the point null and all other possible values of our population parameter. Rather, we're simply reserving judgment as to which of the directional alternatives is correct until and unless we have cumulated very strong evidence for a particular direction of departure from H_0. I hypothesize, in other words, that users exposed to three-alternative NHST will be less likely than those exposed to the traditional presentation of NHST to make the error of treating nonrejection as equivalent to acceptance of H_0.

I also hope that the need to present the *three* possible outcomes of NHST will discourage textbook authors from the currently popular practice of introducing NHST via examples in which the population parameter being examined has only two possible values (e.g., the urn you're drawing from has either exactly .7 or exactly .3 red balls, or every member of the population either has or doesn't have TB). Such examples can be useful (e.g., Cohen, 1994) in demonstrating, for example, the difference between the probability of a t ratio as large as we obtained, given that H_0 is true—Pr(our t ratio | H_0)—and the probability that H_0 is true, given our obtained t ratio—Pr(H_0 | our t ratio). They are, however, unrepresentative of the vast majority of applications of NHST (where our population parameter has an infinite number of possible values). Further, they foster the illusion that "acceptance" (nonrejection) of H_0 has the same evidential status as acceptance of H_1 or of H_2.

WHY WASN'T THREE-ALTERNATIVE HYPOTHESIS TESTING ADOPTED 37 YEARS AGO?

The reader may at this point share an anonymous reviewer's reaction: "Why hasn't [the three-valued approach to NHST] gained more widespread use? . . . The concept has been around for over 30 years [but] two-valued significance testing remains the norm." Or, as Hunter (1997) put it, "[This] scheme was put forward 35 years ago by Henry Kaiser and was adopted by no one. So even though [three-alternative NHST] would be an improvement, we already know that it will not work in practice." Explaining the fate of Kaiser's 1960 article would be an interesting exercise in the sociology of (non)dissemination of innovation, and such a study might help assuage my embarrassment at having overlooked Kaiser's article in my own book (Harris, 1994) and poster (Harris, 1995), in which I reinvented the statistical wheel of three-alternative significance-testing logic. As a first installment toward such an analysis, I examined 20 of the 24 papers identified in the *Science Citation Index* or the *Social Science Citation Index* for 1960 through 1995 as having included Kaiser (1960) in their reference lists. (The titles of the four articles I could not locate suggested applied studies citing Kaiser in support of some aspect of their data analysis.) Many of these articles make rather minimal use of three-alternative logic, such as (a) simply citing Kaiser (1960) as a source of the concept of Type III error (Astin, 1970a; Games, 1966; Marascuilo & Levin, 1970; Perloff, Perloff, & Sussna, 1976) or of the idea of weighting particular contrasts unequally (Rosenthal & Rubin, 1984), (b) including Kaiser only in a "laundry list" of articles that have discussed "the use of the null hypothesis in psychological research" (Hays, 1968) or of those that have discussed Type III error (Finner, 1994), (c) including Kaiser in the references list but not in the body of the article (Astin, 1970b), and even (d) citing Kaiser's article as "a classic justification of the use of one-tailed tests in the kinds of research reported here" (Mahler, 1981). However, I found no article that was critical of three-alternative NHST. The closest to a criticism was Bakan's (1966) citing Kaiser as having reduced "hypothesis testing" to absurdity by pointing out that directional conclusions are not possible with two-valued logic—but, as Peizer (1967) pointed out, Bakan failed to mention that Kaiser had offered three-alternative hypothesis testing as an effective solution to the problem, perhaps because Bakan was focused on justifying his espousal of Bayesian inference as the alternative to traditional NHST.

On the positive side, LaForge (1967) voiced general support for Kaiser's suggestions over Bakan's (without explicitly mentioning three-valued logic), and a number of other authors build on or further develop aspects of three-valued NHST: Braver (1975) expanded Kaiser's suggestion that α_{pred} and $\alpha_{opp.pred}$ need not be of equal size into the split-tailed test procedure discussed earlier, whereas

Nosanchuk (1978, apparently independently) recommended a split-tailed test with a .045/.005 division of overall alpha between the predicted and opposite-to-prediction tails as providing optimal balance between power for a priori predictions and sensitivity to what your data are trying to tell you. (Nosanchuk referred to the rejection region on the nonpredicted side of the distribution as a "serendipity tail.") Shaffer (1972; see also Shaffer, 1974 and 1980, which articles were not uncovered in the *SCI/SSCI* search) endorsed three-alternative NHST and extended it to multiple comparisons, but preferred to represent it as a pair of simultaneous one-tailed tests. (See Footnote 3 of the present chapter.) Bohrer (1979) supported the need for three-alternative NHST by pointing out that no two-decision hypothesis-testing procedure can guarantee, even for very large sample size, that the probability of rejecting H_0 in the correct direction will be > .5. Rather, to achieve this, a third decision must be included, "namely, that the data are inconclusive" (p. 432).

It is clear, then, that Kaiser's three-valued NHST procedure has not been tried and found wanting, as Hunter would have us believe. Why, then, has it not heretofore found its way into statistics textbooks and curricula? One possibility is that it *has* been espoused by textbook authors and incorporated into curricula, but that my anecdotal approach of examining statistics texts as they arrive from publishers (sorting them into the "espouse one-tailed tests" reject pile and the "worth closer examination" pile) has simply missed those worthy exemplars. Bob Pruzek (personal communication, July 10, 1996), for instance, pointed out to me that Bock's multivariate text devotes a page (1975, p. 16) to presentation and endorsement of "an inferential rule directing the investigator to one of three actions . . . ," citing Hodges and Lehmann (1954), Kaiser (1960), and Peizer (1967) in support. And Abelson's (1995) paperback shares the present chapter's (and Tukey's, 1991) view that NHST is a matter of establishing the sign of the population effect, rather than of testing the almost-certainly false null hypothesis. Nonetheless, I have yet to find an introductory or intermediate statistics or design textbook other than Harris (1994) that grounds NHST in three-valued, rather than two-valued, logic.

I could at this point discuss the impact of information overload on the research community's difficulty in keeping abreast of and adopting even important developments. Or I could cite examples of other ways in which we behavioral researchers display a lack of concern for consistency between logic and research behavior (e.g., Harris, 1976, 1989). Instead, let me simply express the hope that the present round of debates over the proposed demise of NHST will bring Kaiser's contribution "above threshold," thereby rendering this whole section's discussion moot.

SUSCEPTIBILITY OF NHST ALTERNATIVES TO
MISINTERPRETATION

It is not immediately clear what alternative system NHST-ban proponents would have us adopt. Schmidt (1996) said that "individual studies should be analyzed using not significance tests but point estimates of effect sizes and confidence intervals" (p. 124). But confidence intervals (CIs) can be employed so as to essentially mimic NHST (cf. the following section on Equivalence of Error Rates for NHST, Confidence Intervals), or to help choose between low power and small population effect size as the reason for nonsignificance (or failure of the CI to exclude zero), or simply as raw data for subsequent meta-analyses, with no attempt at interpretation. Schmidt appears to favor this last use, as when he said that "any single study is rarely adequate by itself to answer a scientific question. Therefore each study should be considered [merely?] as a data point to be contributed to a later meta-analysis" (p. 124).

Despite our uncertainty as to exactly how the CIs that are to replace NHST are to be used, we can examine the comments that have been made by ban proponents to see whether the proposed significance-test-free world is indeed likely to be less susceptible to misinterpretation than the current NHST-bedeviled researcher's world.

Let's start with what Schmidt (1996) regarded as the most pernicious misinterpretation of significance tests, namely the tendency to interpret nonsignificance as establishing the validity of the null hypothesis. ("This belief has probably done more than any of the other false beliefs about significance testing to retard the growth of cumulative knowledge in psychology" [p. 126].) Schmidt severely criticized authors who summarize nonsignificant findings by saying that there was "no effect" of a given manipulation, solely on the basis of a lack of statistical significance. Schmidt pointed out that the resulting tabulation of studies that have found "no effect" versus those that yielded significance leads to "wasted research efforts to identify non-existent [sic] moderator variables" (p. 118). Similarly, Jack Hunter (1997, p. 3) claimed that each review based on such a search for moderator variables "can delay progress in that area of research for decades. In personnel selection (such use) has caused a 50 year delay in research progress!" But in declaring moderator effects nonexistent Schmidt and Hunter were making exactly the same error of affirming the null hypothesis with respect to interaction effects as they excoriated with respect to main effects. Interactions with type of firm or other situational variables may be orders of magnitude smaller than the main effects of the variables being studied, but they are almost certainly not precisely zero.

Of even greater danger to the unwary reader is some NHST-ban proponents' perilously close approach to declaring meta-analytic results impervious to sampling error. Thus, for instance, Schmidt (1996) stated that in meta-analysis "Only effect sizes are used, and significance tests are not used in analyzing the effect sizes" (p. 119), and "meta-analysis tells us that there is only one population correlation, and that value is .22" (p. 122). Careful reading reveals that what this latter statement is actually based on is an ANOVA-like decomposition of the proportion of variability in the sample correlations that is attributable to sampling error versus between-study variation, with the resulting estimate of between-study variation being close to (Schmidt claimed exactly) zero. This result implies that each study is estimating the same underlying population correlation, and that the average across all studies is the *best available estimate* of (not necessarily identical to) the true population correlation common to all 21 studies. Yes, meta-analyses, being based on larger total Ns, will yield lower standard errors than the individual studies that form their database, but the standard errors still will be nonzero. We clearly need a confidence interval around that .22—except that this was a contrived example in which the 21 samples of 68 cases each were drawn at random and *without replacement* from a single large study of 1,428 subjects and thus (a) completely exhausted the population, so that the average of the 21 equal-size samples was guaranteed to match the average of the original 1,428 observations, and (b) were not in fact subject to cross-study variability, having been drawn at random from a single study. Remember that I earlier said that there were no true null hypotheses *except by construction*, as in the present case. For real data that do not exhaust the population to which you wish to generalize, estimates of a near-zero component of variation can be expected to vary randomly around zero (and thus come out negative about half the time, as in expected mean squares in mixed-design ANOVA). Even if our best estimate of cross-study variability comes out zero or negative, this does not imply that our meta-analytic estimate of the common effect size is free of sampling error. Again, the main point is that these claims about meta-analysis, based in the present case on a contrived example where they were in fact constrained to be true, could easily be misinterpreted by unwary readers as endorsing the claim that meta-analytic results are not subject to sampling error.

Banning significance tests is clearly not going to guarantee that misunderstandings of the role of sampling error and the strength of evidence required to establish the validity of a null hypothesis won't continue to bedevil us.

EQUIVALENCE OF ERROR RATES FOR NHST, CONFIDENCE INTERVALS

Schmidt (1996) pointed out that confidence intervals (his preferred alternative to NHST in single studies) can be used to make the same decision between H_0 and

H_1 that NHST does. Extending the comparison to three-alternative NHST, we would simply adopt the following decision rule:

Three-Alternative, CI-Based Decision Rule

Given a $100(1-\alpha)\%$ confidence interval around $(\mu_1 - \mu_2)$,
namely $L \leq \mu_1 - \mu_2 \leq U$,

If L (lower) and U (upper) are both positive
(that is, our CI includes only positive values of
$\mu_1 - \mu_2$),
conclude $\mu_1 > \mu_2$;
If L and U are both negative,
conclude $\mu_1 < \mu_2$;
If L < 0 < U (that is, our CI includes both positive
and negative values of $\mu_1 - \mu_2$),
conclude that we have insufficient evidence to be
confident of the sign of $\mu_1 - \mu_2$.

It is easily shown that every possible outcome of our study will lead to the same conclusion whether we apply this CI-based decision rule or instead use a three-alternative two-tailed NHST. Indeed, one definition of a confidence interval is "that set of values of $\mu_1 - \mu_2$ that would not be rejected by a NHST." The aforementioned procedure can also be matched to the three-alternative split-tailed test, provided that we employ an asymmetric CI such that $L = (\overline{Y}_1 - \overline{Y}_2) - t_{crit,pred} s_{\overline{Y}_1 - \overline{Y}_2}$ whereas $U = (\overline{Y}_1 - \overline{Y}_2) + t_{crit,opp.pred} s_{\overline{Y}_1 - \overline{Y}_2}$. (Constructing the CI corresponding to a one-tailed test is more problematic, in that the union-of-nonrejected-parameter-values definition of such a CI would lead us, whenever $\overline{Y}_1 - \overline{Y}_2$ falls short of statistical significance, to include in our CI some negative values of $\mu_1 - \mu_2$ that our test procedure declares impossible, and exclusion of negative values from our CI leads to a zero probability that our CI encloses the true value of $\mu_1 - \mu_2$ whenever that true value is opposite to prediction.)

This equivalence of CI-based and NHST-based decisions as to the sign of $\mu_1 - \mu_2$ has been cited as evidence that NHST can be dispensed with in favor of reporting only a point estimate $(\overline{Y}_1 - \overline{Y}_2)$ of our parameter and the CI around it. However, if we do adopt the CI-based procedure for deciding on the sign of $\mu_1 - \mu_2$, we will find that we are subject to exactly the same Type I, Type II, and Type III (rejecting H_0 in the wrong direction) error rates as if we had used NHST. If we conduct a study with only 40% power (the level assumed throughout Schmidt's and Hunter's articles) then the CI-based procedure will have the same

60% probability of failing to provide a conclusion as to the sign of our effect that NHST does. The claim (in, e.g., Schmidt, 1996) that the overall rate for the confidence-interval procedure in this situation (and every other situation in which we report a 95% CI) is only 5% comes from comparing two very different kinds of error. It is true that only 5% of the CIs we construct in exact replications of such a study will fail to include the true value of $\mu_1 - \mu_2$—but a large percentage of the "correct" 95% of these statements will be vacuously correct, that is, will include both positive and negative values of $\mu_1 - \mu_2$ and will thus fail to provide a decision as to the sign of the population effect, without which not even the most basic comparison between competing theories as to the underlying process is possible. The invidious comparison between "overall error rate" of 60% for NHST and 5% for CIs is based on two very different error rates and gives the CI-based procedure "credit" for a high probability of being uselessly correct. It also implies an inappropriate criterion for the performance of CI-based procedures. If it is indeed the overall error rate of CI-based procedures, why not set that error rate even lower by employing, say, $\alpha = .001$ or $\alpha = $ zero? In this latter case, we would have an "overall error rate" of zero (by Schmidt's and Hunter's definition of that error rate) and a 100% probability of making the correct but totally vacuous statement that our population difference lies somewhere between plus and minus infinity, and we would never come to a decision about the sign of that population difference.

Clearly, the traditional Type I, Type II, and Type III error rates are the appropriate criteria for assessing the performance of CI-based decisions, just as they are for assessing NHST-based decisions. If, then, we wish to retain in a CI-based alternative to significance testing the kind of social control over (over-)interpretation of our data that NHST has provided over the past several decades, we will find that the error rates of the alternative system in this respect are identical to those of the system it replaces.

TWO WAYS IN WHICH *P*-VALUES ARE MORE INFORMATIVE THAN CI'S

There are actually two respects in which the p value associated with a NHST provides useful information that is not easily gleaned from the corresponding CI: degree of confidence that we have not made a Type III error, and likelihood that our sample result is replicable. (We *can* compute the p value from the CI by reconstructing the t ratio from the midpoint and width of the CI, but . . .) The probability of a Type III error (rejecting H_0 in the wrong direction) equals $\alpha/2$ when H_0 is true and drops precipitously (for two-tailed and split-tailed tests) as the true value of our parameter departs from its null-hypothesized value. Thus, although a highly significant (e.g., $p < .001$) result does not necessarily imply that the effect tested is large or important, it *does* indicate that you are considerably less likely to be wrong in your conclusion about the sign of the population effect than if your significance test had yielded a p value of, say, .049. No conclusion based on variable data (whether single-study or meta-analytic) is error-free, but a researcher is justified in feeling less nervous about asserting that the population effect matches in sign that of the sample result if he or she has a highly significant result, rather than a barely significant one. Patrick Onghena made essentially this same point in a posting to the exact statistics bulletin board.[4]

One of the major misinterpretations of significance tests cited by proponents of an NHST ban is that a p value of .05 indicates that there is a 95% chance that this result would replicate (again be statistically significant in the same direction). Ban proponents are certainly right that significance at the α level doesn't imply a replication probability of $1 - \alpha$—in fact, even in the absence of a file-drawer effect, the probability that a result that achieves a p value of exactly .05 in one study comes out statistically significant at the .05 level (in the same direction) in an exact replication is very close to .50. However, with N and σ fixed (or N fixed and effect size expressed in standard-deviation units) the larger the population effect size, the lower the average p value across a set of studies. Similarly, the larger the effect size, the higher the probability that two successive studies will yield statistical significance at a given α level in the same direction. Thus there will be a negative correlation between p value and probability that an effect will replicate in the sense just described. It has been shown (Greenwald, Gonzalez, Harris, & Guthrie, 1996) that a reasonable set of assumptions leads to the conclusion that a p value of .005 (note the extra zero) is associated with about an 80% chance of successful replication. The relationship between p value and replication probability is very nearly independent of population effect size and N, whereas the relationship between replication probability and sample effect size is much more complex.

SOME AREAS WHERE NHST ALONE WOULD
BE AN IMPROVEMENT

As suggested earlier, confidence intervals can provide a very useful supplement to NHST. The later section on encouraging power analysis discusses, for example, the use of your CI to distinguish between low power and small population

---

[4] The note was posted originally on exact-stats@mailbase.ac.uk, 12/2/95, and was forwarded to SMEPNet (smep@pmc.psych.nwu.edu, 12/6/95).

effect size as possible causes of a nonsignificant result. However, there are also areas of research where even NHST alone would be an improvement over the current lack of attention to sampling error. I mentioned one such area already in the previous section's discussion of the downplaying of attention to sampling error in meta-analyis.

Another example is provided by the area of Monte Carlo simulations of statistical procedures. Most researchers who employ the technique are aware that Monte Carlo simulations are subject to case-to-case random variation, just as are data collected from real subjects—but simulation results seldom incorporate this insight in more than an offhand way. It would be very nice to include CIs around, say, the difference in Type I error rates for two alternative tests. (This is *not* the same, by the way, as asking to what extent the separate CIs for the two αs overlap.) It would nonetheless be a considerable improvement over current practice to at least report whether that difference is statistically significant—that is, whether we have run enough replications to be confident of the *direction* (sign) of the difference between the two procedures' αs. Instead we have such wonders as the development of the myth that salient-loadings scoring is superior to regression-based factor scoring, based in part on a .965 versus .960 difference in validities when averaged over 12 (!) samples from a known population (Wackwitz & Horn, 1971). Or the conclusion that the residual-lambda test more accurately identifies the number of nonzero population canonical r's than does the step-down g.c.r. (Greatest Characteristic Root) test, based on four versus two correct identifications in 1,000 replications (Mendoza, Markos, & Gonter, 1978). Or a parallel-analysis determination of whether our third principal factor should be retained, based on the median value of the third lambda in as few as 10 replications—or even a single sample (as pointed out by Montanelli & Humphreys, 1976). By all means put CIs around the differences between your Monte Carlo performance statistics, but don't pooh-pooh the significance tests provided by chi-square or ANOVA analyses of your sampling design until your own basis for coming up with discussion-section recommendations achieves at least the level of objective support significance testing would have provided.

THERE'S STILL HOPE FOR IMPROVING ATTENTION TO POWER

An obvious corrective to the high Type II error rate (low power) typical of published psychological research is to require that authors precede and supplement their significance tests with explicit power analyses. The preliminary power analysis might encourage authors to employ Ns sufficient to lower the probability of "coming up empty" to a more acceptable level, and the post hoc power analysis would aid in determining whether a nonsignificant result implied a near-zero population effect or instead resulted from insufficient power to detect even large effects. NHST-ban proponents have advanced two arguments against the adequacy of such a reform. First, given constraints on resources (e.g., low availability of leukemic children who have undergone radiation therapy or the high cost of MRI scans), the inevitably low power of the study any one lab could afford to run might discourage the collection of important data in the first place, even though meta-analytic compilation of these low-power results would have permitted meaningful conclusions (Schmidt, 1996). This is essentially an argument against any censoring of data collection or data publication, and will be addressed in the next section.

Second, to quote from the in-press version of John Hunter's contribution to an APS symposium on the NHST-ban issue, "We now have 30 years of experience showing that power analysis cannot be successfully taught in the present environment. Authors just do not learn and do not use power analysis." I suspect that this low rate of use of power analysis is largely due to the lack of proportionality between the effort required to learn and execute power analyses (e.g., dealing with noncentral distributions or learning the appropriate effect-size measure with which to enter the power tables in a given chapter of Cohen, 1977) and the low payoff from such an analysis (e.g., the high probability that resource constraints will force you to settle for a lower N than your power analysis says you should have)—especially given the uncertainties involved in a priori estimates of effect sizes and standard deviations, which render the resulting power calculation rather suspect. If calculation of the sample size needed for adequate power and for choosing between alternative interpretations of a nonsignificant result could be made more nearly equal in difficulty to the effort we've grown accustomed to putting into significance testing itself, more of us might in fact carry out these preliminary and supplementary analyses. There is in fact hope that such improvement in "user-friendliness" can be achieved.

One basis for hope is the increasing availability of computer programs for power analysis and the incorporation of such analyses in packages of statistical programs. Two much lower tech solutions are also available, one for the a priori analysis and one for the post hoc analysis. With respect to interpretation of a nonsignificant result as due to low power versus small population effect size, reporting of the CI is a much easier and more direct route to this choice than doing a formal power calculation. Calculation of the CI requires recombining of the same numbers we used in our t test: CI = numerator ± (denominator × critical value). If the CI includes no theoretically or practically important values, the nonsignificance was due to low population effect size. If, on the other hand, the CI includes some values of the population parameter that would clearly be of theoretical or practical (clinical?) importance (as well as zero), the nonsignificance may be due to having conducted too low-power a study. (The fact that the

CI includes zero and values close to zero tells us that a low population effect size may also have contributed to nonsignificance—we simply don't have sufficient power to resolve the difference between important and unimportant effect sizes.)

With respect to the calculation of necessary sample size, two methods that involve carrying out on hypothetical data the same computations you will subsequently apply to your obtained data were provided by Harris and Quade (1992). The MIDS (*M*inimally *I*mportant *D*ifference *S*ignificant) criterion sets your sample size at that value (N_{MIDS}) that would be barely sufficient to yield statistical significance if your sample effect size is "minimally important," that is, right on the borderline between having and not having practical or theoretical importance. For any single-degree-of-freedom effect this will give you 50% power if the true population effect size is just barely worth talking about—and we wouldn't want to have better than a 50-50 chance of getting significance if the population effect is supra-minimal—and at least 97% power if the population difference is twice as large as the MID (84% or higher power for a population difference 1.5 times as large as the MID). For overall tests of multiple-degree-of-freedom effects, using the N computed as in the preceding for a particular, minimally important pattern of (e.g.) means gives a considerably higher than .50 probability that the overall test will be significant—but our focus should be on specific, single-degree-of-freedom contrasts, not overall tests.

Let's try to make the preceding a bit more concrete by way of:

A MIDS Example: Blood Doping. Assume that we wish to examine the effects of blood "doping" on 10-kilometer (10K) running time (as did Brien & Simon, 1987; see also Brien, Harris, & Simon, 1989). We plan to have n runners (the Control group) do a 10K run after having received an infusion of a saline solution, whereas another n will run their 10K after receiving an infusion of their own blood (collected some weeks earlier). Examination of running times in collegiate meets leads us to expect the standard deviation of 10K running times to be about 1.0 minutes. Interviews with coaches and runners convince us that a lowering of 10K running times by 15 seconds or more would be considered important enough to justify the expense and inconvenience of the "doping" procedure, while a smaller effect would not. Thus our MID is 0.25 minutes. We now pretend that our data are in hand and that they have yielded a mean difference of .25 minutes (the MID) between our two groups, and we proceed to carry out an independent-means t test on these data; that is, we compute

$$t = \frac{0.25}{\sqrt{1.0(2/n)}}$$

Of course, we can't complete the calculation of the t ratio until we know our sample size. The MIDS criterion enjoins us to use the n that makes the preceding t just barely statistically significant, that is, that yields a t of about 2.0. This requires that $.25 / \sqrt{2/n} = 2$, whence $n/2 = 8$, whence $n = 128$.

This value of n, 128 runners per group, is n_{MIDS}, the sample size we would need to have a 50-50 chance of achieving a statistically significant difference between our groups if the population difference is indeed .25 minutes (and our estimate of the population standard deviation is accurate).

However, recruiting and carrying out the complex doping procedure on 256 runners is beyond our resources, so we rethink our design. Reexamining our data on running times, we discover that 10K running times, although highly variable from one runner to the next, are also highly reliable within runners, yielding a 1-week run-rerun reliability of .96. What if we were to have each of a single group of N runners do two 10K runs a week apart, once after a saline infusion and once after an own-blood infusion? Given the same sample mean effect of a .25-minute lower time after doping (that is, a sample effect equal to the MID), our t ratio now will be a correlated-means t,

$$ t = \frac{0.25}{\sqrt{\dfrac{2(1.0)(1-.96)}{N}}} \ , $$

which equals 2.0 (our first guess at the critical value of our t) if and only if (iff) $\sqrt{N/.08} = 8$, that is, iff $N = 5.12$. However, an N of 6 would require df (degrees of freedom) = 5 and a critical value of 2.571, so, having initially equated our t to 2.0, we have to redo our calculation with a higher critical value. A bit of trial-and-error computation reveals that an N of 8 and the corresponding critical value of 2.365 provide a consistent solution to our problem. Thus our switch to a within-subjects design permits us to run a study with only 8 runners, rather than the 256 a between-subjects design would require. This N_{MIDS} of 8 will provide 50% power if the true population effect of doping is a 15-second decrease, and considerably higher power if the actual population effect is substantially larger than this "jnd."

If you find it impossible to specify the MID (because, e.g., you would consider any nonzero population effect important), or if you simply prefer to focus on the likelihood of being able to publish your results, then you can employ the FEDS (*F*raction of *E*xpected *D*ifference *S*ignificant) criterion, which, though not explicitly stated by Harris and Quade (1992), is implied by their finding that the power of a NHST depends almost entirely on α, N, and the ratio of population effect size to the sample effect size used in computing your significance test on hypothetical data. Thus, for instance, all we have to do to ensure 80% power for a .05-level test is to select an N (N_{FEDS}) such that a sample effect size .7 as large as the true population effect size would just barely reach statistical significance—assuming, of course, that the estimate of the population standard deviation you employed is accurate and that the population effect size really is as large as you anticipated.

Blood-Doping Example (Second Installment). For instance, in the blood-doping example given previously, let's assume that we feel uncomfortable about the assumption that the MID is 15 seconds—or that our source of funds wants to know what our chances of getting statistical significance (our power) *will* be, given our best estimate of the actual population effect. Confidential interviews with runners who have used blood doping lead us to believe that the true population effect is about a 45-second improvement—our Expected Difference. The FEDS criterion tells us that, if we want actual power of .80 to detect the expected effect of a .75-minute decrease, we need to use an N that makes a *sample* effect of .7(.75) = .525 minutes just barely significant. Our revised calculation thus becomes

$$t = \frac{.525}{\sqrt{.08 / N}}$$

which equals, say, 2.5 iff $\sqrt{N/.08} = 4.762$, whence $N = 1.814$. But, once again our initial assumption about the critical value corresponding to the N we would need was too low, so we increase our critical value until the N we calculate is consistent with the critical value used (that is, we solve the equation for t, which unfortunately involves N on both sides of the equation), leading to the conclusion that an N of four runners will be sufficient to yield 80% power if the population effect is indeed 45 seconds. (Brien & Simon, 1987, in fact used six runners, with three of them completing their runs in each of two orders [saline infusion preceding versus following own-blood infusion], and obtained a highly significant doping effect of close to 1.0 minutes.)

Using the MIDS criterion requires no computations or critical values beyond those you would use for your significance test, anyway, and using the FEDS criterion to achieve 80% (97%) power for a given true population effect size requires in addition only that you remember (or look up in the only table of Harris, in prep) the "magic fraction" .7 (.5). This simplicity gives at least me hope that researchers can be induced to carry out meaningful power analyses and that this aspect of NHST can be reformed, rather than eliminating NHST altogether.

CENSORING OF DATA VERSUS CENSORING OF INTERPRETATIONS

This brings us to the other major argument against increased use of power as an alternative to the proposed ban on NHST, namely that constraints on resources may lead one to refrain from conducting studies in important areas when your calculation of N_{MIDS} or N_{FEDS} tells you that you need to run more subjects than you can afford. Schmidt (1996) pointed out that this precollection censoring of data leads to a more meager (or even nonexistent) database for any subsequent meta-analysis of the effect in question, when in fact a cumulation of the knowledge provided by confidence intervals (and point estimates, which for two-tailed tests are just the midpoints of those confidence intervals) over several such low-power studies could provide a useful estimate of the effect size in question. Schmidt raised a similar but even stronger complaint about the postcollection censoring of data we impose when we set statistical significance as a necessary condition for publication. If only those results that (partly by chance) achieve statistical significance get published, the corpus of data available for eventual meta-analysis of a given effect not only will be smaller (due to all of the file-drawer studies) but also will provide a positively biased estimate of the true population effect size.

In short, what is being proposed as the alternative to NHST is that researchers be encouraged to carry out well-designed studies of any effects of potential importance without regard to the (possibly very low) power of what would have been their now-banned significance tests (and thus the possibly very low precision of their point estimates and wide width of their CIs), and that editors be asked to publish the resulting CIs and point estimates without regard to statistical significance, power, or precision of estimate. Effectively (from the point of view of a preban significance tester) we would be resetting our alpha to 1.0.

In addition to the massive increase in journal space such an overhaul of research practice and editorial policy would entail, it would also greatly increase the frequency with which the elaborate theory that explained the direction of effect observed in one study had to be overhauled when that direction reversed itself in the next study. This is not an issue of validity of NHST (whether correctly or incorrectly interpreted) for the purpose for which it is intended, namely determining whether we have sufficient evidence of the sign of an effect to justify using that direction of effect as a criterion in selecting an explanation of or choosing among alternative explanations of that effect. It is, rather, the entirely separate issue of whether setting such a precondition on our explanatory behavior (or the corresponding precondition on our data-collection behavior that the study have a reasonable chance of meeting the significance criterion) is desirable at all. Those proposing a ban suggest that any precondition for launching explanations is undesirable at the single-study level if it carries with it a ban on publishing the data. This permissiveness with respect to publication of data is accompanied, however, by an essentially total ban on interpretation of single-study results, deferring any conclusions about effect size and direction to the subsequent meta-analytic study in which the uncensored data will be incorporated. (Cf. the earlier quote in the Susceptibility to Misinterpretation section of the current chapter, together with Schmidt's comments in a posting to the SMEPNet that "there is no scientific reason to have or want binary decisions [how about trichotomous decisions?] to accept or reject hypotheses in individual studies—because . . . decisions to accept or reject are based on results integrated across all studies that have tested that hypothesis . . . through meta-analysis;"[5].) This still leaves open the possibility of requiring statistical significance (or absence of zero from the CI) at the meta-analytic level—except that, as pointed out in earlier sections of this chapter, Schmidt (1996) appears to believe that no such control is needed for meta-analytic results.

It seems unrealistic to expect authors and editors to completely avoid interpretation of results of single studies. After all, although any meta-analysis must as a matter of logic have a higher N than any of the single studies it integrates, a single study of one effect based on an N of 10,000 is very likely to provide a more precise and more replicable estimate of that effect than a meta-analytic study of some effect associated with attempts to educate feral children based on all 12 (?) available cases. A compromise that avoids both sets of negative consequences would be to provide a medium for publication of nonsignificant results (presumably sheared of abstracts and discussion sections that discuss the effect as if its sign had been definitely established), while reserving publication in archival journals for articles that, because of adequate attention to power and/or inclusion of evidence as to the replicability of the result, can reasonably claim to provide convincing evidence as sign of effect. We can't expect journals that maintain 80%-90% rejection rates to suddenly drop that rate to zero, but there are now (probably) mass-storage systems with sufficient capacity to handle the deluge. Someone would have to work out a good enough cataloging system (key words, etc.) so that all studies relevant to a given effect could be retrieved by the meta-analyst, but surely the legion of meta-analysts Schmidt (1996) saw cropping up everywhere would be willing to support the development of such a system.

---

[5] smep@pmc.psych.nwu.edu, 11/8/95

SUMMARY

I outlined in the opening section of this chapter the major points I wished to make. I hope that the support for these points has been made clear in the intervening sections. The upshot of all this is that I remain optimistic that converting our presentations of null hypothesis significance testing (NHST) to three-valued logic will make NHST more consistent with sound research practice; will thus avoid many of the misinterpretations of NHST that have arisen over the decades; and will make clearer that any replacement of NHST will need to retain its element of social and self-control over our tendency to overinterpret nearly random aspects of our data. I am also hopeful that the simpler procedures for introducing power considerations into our research planning that the MIDS and FEDS criteria provide will help reform this aspect of NHST, whether it is retained in its present form or incorporated into reports of confidence intervals. Finally, the point made by proponents of a NHST ban that making statistical significance a requirement for publication of results leads to a positive bias in subsequent meta-analytic results suggests needs to be attended to. My preferred solution would be to impose statistical significance (or a zero-excluding CI) as a condition for "full-blown" interpretation of one's results, but to provide a means of archiving for subsequent use in meta-analyses all methodologically sound studies of a given effect, whether statistically significant or not.

REFERENCES

Abelson, R. P. (1995). *Statistics as principled argument.* Hillsdale, NJ: Lawrence Erlbaum Associates.

American Psychological Association (1994). *Publication manual of the American Psychological Association* (4th ed.). Washington, DC: Author.

Astin, A. W. (1970a). The methodology of research on college impact, Part one. *Sociology of Education, 43,* 223–254.

Astin, A. W. (1970b). The methodology of research on college impact, Part two. *Sociology of Education, 43,* 437–450.

Bakan, D. (1966). The test of significance in psychological research. *Psychological Bulletin, 66,* 423–437.

Biller, H. R. (1968). A multiaspect investigation of masculine development in kindergarten age boys. *Genetic Psychology Monographs, 78,* 89–138.

Bohrer, R. (1979). Multiple three-decision rules for parametric signs. *Journal of the American Statistical Association, 74,* 432–437.

Braver, S. L. (1975). On splitting the tails unequally: A new perspective on one-versus two-tailed tests. *Educational and Psychological Measurement, 35,* 283–301.

Brien, A. J., & Simon, T. L. (1987). The effects of red blood cell infusion on 10-km race time. *Journal of the American Medical Association, 257,* 2761–2765.

Brien, A. J., Harris, R. J., & Simon, T. L. (1989). The effects of an autologous infusion of 400 ml red blood cells on selected haematological parameters and 1,500 m race time in highly trained runners. *Bahrain Medical Bulletin, 11,* 6–16.

Cohen, J. (1977). *Statistical power analysis for the behavioral sciences* (Rev. ed.). NY: Academic Press.

Cohen, J. (1994). The earth is round ($p < .05$). *American Psychologist, 49,* 997–1003.

Finner, H. (1994). Two-sided tests and one-sided confidence bounds. *Annals of Statistics, 22,* 1502–1516.

Games, P. A. (1966). Comments on "A power comparison of the F and L tests—I." *Psychological Review, 73,* 372–375.

Greenwald, A. G., Gonzalez, R., Harris, R. J., & Guthrie, D. (1996). Effect sizes and *p* values: What should be reported and what should be replicated? *Psychophysiology, 33,* 175–183.

Harris, R. J. (1976). The uncertain connection between verbal theories and research hypotheses in social psychology. *Journal of Experimental Social Psychology, 12,* 210–219.

Harris, R. J. (1989). A canonical cautionary. *Multivariate Behavioral Research, 24,* 17–39.

Harris, R. J. (1994). *An analysis of variance primer.* Itasca, IL: F. E. Peacock.

Harris, R. J. (1995, November). *The need for three-valued logic in hypothesis testing.* Paper presented at meetings of the Judgment/Decision Making Society, Los Angeles.

Harris, R. J. (in prep.). *The FEDS (Fraction of Expected Difference Significant) criterion for sample size, and the magic fraction .7.* Manuscript in preparation.

Harris, R. J., & Quade, D. (1992). The Minimally Important Difference Significant criterion for sample size. *Journal of Educational Statistics, 17,* 27–49.

Hays, W. L. (1968). Statistical theory. *Annual Review of Psychology, 19,* 417–436.

Hodges, J. L., & Lehmann, E. L. (1954). Testing the approximate validity of statistical hypotheses. *Journal of the Royal Statistical Society (B), 16,* 261–268.

Hunter, J. E. (1997). Needed: A ban on the significance test. *Psychological Science, 8*, 3–7.

Kaiser, H. F. (1960). Directional statistical decisions. *Psychological Review, 67*, 160–167.

LaForge, R. (1967). Confidence intervals or tests of significance in scientific research? *Psychological Bulletin, 68*, 446–447.

Mahler, V. A. (1981). Mining, agriculture, and manufacturing: The impact of foreign investment on social distribution in third world countries. *Comparative Political Studies, 14*, 267–297.

Marascuilo, L. A., & Levin, J. R. (1970). Appropriate post hoc comparisons for interaction and nested hypotheses in analysis of variance designs: The elimination of Type IV errors. *American Educational Research Journal, 7*, 297–421.

Mendoza, J. L., Markos, V. H., & Gonter, R. (1978). A new perspective on sequential testing procedures in canonical analysis: A Monte Carlo evaluation. *Multivariate Behavioral Research, 13*, 371–382.

Montanelli, R. G. & Humphreys, L. G. (1976). Latent roots of random data correlation matrices with squared multiple correlations on the diagonal: A Monte Carlo study. *Psychometrika, 41*, 341–348.

Nosanchuk, T. A. (1978). Serendipity tails: A note on two-tailed hypothesis tests with asymmetric regions of rejection. *Acta Sociologica, 21*, 249–253.

Peizer, D. B. (1967). A note on directional inference. *Psychological Bulletin, 68*, 448.

Perloff, R., Perloff, E., & Sussna, E. (1976). Program evaluation. *Annual Review of Psychology, 27*, 569–594.

Rosenthal, R., & Rubin, D. B. (1984). Multiple contrasts and ordered Bonferroni procedures. *Journal of Educational Psychology, 76*, 1028–1034.

Schmidt, F. L. (1996). Statistical significance testing and cumulative knowledge in psychology: Implications for training of researchers. *Psychological Methods, 1*, 115–129.

Shaffer, J. P. (1972). Directional statistical hypotheses and comparisons between means. *Psychological Bulletin, 77*, 195–197.

Shaffer, J. P. (1974). Bidirectional unbiased procedures. *Journal of the American Statistical Association, 69*, 437–439.

Shaffer, J. P. (1980). Control of directional errors with stagewise multiple test procedures. *Annals of Statistics, 8*, 1342–1347.

Tukey, J. W. (1991). The philosophy of multiple comparisons. *Statistical Science, 6*, 100–116.

Wackwitz, J. H. & Horn, J. L. (1971). On obtaining the best estimates of factor scores within an ideal simple structure. *Multivariate Behavioral Research, 6,* 389–408.

Chapter 7

A Case Study in the Failure of Psychology as a Cumulative Science: The Spontaneous Recovery of Verbal Learning

Joseph S. Rossi

Cancer Prevention Research Center
University of Rhode Island

Many observers have noted the failure of psychology as a cumulative science. Although many reasons can be advanced for this problem, perhaps the most important is the dependence of the behavioral sciences on the paradigm as the basis for assessing evidence and establishing the existence of effects. The paradigm too easily gives rise to the practice of dichotomous interpretation of significance levels, resulting in over reliance on p values as the main evidence contained in a study and the dismissal of nonsignificant p values. However, where some see significance testing as inherently at fault, I believe the problem is better characterized as the misuse of significance testing. The history of research on the spontaneous recovery of verbal associations provides an interesting example of how reliance on significance testing can create inconsistencies among the results of research studies and controversy over the existence of an effect. Also shown is how the appropriate use of statistical techniques such as meta-analysis and power analysis might have resolved the controversy and helped establish a consensus on the magnitude and theoretical importance of the effect of spontaneous recovery. A brief survey of the results of several other meta-analyses suggests that the case of spontaneous recovery is not an isolated one. The technique of using power analysis to estimate probable upper bounds on the magnitude of effect sizes is described and illustrated. This procedure is suggested as a practical means of evaluating the results of studies that fail to reject the null hypothesis and incorporating such results into the larger body of scientific evidence. Together with alternative statistical methods such as meta-analysis, effect-size estimation, and confidence intervals, the social and behavioral sciences may yet embark on the path that the more developed sciences have already discovered.

–The Truth Is Out There

Lively debate on a controversial issue is often regarded as a healthy sign in science. Anomalous or conflicting findings generated from alternative theoretical viewpoints often precede major theoretical advances in the more developed sciences (Kuhn, 1970), but this does not seem to be the case in the social and behavioral sciences. As Meehl (1978) pointed out nearly 20 years ago, theories in the behavioral sciences do not emerge healthier and stronger after a period of challenge and debate. Instead, our theories often fade away as we grow tired, confused, and frustrated by the lack of consistent research evidence. The reasons are many, including relatively crude measurement procedures and the lack of strong theories underlying our research endeavors (Platt, 1964; Rossi, 1985, 1990). But not least among our problems is that the accumulation of knowledge in the behavioral sciences often relies upon judgments and assessments of evidence that are rooted in statistical significance testing.

At the outset I should point out that I do not intend here to enumerate yet again the many problems associated with the significance testing paradigm. Many competent critiques have appeared in recent years (Cohen, 1994; Folger, 1989; Goodman & Royall, 1988; Oakes, 1986; Rossi, 1990; Schmidt, 1996; Schmidt & Hunter, 1995); in fact, such criticisms are almost as old as the paradigm itself (Berkson, 1938, 1942; Bolles, 1962; Cohen, 1962; Grant, 1962; Jones, 1955; Kish, 1959; McNemar, 1960; Rozeboom, 1960). However, one consequence of significance testing is of special concern here. This is the practice of dichotomous interpretation of p values as the basis for deciding on the existence of an effect. That is, if $p < .05$, the effect exists. If $p > .05$, the effect does not exist. Unfortunately, this is a common decision-making pattern in the social and behavioral sciences (Beauchamp & May, 1964; Cooper & Rosenthal, 1980; Cowles & Davis, 1982; Rosenthal & Gaito, 1963, 1964).

The consequences of this approach are bad enough for individual research studies: All too frequently, publication decisions are contingent on which side of the .05 line the test statistic lands. But the consequences for the accumulation of evidence across studies is even worse. As Meehl (1978) has indicated, most reviewers simply tend to "count noses" in assessing the evidence for an effect across studies. Traditional vote-counting methods generally underestimate the support for an effect and have been shown to have low statistical power (Cooper & Rosenthal, 1980; Hedges & Olkin, 1980). At the same time, those studies that find a statistically significant effect (and that are therefore more likely to be published) are in fact very likely to overestimate the actual strength of the effect (Lane & Dunlap, 1978; Schmidt, 1996). Combined with the generally poor power characteristics of many primary studies (Cohen, 1962; Rossi, 1990), the prospects for a meaningful cumulative science seem dismal.

This last point is worth emphasizing. If published studies result in overestimates of effect sizes, then replication attempts will generally be underpowered, because the true effect size will be smaller than expected. The situation is especially problematic when the statistical power of tests designed to detect an effect is about .50. Because power is the probability that a statistical test will find statistically significant results, the results of some tests will be significant and some will not. Under these circumstances, it is easy to see how inconsistencies might arise among study outcomes, resulting in controversy among researchers. But the inconsistencies would be essentially artifactual. By this I mean only that the controversy arises not from the strength of competing theoretical models, but rather from the inadequacy of the underlying statistical power functions that characterize the research.

A HYPOTHETICAL EXAMPLE

The problem is well illustrated using an example. Suppose a researcher discovers that a brief training program based on a radical new model of learning increases scores on the verbal section of the Scholastic Aptitude Test (SAT-V) by 50 points among a sample of 50 11th-graders compared to 50 controls. The results are easily statistically significant, $t(98) = 2.5$, $p < .05$. As this is a rather startling finding, several other investigators steeped in orthodoxy fervently wish to confirm the effect (actually, they wish to disconfirm it). All across the country, researchers purchase copies of the training manual and accompanying CD-ROM. Ten exact replications of the original study are quickly conducted, in each of which 50 students are given the training while an additional 50 are used as controls. The statistical test is conducted as a directional test at the .01 level of significance.

Assume that the training program really does work. What is the probability that each study will yield a statistically significant result? Because we are assuming that the training program does increase SAT-V scores, a naive expectation is that all 10 studies would result in statistically significant differences, with the treatment group outperforming the controls every time. This is exactly what would occur if samples perfectly representative of the two populations were drawn for all 10 studies. In fact, sampling error will reduce the likelihood of obtaining statistically significant results in each study, as defined by the underlying statistical power function based on the study's design parameters.

To determine the power of each replication study we need to know not only the sample size and alpha level of the statistical test, but also the magnitude of the treatment effect. Effect sizes can be represented in many different ways, but perhaps the simplest and most meaningful measure is Cohen's (1962, 1988) d. The value of d is computed by taking the difference in means between the treatment and control groups and dividing by the pooled within-groups standard deviation. Assuming a typical within-groups standard deviation of 100 for the SAT-V, the effect size works out to be one half of a standard deviation, that is, d = 50/100 = 0.50. Taking this as our best estimate of the population effect size, the resulting statistical power of each replication is .55. Thus, we should expect only five or six studies to achieve statistical significance, even assuming that the training program actually works as described. It is easy to see how controversy concerning the effectiveness of the training program and the validity of the underlying theory might develop under these circumstances. Ideological warfare might quickly break out, especially if some of those researchers who were predisposed to accept the radical new theory were among the lucky ones who had obtained a significant effect.

Although this example is contrived, there is every reason to believe that it can and does happen in actual research applications. Cohen (1962) was the first to systematically demonstrate that behavioral research was characterized by low levels of statistical power. His survey of research published in the *Journal of Abnormal and Social Psychology* for the year 1960 found power of only .48 for medium-size effects (defined as d = 0.50). Almost 30 years later, two independent studies found little or no meaningful increase in the statistical power of psychological research (Rossi, 1990; Sedlmeier & Gigerenzer, 1989) . In addition, a study of 25 power surveys across a wide range of social science disciplines, including over 1,500 journal articles and 40,000 statistical tests, found that power was only .64 for medium-size effects (Rossi, 1990). Very few surveys of effect sizes have been conducted, but those that have indicate that medium-size effects are typical of research in the social and behavioral sciences (Cooper & Findley, 1982; Haase, Waechter, & Solomon, 1982). Thus, it seems plausible that at least some controversies in the social and behavioral sciences may be artifactual in nature.

SPONTANEOUS RECOVERY: A CASE STUDY

The history and fate of the spontaneous recovery of previously extinguished or unlearned verbal associations provides an enlightening example of real-world artifactual controversy. Although spontaneous recovery occupied an important position in the interference theory of memory, the question of the existence of the effect enjoyed controversial status for many years (Brown, 1976; Postman & Underwood, 1973; Underwood & Postman, 1960). The underlying questions were both subtle and complex, so that the following description of the problem is necessarily a simplification. At issue was the assumption that the learning of a list of words required the unlearning of competing pre-experimental natural language associations to the list items. The unlearning hypothesis was interesting in

that it suggested an analogy with the concept of extinction from classical learning theory (Underwood, 1948a). By extending the extinction analogy, researchers concluded that it should be possible to observe the spontaneous recovery of
the unlearned responses, as is usually obtained in simple animal-conditioning
experiments. (The extension of the principles of simple animal learning to complex human verbal learning was, of course, something of a big deal.) The recovery of these unlearned or extinguished associations should occur during a reten-
tion interval, thus competing with the more recently learned associations at recall and resulting in the forgetting of some list responses. This constitutes a kind
of proactive inhibition paradigm. In fact, these and other observations led to the
identification of proactive inhibition as a major cause of recall interference
(Underwood, 1957). Obtaining spontaneous recovery experimentally was therefore considered one of the critical issues on which a viable unlearning model of
interference theory was based.

Approximately 40 studies were published on spontaneous recovery during the
period of most intensive investigation (1948–1969). Unfortunately, the effect
was found in only about half of these studies. The resulting ambiguity led to the
conclusion in most texts and literature reviews that the evidence for spontaneous
recovery was not convincing (Baddeley, 1976; Crowder, 1976; Keppel, 1968;
Klatzky, 1980; Postman, Stark, & Fraser, 1968; Postman & Underwood, 1973). I
even concluded so myself during my graduate student days (Rossi, 1977)! Some
researchers went so far as to blame the analysis of variance as an inadequate
analytical technique (although not for reasons relating to significance testing or
statistical power), and several alternative procedures were suggested (Brown,
1976; Coleman, 1979). Ultimately, the effect was considered ephemeral, and the
issue was not so much resolved as it was abandoned: a classic example of
Meehl's (1978) thesis of theories in psychology fading away, though in this case,
not in one of psychology's "softer" areas.

META-ANALYSIS AND POWER ANALYSIS OF SPONTANEOUS RECOVERY RESEARCH

Some critics of the significance testing paradigm seem to suggest that significance tests are inherently incapable of contributing to a cumulative knowledge
base. Recently, this position has been most forcefully argued by Schmidt (1996;
Schmidt & Hunter, 1995). I think it may be fairer to say that it is primarily the
abuse of the paradigm that is problematic. In particular, the uncritical adherence
to a standard criterion of significance (be it .05 or any other level) and especially
the subsequent dichotomous interpretation of p values certainly constitutes
abuse. The irony is that the significance testing paradigm also provides the tools

for establishing cumulative knowledge in the social and behavioral sciences. That it has not done so simply suggests these tools have not yet been adequately used or appreciated. Recent critics of significance tests have therefore provided a great service by focusing attention on many of these alternative tools, including measures of effect size, confidence intervals, meta-analysis, and power analysis. But it seems to me undeniable that all of these procedures arose as elements of the significance testing paradigm, and not always in opposition to it, and they now form an essential part of the paradigm. Measures of effect size can be and often are computed from the results of significance tests; similarly, meta-analysis is often performed on the results of significance tests. Well, perhaps this is a chicken-and-egg problem. In any event, whether one thinks of these techniques as part and parcel of the significance testing paradigm or as revolutionary new approaches to data analysis, the employment of several of these procedures can bring a great deal of clarity and understanding to the history and fate of spontaneous recovery.

An analysis of the statistical power of the research on spontaneous recovery is especially instructive. Such an analysis first requires specification of the expected magnitude of the spontaneous recovery effect. The approach taken in most power surveys, starting with Cohen (1962), is to estimate power for a wide range of effect sizes (e.g., small, medium, and large effects). Although this approach has worked well, it is not without its drawbacks, especially when a specific research literature is of primary interest (Rossi, 1990). A more appropriate, though less frequently used approach is to estimate power based on the obtained effect size for the series of studies in question (Rossi, 1982, 1983a, 1984, 1990). This may be achieved by using data synthesis procedures such as meta-analysis (Cooper & Hedges, 1994; Eddy, Hasselblad, & Shachter, 1992; Hedges & Olkin, 1985; Hunter & Schmidt, 1990; Rosenthal, 1991) .

Method

Selection of Studies. Spontaneous recovery was first demonstrated by Underwood (1948a, 1948b). Such a well-marked origin provides a convenient point of departure for a bibliographic search. Two general indices were searched using *spontaneous recovery, interference theory, retroactive interference, retroactive inhibition, proactive interference,* and *proactive inhibition* as key words: *Psychological Abstracts* and *Social Science Citation Index.* In addition, 11 journals that published research on human learning and memory were searched exhaustively: *American Journal of Psychology, Bulletin of the Psychonomic Society, Journal of Experimental Psychology, Journal of Psychology, Journal of Verbal Learning and Verbal Behavior, Memory & Cognition, Perceptual and Motor Skills, Psychological Record, Psychological Reports, Psychonomic Science,* and the *Quarterly Journal of Experimental Psychology*. The potential effect of publication bias was considered minimal for this analysis, given the large proportion of published studies that reported nonsignificant results. Nevertheless, in order to include as many studies from as wide a variety of sources as possible, *Dissertation Abstracts* and relevant conference proceedings (e.g., American Psychological Association, Eastern Psychological Association) were also searched, though availability of conference reports was limited. The period of the search covered the years from 1948 to 1981.

The search revealed a total of 39 spontaneous recovery studies conducted between 1948 and 1979. Most of the studies were retrieved from the published research literature ($N = 35$). The remaining sources included dissertations ($N = 3$) and conference proceedings ($N = 1$). The 39 studies included 47 separate experiments and 4,926 subjects. Of the 47 experiments, 20 (43%) reported statistically significant results ($p < .05$). Because similar results were obtained using either studies or experiments as the unit of analysis, only the results based on experiments are reported. Additional results and a list of the studies included in the analysis is given in Rossi (1984).

Results

Meta-Analysis. Because more than 30 years of research on spontaneous recovery resulted in no consensus among researchers concerning even the existence of the phenomenon, the first step in the meta-analysis was simply to determine the overall level of statistical support for the effect. Several techniques described by Rosenthal (1978) were used for this purpose, including the method of adding z scores, testing the mean p value, testing the mean z, and the Fisher χ^2 procedure. All gave essentially the same results so only the first is reported. A z score of zero was assigned if the study reported nonsignificant results without specifying a test statistic or p value for the spontaneous recovery effect.

The z score for the combination of all 47 spontaneous recovery experiments was 8.5 ($p < .001$). Because it appeared that experiments with larger sample sizes tended to produce more nonsignificant results, the combined z weighted by sample size also was determined. The result was only slightly smaller ($z = 8.1, p < .001$). As protection against the file drawer problem, the fail-safe N for spontaneous recovery also was computed, using the procedure described by Rosenthal (1979). The fail-safe N specifies the minimum number of unpublished or undiscovered studies that might be squirreled away in file drawers and that might have obtained nonsignificant results. If included in the meta-analysis, these studies would reduce the overall meta-analysis z score to nonsignificance (i.e., $p > .05$). The fail-safe N for spontaneous recovery was 1,212, more than 25 times the number of studies retrieved by the literature search. Given the difficulty of conducting spontaneous recovery research and that many nonsignificant studies were in fact published, the likelihood of there being more than 1,200 additional unpublished null results in file drawers seems remote.

Each study then was assessed for the magnitude of the spontaneous recovery effect. Not surprisingly, no direct estimates of effect size were reported in any of the studies. Therefore, effect sizes were estimated from summary data, including group means and standard deviations and analysis of variance F test results. Studies reporting no significant effects but otherwise providing no data on which to base an effect-size estimate were assigned an effect size of zero. Studies reporting significant effects but providing no other data than the p value for the effect were assigned the minimum effect size consistent with the stated p value and sample size. Studies finding evidence in the direction opposite to that predicted by the hypothesis of spontaneous recovery were weighted negatively. Multiple effect sizes within experiments were averaged so that each experiment contributed only one estimate of the magnitude of the spontaneous recovery effect. Additional details are reported elsewhere (Rossi, 1984). Despite these efforts, it was not possible to obtain an estimate of effect size for every study. In all, effect sizes were estimated for 40 experiments from 36 studies. The average effect size was $d = 0.39$ (range = –0.42–1.03; 95% confidence interval = 0.27–0.48).

Power Analysis. Using the average spontaneous recovery effect-size estimate as the basis for the alternative hypothesis, power was determined for each experiment based on the degrees of freedom for the significance test used in the original analysis. Power calculations were based on the cube root normal approximation of the noncentral F distribution (Laubscher, 1960; Severo & Zelen, 1960) using computer programs developed by the author (Rossi, 1984, 1990). The accuracy of this approximation has been found to be quite good (Cohen & Nee, 1987). Additional details on the computer programs are reported elsewhere (Rossi, 1984, 1990). Power also was computed for each experiment using Cohen's (1988) definitions of small, medium, and large effect sizes ($d = 0.20, 0.50, 0.80$, respectively). Alpha was set to .05 (two-tailed) for all power calculations. Sample size was unavailable for only 3 of the 47 spontaneous recovery experiments. Average power for the remaining 44 experiments was .38 (range = .12–.78; 95% confidence interval = .33–.43). Power against small, medium, and large effect size alternatives was .15, .62, and .93, respectively.

Discussion

Spontaneous recovery has been a controversial phenomenon throughout most of its history. Meta-analysis and power analysis of spontaneous recovery studies suggest that this controversy may be primarily statistical in nature. Meta-analysis reveals that the magnitude of the spontaneous recovery effect is quite small, especially in the context of laboratory studies of human learning and memory. Power analysis suggests that the sample sizes of spontaneous recovery studies have been inadequate to ensure the detection of the effect in most studies, although sufficient to produce some significant results. In fact, power was less than the usually recommended value of .80 for every one of the 44 spontaneous recovery experiments included in the analysis. The average power across all experiments was .38, in good agreement with the observed proportion of significant results of .43 (20 of 47 experiments significant at $p < .05$). It is easy to see how controversy over the existence of the effect might occur under these circumstances.

These results suggest that the inconsistency among spontaneous recovery studies may have been due to the emphasis reviewers and researchers placed on the level of significance attained by individual studies, rather than that attained by the entire series of spontaneous recovery studies. In fact, meta-analysis demonstrates convincing support for the existence of the phenomenon. Although fewer than half of the studies yielded statistically significant results, many of the nonsignificant outcomes were in the direction predicted by the spontaneous recovery hypothesis. Brown (1976) was one of the few reviewers of this literature who noted this effect and correctly concluded that there was sufficient evidence for the phenomenon. Presumably, most other reviewers did not discern any support for spontaneous recovery among the nonsignificant studies, despite evidence beyond mere statistical significance that supported the existence of the effect. Instead, they simply "counted noses" and were persuaded by the relative proportion of significant and nonsignificant results. A cumulative science will be difficult to achieve if only some studies are counted as providing evidence.

It is very unlikely that spontaneous recovery researchers ever considered the possibility that their problems had a statistical basis. None of the studies included a discussion of either effect size or statistical power, either as an a priori design feature or in the evaluation of negative results. As a laboratory endeavor, it was probably assumed that sufficient control of the experimental situation would be all that was necessary to elucidate the effect. Small effects are unusual in laboratory studies of human learning and memory, and sample sizes frequently are selected on the basis of what has worked well in the past. Probably, there was an implicit expectation that any new phenomenon would be similar in magnitude to other previously studied effects. The problem was that spontaneous recovery was a much smaller effect than certain related phenomena, such as proactive and retroactive inhibition.

The average sample size of research in spontaneous recovery was about 80, somewhat larger than research in other areas of psychology (Holmes, 1979;

Holmes, Holmes, & Fanning, 1981). Unfortunately, this was not large enough to consistently detect the effect. In fact, the power of spontaneous recovery studies was inadequate for all but relatively large effect sizes. Average sample sizes would have to have been about three times larger to achieve power of .80. Such sample sizes are unusual in laboratory studies of human learning and memory. For sample sizes typical of spontaneous recovery studies, power would have been .80 only if the effect had been substantially larger ($d = 0.63$) than actually obtained ($d = 0.39$).

Might Controversy Have Been Avoided?

It seems reasonable to suppose that much of the controversy surrounding the existence of spontaneous recovery was based on researchers' reliance on p values to resolve the question. Unfortunately, circumstances conspired to subvert the trust on which that reliance was based. A much smaller effect size than researchers had been accustomed to investigating in combination with a general disregard or even ignorance of the roles of effect size and statistical power were the asteroids that killed the spontaneous recovery dinosaur. Given that researchers are likely to remain wedded to a significance-testing approach, it is instructive to consider how inconsistent findings and controversy might have been avoided even within the paradigm.

As noted earlier, the simplistic answer is the use of much larger sample sizes, so that most studies would have had a good chance at finding the effect. It is worth noting, however, that problems also would have been avoided had *smaller* sample sizes been used, because the effect then only rarely would have been detected (Harris & Quade, 1992; Rossi, 1990). This is an important point, because the null hypothesis is essentially always false, insofar as the means of two groups are never exactly equal. Thus, it is important for researchers to consider the power of their experiments not only to detect the effects they seek, but also to avoid detecting trivially small effects. Trying to define how small an effect is too small is admittedly an arbitrary judgment and likely to vary across situations and researchers. A small effect may be important from a theoretical standpoint, but may contribute little for predictive purposes (Rossi, 1990). Abelson (1985) and Rosenthal (1990) have provided interesting and dramatic examples of how even very small effects can be quite important. The current debate on the meaning of cognitive gender differences provides a good example of small effects that may not be particularly useful from a prediction or classification standpoint (e.g., Benbow & Stanley, 1980; Hyde, 1981; Rossi, 1983b).

Of course, there is no substitute for direct assessment and consideration of effect size, and spontaneous recovery researchers would have been well advised to have done so. But there are potential pitfalls here too. Suppose after the first few studies researchers had noticed that the magnitude of the spontaneous recovery effect was very small. Upon first discovery, many effects are quite small, and researchers are often loath to report effect sizes precisely because small effects are frequently equated with unimportant effects. The effect might well have been dismissed as meaningless. Inasmuch as spontaneous recovery occupied a critical position in the interference theory of forgetting, it may be that even a small effect would have been worth pursuing. As research continued, improvements in understanding the phenomenon would be expected to lead to more sensitive and precise experimental tests, thus increasing the effective magnitude of the effect. This process has worked well in the physical sciences, where the investigation of small effects is a routine business and measurement has reached impressive levels of precision, often as a prelude to significant advancement in knowledge (Holton, 1996; Pipkin & Ritter, 1983; Rossi, 1984, 1985; Will, 1990).

Estimation of Probable Upper Bounds on Effect Size

As many have noted, the cumulative nature of the more developed sciences is lacking in the social and behavioral sciences (Cohen, 1994; Meehl, 1967, 1978; Rossi, 1990; Schmidt, 1996; Schmidt & Hunter, 1995). Ultimately, this is the problem underlying the failure of researchers to document the spontaneous recovery effect. The logic of null hypothesis testing using a sharp decision-making criterion based on an arbitrary alpha-level cutoff point requires researchers to conclude that their data either do or do not support their research hypothesis. No in-between conclusions are permitted. The degree of support for the research hypothesis cannot be assessed easily using p values, so the only option left is to count noses. Based on the lack of consistent support for the phenomenon, researchers in the learning and memory field dutifully followed the path of the paradigm, straight to their demise. Eventually, they came to accept the null hypothesis with regard to spontaneous recovery. Even within the context of significance testing, this was an incorrect conclusion, as the meta-analysis of spontaneous recovery studies demonstrates.

Lack of evidential consistency is not just a problem in the social and behavioral sciences. Even in the physical sciences, data in support of theory can be contradictory. Many suspected phenomena are quite controversial, and the evidence in support of an effect is not always consistent. Indeed, sometimes the support for a phenomenon is entirely theoretical, without any empirical support whatsoever! Some examples include such physical exotica as the mass of the photon (Davis, Goldhaber, & Nieto, 1975; Goldhaber & Nieto, 1976) , proton decay (Weinberg, 1981), neutrino mass (Dar, 1990), and until surprisingly recently, black holes (Charles & Wagner, 1996). None of these phenomena has been directly detected, although there have been many unsuccessful attempts.

Yet, physical scientists do not necessarily conclude that these things do not exist, only that if they do exist, their measurable effects must be smaller than a certain magnitude, as determined by the degree of experimental measurement error (Rossi, 1984, 1985, 1990).

The situation is not unlike that which frequently confronts the hypothesis-testing behavioral scientist: the failure to reject the null hypothesis. The behavioral scientist in this situation often asserts that there is no effect. The physical scientist, on the other hand, suspends judgment and simply assigns an upper limit on the magnitude of the effect, leaving the question of its existence to future research. Such an approach might have been helpful in avoiding the controversy over spontaneous recovery. Rather than simply conclude that spontaneous recovery did not exist, researchers might have set an upper limit on the magnitude of the effect as a guide for future researchers.

Statistical power analysis provides a means for determining such upper bounds on effect sizes (Rossi, 1990), as demonstrated in Table 7.1. This table shows the Type II error rates for a range of possible effect sizes, based on the average sample size of spontaneous recovery studies and assuming $\alpha = .05$. For example, assuming that the true magnitude of the spontaneous recovery effect is $d = 0.59$, the corresponding Type II error rate would be .25. This means that the probability is .25 that a spontaneous recovery effect of this magnitude exists and was missed by researchers. Another way of thinking about this is that the table helps set the probable upper bound on the magnitude of the effect size for spontaneous recovery. Thus, there is only a 25% chance that the accumulated evidence for spontaneous recovery supports the existence of an effect larger than $d = 0.59$.

Rather than conclude that there is no spontaneous recovery effect, a more appropriate conclusion might be that, if the effect exists, there is a 75% chance that

TABLE 7.1

Type II Error Rates as Probable Upper Bounds on
the Effect Size (d) for Spontaneous Recovery

Type II Error	d
.50	0.44
.25	0.59
.20	0.63
.15	0.68
.10	0.74
.05	0.82
.01	0.97

it is smaller than $d = 0.59$ and only a 25% chance that it is larger than $d = 0.59$. The choice of an appropriate level of confidence is left to the individual researcher, as is the assessment of what constitutes a plausible effect size for spontaneous recovery. Researchers in this field could conclude with the same degree of confidence that they typically use to reject the null hypothesis (i.e., .05) that the spontaneous recovery effect is not larger than $d = 0.82$. This procedure provides a sensible means of evaluating null results, and is the closest anyone can come to accepting the null hypothesis.

IS THE CASE OF SPONTANEOUS RECOVERY UNIQUE?

Finally, we might ask if all this is making a great deal out of a single unfortunate episode. Was the tragic history of spontaneous recovery a one-time confluence of events, or have statistical power functions conspired to visit the same fate on other unsuspecting research literatures? This question gets no definitive answer here. But certainly spontaneous recovery is not the only research plagued with inconsistent findings. And although it is certainly possible that the conflicting results found among spontaneous recovery studies may be to some degree due to additional and as yet undiscovered sources, it seems clear enough that the power of spontaneous recovery research was too low.

Identifying research areas in which there are conflicting findings was not as difficult as might be imagined: It is often precisely the purpose of meta-analysis to ascertain the overall level of support for an effect for which previous studies have provided inconsistent evidence. Use of published meta-analyses as a source is particularly convenient inasmuch as the exhaustive literature searches and effect-size calculations that are the defining features of meta-analysis have already been completed!

Method

Selection of Studies. The search for candidate meta-analyses was conducted using the subject indices of *Psychological Abstract* and the *Social Science Citation Index*, as well as several journals that typically publish such studies, including the *American Educational Research Journal, American Psychologist, Journal of Consulting and Clinical Psychology, Journal of Educational Psychology, Journal of Personality and Social Psychology, Personality and Social Psychology Bulletin, Psychological Bulletin,* and the *Review of Educational Research.*

To be suitable for power analysis, a meta-analysis must provide certain minimum information. In particular, sample-size and effect-size information must be explicitly given for all (or nearly all) of the primary studies included in the analysis. These data are necessary to compute the statistical power of each primary study. Unfortunately, of the 95 meta-analyses that resulted from the search, only 6 provided the required information! Most analyses did not report any individual study data, only the relationships between effect size and suspected moderator variables. Thus, the results that follow should not be considered definitive. Fortunately, the search for meta-analyses was not intended to be either exhaustive or representative, but only to supply a few examples for inspection. The six meta-analyses included five journal publications and one dissertation.

Four of the studies contained more than one research synthesis, so that a total of 17 separate meta-analyses were available for examination. Of these, four were excluded because they were conducted on areas of minimal controversy, which was defined as whenever more than 80% of the primary studies reached the same conclusion. One additional meta-analysis was excluded because it consisted of only four primary studies. The remaining 12 meta-analyses were based on a total of 215 primary studies and over 160,000 subjects.

Results

Meta-Analyses. All of the meta-analyses used Cohen's (1988) d as the index of effect size. The average effect size for each meta-analysis was recomputed for this study for two reasons: (a) as a check on the results reported in the analysis (cf. Rossi, 1987), and (b) because several authors simply omitted from their calculations any primary studies for which d could not be directly computed, even when indirect means of computing results were available. For example, studies not reporting an effect size but reporting nonsignificant results were assigned $d = 0$. Studies not reporting an effect size but reporting statistically significant results were assigned the lowest d value that would have resulted in the stated p value, based on the sample size of the test. For some primary studies, the value of d was computed from other measures of effect size (e.g., η^2, ω^2). Thus, the average effect size reported here may differ from that reported in the original study.

Power Analyses. Using the average effect size as the alternative to detect, power was computed for each of the primary studies in the meta-analysis, based on the sample size of the study and assuming $\alpha = .05$. A traditional power survey using small, medium, and large effect sizes ($d = 0.20$, 0.50, and 0.80, respectively) also was conducted, but these results are reported elsewhere (Rossi, 1983a, 1984). Results are given in Table 7.2. Also shown is the number of primary studies in the analysis, the total and median sample sizes of the primary

TABLE 7.2
Power Analysis of Meta-Analyses

Source	Sample Size[a]			d [c]	Prop. Sig.[d]	Power [e]
	N [b]	Total	Mdn.			
Arkin et al. (1980) Study 1	8	709	88	.578	.625	.754
Arkin et al. (1980) Study 2	7	553	80	.744	.714	.895
Arkin et al. (1980) Study 3	8	549	68	.508	.500	.522
Burger (1981)	22	4404	160	.273	.273	.420
Cooper (1979) Study 1	16	2274	116	.277	.438	.353
Cooper (1979) Study 2	8	992	100	.094	.250	.082
Hall (1978) Study 1	55	12253	115	.171	.236	.214
Hall (1978) Study 2	13	1896	119	.162	.385	.161
Hasenfeld (1983)	11	768	80	.420	.455	.394
Hyde (1981) Study 1	27	68899	528	.166	.444	.502
Hyde (1981) Study 2	16	65193	620	.266	.688	.878
Hyde (1981) Study 3	24	1632	54	.413	.458	.358
Totals/Averages	215	160122	115	.278	.400	.397

[a]Sample size refers to the total number of subjects in each meta-analysis and to the median number of subjects included in each primary study.

[b]N is the number of primary studies included in each meta-analysis.

[c]d is the average effect size for each meta-analysis. The average effect size for all meta-analyses was weighted by N.

[d]Prop. Sig. is the proportion of all primary studies in each meta-analysis reporting statistically significant effects ($p < .05$).

[e]The power of each primary study in each meta-analysis was computed based on the average effect size for that meta-analysis, on the sample size of the study, and assuming an α level of .05. Power estimates were converted to z scores before being averaged. Average power for all meta-analyses was weighted by N.

studies, the average effect size, and the proportion of primary studies for which the reported results were statistically significant ($p < .05$).

Discussion

If the inconsistent findings in any particular research area are due to inadequate statistical power, then we may expect the average power for that area to be a reasonably good estimate of the proportion of studies that resulted in statistically significant effects. These data are given in the last two columns of Table 7.2. The correlation between these data is quite good ($r = .904$). The average power for all 215 studies (.397) closely matches the proportion of all studies that obtained significant results (.400).

Consideration of the power results for each meta-analysis separately gives an indication of the extent to which the case of spontaneous recovery is an isolated one. For seven of the meta-analyses, the correspondence between the power estimate and the significance rate seems reasonably good. For two of the meta-analyses, power was substantially lower than the significance rate (Cooper, 1979, Study 2; Hall, 1978, Study 2). This is not a surprising outcome, because significant studies are more likely to be published than nonsignificant ones. For the remaining three meta-analyses, power was substantially greater than the significance rate. For these three areas of research, then, it would seem that inadequate statistical power cannot account completely for the existence of inconsistent findings, although the power for one of these areas is clearly very low (Burger, 1981). For the other two studies (Arkin, Cooper, & Kolditz, 1980, Study 2; Hyde, 1981, Study 2), power is quite good, nearly .90. Inconsistency in these areas is most likely to be due to any of the various sources researchers investigate when trying to ascertain why some studies are significant and others not: different methodologies or measures, differential failure to control extraneous sources of error, incompatible operational definitions, conflicting theoretical orientations, and so on.

The most disappointing aspect of the findings presented here is that only for these last two studies does statistical power reach conventional levels of acceptability (i.e., greater than .80). Thus, only for these two areas of research can inadequate power be ruled out as a source of the conflicting findings. For the 10 remaining areas, inadequate power appears to be at least partially responsible for the inconsistencies, although only further research within each specific area can determine whether there are yet additional sources contributing to the existence of the conflicting findings.

Contributing to this sad state of affairs is the size of the effects under investigation. The average effect size across all of the meta-analyses was estimated at only $d = 0.278$. These are small effects indeed, and it should not be surprising that there may be difficulties in reaching traditional levels of statistical significance in these areas. What is surprising is that in no case was statistical power mentioned in these meta-analyses as a potential source of the inconsistencies in the primary studies; this despite the fact that researchers who conduct meta-analyses are probably more aware of statistical issues than other behavioral researchers. This is particularly ironic in that increased statistical power often is given as one of the primary reasons for conducting meta-analysis in the first place.

SUMMARY

Spontaneous recovery is dead. At least, it is as a topic of serious scientific investigation. In current textbooks on human learning and memory, the interference theory of forgetting still is discussed. But spontaneous recovery generally is considered ephemeral, and that aspect of interference theory dealing with the phenomenon rarely is mentioned. One of the few recent texts that does mention spontaneous recovery refers to it as "one of the unresolved issues of interference theory" (Zechmeister & Nyberg, 1982, p. 112). Indeed, the very term spontaneous recovery seems to have disappeared from textbook subject indexes. Even the discoverer of the effect does not mention it in his recent text, despite an entire chapter on the interference theory of forgetting (Underwood, 1983). Instead, the issue of spontaneous recovery seems to have slowly withered during the 1970s, as the once dominant stimulus-response theory of human learning and memory gave way to the cognitive paradigm. The entire episode is reminiscent of Meehl's (1978) characterization of the fate of theories in soft psychology as never dying a quick clean death, but just slowing fading away as researchers lose interest to pursue new theories and models. Unfortunately, such fates are not uncommon in the behavioral sciences, though perhaps a bit more unusual in psychology's laboratory disciplines.

Although there no longer may be any reason to mourn the demise of spontaneous recovery, the killer should concern us greatly, for it is still at large! Spontaneous recovery was killed by our over-reliance on interpreting p values within the context of the paradigm. Beset by a series of inconsistent and contradictory findings that seemed to defy theoretical explanation, researchers became confused and frustrated. The plethora of null findings was especially problematical for researchers. Within the traditional paradigm, failure to reject the null hypothesis leaves researchers in an awkward position. Often there is not much to say. About all that can be said with confidence is that there is insufficient evidence to reject the null hypothesis. It's no wonder few failures to reject the null are published.

Although this happened not to be the case for research on spontaneous recovery, failure to publish null results is a substantial problem for the behavioral sciences, as many have noted (Bakan, 1966; Cohen, 1994; Greenwald, 1975; Meehl, 1978; Rossi, 1990; Rozeboom, 1960; Sterling, 1959). In particular, it seriously compromises the accumulation of knowledge across studies. Greater reliance on alternative methods, such as estimating effect sizes and associated confidence intervals as well as the procedures described here for establishing probable upper bounds on effect sizes, can provide a sensible means of incorporating null results into the larger body of scientific evidence. Together with powerful data accumulation procedures such as meta-analysis, these techniques may be able to set the social and behavioral sciences on the path that the more developed sciences already have discovered.

ACKNOWLEDGMENTS

This research was partially supported by National Institutes of Health Grants AR43051, CA27821, and CA50087. Portions of this chapter are based on a doctoral dissertation submitted at the University of Rhode Island. Earlier versions of this research were presented at the 53rd annual meeting of the Eastern Psychological Association, Baltimore, MD, April 1982, the 54th annual meeting of the Eastern Psychological Association, Philadelphia, PA, April 1983, the 150th annual meeting of the American Association for the Advancement of Science, New York, NY, May 1984, the 56th annual meeting of the Eastern Psychological Association, Boston, MA, March 1985, and the annual meeting of the Psychometric Society, Toronto, Ontario, Canada, June 1986.

Correspondence and requests for reprints should be addressed to Joseph S. Rossi, Cancer Prevention Research Center, University of Rhode Island, 2 Chaffee Road, Kingston, RI 02881. E-mail: kzp101@uriacc.uri.edu.

REFERENCES

Abelson, R. P. (1985). A variance explanation paradox: When a little is a lot. *Psychological Bulletin, 97*, 129–133.

Arkin, R., Cooper, H. M., & Kolditz, T. (1980). A statistical review of the literature concerning the self-serving attribution bias in interpersonal influence situations. *Journal of Personality, 48*, 435–448.

Baddeley, A. D. (1976). *The psychology of memory*. New York: Basic Books.

Bakan, D. (1966). The test of significance in psychological research. *Psychological Bulletin, 66*, 423–437.

Beauchamp, K. L., & May, R. B. (1964). Replication report: Interpretation of levels of significance by psychological researchers. *Psychological Reports, 14*, 272.

Benbow, C. P., & Stanley, J. C. (1980). Sex differences in mathematical ability: Fact or artifact? *Science, 210*, 1262–1264.

Berkson, J. (1938). Some difficulties of interpretation encountered in the application of the chi-square test. *Journal of the American Statistical Association, 33*, 526–542.

Berkson, J. (1942). Tests of significance considered as evidence. *Journal of the American Statistical Association, 37*, 325–335.

Bolles, R. C. (1962). The difference between statistical hypotheses and scientific hypotheses. *Psychological Reports, 11*, 639–645.

Brown, A. S. (1976). Spontaneous recovery in human learning. *Psychological Bulletin, 83*, 321–338.

Burger, J. M. (1981). Motivational biases in the attribution of responsibility for an accident: A meta-analysis of the defensive-attribution hypothesis. *Psychological Bulletin, 90*, 496–512.

Charles, P. A., & Wagner, R. M. (1996). Black holes in binary stars: Weighing the evidence. *Sky & Telescope, 91*(5), 38–42.

Cohen, J. (1962). The statistical power of abnormal-social psychological research: A review. *Journal of Abnormal and Social Psychology, 65*, 145–153.

Cohen, J. (1988). *Statistical power analysis for the behavioral sciences* (2nd ed.). Hillsdale, NJ: Lawrence Erlbaum Associates.

Cohen, J. (1994). The earth is round ($p < .05$). *American Psychologist, 49*, 997–1003.

Cohen, J., & Nee, J. C. M. (1987). A comparison of two noncentral *F* approximations with applications to power analysis in set correlation. *Multivariate Behavioral Research, 22*, 483–490.

Coleman, E. B. (1979). The Solzhenitsyn Finger Test: A significance test for spontaneous recovery. *Psychological Bulletin, 86*, 148–150.

Cooper, H. M. (1979). Statistically combining independent studies: A meta-analysis of sex differences in conformity research. *Journal of Personality and Social Psychology, 37*, 131–146.

Cooper, H. M., & Findley, M. (1982). Expected effect sizes: Estimates for statistical power analysis in social psychology. *Personality and Social Psychology Bulletin, 8*, 168–173.

Cooper, H. M., & Hedges, L. V. (Eds.). (1994). *The handbook of research synthesis*. New York: Russel Sage Foundation.

Cooper, H. M., & Rosenthal, R. (1980). Statistical versus traditional procedures for summarizing research findings. *Psychological Bulletin, 87*, 442–449.

Cowles, M. P., & Davis, C. (1982). Is the .05 level subjectively reasonable? *Canadian Journal of Behavioral Science, 14*, 248–252.

Crowder, R. G. (1976). *Principles of learning and memory*. Hillsdale, NJ: Lawrence Erlbaum Associates.

Dar, A. (1990). Astrophysics and cosmology closing in on neutrino masses. *Science, 250*, 1529–1533.

Davis, L., Goldhaber, A. S., & Nieto, M. M. (1975). Limit on the photon mass deduced from Pioneer-10 observations of Jupiter's magnetic field. *Physical Review Letters, 35*, 1402–1405.

Eddy, D. M., Hasselblad, V., & Shachter, R. (1992). *Meta-analysis by the confidence profile method: The statistical synthesis of evidence.* San Diego: Academic Press.

Folger, R. (1989). Significance tests and the duplicity of binary decisions. *Psychological Bulletin, 106*, 155–160.

Goldhaber, A. S., & Nieto, M. M. (1976). The mass of the photon. *Scientific American, 234*(5), 86–91, 94–96.

Goodman, S. N., & Royall, R. (1988). Evidence and scientific research. *American Journal of Public Health, 78*, 1568–1574.

Grant, D. A. (1962). Testing the null hypothesis and the strategy and tactics of investigating theoretical models. *Psychological Review, 69*, 54–61.

Greenwald, A. G. (1975). Consequences of prejudice against the null hypothesis. *Psychological Bulletin, 82*, 1–20.

Haase, R. F., Waechter, D. M., & Solomon, G. S. (1982). How significant is a significant difference? Average effect size of research in counseling psychology. *Journal of Counseling Psychology, 29*, 58–65.

Hall, J. A. (1978). Gender effects in decoding nonverbal cues. *Psychological Bulletin, 85*, 845–857.

Harris, R. J., & Quade, D. (1992). The minimally important difference significant criterion for sample size. *Journal of Educational Statistics, 17*, 27–49.

Hasenfeld, R. (1983). *Empathy and justification: Two contextual cues related to gender differences in aggressive behavior.* Unpublished doctoral dissertation, University of Rhode Island, Kingston.

Hedges, L. V., & Olkin, I. (1980). Vote counting methods in research synthesis. *Psychological Bulletin, 88*, 359–369.

Hedges, L. V., & Olkin, I. (1985). *Statistical methods for meta-analysis.* Orlando, FL: Academic Press.

Holmes, C. B. (1979). Sample size in psychological research. *Perceptual and Motor Skills, 49*, 283–288.

Holmes, C. B., Holmes, J. R., & Fanning, J. J. (1981). Sample size in non-APA journals. *Journal of Psychology, 108*, 263–266.

Holton, G. (1996). *Einstein, history, and other passions: The rebellion against science at the end of the twentieth century.* Reading, MA: Addison-Wesley.

Hunter, J. E., & Schmidt, F. L. (1990). *Methods of meta-analysis: Correcting error and bias in research findings.* Newbury Park, CA: Sage.

Hyde, J. S. (1981). How large are cognitive gender differences? A meta-analysis using ω^2 and d. *American Psychologist, 36,* 892–901.

Jones, L. V. (1955). Statistics and research design. *Annual Review of Psychology, 6,* 405–430.

Keppel, G. (1968). Retroactive and proactive inhibition. In T. R. Dixon & D. L. Horton (Eds.), *Verbal behavior and general behavior theory* (pp. 172–213). Englewood Cliffs, NJ: Prentice-Hall.

Kish, L. (1959). Some statistical problems in research design. *American Sociological Review, 24,* 328–338.

Klatzky, R. L. (1980). *Human memory: Structures and processes* (2nd ed.). San Francisco: Freeman.

Kuhn, T. S. (1970). *The structure of scientific revolutions* (2nd ed.). Chicago: University of Chicago Press.

Lane, D. M., & Dunlap, W. P. (1978). Estimating effect size: Bias resulting from the significance criterion in editorial decisions. *British Journal of Mathematical and Statistical Psychology, 31,* 107–112.

Laubscher, N. F. (1960). Normalizing the noncentral t and F distributions. *Annals of Mathematical Statistics, 31,* 1105–1112.

McNemar, Q. (1960). At random: Sense and nonsense. *American Psychologist, 15,* 295–300.

Meehl, P. E. (1967). Theory testing in psychology and physics: A methodological paradox. *Philosophy of Science, 34,* 103–115.

Meehl, P. E. (1978). Theoretical risks and tabular asterisks: Sir Karl, Sir Ronald, and the slow progress of soft psychology. *Journal of Consulting and Clinical Psychology, 46,* 806–834.

Oakes, M. (1986). *Statistical inference: A commentary for the social and behavioural sciences.* New York: Wiley.

Pipkin, F. M., & Ritter, R. C. (1983). Precision measurements and fundamental constants. *Science, 219,* 913–921.

Platt, J. R. (1964). Strong inference. *Science, 146,* 347–353.

Postman, L., Stark, K., & Fraser, J. (1968). Temporal changes in interference. *Journal of Verbal Learning and Verbal Behavior, 7,* 672–694.

Postman, L., & Underwood, B. J. (1973). Critical issues in interference theory. *Memory & Cognition, 1,* 19–40.

Rosenthal, R. (1978). Combining results of independent studies. *Psychological Bulletin, 85,* 185–193.

Rosenthal, R. (1979). The "file drawer problem" and tolerance for null results. *Psychological Bulletin, 86,* 638–641.

Rosenthal, R. (1990). How are we doing in soft psychology? *American Psychologist, 45*, 775–777.

Rosenthal, R. (1991). *Meta-analytic procedures for social research* (Rev. ed.). Newbury Park, CA: Sage.

Rosenthal, R., & Gaito, J. (1963). The interpretation of levels of significance by psychological researchers. *Journal of Psychology, 55*, 33–38.

Rosenthal, R., & Gaito, J. (1964). Further evidence for the cliff effect in the interpretation of levels of significance. *Psychological Reports, 15*, 570.

Rossi, J. S. (1977). *On the generality of the laws of unlearning: Spontaneous recovery?* Unpublished manuscript, University of Rhode Island, Kingston.

Rossi, J. S. (1982, April). *Meta-analysis, power analysis and artifactual controversy: The case of spontaneous recovery of verbal associations.* Paper presented at the 53rd annual meeting of the Eastern Psychological Association, Baltimore.

Rossi, J. S. (1983a, April). *Inadequate statistical power: A source of artifactual controversy in behavioral research.* Paper presented at the 54th annual meeting of the Eastern Psychological Association, Philadelphia.

Rossi, J. S. (1983b). Ratios exaggerate gender differences in mathematical ability. *American Psychologist, 38*, 348.

Rossi, J. S. (1984). *Statistical power of psychological research: The artifactual basis of controversial results.* Unpublished doctoral dissertation, University of Rhode Island, Kingston.

Rossi, J. S. (1985, March). *Comparison of physical and behavioral science: The roles of theory, measurement, and effect size.* Paper presented at the 56th annual meeting of the Eastern Psychological Association, Boston.

Rossi, J. S. (1987). How often are our statistics wrong? A statistics class exercise. *Teaching of Psychology, 14*, 98–101.

Rossi, J. S. (1990). Statistical power of psychological research: What have we gained in 20 years? *Journal of Consulting and Clinical Psychology, 58*, 646–656.

Rozeboom, W. W. (1960). The fallacy of the null hypothesis significance test. *Psychological Bulletin, 57*, 416–428.

Schmidt, F. L. (1996). Statistical significance testing and cumulative knowledge in psychology: Implications for training of researchers. *Psychological Methods, 1*, 115–129.

Schmidt, F. L., & Hunter, J. E. (1995). The impact of data-analysis methods on cumulative research knowledge: Statistical significance testing, confidence intervals, and meta-analysis. *Evaluation & the Health Professions, 18*, 408–427.

Sedlmeier, P., & Gigerenzer, G. (1989). Do studies of statistical power have an effect on the power of studies? *Psychological Bulletin, 105,* 309–316.

Severo, N. C., & Zelen, M. (1960). Normal approximation to the chi-square and non-central *F* probability functions. *Biometrika, 47,* 411–416.

Sterling, T. D. (1959). Publication decisions and their possible effects on inferences drawn from tests of significance—or vice versa. *Journal of the American Statistical Association, 54,* 30–34.

Underwood, B. J. (1948a). Retroactive and proactive inhibition after five and forty-eight hours. *Journal of Experimental Psychology, 38,* 29–38.

Underwood, B. J. (1948b). "Spontaneous recovery" of verbal associations. *Journal of Experimental Psychology, 38,* 429–439.

Underwood, B. J. (1957). Interference and forgetting. *Psychological Review, 64,* 49–60.

Underwood, B. J. (1983). *Attributes of memory.* Glenview, IL: Scott, Foresman.

Underwood, B. J., & Postman, L. (1960). Extra-experimental sources of interference in forgetting. *Psychological Review, 67,* 73–95.

Weinberg, S. (1981). The decay of the proton. *Scientific American, 244*(6), 64–75.

Will, C. M. (1990). General relativity at 75: How right was Einstein? *Science, 250,* 770–776.

Zechmeister, E. B., & Nyberg, S. E. (1982). *Human memory: An introduction to research and theory.* Monterey, CA: Brooks/Cole.

Chapter 8

Goodness of Approximation in the Linear Model

Roderick P. McDonald
University of Illinois

A demonstration is given, based on well-known theory, that measures of effect sizes in a linear (ANOVA-type) model can be reinterpreted as measures of goodness of approximation when the effect is omitted from the model. Specifically, in the linear model the geometric mean of the likelihood ratio reduces to the conventional standardized effect size, and constitutes a measure of goodness of approximation. Discussion focuses on the problem of a statistically significant interaction term that we might wish to regard as negligible. Because it is not yet settled how, or even whether, indices of goodness of approximation can be used in the context of structural equation models where they originate, the cautious conclusion is drawn that their application to linear models may provide support for an investigator's decision to retain a restrictive model—for example, a model without interaction—but cannot be a substitute for judgment.

If a first-person opening is permitted here, I may begin by noting that for much of my teaching life (shared about evenly between education and psychology) I have led a double life, teaching (without entire conviction) reluctant undergraduates how to use t and F to reject restrictive hypotheses, and teaching (also without entire conviction) not-so-reluctant graduates how to use goodness-of-fit indices in structural models for multivariate data to retain restrictive hypotheses. It does not take any heavy algebra to resolve the schism between these classes of problem, by showing how a treatment of goodness of approximation can be applied to both, but it does require putting a slight twist on the obvious, and a few minor technicalities. The object of this chapter is to give such a treatment, including a simple account of the technicalities, and some discussion of the limitations of the treatment of goodness of approximation to be offered.

As an aside, I remark that in one of my earliest publications (McDonald & O'Hara, 1964), on size-distance invariance, I had an eight-factor split-split plot design, which gave me a technically significant seventh-order interaction involving apparatus-counterbalancing conditions, and some huge desired main effects. I cheated by reporting individual tests on the main effects. I have never lost sleep over this, but 30 years later I possibly am inventing excuses. A central motive and a central focus for the following remarks is the problem of ignoring a statistically significant interaction in order to interpret main effects.

In the current resurgence of criticism directed at significance testing, the question is being examined from a variety of perspectives in this volume and elsewhere. I think I must begin by restating the best case, as I see it, for testing the significance of a null hypothesis. This has always been, for me as for many, close to the account critiqued by Cohen (1994). With the aid of the humble t test I explain to my students that statistical tests are patterned after the classical *modus tollens*: if null hypothesis (H_0) then not-these-data (not-D), but D therefore not-H_0. In the statistical context this is modified into: If H_0 then D improbable ($< \alpha$), therefore either not-H_0 or the improbable has occurred. It is then rational though possibly an error to conclude not-H_0, rather than conclude that the improbable has occurred. Like, I trust, almost all instructors, I teach my students why we may not conclude that H_0 is "improbable"/ "unlikely." It is perhaps not our fault if they do not learn what we teach them, and fall into what Cohen has described as the common error of treating α as the probability of H_0 (See also Falk & Greenbaum, 1995). I also attempt to teach my reluctant undergraduates that the only good thing about null/nil hypotheses is that they imply a definite probability for our data, whereas the alternative hypotheses do not. The next delicate task for the instructor (as I see it) is to let the students in on the not-so-well-kept secret that all point hypotheses are false, so the null/nil hypothesis is just a *facon de parler*, and the test of significance is just a formal move in a game directed at publishing. One then moves rapidly on to the important part, the estimation of effect sizes, with standard errors/confidence intervals (noting that the intervals possibly contain the null point), and makes contextual remarks about the objectives of pure/scientific behavioral research—the identification of causes and the magnitude of their effects—and the much more varied objectives of applied research.

At this point, for some of us, the restrictive hypothesis can be safely left behind. However, it returns, whether we notice this or not, when we move on to more complex models, as for example in multifactorial designs, with their potential for significant(?)/non-negligible(?) interactions. In a true experiment with just two treatment conditions, to which subjects are randomly assigned, most investigators will suppose they are studying the contrasting (causal) effects of the conditions. As anyone familiar with causal modeling knows, the paradigmatic control-treatment (t test) situation lacks several kinds of generality. One kind of generality can be approached by adding further potentially causal factors to make a multifactorial design (preferably balanced). In many applications of such designs, whether with or without strong theoretical backing, the investigator will be hoping to find that the effects are additive, yielding a simple model for the causal relations. (Of course, there are exceptions, where the investigator theoretically hopes for an interaction.) Suppose we analyze a factorial design in the traditional way, at some sample size, and find highly "significant" main effects and a technically "significant" interaction, with $\alpha = .05$! (Suppose also that the interaction is disordinal, and so certainly cannot be removed by rescaling the response measure.) What the experimenter might wish to do, if it could be permitted by the rules of the game, is to regard the interaction as negligible, though technically significant, and retain a simple intelligible model of additive effects, that is, retain a theoretically satisfactory restrictive model that sufficiently approximates the behavior under study. Of course, at a sufficiently large sample size, all interactions will be "highly significant." A possible tactic is to compute the size of the interaction and judge it to be "small," but we see here a hint that we might wish to ask about the goodness of approximation of the additive model to the actual, not-quite-additive process that generated the data. For one way of doing this, we turn to structural models for multivariate responses. An embarrassing aspect of the following exposition (which makes no particular claim to originality) is that we soon see that the treatment of goodness of fit in structural models comes directly out of the counterpart results for the linear analysis of variance (ANOVA) cases, and the only reason why these have not been fully developed in that context is that mathematical statisticians have seemingly not regarded the question as interesting.[1] Before we consider ANOVA applications of these ideas, some general review of goodness of approximation in the context of structural equation models is necessary.

Jöreskog's (1967) maximum likelihood (ML) treatment of the common factor model, and the elaboration of this and more general linear structural relations models in commercially available computer programs was greeted enthusiastically by many of us, as bringing these models into a respectable statistical form, primarily through the availability of an asymptotic chi-square test for the "acceptance"/"rejection" of a restrictive multivariate model. Examples include a specified number of factors in an exploratory factor model, or a specified confirmatory factor pattern, or a carefully specified set of equations representing a hypothesis of presence versus absence of causal pathways in nonexperimental data. It is convenient from here on to refer to the researcher using an ANOVA-type model—the classical linear model—as an *experimentalist*, and the researcher using structural models in nonexperimental data as a *structural*

---

[1] I understand that unpublished work by Steiger (1990a, 1990b) has addressed this question, but I am not aware of its nature. McDonald (1989) noted that such a development should be straightforward. The present account is essentially what was meant by that remark.

modeler, and regard them as dealing, respectively, with *experimental* and *structural* data. Our objective is to study the relationship between measures of (mis-)fit in structural data and in experimental data. The boundaries of these classes of situation are not, in this nontechnical account, being made absolutely clear, but at least the reader will recognize representative examples.

After the introduction of technology for fitting structural models by ML, it soon became apparent that the structural modeler has, in some sense, the opposite intention to the experimentalist. The latter hopes to "reject" a restrictive hypothesis of the absence of certain causal effects in favor of their presence—rejection permits publication. If it appears that no factor in the experiment has an effect, the experimentalist has nothing to say. The former wishes to "accept" a restrictive model of the absence of certain causal effects—acceptance permits publication. If every variable has a causal effect on every other, we have a model that trivially fits and unintelligibly accounts for every data set, and the structural modeler has nothing to say.

In the context of a science of the determination of behavior by treatments/specific causes, the belief that all restrictive hypotheses are false is equivalent in applications to the belief that all treatments have effects on all responses. (I recall a not very good line of Victorian poetry: "Thou canst not stir a flower without troubling a star.") A moment's reflection (here substituting for the hundred pages or so that we could expect from a philosopher of science on this issue) reveals that if all treatments affect all responses, neither experimental nor structural studies can possibly tell us anything usefully intelligible. It also reveals that if scientific inquiry can proceed it is because some treatment effects are small enough to be negligible, at least to a "first approximation." (The star will not be greatly troubled. And please, let us not invoke notions from chaos theory here!)

From 1967 on, structural modelers, with varying reaction times and varying degrees and forms of insight, came to realize that the asymptotic chi-square test cannot be used (even supposing that the experimentalists' t's and F's could be), because it is no better than an indirect measure of sample size (which they need to know to get the chi-square). For a sufficiently small sample size, the simplest structural model cannot be rejected. For a sufficiently large sample size, every restrictive model will be rejected. (There may be some very pure psychometric theorists, kept aseptically free from empirical data, and inhabiting a lab devoted entirely to computer simulations, who have not yet made this discovery.)

The problem thus arising was clearly and beautifully stated in a classic of the psychometric literature—the seminal article by Tucker and Lewis (1973), in which they defined a measure of goodness of approximation based on the limiting value of a function of the likelihood ratio as the sample size becomes indefinitely large. (In general the likelihood ratio itself will go to zero in the limit.) In fitting a structural model to multivariate data we collect measures on p variables from a sample of subjects of size N, and compute the sample covariance matrix **S**. (Often, in applications, this is the sample correlation matrix.) The sample is drawn from a population with unknown covariance matrix Σ, which, we now recognize, will not fit any restrictive model except approximately, in general. To fit a restrictive, approximating model, Σ_0, by ML, we set the computer program to minimize a *discrepancy function*, given by

$$g = \operatorname{Tr}(\mathbf{S}\Sigma_0^{-1}) - \ln|\mathbf{S}\Sigma_0^{-1}| - p. \tag{8.1}$$

Nonspecialist readers may be content to take on trust the following statements:

1. The value of g depends on **S** and is a function of Σ_0, which in turn is a function of the m parameters in the structural model—factor loadings, factor correlations, and unique variances in the common factor model, or path coefficients and residual variances/covariances in a causal path model—so the function is minimized with respect to these parameters.

2. The value of g is necessarily positive, is equal to zero if and only if **S** is exactly reproduced by Σ_0, and in a sense is large or small according as the differences (discrepancies) between the p^2 elements of Σ_0 and the corresponding elements in **S** are large or small. It is a "discrepancy function" because it is one possible global measure of these discrepancies.

3. The quantity g is derived as

$$g = -(2/N)\ln L, \tag{8.2}$$

where L is the ratio of the likelihood of the data under the restrictive hypothesis to their likelihood under the alternative supposition of no restriction.

We here ignore mathematical pedantries and regard the likelihood of the data as simply their probability for a given set of values of the parameters. The likelihood ratio is necessarily a number between zero and unity, because it is a ratio of probabilities and because the probability of data under a restriction cannot be greater than its probability without the restriction, hence correspondingly g is necessarily nonnegative.

4. After minimization,

$$v = Ng \tag{8.3}$$

is distributed as chi-square in large samples with degrees of freedom given by

$$q = \frac{p(p+1)}{2} - m \tag{8.4}$$

(if the model is identified), provided that the restrictive hypothesis is true.

The early naive application of these results was to the acceptance/rejection of the restrictive hypothesis at some level of significance α. However, it is now widely recognized that, in applications, even if we had the entire population, its actual covariance matrix Σ would be different from the restricted Σ_0, which is at best an approximation to it, so we have two discrepancies to consider: that between sample S and population Σ—the error of sampling—and that between Σ and Σ_0—the error of approximation. (For an excellent account of aspects of this problem, see Browne & Cudeck, 1993.) In the special case of the common factor model, Tucker and Lewis (1973) noted that, by a mathematical result in Lawley (1940), the discrepancy function g closely approximates a sum of squares of residual correlations after fitting the model, thus giving a more readily understandable meaning to it as a global measure of the discrepancies. Steiger and Lind (1980) also noted this fact and suggested accordingly that g calculated with the (unknown) population Σ substituted for the known sample S is a natural measure of population badness of fit—or, we now call it, the error of approximation—to a given common factor model. We denote the population counterpart of g by γ. The quantity g is a consistent estimator of γ, but is biased in small samples. McDonald (1989) pointed out that an unbiased estimate of the error of approximation, γ, is given by

$$\hat{\gamma} = g - \left(\frac{q}{N}\right), \tag{8.5}$$

or

$$\hat{\gamma} = \frac{(v - q)}{N}, \tag{8.6}$$

that is, chi-square minus degrees of freedom, re-scaled by dividing by sample size. (The quantity γ can also be recognized as a re-scaled version of the noncentrality parameter used in power calculations in connection with the chi-square test of significance, but that is not our present concern.) The error of approximation γ is a necessarily nonnegative number, zero if there is no approximation error, and increasing with the general global amount of discrepancy between the unrestricted Σ and the restricted (modeled) Σ_0. The estimate can take small negative values due to sampling. One way to understand the quantity γ is to recognize it, by Equation 8.2, as minus twice the limit, as the sample size increases, of the arithmetic mean of the contributions of the N observations to the (negative) log likelihood—a "natural" measure of "distance" between the restricted model and the actual distribution.

McDonald (1989) accordingly suggested as an index of *goodness of approximation* the corresponding (geometric) mean in the population of the likelihood ratio itself, that is, the population limit of $L^{(1/N)}$ in Equation 8.2, which we denote here by Λ_g, and refer to as the GMLR (geometric mean likelihood ratio). This goodness of approximation measure ranges from zero to unity, being equal to unity when the approximation is perfect. The sample quantity $L^{(1/N)}$ is (tautologically) a consistent estimator of Λ_g, but a better estimate is given by what some colleagues have kindly referred to as McDonald's index of goodness of approximation,

$$\begin{aligned} M_c &= \exp[-(1/2)\hat{\gamma}] \\ &= \exp[-(1/2)(v-q)/N] \end{aligned} \tag{8.7}$$

(See McDonald, 1989.)

A number of indices of goodness of fit, some of which are interpretable as measures of goodness or badness of approximation, have been suggested by now. Some are *absolute*, whereas others are *relative* to another model, chosen to be more restrictive, referred to as a "null" model. Some indices are designed to incorporate an intuitive notion of parsimony, usually represented by some arbitrarily though plausibly created function combining $\hat{\gamma}$ or g with q, the degrees of freedom, or with m, the number of parameters. The algebraic properties of a number of these have been studied by McDonald and Marsh (1990). It is not necessary to consider these alternatives here. Instead, we turn to the question of defining counterpart global measures of approximation for general ANOVA applications. The results presented are extremely obvious, but do not seem to be widely known.

Most textbook accounts of the general linear model and the associated technology of analysis of variance are based on the least squares (LS) principle, often with a remark on the side that "obviously," or by brief demonstration, ML estimators under usual assumptions are equivalent to LS and need not be considered further. Then well-known properties of chi-square are invoked for the distribution of the Mean Squares to arrive at the necessary (Snedecor) F ratios. Here we call on some results based on the application of ML estimation that are well known, yet not as widely known among practitioners as they should be. For simplicity we consider a fixed-factor model with equal cell sizes. For a set of possible observations $Y_{ij}, j = 1,..., J$ treatment conditions or treatment combinations in a multifactorial design, $i = 1,..., N$ replications per cell, we compare two models. The first is the simple nonrestrictive model

$$M_u: \ Y_{ij} = \mu + \alpha_j + E_{ij}, \tag{8.8}$$

with the usual side condition

$$\sum_j \alpha_j = 0, \tag{8.9}$$

where the residuals E_{ij} are independently and identically distributed normally with mean zero, variance σ_E^2. (In choosing to regard the distribution of Y_{ij} as characterized by the parameters of M_u and the assumption of normality and homoscedasticity, there are still restrictions, but generally these would be regarded as not in question.) The second is the restrictive model

$$M_r: \ Y_{ij} = \mu + E_{ij}. \tag{8.10}$$

(Because our concern is with the goodness of approximation of M_r to M_u, these models have not been labeled H_1, H_0.)

The distribution of Y_{ij} under M_u for some value of α_j is

$$\Pr(Y_{ij}|\alpha_j) = (2\pi\sigma)^{-\frac{1}{2}} \exp\left\{-(Y_{ij} - \mu - \alpha_j)^2 / (2\sigma_E^2)\right\} \tag{8.11}$$

and the likelihoods of the sample are, respectively, L_u, the product of these probabilities over i and j under M_u, and L_r, the corresponding product with $\alpha_j = 0$ under M_r. By standard methods it is known—see, for example, Scheffe (1959)—that in the unrestricted model the ML estimators of the parameters are, as in LS theory,

$$\hat{\mu} = \sum_i \sum_j Y_{ij} / (NJ) = \overline{Y}_{..},$$

$$\hat{\alpha}_j = \sum_i Y_{ij}/N - \sum_i \sum_j Y_{ij}/(NJ) = \overline{Y}_{.j} - \overline{Y}_{..} \qquad (8.12)$$

$$\hat{\sigma}_E^2 = \sum_j \sum_i (Y_{ij} - \overline{Y}_{.j})^2 \Big/(NJ) = SS_W/(NJ) \qquad (8.13)$$

and in the restrictive model they are

$$\hat{\mu} = \sum_j \sum_i Y_{ij} \Big/(NJ) = \overline{Y}_{..}, \qquad (8.14)$$

and

$$\hat{\sigma}_E^2 = \sum_j \sum_i (Y_{ij} - \overline{Y}_{..})^2 \Big/(NJ) = SS_T/(NJ). \qquad (8.15)$$

(We use SS_T etc. here following universally accepted notational conventions.) Of more interest to us here than the equivalence of the ML to the LS estimates is the further result that at the ML/LS values of the parameters, we have

$$L_r = (2\pi SS_T)^{-N/2} \exp(-N/2) \qquad (8.16)$$

and

$$L_u = (2\pi SS_W)^{-N/2} \exp(-N/2), \qquad (8.17)$$

so

$$L_r/L_u = (SS_T/SS_W)^{-N/2}. \qquad (8.18)$$

As in the derivation of McDonald's index of goodness of approximation given earlier, we define the geometric mean likelihood ratio (GMLR) as the limit Λ_g as N increases, of

$$(L_r/L_u)^{1/N} = (SS_W/SS_T)^{1/2}. \qquad (8.19)$$

It can be shown that this (nonvanishing) limit is given by

$$\Lambda_g = \sqrt{\frac{\sigma_E^2}{\sigma_E^2 + \dfrac{1}{J}\sum_j \alpha_j^2}} . \tag{8.20}$$

We have thus arrived, by a rather roundabout route, in familiar territory. The index

$$f = \sqrt{\frac{\sum_j \alpha_j^2}{J\sigma_E^2}} \tag{8.21}$$

has been given by Cohen (1988) as a global measure of effect size in a suitable ("standardizing") metric. We see that f^2 can be written as a function of the GMLR, namely

$$f^2 = \frac{1 - \Lambda_g^2}{\Lambda_g^2}, \tag{8.22}$$

and conversely

$$\Lambda_g = \left(1 + f^2\right)^{-\frac{1}{2}}. \tag{8.23}$$

The proportion of the total variance of Y due to treatments has been recommended (see Hays, 1994) as a general measure of association between the treatments and the response. This may be written as

$$\omega^2 = \frac{\sum_j \alpha_j^2}{J\sigma_Y^2}, \tag{8.24}$$

where

$$\sigma_Y^2 = \sigma_E^2 + \frac{1}{J}\sum_j \alpha_j^2, \tag{8.25}$$

or as

$$\omega^2 = \frac{f^2}{1 + f^2}. \tag{8.26}$$

When cell membership corresponds to levels of a quantitative treatment, ω^2 can be identified with the (population) correlation ratio, commonly denoted by η^2. We see that ω^2 can be written as

$$\omega^2 = 1 - \Lambda_g^2. \tag{8.27}$$

(We are not yet concerned with sample estimates—possibly unbiased—of these indices.) The point hypothesis that the restrictive model is "true" can be expressed, equivalently, as $f = 0$, $\omega^2 = 0$, and—we now further observe—as $\Lambda_g = 1$, against the alternative that $f > 0$, $\omega^2 > 0$, $\Lambda_g < 1$.

Further restrictive models can be defined by setting some specific α_j values to zero—without loss of generality, the first R of them, say. These can be expressed as

$$\sum_{j=1}^{R} f_j^2$$

or

$$\sum_{J=1}^{R} \omega_j^2$$

In a slightly more general account of Equations 8.10 through 8.20, we replace M_r in Equation 8.10 by

$$M_r : Y_{ij} = \mu + \alpha_{R+1} +, \ldots, + \alpha_J + E_{ij}, \tag{8.28}$$

which leads by a parallel argument, to

$$\Lambda_g \{\alpha_1 = 0, \ldots, \alpha_R = 0\} = \frac{\sigma_E^2}{\sigma_E^2 + \dfrac{1}{J-R} \displaystyle\sum_{j=R+1}^{J} \alpha_j^2}, \tag{8.29}$$

with obvious notation.

In this more general model, the GMLR is no longer the unit complement of

$$\omega^2 \{\alpha_1 = 0, \ldots, \alpha_R = 0\} = \frac{\dfrac{1}{J-R} \displaystyle\sum_{j=R+1}^{J} \alpha_j^2}{\sigma_Y^2}, \tag{8.30}$$

because the denominator in this last expression is still that given by Equation 8.25.

The modest proposal being made here is simply to turn the regular notions of measures of effect size and association upside-down. Here we regard Λ_g—the geometric mean likelihood ratio—as a measure of goodness of approximation of a false but possibly adequate restrictive model to the distribution of Y_{ij}. We accordingly reinterpret f or f^2 as a measure of error of approximation, as well as a measure of effect size in the unrestricted alternative hypothesis.

It may be shown that f^2 fits into the same general framework as the *discrepancy due to approximation* discussed by Browne and Cudeck (1993) in the context of structural models, and is, in the same sense, a measure of error of approximation. Because the context of application is very different, we cannot assume simply that all theory of or empirical experience with such measures carries over from structural models to the linear/ANOVA context.

The motivation/excuse for arriving at these results via the GMLR was simply to bring back to the classical statistical model the treatment of error/goodness of approximation that was carried from it into the structural modeling literature. The remaining tasks here are to comment on procedures for estimating these indices and to consider how they might be used in applications.

It should suffice to present the remaining results for the special case of a two-way factorial design with equal numbers of replications per cell, from which more general principles can be seen.[2] Following Hays (1994) for notation, we consider the model

$$Y_{ijk} = \mu + [\alpha\beta]_{jk} + E_{ijk} , \tag{8.31}$$

or

$$Y_{ijk} = \mu + \alpha_j + \beta_k + (\alpha\beta)_{jk} + E_{ijk} , \tag{8.32}$$

$i = 1,...,N$, $j = 1,..., J$, $k = 1,...,K$, where Equation 8.31 represents the simple between/within decomposition, with $[\alpha\beta]_{jk}$ as cell effects, which are further decomposed in Equation 8.32 as main effects and interaction. (Note that in Hays'

---

[2]A major limitation of this discussion is that it omits all consideration of the precision of sample estimates of effect sizes and derived measures of goodness of approximation. I understand that work by Steiger and Fouladi (1997, Chapter 9 of this volume) addresses this question *inter alia*.

TABLE 8.1
ANOVA Expressions

Source	df	SS	MS	E(MS)
A	$J-1$	SS_A	$SS_A / (J-1)$	$\sigma_E^2 + \dfrac{KN \sum_j \alpha_j^2)}{J-1}$
B	$K-1$	SS_B	$SS_B / (K-1)$	$\sigma_E^2 + \dfrac{JN \sum_j \beta_j^2}{K-1}$
AB	$(J-1)(K-1)$	SS_{AB}	$SS_{AB} / [(J-1)(K-1)]$	$\sigma_E^2 + \dfrac{N \sum_j \sum_k (\alpha\beta)_{jk}^2}{(J-1)(K-1)}$
Bet	$JK-1$	SS_{Bet}	$SS_{Bet} / (JK-1)$	$\sigma_E^2 + \dfrac{\sum_j \sum_k [\alpha\beta]_{jk}^2)}{JK-1}$
W	$JK(N-1)$	SS_W	$SS_W / [JK(N-1)]$	σ_E^2
T	$JKN-1$	SS_T		

notation parentheses enclose an interaction whereas square brackets enclose a cell mean.) As usual we impose, in Equation 8.32, the identification conditions

$$\sum_{j=1}^{J} \alpha_j = \sum_{k=1}^{K} \beta_k = \sum_{j=1}^{J} \sum_{k=1}^{K} (\alpha\beta)_{jk} = 0.$$

With these conditions

$$\sum_{j=1}^{J} \sum_{k=1}^{K} [\alpha\beta]_{jk}^2 = K \sum_{j=1}^{J} \alpha_j^2 + J \sum_{k=1}^{K} \beta_k^2 + \sum_{j=1}^{J} \sum_{k=1}^{K} (\alpha\beta)_{jk}^2. \tag{8.33}$$

Table 8.1 represents the ANOVA for these models.

Table 8.2 gives a simple 2×2 numerical example, constructed so that the interaction is technically significant ($p < .05$), and the main effect of A gives $p < .001$, whereas that of B gives $p < .01$.

The conventional position would be that we cannot interpret the "main effects" in the presence of "significant" interaction. Here, we wish to ask if the model with zero interaction can be considered an acceptable approximation. From the expected values in Table 8.1, unbiased estimators of the quantities we need are easily obtained. They may be listed as follows, together with their values as obtained from the example of Table 8.2:

$$\hat{\sigma}_E^2 = MS_W = 1.0, \tag{8.34}$$

$$\sum_j \hat{\alpha}_j^2 = [SS_A - (J-1)MS_W]/(KN) = .6145 \tag{8.35}$$

$$\sum_j \hat{\beta}_k^2 = [SS_B - (K-1)MS_W]/(JN) = .328 \tag{8.36}$$

$$\sum_j \sum_k (\widehat{\alpha\beta})_{jk}^2 = [SS_{AB} - (J-1)(K-1)MS_W]/N = .317 \tag{8.37}$$

$$\sum_j \sum_k [\widehat{\alpha\beta}]_{jk}^2 = [SS_{Bet} - (JK-1)MS_W]/N = 2.202 \tag{8.38}$$

The unbiased estimate of the total variance of Y_{ijk} in Equation 8.25 is given by

$$\hat{\sigma}_Y^2 = (SS_T + MS_W)/(JKN) = 1.5505. \tag{8.39}$$

Not surprisingly, the sample estimators are easily seen to satisfy the sample counterpart of Equation 8.33.

The resulting estimates of f^2, ω^2, Λ_g^2, and Λ_g are given in Table 8.3. Note that in this table f^2 has a dual interpretation. The sources listed at the top are thought of (a) as sources of the proportions of variance ω^2, (b) as sources of the effect sizes f^2, (c) as yielding errors of approximation f^2 and the remaining goodness or badness of approximation measures when these sources are omitted

TABLE 8.2

ANOVA Example

Source	df	SS	MS	F
A	1	13.29	13.29	13.29
B	1	7.56	7.56	7.56
AB	1	4.17	4.17	4.17
Bet	3	25.02	8.34	8.34
W	3	36.00	1.00	
T	3	61.02		

TABLE 8.3
Estimated Coefficients

	AB	B	A	AB&B	AB, A&B
df	1	1	1	2	3
π	1/3	1/3	1/3	2/3	1
f^2	.079	.164	.307	.243	.550
ω^2	.051	.106	.198	.157	.355
Λ_g^2	.927	.859	.765	.804	.645
Λ_g	.962	.930	.875	.897	.803
ρ	.144	.298	.538	.442	1
h	.856	.702	.456	.558	0
$h^{(\rho)}$	.285	.234	.152	.372	0

to yield a restrictive model.

At the time of writing, quite a large number of indices of goodness/badness of fit/approximation have been invented, and one can expect to see an indefinite number of further indices, because it is not in fact a difficult task to create a plausible global norm on the misfit of a model. I intend to use restraint here and not survey the possibilities, or even many of those so far thought of. It seems necessary, however, to show how a few further indices might be considered in the context of the linear model, if only to recommend against their proliferation. As already mentioned, some indices have been introduced to represent *relative fit*—the fit of a restrictive model relative to some more restrictive model, conventionally referred to as the null model. Some indices are intended to capture the intuitive notion of "parsimony" by including degrees of freedom or number of parameters estimated in the index. In the present context, a likely choice for a null model would be the model in which all effects are zero. To understand how we might transfer some of the indices developed in structural modeling work to the present type of application, we define a *badness-of-fit* ratio (McDonald & Marsh, 1990), as

$$\rho = f^2 / f_0^2 \tag{8.40}$$

where, in the present application, f^2 is the error of approximation Equation 8.22 in the restrictive model considered, and f_0^2 is the error of approximation in the model of all-zero-effects. We also may define a *parsimony ratio* as

$$\pi = d_r / d_0 \qquad (8.41)$$

where d_r, d_0 are the corresponding degrees of freedom. In counterpart structural modeling applications, McDonald & Marsh showed that a number of relative indices are at least consistent estimators of the index

$$h = 1 - \rho, \qquad (8.42)$$

which is defined to measure (relative) goodness of approximation. One was given independently by McDonald & Marsh (1990) and Bentler (1990), and referred to respectively as an "unbiased relative fit index" (URFI) and a "comparative fit index" (CFI). The Tucker-Lewis Index is a consistent estimator of

$$\tau = 1 - (\rho / \pi). \qquad (8.43)$$

Both the Tucker-Lewis Index and the URFI/CFI approach unity as the error of approximation f^2 approaches zero, at a rate that depends on the error of approximation for the chosen null model. (See Browne & Cudeck, 1993, for a cogent argument favoring an absolute index of badness/goodness of fit over one relative to a chosen null model.) McDonald and Marsh were not so much offering the URFI for possible use as showing how its algebra compared with that of other indices in their survey. James, Mulaik & Brett (1982)—see also Mulaik et al. (1989)—pointed out that (relative) *parsimonious goodness-of-fit indices* can be obtained by multiplying a (relative) goodness-of-fit index defined on the interval from zero to unity (where unity represents perfect fit) by the parsimony ratio. An example is Jöreskog's "adjusted goodness-of-fit index." (See Tanaka, 1993, for a good account of this and similar indices.) Here we could, if we wish, easily apply this principle to h in Equation 8.42, yielding

$$h^{(\rho)} = \pi h. \qquad (8.44)$$

(It would not make sense to apply it to Λ_g, which is an absolute index.) McDonald and Marsh (1990) pointed out that the parsimonious form of the Tucker-Lewis Index may be written as

$$\pi \tau = \pi - \rho, \qquad (8.45)$$

wherein the parsimony ratio enters additively, whereas it enters the original Tucker-Lewis Index as a divisor. There seems no theoretical ground for choosing between an additive, a multiplicative, or a divisor adjustment, or indeed any other function combining error of approximation with a parsimony ratio or degrees of freedom. Table 8.3 contains estimates of the three additional indices, p, h, and $h^{(p)}$. Note that the last column represents also the null model.

We can certainly estimate these measures of approximation (and effect size). The question remains whether recommendations can be made for their use, as bases for the possible acceptance of a restrictive, false, approximating model. This is a much more difficult problem than that of defining and estimating them, because the question is unclear, so we do not know what would count as an answer. In commercial programs for structural equation modeling, we find a large number of goodness-/badness-of-fit indices computed and printed. These are not all in one-to-one correspondence and they do not all have clear guidelines, whether based on rational/experiential grounds or the authority of the manual or of the originator, so the user has some freedom (which is open to abuse) to choose the most pleasing index post facto to justify acceptance of an approximating model for the purpose of publication. In applications to the linear/ANOVA model, Cohen (1988) has suggested guidelines for f, with

> $f = .1$ a "small" effect size
>
> $f = .25$ a "medium" effect size
>
> $f \geq .4$ a "large" effect size.

(These guidelines are offered for use only in the absence of better knowledge. Cohen's text contains much careful and wise advice that should warn readers against the simple mechanical application of such criteria.) If, contrary to Cohen's intent, we took "small" to mean "negligible," in the present example, with a smallest f of .281, we would find little excuse for neglecting the technically significant interaction, for the sake of adopting a simple additive model. For such an excuse one might turn to the estimated GMLR, and claim that the mean likelihood ratio of .962 for omitting the interaction is very close to unity. Any reader who has experienced the socializing practices of courses on research methods in behavioral science will reflexively respond to an index defined on the range from zero to unity, with unity representing the ideal. It is left to the reader to judge whether the probability-ratio metric contained in the GMLR carries more authority than the metric of other indices.

Taking a cautious, scholarly attitude, one would conclude from what has been shown that the same devices can be used in the classical linear model for experimental treatments as in structural modeling to get global measures of approximation, and that the logic that makes us seek approximating models rather than reject null hypotheses applies in the same way to both. There is no purely theoretical ground for offering guidelines for the use of such global measures.

And it is not clear what kind of experience—in the absence of a theoretical basis—could be used for the development of guidelines. It might seem that if there are other bases for judgment that can be used to validate the use of a goodness/badness of approximation index, these judgments might be better used instead. (For example, in structural models it is commonly much more informative to examine the individual discrepancies than to look only at a global index.) As to the use of indices relative to a null model, or indices attempting to take account of differential model complexity, it seems that these are still awaiting the necessary critical work in the context of structural modeling where they originate.

I propose to end as I began, with some first-person remarks of a more speculative character. In the example of Tables 8.2 and 8.3, I am biased in favor of the evidence given by the GMLR, with its probability-ratio metric, as giving some legitimacy to a prior wish to regard an additive model as a sufficient approximation to the (causal) process that generates the distribution of Y_{ijk}. I weigh this against the f value of .281—rated by Cohen's guidelines as a "medium" effect size. I would find it entirely understandable if many readers disagree. My a priori bias in favor of the additive model as a first approximation rests on the belief that additive models commonly express intelligible behavioral laws and allow accumulation of evidence from similar but distinct studies.

I refer again to Browne and Cudeck (1993) for the reasons why I do not recommend, and would not, in the example, take evidence from, the relative indices. I am *a fortiori* not tempted to conclude from the parsimonious relative fit index $h^{(\rho)}$ in Table 8.3 that the "best" model omits both the interaction and the main effect of B. More generally, I remain unconvinced that we have any indices (nonmonotone functions of some measure of "model complexity") that can be used for the objective selection of a "best-fitting" model from a set of given models. (See Browne & Cudeck, 1993; McDonald and Marsh, 1990.) With arguments similar to those against the incorporation of a null model, I presently recommend against incorporating any measure of model complexity in an index of goodness/badness of approximation. Instead, we can take account of model complexity separately, leaving greater latitude for contextual judgment by the investigator. Further critical work is needed.

A final speculative remark: If we are to develop a truly integrated behavioral science, given that experiments are rarely replicated but sometimes imitated, it is appropriate to ask what are the expected invariants across similar but distinct experimental studies. Standardized effect sizes, as discussed here—or, an equivalent, the errors of approximation—involve the residual variance (i.e., the error variance) in each experiment. This variance includes errors of measurement—due to the instrument/test device used to obtain the response—and the effects of omitted variables—including, let us say, "individual differences" in response characterizing members of the subject pools. Experiments that are otherwise comparable will differ in standardized effect sizes/coefficients of association when circumstances alter the error variance of the experiment, whereas unstandardized effect sizes may be expected to remain invariant. (This is part of the more general problem of noninvariance of correlations and of standardized regressions across distinct populations when the unstandardized regressions are invariant.) If behavioral science is to be integrative and theoretically intelligible—that is, not mindlessly empiricist—some way must be found to deal with the problems of non-invariance that inevitably must arise.

APPLICATION IDEAS

The reader of this chapter has a right to be disappointed, as all I have shown is that conventional measures of effect sizes can be reinterpreted as measures of approximation when those effects are omitted from the model. It follows that if we knew how to use goodness-of-approximation indices in structural equation models we could apply that knowledge to the linear models of ANOVA and to other restricted statistical models. I do not believe that we presently know how to use such indices and in particular I do not believe on current evidence that global indices of approximation can or should be used as the sole basis for a decision that a restrictive model is acceptable. Thus the only application idea offered here is that the investigator should use judgment as to the acceptability of an approximating model, or, equivalently, whether specific effects are or are not negligible, and should give the grounds of the judgment in any report of the work. The estimated GMLR, or other appropriate indices, will help support judgment, but will not substitute for it. *Caveat emptor.*

ACKNOWLEDGMENTS

I would like to thank David Budescu, Michael Browne, Larry Hubert, and Larry Jones for their comments on the manuscript. Remaining errors are my own responsibility.

REFERENCES

Bentler, P. M. (1990). Comparative fit indexes in structural models. *Psychological Bulletin, 107,* 238–246.

Browne, M. W., & Cudeck, R. (1993). Alternative ways of assessing model fit. In K. A. Bollen & J. S. Long (Eds.), *Testing structural equation models.* Newbury Park, CA: Sage.

Cohen, J. (1988). *Statistical power analysis for the behavioral sciences* (2nd ed.). Hillsdale, NJ: Lawrence Erlbaum Associates.

Cohen, J. (1994). The earth is round (p<.05). *American Psychologist, 49,* 997–1003.

Falk, R., & Greenbaum, C. W. (1995). Significance tests die hard. *Theory & Psychology, 5,* 75–98.

Hays, W. L. (1994). Statistics. (4th ed.). New York: Holt, Rinehart & Winston.

James, L. R., Mulaik, S. A., & Brett, J. M. (1982). *Causal analysis: Assumptions, models, and data.* Beverly Hills, CA: Sage.

Jöreskog, K. G. (1967). Some contributions to maximum likelihood factor analysis. *Psychometrika, 32,* 443–482.

Lawley, D. N. (1940). The estimation of factor loadings by the method of maximum likelihood. *Proceedings of the Royal Society of Edinburgh,* Section A, *60,* 64–82.

McDonald, R. P. (1989). An index of goodness-of-fit based on noncentrality. *Journal of Classification, 6,* 97–103.

McDonald, R. P., & Marsh, H. W. (1990). Choosing a multivariate model: Noncentrality and goodness of fit. *Psychological Bulletin, 107,* 247–255.

McDonald, R. P., & O'Hara, P. T. (1964). Size-distance invariance and perceptual constancy. *American Journal of Psychology, 77,* 276–280.

Mulaik, S. A., James, L. R., Van Alstine, J., Bennett, N., Lind, S., & Stillwell, C. D. (1989). An evaluation of goodness of fit indices for structural equation models. *Psychological Bulletin, 105,* 430–445.

Scheffe, H. (1959). *The analysis of variance* New York: Wiley.

Steiger, J. H. (1990a). Noncentrality interval estimation and the evaluation of statistical models. Paper presented at the annual meeting of the Psychometric Society, Princeton, July.

Steiger, J. H. (1990b). Noncentrality interval estimation and the evaluation of statistical models. Paper presented at the annual meeting of the Society for Multivariate Experimental Psychology. Newport, R. I., October.

Steiger, J. H., & Lind, J. C. (1980). Statistically-based tests for the number of common factors. Paper presented at the Annual Meeting of the Psychometric Society.

Steiger, J. H., & Fouladi, R. T. (1997). Noncentrality interval estimation and the evaluation of statistical models. In L. Harlow, S. A. Mulaik, & J. H. Steiger (Eds.), *What if there were no significance tests?* Mahwah, NJ: Erlbaum.

Tanaka, J. S. (1993). Multifaceted conceptions of fit in structural equation models. In K. A. Bollen & J. S. Long (Eds.), *Testing structural equation models.* Newbury Park, CA: Sage.

Tucker, L. R., & Lewis, C. (1973). The reliability coefficient for maximum likelihood factor analysis. *Psychometrika, 38,* 1–10.

Chapter 9

Noncentrality Interval Estimation and the Evaluation of Statistical Models

James H. Steiger
University of British Columbia

Rachel T. Fouladi
University of Texas at Austin

Noncentrality-based confidence interval estimates provide a superior alternative to significance testing for assessing model fit in most standard areas of behavioral statistics, from the t test through multiple regression and analysis of variance to the analysis of covariance structures. These confidence intervals provide all the information inherent in a significance test, and more, and deal with situations more traditional interval estimates cannot handle. For example, in the analysis of variance, noncentrality interval estimation allows computation of exact confidence intervals for (a) standardized measures of effect size and (b) statistical power. In multiple regression, one can compute an exact confidence interval on the squared multiple correlation. Because of computational complexities, noncentrality-based confidence intervals seldom have been computed, except in the analysis of covariance structures. Most of the reasons for not using these interval estimates are no longer relevant in the microcomputer age. In this chapter, we review some of the standard techniques, and provide computational examples.

Behavioral statistics has been, and continues to be, dominated by the significance testing tradition. Nearly every major textbook in behavioral statistics spends far more time and energy on the theory and mechanics of significance testing than on any other topic. Periodically, some of the more authoritative writers in our field have questioned this. The list of names includes many (Cohen, Meehl, Guttman, Rozeboom, to name just a few) who have imposing reputations for technical expertise, but also share a common reputation for *perspective*, manifested in an ability to sort out what is important and what is right.

Some important early contributions to the literature on hypothesis testing and interval estimation were reviewed recently by Cohen (1994). Most of the authors, including Cohen, concentrate on the fundamental logical problems and limitations of significance testing, and make broad suggestions for improving the status of practice. A key suggestion that has surfaced repeatedly in these writings is that, as an analytic tool, the *confidence interval* is superior to the significance test. Schmidt and Hunter (1997) echo this view in chapter 3 of this volume, while providing a succinct critique of many of the arguments often used to defend significance testing. Because we agree fundamentally with many of the opinions of Rozeboom (1960), Meehl (1978), Guttman (1977), Cohen (1994), and Schmidt and Hunter (1997), we see no need to review all of their arguments here; but to keep the account relatively self-contained, we review a few key advantages of confidence intervals. Our fundamental contribution, however, is to suggest a significant change in the statistical methodology routinely employed in the most common situations in behavioral statistics. We suggest improved techniques that we think have real merit, and that, if given wide use, offer such substantial advantages that they will surely accelerate the ascendancy of interval estimation. Some of these implementations (such as the noncentrality-based techniques in structural modeling) are relatively new but already quite popular. Some are old, but hardly ever discussed in textbooks. All offer substantial advantages over the significance tests, and in some cases over other interval estimates currently in use. All are computer intensive, and require *very* careful software implementation. This latter fact explains why they have seldom been employed, but why their time finally may have arrived.

We begin by reviewing a situation familiar to us all—the simple two-group experiment based on two independent samples. We review the standard interval estimation procedures, then discuss an alternative *standardized* confidence interval discussed by Hedges and Olkin (1985), but not computationally practical at the time their book was written. We show why this interval estimation approach is superior, not only to the standard *t* test, but also to the standard confidence interval on mean differences discussed in textbooks. We then extend this idea through the analysis of variance, to the analysis of covariance structures, to multiple regression and beyond. So our scope is quite broad. Almost all the significance testing procedures currently recommended in major behavioral statistics books could be replaced with the superior confidence interval approaches we discuss here.

USE AND ABUSE OF SIGNIFICANCE TESTING LOGIC

In this section, we argue, as do numerous colleagues, that significance tests, though almost always reported in the analysis of social science data, are seldom to be preferred, and often simply inappropriate. We begin by returning briefly to first principles. Suppose we are performing a simple two-group experiment in

TABLE 9.1
2 × 2 Table for Statistical Decisions

		State of the World	
		H_0	H_1
Decision	H_0	Correct Acceptance	Type II Error β
	H_1	Type I Error α	Correct Rejection

which an experimental group is compared to a control group. The theoretical question of interest is frequently phrased as, "Has the experimental treatment made any difference?"

In this case, the statistical null and alternative hypotheses are

$$H_0: \mu_1 = \mu_2 \qquad H_1: \mu_1 \neq \mu_2.$$

We test this hypothesis, in practice, by taking two samples, often (but not necessarily) of equal size, and computing a two (independent) sample Student's t statistic. If the statistic's absolute value is sufficiently large, we reject H_0. Otherwise, loosely speaking, we "accept" (or, perhaps more appropriately, "fail to reject") H_0.

Back in our undergraduate statistics course, we were taught that, in the significance testing approach, four things can happen, two of them bad. We all memorized a little 2 × 2 table that summarized the possibilities and attached statistical jargon to them (See Table 9.1).

Most of us were steeped in the grand tradition of Educational and Psychological Statistics, i.e., that α, the Type I error rate, must be kept at or below .05, and that, if at all possible, β, the Type II error rate, must be kept low as well.

The conventions are, of course, much more rigid with respect to α than with respect to β. Seldom, if ever, is α allowed to stray above the magical .05 mark. Let's review where that tradition came from.

In the context of significance testing, we can define two basic kinds of situations, reject-support (RS) and accept-support (AS). In RS testing, *the null hypothesis is the opposite of what the researcher actually believes*, and rejecting it supports the researcher's theory. In a two group RS experiment, the experimenter believes the treatment has an effect, and seeks to confirm it through a significance test that rejects the null hypothesis.

In the RS situation, a Type I error represents, in a sense, a "false positive" for the researcher's theory. From society's standpoint, such false positives are particularly undesirable. They result in much wasted effort, especially when the false positive is interesting from a theoretical or political standpoint (or both), and as a result stimulates a substantial amount of research. Such follow-up research will usually not replicate the (incorrect) original work, and much confusion and frustration will result.

In RS testing, a Type II error is a tragedy from the researcher's standpoint, because a theory that is true is, by mistake, not confirmed. So, for example, if a drug designed to improve a medical condition is found (incorrectly) not to produce an improvement relative to a control group, a worthwhile therapy will be lost, at least temporarily, and an experimenter's worthwhile idea will be discounted.

As a consequence, in RS testing, society, in the person of journal editors and reviewers, insists on keeping α low. The statistically well-informed researcher makes it a top priority to keep β low as well. Ultimately, of course, everyone benefits if *both* error probabilities are kept low, but unfortunately there is often, in practice, a trade-off between the two types of error.

The RS situation is by far the more common one, and the conventions relevant to it have come to dominate popular views on statistical testing. As a result, the prevailing views on error rates are that relaxing α beyond a certain level is unthinkable, and that it is up to the researcher to make sure statistical power is adequate. One might argue how appropriate these views are in the context of RS testing, but they are not altogether unreasonable.

In AS testing, the common view on error rates we described above is clearly inappropriate. In AS testing, H_0 *is what the researcher actually believes*, so accepting it supports the researcher's theory. In this case, a Type I error is a false negative for the researcher's theory, and a Type II error constitutes a false positive. Consequently, acting in a way that might be construed as highly *virtuous* in the RS situation, for example, maintaining a very low Type I error rate like .001, is actually "stacking the deck" in favor of the researcher's theory in AS testing.

In both AS and RS situations, it is easy to find examples where significance testing seems strained and unrealistic. Consider first the RS situation. In some such situations, it is simply not possible to have very large samples. An example that comes to mind is social or clinical psychological field research. Researchers in these fields sometimes spend several days interviewing a single subject. A year's research may only yield valid data from 50 subjects. Correlational tests, in particular, have very low power when samples are that small. In such a case, it probably makes sense to relax α beyond .05, if it means that reasonable power can be achieved.

On the other hand, it is possible, in an important sense, to have power that is too high. For example, one might be testing the hypothesis that $\mu_1 = \mu_2$ with sample sizes of a million in each group. In this case, even with trivial differences between groups, the null hypothesis would virtually always be rejected.

The situation becomes even more unnatural in AS testing. Here, if n is too high, the researcher almost inevitably decides against the theory, even when it turns out, in an important sense, to be an excellent approximation to the data. It seems paradoxical indeed that in this context experimental precision seems to work against the researcher.

To summarize, in RS research:

1. The researcher wants to reject H_0.
2. Society wants to control Type I error.
3. The researcher must be very concerned about Type II error.
4. High sample size works for the researcher.
5. If there is "too much power," trivial effects become "highly significant."

In AS research:

1. The researcher wants to accept H_0.
2. "Society" should be worrying about controlling Type II error, although it sometimes gets confused and retains the conventions applicable to RS testing.
3. The researcher must be very careful to control Type I error.
4. High sample size works against the researcher.
5. If there is "too much power," the researcher's theory can be "rejected" by a significance test even though it fits the data almost perfectly.

Strictly speaking, the outcome of a significance test is the dichotomous decision whether or not to reject the null hypothesis. This dichotomy is inherently dissatisfying to psychologists and educators, who frequently use the null hypothesis as a statement of no effect, and are more interested in knowing how big an effect is than whether it is (precisely) zero. This has led to behavior like putting one, two, or three asterisks next to results in tables, or listing p levels next to results, when, in fact, such numbers, across (or sometimes even within!) studies need not be monotonically related to the best estimates of strength of experimental effects, and hence can be extremely misleading. Some writers (e.g., Guttman, 1977) view asterisk-placing behavior as inconsistent with the foundations of significance testing logic.

Probability levels can deceive about the "strength" of a result, especially when presented without supporting information. For example, if, in an ANOVA table, one effect had a p level of .019, and the other a p level of .048, *it might be an error* to conclude that the statistical evidence supported the view that the first effect was stronger than the second. A meaningful interpretation would require additional information. To see why, suppose someone reports a p level of .001. This *could* be representative of a trivial population effect combined with a huge sample size, or a powerful population effect combined with a moderate sample size, or a huge population effect with a small sample. Similarly a p level of .075 *could* represent a powerful effect operating with a small sample, or a tiny effect with a huge sample. Clearly then, we need to be careful when comparing p levels.

In AS testing, which occurs frequently in the context of model fitting in factor analysis or "causal modeling," significance testing logic is basically inappropriate. Rejection of an "almost true" null hypothesis in such situations frequently has been followed by vague statements that the rejection shouldn't be taken too seriously. Failure to reject a null hypothesis usually results in a demand for cumbersome power calculations by a vigilant journal editor. Such problems can be avoided by using confidence intervals.

THE VALUE OF INTERVAL ESTIMATES

Much psychological research is exploratory. The fundamental questions we are usually asking are "What is our best guess for the size of the population effect?" and "How precisely have we determined the population effect size from our sample data?" Significance testing fails to answer these questions directly. Many a researcher, faced with an "overwhelming rejection" of a null hypothesis, cannot resist the temptation to report that it was "significant *well beyond* the .001 level." Yet we have seen previously (and demonstrate conclusively with numerical examples in a subsequent section) that a p level following a significance test can be a poor vehicle for conveying what we have learned about the strength of population effects.

Confidence interval estimation provides a convenient alternative to significance testing in most situations. Consider the 2-tailed hypothesis of no difference between means. Recall first that the significance test rejects at the α significance level if and only if the $1 - \alpha$ confidence interval for the mean difference excludes the value zero. Thus the significance test can be performed with the confidence interval. Most undergraduate texts in behavioral statistics show how to compute such a confidence interval. The interval is exact under the assumptions of the standard t test. However, the confidence interval contains information about experimental precision that is not available from the result of a significance test. Assuming we are reasonably confident about the metric of the

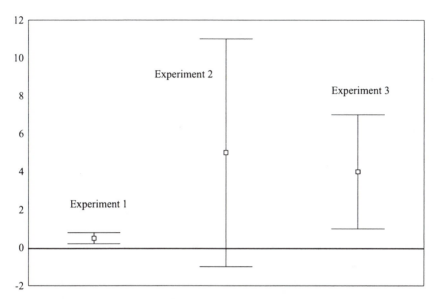

FIGURE 9.1   Confidence intervals reflecting different degrees of precision
of measurement.

data, it is much more informative to state a confidence interval on $\mu_1 - \mu_2$ than
it is to give the p level for the t test of the hypothesis that $\mu_1 - \mu_2 = 0$. In summary, we might say that, in general, a confidence interval conveys more information, in a more naturally usable form, than a significance test. This is seen
most clearly when confidence intervals from several studies are graphed alongside one another, as in Figure 9.1.

Figure 9.1 shows confidence intervals for the difference between means for 3
experiments, all performed in the same domain, using measures with approximately the same variability. Experiments 1 and 3 yield a confidence interval that
fails to include zero. For these experiments, the null hypothesis was rejected.
The second experiment yields a confidence interval that includes zero, so the
null hypothesis of no difference is not rejected. A significance testing approach
would yield the impression that the second experiment did not agree with the
first and the third.

The confidence intervals suggest a different interpretation, however. The first
experiment had a very large sample size, and very high precision of measurement, reflected in a very narrow confidence interval. In this experiment, a small
effect was found, and determined with such high precision that the null hypothesis of no difference could be rejected at a stringent significance level.

The second experiment clearly lacked precision, and this is reflected in the very wide confidence interval. Evidently, the sample size was too small. It may well be that the actual effect in conditions assessed in the second experiment was larger than that in the first experiment, but the experimental precision was simply inadequate to detect it.

The third experiment found an effect that was statistically significant, and perhaps substantially higher than the first experiment, although this is partly masked by the lower level of precision, reflected in a confidence interval that, though narrower than Experiment 2, is substantially wider than Experiment 1.

Suppose the 3 experiments involved testing groups for differences in IQ. In the final analysis, we may have had *too much power* in Experiment 1, as we are declaring "highly significant" a rather miniscule effect substantially less than a single IQ point. We had far too little power in Experiment 2. Experiment 3 seems about right.

Many of the arguments we have made on behalf of confidence intervals have been made by other authors as cogently as we have made them here. Yet, confidence intervals are seldom reported in the literature. Most important, as we demonstrate in the succeeding sections, there are several extremely useful confidence intervals that virtually *never* are reported. In what follows, we discuss *why* the intervals are seldom reported, *how* they can be computed, and *where* software performing all these techniques may be obtained.

REASONS WHY INTERVAL ESTIMATES ARE SELDOM REPORTED

In spite of the obvious advantages of interval estimates, they are seldom employed in published articles in psychology. On those infrequent occasions when interval estimates are reported, they are often not the optimal ones. There are several reasons for this status quo:

1. *Tradition.* Traditional approaches to psychological statistics emphasize significance testing much more than interval estimation.

2. *Pragmatism.* In RS situations, interval estimates are sometimes embarrassing. When they are narrow but close to zero, they suggest that a "highly significant" result may be statistically significant but trivial. When they are wide, they betray a lack of experimental precision.

3. *Ignorance.* Many people are simply unaware of some of the very valuable interval estimation procedures that are available. For example, the vast majority of psychologists are simply not aware that it is possible to compute a confidence interval on the squared multiple correlation coefficient.

The procedure is not discussed in standard texts, and it is not implemented in major statistical packages.

4. *Lack of availability.* Some of the most desirable interval estimation procedures are computer intensive, and are not implemented in major statistical packages like SAS, SPSS, STATISTICA, and so on. This makes it unlikely that anyone will try the procedure.

CONFIDENCE LIMITS, CONFIDENCE INTERVALS, AND THE INVERSION APPROACH TO INTERVAL ESTIMATION

In this section, we review the basic definition of a confidence interval, and the simple approach used to generate the simple confidence intervals found in most textbooks. Then we describe the less conventional, more computer-intensive approach which allows much more interesting and useful intervals to be derived. Here the discussion becomes somewhat more technical, and we employ notations that are common in mathematical statistics texts, but that the typical reader with a basic background in introductory applied statistics texts may find slightly intimidating. We try to strike a balance that provides sufficient, but not extraneous, detail. To begin, suppose we have a sample on n independent observations from some population. The "observations" can be individual numbers (e.g., measuring the heights of n people) or lists of numbers (measuring the height, weight, and age of n people). Suppose we use the letter X to stand for the data. A "statistic" is any function of the numbers in X. We can refer to statistics generically by using the standard mathematical notation for functions. So, for example, if we wish to discuss "statistics calculated on X" in very general terms, we could use a notation like $A(X)$. One can calculate numerous different statistics on the same data. For example, the sample mean of the heights would be one function, the correlation between height and weight another.

A common problem in statistics is to try to put limits on the value of an unknown parameter on the basis of fallible data. (We use the term *parameter* in the broad sense to refer to some numerical characteristic of a statistical population, as opposed to the strict sense, i.e., a formal argument of a probability distribution function.) For example, a politician might wish to estimate, on the basis of a modest opinion poll, the maximum level of support he or she is likely to receive in an upcoming election. *Confidence limits* and *confidence intervals* are techniques that frequently are employed to construct such limits.

An *upper confidence limit* (or *upper confidence bound*) is a statistic that, over repeated samples of size n, exceeds an unknown parameter θ a certain proportion of the time. For example, function $B(X)$ is a $1 - \alpha$ upper confidence limit for θ if, over repeated samples, the probability that $B(X)$ is greater than or equal to θ is equal to $1 - \alpha$, or, in mathematical notation,

$$\Pr(B(X) \geq \theta) = 1 - \alpha. \tag{9.1}$$

The basic reason behind the use of an upper confidence limit is to arrive at a number that one is quite confident exceeds the parameter. Note, one can seldom if ever be absolutely sure a statistic is greater than the unknown parameter, because the data may, through bad luck, be extremely unrepresentative of the population. Think of α in the preceding expression as an error rate. Suppose, for example, it is .05, and so $1 - \alpha = .95$. Then the preceding equation says that, if one takes a sample of data X and computes the statistic $B(X)$, it will, in the long run, be above the parameter value with probability .95, or 95% of the time. If $B(X)$ is used as a "statistical upper bound" for the parameter, it will be wrong about 5% of the time. It is common, after computing $B(X)$, to say that one is "95% confident that θ is below $B(X)$," or that one is "95% confident that θ does not exceed $B(X)$." To see why this might be useful, consider the opinion poll discussed earlier. Suppose the 95% upper confidence limit on the proportion of people intending to vote for the candidate is .65. The pollster could report back to the politician that "we are 95% confident your current support level is no greater than 65%." As another example, suppose an item is manufactured, and the parameter θ of interest is the failure rate for the item. The goal is to be reasonably certain that the failure rate is below a certain value.

In this case, one would frequently perform "reliability testing," by taking a sample X and computing an upper confidence limit for θ, the proportion of items that are defective. Suppose the upper limit is .001, or .1%. Then you might say "I am 95% confident that the defect rate is less than or equal to .1%."

Similar situations exist when one is establishing lower boundaries for a parameter, in which case *lower confidence limits* are computed.

A *lower confidence limit* (or *lower confidence bound*) is a statistic that is less than the unknown parameter a certain proportion of the time. A function $A(X)$ of the observed data X is a $1 - \alpha$ lower confidence limit for θ if, over repeated samples,

$$\Pr(A(X) \leq \theta) = 1 - \alpha. \tag{9.2}$$

For example, a pollster might report to a politician that "I am 95% confident your support level is no worse than 47%." The problem with confidence limits is that they provide, by themselves, no indication of precision of measurement. In general, the less authoritative your database, the further you have to move a confidence limit up (in the case of an upper limit) or down (in the case of a lower limit) in order to bound the parameter reliably. Returning to the political opinion poll, if the sample is moderately large, the pollster might report a lower limit of 44%, whereas in the same situation if the sample is quite small, the lower limit might have to be reported as 35% in order to gain the same degree of confidence. So, in order to be 95% confident, the political pollster would have to report a "minimum level of support" that is unduly pessimistic. Consequently, upper and lower confidence limits usually are combined to yield a *confidence interval* $(A(X), B(X))$, whose endpoints surround the parameter θ a certain proportion of the time. $A(X)$ and $B(X)$ bound a $1 - \alpha$ confidence interval for θ if, over repeated samples,

$$\Pr\big(A(X) \le \theta \le B(X)\big) = 1 - \alpha. \tag{9.3}$$

In practice, one usually constructs the confidence interval by choosing $A(X)$ and $B(X)$ to be, respectively, lower and upper $1 - \alpha/2$ confidence limits so that the confidence interval is symmetric.

The advantage of a confidence interval is that the width of the interval provides a ready indication of precision of measurement. That is, if the sample estimate has low sampling variability and high precision of estimate, then even a narrow confidence interval will bracket the true parameter a high percentage of the time, over repeated samples. Thus, the outcome of the confidence interval calculation is a report of a parameter value, together with an indication of how precisely it has been determined. In many situations involving exploratory research, this outcome more accurately reflects what an experimenter is hoping to learn from the data than a significance test does. So, for example, if the pollster reports "I am 95% confident that your support level is between 46% and 54%," the politician realizes that the election is up for grabs and that the support level is roughly 50% give or take 4%. This is probably more useful to the politician than being told that "a test of the hypothesis that your support level is 50% was not rejected." The politician is not really interested in whether the support level is exactly 50%—there is something artificial about testing for the significance of such a hypothesis. Rather, the key interest is in the best estimate of the support level, and how precise that estimate is. The location of the confidence interval, and its width, provide such information. If the politician feels that level of precision is inadequate, the pollster can report (based on statistical theory) that halving the width of the confidence interval will require quadrupling the size of the opinion poll!

Most confidence intervals discussed in standard textbooks are derived by simple manipulation of a statement about interval probability of a sampling distribution. For example, confidence intervals are usually introduced in terms of a simple Z statistic for testing the hypothesis $\mu = a$ when the population distribution is normal and the population standard deviation σ is known. If n is the sample size, and $\overline{X}$ is the ordinary sample mean based on the n observations, then the sampling distribution of the sample mean is normal, with a mean of μ, and a standard deviation (usually called the "standard error of the mean") of $\sigma/\sqrt{n}$. In any normal distribution, the probability that a score will fall between standard score values of -1.96 and $+1.96$ is .95. To convert the sample mean to its standard score equivalent, one subtracts its mean (μ) and divides by its standard deviation ($\sigma/\sqrt{n}$) to construct a test statistic Z,

$$Z = \frac{\overline{X} - \mu}{\sigma/\sqrt{n}}. \tag{9.4}$$

The resulting test statistic, in the long run, will fall between the 2.5% and 97.5% points of the standard normal curve (values of -1.96 and $+1.96$) with probability .95. As an inequality, these facts can be stated

$$\Pr(-1.96 \le Z \le +1.96) = .95, \tag{9.5}$$

or

$$\Pr\left(-1.96 \le \frac{\overline{X} - \mu}{\sigma/\sqrt{n}} \le +1.96\right) = .95. \tag{9.6}$$

The confidence interval for μ is derived by manipulating this interval algebraically. Because σ and n are both positive, we may multiply all three sections of the inequality by $\sigma/\sqrt{n}$ without altering its correctness. We then obtain

$$\Pr\left(-1.96\frac{\sigma}{\sqrt{n}} \le \overline{X} - \mu \le +1.96\frac{\sigma}{\sqrt{n}}\right) = .95. \tag{9.7}$$

One way of interpreting this inequality statement is that 95% of the time, the distance between μ and $\overline{X}$ is less than $1.96\sigma/\sqrt{n}$. That is, 95% of the time μ is within a certain distance of $\overline{X}$. Of course, this also means that 95% of the time $\overline{X}$ is within the same distance of μ. (If you and I are walking down the street and 95% of the time you are within 3 feet of me, then 95% of the time I am within 3 feet of you.) What this means, in turn, is that if we take $\overline{X}$ and construct an interval by adding and subtracting $1.96\sigma/\sqrt{n}$ from it, that interval will have μ within its endpoints 95% of the time in the long run. Such insight is not necessary to derive the confidence interval, however. One may simply continue manipulating the interval algebraically. First, subtract $\overline{X}$ from all three sections of the inequality. Then multiply all three sections by -1, and reverse the direction of the inequality. This leads to the following expression:

$$\Pr\left(\overline{X} - 1.96\frac{\sigma}{\sqrt{n}} \le \mu \le \overline{X} + 1.96\frac{\sigma}{\sqrt{n}} \right) = .95. \qquad (9.8)$$

The expression states that if one constructs an interval with endpoints $\overline{X} \pm 1.96\sigma/\sqrt{n}$, this interval will contain the true parameter (μ) 95% of the time in the long run.

A number of simple inequalities can be converted into confidence intervals in this way. Typically, one finds, in elementary to intermediate texts, confidence intervals for (a) a single mean, (b) the difference between two means, (c) a single contrast on means, (d) a single variance, (e) the ratio of two variances, (f) a single correlation, and (g) a single proportion. An element common to the preceding intervals is that an interval statement about the distribution of the null distribution of a test statistic can be manipulated easily to yield the desired confidence interval. Situations where (a) the distribution of the test statistic changes as a function of the parameter to be estimated, and (b) simple interval manipulation does not yield a convenient confidence interval, are generally not discussed. As an example, consider the sample squared multiple correlation, whose distribution changes as a function of the population squared multiple correlation. Confidence intervals for the squared multiple correlation are very informative, yet are not discussed in standard texts, because a single simple formula for the direct calculation of such an interval cannot be obtained in a manner analogous to the way we obtain a confidence interval for μ.

A general method for confidence interval construction is available that includes the method discussed earlier as a special case, but also allows confidence limits and confidence intervals to be constructed when the aforementioned method cannot be applied. This method combines two general principles, which we call the *confidence interval transformation* principle and the *inversion confidence interval* principle. The former is obvious, but seldom discussed formally. The latter is referred to by a variety of names in several classic references (Kendall & Stuart, 1979; Cox & Hinckley, 1974), yet does not seem to have found its way into the standard textbooks, primarily because its implementation involves some difficult computations. However, the method is easy to discuss *in principle*, and no longer impractical. Interestingly, when the two principles are combined, a number of very interesting confidence intervals result.

First we discuss the confidence interval transformation principle.

Proposition 1. Confidence Interval Transformation Principle. Let $f(\theta)$ be a monotonic, strictly increasing continuous function of θ. Let l_1 and l_2 be endpoints of a $1 - \alpha$ confidence interval on quantity θ. Then $f(l_1)$ and $f(l_2)$ are endpoints of a $1 - \alpha$ confidence interval on $f(\theta)$.

To prove the proposition, recall that a function is monotonic and strictly increasing if, when plotted in the plane, the graph "keeps going up" from left to right, that is, it never flattens out or goes down. A monotonic, strictly increasing function is *order preserving*. Because the plot never flattens out, if $x > y$, then $f(x) > f(y)$. This can be seen easily by examining Figure 9.2.

If l_1 and l_2 are endpoints of a valid .95 confidence interval on quantity θ, then 95% of the time in the long run, θ is between l_1 and l_2. If $f(\ )$ is a monotonic strictly increasing function, l_2 is greater than θ, and θ is greater than l_1, then it must also be the case that $f(l_2) > f(\theta)$, and $f(\theta) > f(l_1)$. Consequently, if l_1 and l_2 are endpoints of a $1 - \alpha$ confidence interval for parameter θ then $f(l_1)$ and $f(l_2)$ are endpoints of a valid $1 - \alpha$ confidence interval on $f(\theta)$.

Here are two elementary examples of the confidence interval transformation principle.

Example 1. A Confidence Interval for the Standard Deviation. Suppose you calculate a confidence interval for the population variance σ^2. Such a confidence interval is discussed in many elementary textbooks. You desire a confidence interval for σ. Confidence intervals for σ are seldom discussed in textbooks. However, one may be derived easily. Because σ takes on only nonnegative values, it is a monotonic increasing function of σ^2 over its domain. Hence, the confidence interval for σ is obtained by taking the square root of the endpoints for the corresponding confidence interval for σ^2.

Example 2. Inverting the Fisher Transform. Suppose one calculates a confidence interval for $z(\rho)$, the Fisher transform of ρ, the population correlation coefficient. Taking the *inverse* Fisher transform of the endpoints of this interval will give a confidence interval for ρ. This is, in fact, the method employed to calculate the standard (approximate) confidence interval for a correlation.

These examples show why the confidence interval transformation principle is very useful in practice. Frequently a statistical quantity we are very interested in (like ρ) is a simple function of a quantity (like $z(\rho)$) we are not so interested in, but for which we can easily obtain a confidence interval.

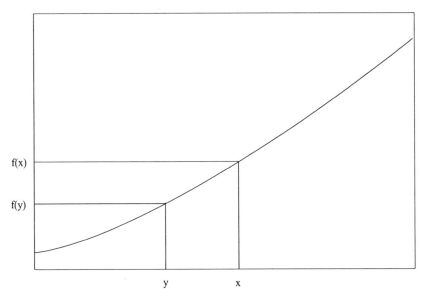

FIGURE 9.2   Order-preserving properties of a monotonic, strictly increasing function.

As an example, suppose we take two independent samples of size n_1 and n_2. We calculate sample means $\bar{x}_1$ and $\bar{x}_2$ and sample variances s_1^2 and s_2^2. Under the standard assumptions of normality and homogeneity of variance, the two-sample t statistic is used to decide whether an experimental and control group differ:

$$t_{n_1+n_2-2} = \frac{\bar{x}_1 - \bar{x}_2}{\sqrt{\left(\dfrac{1}{n_1} + \dfrac{1}{n_2}\right)\left(\dfrac{(n_1-1)s_1^2 + (n_2-1)s_2^2}{n_1 + n_2 - 2}\right)}} \tag{9.9}$$

The traditional approach is to compute the t statistic and perform a significance test. A better, but less frequently employed procedure is to report a confidence interval on the quantity $E = \mu_1 - \mu_2$ using the following standard formula for the endpoints (where $t*$ is the critical value from Student's t distribution):

$$(\bar{x}_1 - \bar{x}_2) \pm t*_{\alpha/2,\, n_1+n_2-2} \sqrt{\left(\frac{1}{n_1} + \frac{1}{n_2}\right)\left(\frac{(n_1-1)s_1^2 + (n_2-1)s_2^2}{n_1 + n_2 - 2}\right)} \tag{9.10}$$

In practice, an even more useful quantity than E is the *standardized* effect size, defined as

$$E_s = \frac{\mu_1 - \mu_2}{\sigma}. \qquad (9.11)$$

E_s is a standardized, or "metric-free" measure of effect size. If one two-group study reports its results in pounds, the other in kilograms, then the unstandardized effect E will not be in the same scale of measurement in the two studies, whereas E_s will be. Consequently, a confidence interval on E_s is more informative than one on E. This is especially true when different studies are compared, or when information is combined across studies.

In the context of meta-analysis, Hedges and Olkin (1985) discussed a variety of methods for estimating E_s, most of which are approximations. The exact method (which they discuss on page 91 of their book) involves the noncentrality interval estimation approach. This approach was considered impractical for general use at the time their book was written, so the authors provided nomographs only for some limited cases involving very small samples.

Before continuing, we digress briefly to recall some mathematical background on the key *noncentral* distributions for the less advanced reader. The normal, t, χ^2, and F distributions are statistical distributions covered in most introductory texts. These distributions can be related to the normal distribution in various ways: for example, squaring a random variable that has a standard normal distribution yields a random variable that has a χ^2 distribution with 1 degree of freedom. The t, χ^2, and F distributions are special cases of more general distributions called the *noncentral t, noncentral χ^2,* and *noncentral F*. Each of these noncentral distributions has an additional parameter, called the *noncentrality parameter*. For example, whereas the F distribution has two parameters (the "numerator" and "denominator" degrees of freedom), the *noncentral F* has these two plus a *noncentrality parameter*. When the *noncentral F* distribution has a noncentrality parameter of zero, it is identical to the F distribution, so it includes the F distribution as a special case. Similar facts hold for the t and χ^2 distributions. What makes the noncentrality parameter especially important is that it is related very closely to the truth or falsity of the typical null hypotheses that these distributions are used to test. So, for example, when the null hypothesis of no difference between two means is correct, the standard t statistic has a distribution that has a noncentrality parameter of zero, whereas if the null hypothesis is false, it has a noncentral t distribution. In general, the more false the null hypothesis, the larger the noncentrality parameter.

Suppose we take data from two independent samples, and calculate the two sample t-statistic shown in Equation 9.9. The statistic has a distribution which is noncentral t, with noncentrality parameter

$$\delta = E_s \sqrt{\frac{n_1 n_2}{n_1 + n_2}} . \tag{9.12}$$

When the null hypothesis is true, δ is zero and is not a particularly interesting quantity. However, E_s is a statistical quantity of considerable interest, and may be obtained from δ by a simple monotonic transformation

$$E_s = \delta \sqrt{\frac{n_1 + n_2}{n_1 n_2}} . \tag{9.13}$$

Hence, if we can obtain a confidence interval for δ, we also can obtain a confidence interval for E_s, using the confidence interval transformation principle.

We now describe how to obtain a confidence interval for δ. When we discuss continuous probability distributions, we often talk in terms of the cumulative distribution function, or CDF, and we use the notation $F( )$ to denote this function. The CDF evaluated at a point x is defined as the probability of obtaining a value *less than or equal to* x, hence the term *cumulative*. Many normal curve tables in the back of standard textbooks are CDF tables. For example, in the unit standard normal distribution, half of the cases fall at or below 0, so $F(0) = .50$. Ninety-five percent of the cases fall at or below 1.645, so $F(1.645) = .95$, and $F(-1.645) = .05$. Sometimes, when solving problems involving the normal curve table, one needs to "reverse" the table. For example, if I asked you what point in the normal curve has 95% of the cases at or below it, you would scan down the table until you found .95, move to the number in the column next to .95, and report back "1.645" as your answer. This process of reversing the roles of the two columns in the table is equivalent to inverting the CDF function. In mathematical notation, we say that the CDF function has an inverse, and that $F^{-1}(.95) = 1.645$. In a similar vein, $F^{-1}(.5) = 0$, and $F^{-1}(.05) = -1.645$.

Obtaining a confidence interval for δ is simple in principle, though not in practice. Consider the graph in Figure 9.3. This graph shows the .05 and .95 cumulative probability points for a noncentral distribution for fixed degrees of freedom, and varying values of the noncentrality parameter δ. These functions, labeled "5th percentile" and "95th percentile" in the graph, can be denoted more formally as $F^{-1}(.05, \delta)$ and $F^{-1}(.95, \delta)$, respectively, because they are the inverse of the CDF of the noncentral t, for fixed probability level, evaluated at δ.

To develop a confidence interval for δ, we need to find functions of the sample data that bracket δ a certain proportion of the time, and Figure 9.3 provides the key to obtaining such a function. Consider the upper curve in the graph. For any value of δ along the X axis, this curve plots the observed value t below which the noncentral t will occur 95% of the time. Now, suppose the *true value*

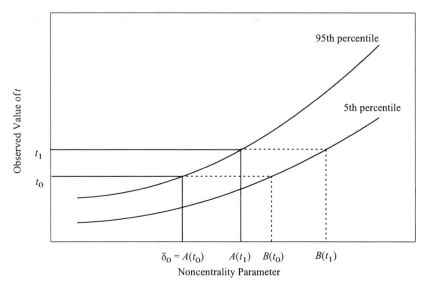

FIGURE 9.3   Noncentrality interval estimation with a confidence belt

of δ is δ_0. This means that 95% of the time the observed t value will be less than the value on the Y-axis marked as t_0.

Careful consideration of the upper curve reveals that its *inverse* (which exists, because the function is monotonic and strictly increasing in δ) can be used to construct a lower confidence limit, or a lower bound on a confidence interval. To see this, move along the Y-axis and, from any value t draw a horizontal line straight out until it intersects with the upper curve, then draw a point straight down until the X-axis is intersected. Call the value obtained this way $A(t)$, because it is a function of the t value chosen from the Y-axis. This value is the *inverse* of the function of the upper curve, evaluated at t. Note that each value of t corresponds to one and only one value of δ.

Imagine that the true noncentrality parameter is δ_0. Imagine further that, for each value of t that is observed, you compute the *inverse* of the upper curve function at t by drawing a line straight over to the upper curve, then straight down to the X-axis. With such a procedure, 95% of the time you will observe a value of t that is less than t_0, and so 95% of the time you will observe a value of $A(t)$ that is less than $A(t_0)$. But $A(t_0) = \delta_0$. Consequently, $A(t)$ produces a 95% lower confidence limit for δ, because it produces numbers that are below δ exactly 95% of the time.

If we call the inverse of the lower curve's function $B(t)$, a similar procedure provides an upper 95% confidence limit for δ. That is, draw a horizontal line from an observed t value on the Y-axis to the lower (5th percentile) curve, then down (perpendicular) to the X-axis. By a similar logic to that discussed previously, the value obtained by this procedure will be above δ 95% of the time, and will therefore be a 95% upper confidence limit. Taken together, $A(t)$ and $B(t)$ provide a 90% confidence interval for δ.

This method works, in general, so long as the $\alpha/2$ and $1 - \alpha/2$ probability points are montonic and strictly increasing as a function of the unknown parameter with the other (known) parameters considered as fixed values. Note that, in practice, one does not have to generate the entire curve of values, because the endpoints of the confidence interval are simply those values of the unknown parameter for which the cumulative probabilities of the observed data are $1 - \alpha/2$ and $\alpha/2$. So if you have a computer routine that can solve for these two values directly, there is no need to plot this curve. (In practice, numerical analysis root-finding techniques like the method of *bisection* are substantially faster than the graphical approach shown here for demonstration purposes. Computer software can calculate the intervals in approximately one second for most practical examples.)

The following proposition expresses succinctly the result of our graphical investigation.

Proposition 2. Inversion Confidence Interval Principle. Let v be the observed value of X, a random variable having a continuous (cumulative) probability distribution expressible in the form $F(v, \theta) = \Pr (X \leq v | \theta)$ for some numerical parameter θ. Let $F(v, \theta)$ be monotonic, and strictly decreasing in θ, for fixed values of v. Let l_1 and l_2 be chosen so that $\Pr (X \leq v \mid \theta = l_1) = 1 - \alpha/2$ and $\Pr (X \leq v | \theta = l_2) = \alpha/2$. Then l_1 is a lower $1 - \alpha/2$ confidence limit for θ, l_2 is an upper $1 - \alpha/2$ confidence limit for θ, and the interval with l_1 and l_2 as endpoints is a $1 - \alpha$ confidence interval for θ.

We call the method we have just described *noncentrality interval estimation*, because in practice one frequently estimates the noncentrality parameter en route to a more interesting statistical quantity. The following numerical example shows how the method is used to estimate standardized effect size in a two-group experiment.

Example 3.   Estimating the Standardized Effect in Two-Group Experiments.   In this example, we apply the noncentrality interval estimation approach to two hypothetical two-group experiments, each involving two independent samples of equal size. Experiment 2 was based on an extremely large sample size of 300 per group, whereas Experiment 1 had only 10 per group. The two-tailed p levels for the experiments were approximately the same, with Experiment 1 having the higher p level (.0181). Experiment 2 had a p level of .0167, and thus was "more

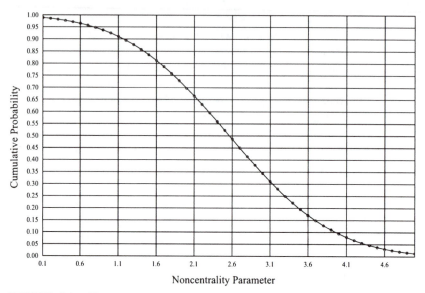

Noncentrality Parameter

FIGURE 9.4   Noncentrality and the cumulative probability of an observed t statistic

significant." Summary statistics for the experiments, along with confidence intervals for the standardized effect size, are shown in Table 9.2.

We now proceed to demonstrate how the confidence interval for E_s may be
calculated. First, we calculate a .95 confidence interval for δ. The t statistic in
Group 1 has an observed value of 2.60 with 18 degrees of freedom. The endpoints of the confidence interval for δ are those values of δ that generate the
unique noncentral $t_{18,\delta}$ distributions in which the observed value of 2.60 has cumulative probability .975 and .025. If a good noncentral t distribution calculation
program is available, and its output can be plotted, these values may be approxi-
mated fairly closely by graphical analysis. Figure 9.4 shows a plot of the cumulative probability of the value 2.60 as a function of δ for the family of noncentral
t distributions with 18 degrees of freedom.

TABLE 9.2
Comparison of confidence intervals for E_s in two experiments.

	Experiment 1	Experiment 2
n per group	10	300
Observed t statistic	2.60	2.40
p level (2-tailed)	.0181	.0167
95% Confidence Interval for E_s	(.1950, 2.1034)	(.0355, .3563)

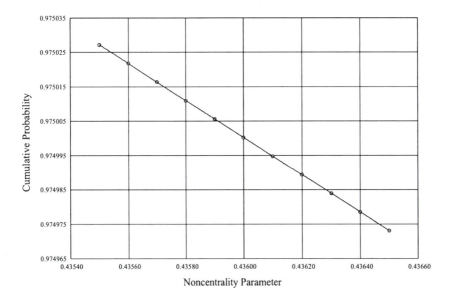

FIGURE 9.5 Calculating the lower confidence limit for the noncentrality parameter

Zooming in on a narrower region of Figure 9.4, we obtain the view shown in Figure 9.5, in which we can pinpoint, with a high degree of accuracy, the value of δ for which the cumulative probability is .975 at approximately .4360. This is the lower endpoint of the .95 confidence interval for δ. In a similar manner, we can determine the value for the upper endpoint as 4.7033.

We recall from Equation 9.13 that, using the confidence interval transformation principle, these endpoints may be transformed into a confidence interval for the standardized effect size E_s by multiplying them by

$$0.44721 = \sqrt{\frac{10+10}{10 \times 10}}.$$

Consequently, the .95 confidence interval for E_s has endpoints .1950 and 2.1034. In a similar manner, we can determine the confidence interval for Experiment 2 to be .0355 and .3563.

The confidence intervals for E_s demonstrate clearly that the experiments have rather different implications. In Experiment 2, a 95% confidence interval for E_s ranges from only .0355 to .3563 standard deviation units. In other words, the experiment determined, with a high degree of precision, that the effect is at best moderate, and quite possibly less than a tenth of a standard deviation. On the other hand, the confidence interval in Experiment 1 demonstrates that the experimental effect has not been determined with precision. The confidence interval for E_s includes such disparate values as .195 (small effect) and 2.10 (very powerful effect). Clearly, the confidence intervals for E_s convey much more useful information than the p levels.

APPLICATIONS OF NONCENTRALITY INTERVAL ESTIMATION

The noncentrality interval estimation approach we illustrated in the preceding section can be applied in a number of common data-analytic situations. Here we examine several, showing how noncentrality interval estimation adds substantial new information to the analysis.

Standardized Effect Size for Planned Orthogonal Contrasts.

As a result of our preceding analysis of Experiments 1 and 2, we might wish to estimate the difference in standardized effect sizes with a confidence interval. We can do this by using a planned orthogonal contrast. Planned orthogonal contrasts are an extension of the two-sample t statistic that can be performed routinely on K independent samples to test hypotheses of the form

$$\Psi = \sum_{k=1}^{K} c_k \mu_k = 0. \tag{9.14}$$

The c_k are referred to as "linear weights," or "contrast weights," and determine the hypothesis being tested. For example, if $K = 2$, and the contrast weights are $+1$ and -1, then $\Psi = \mu_1 - \mu_2$ and the hypothesis being tested is that the two means are equal. Under the standard assumptions of normality and homogeneity of variance, such hypotheses may be tested with a t statistic of the form

$$t = \frac{\hat{\Psi}}{\sqrt{\hat{\sigma}_{\Psi}^2}} = \frac{\sum_{k=1}^{K} c_k \overline{X}_{\bullet k}}{\sqrt{\left(\sum_{k=1}^{K} \frac{c_k^2}{n_k}\right) MS_{error}}}. \tag{9.15}$$

The t statistic has a noncentral t distribution with degrees of freedom equal to those for mean square error, and a noncentrality parameter given by

$$\delta = \frac{\Psi}{\sigma\sqrt{\sum\limits_{k=1}^{K}\frac{c_k^2}{n_k}}} = \frac{\Psi/\sigma}{\sqrt{\sum\limits_{k=1}^{K}\frac{c_k^2}{n_k}}} = \frac{\sum\limits_{k=1}^{K}\frac{c_k\mu_k}{\sigma}}{\sqrt{\sum\limits_{k=1}^{K}\frac{c_k^2}{n_k}}}. \tag{9.16}$$

Confidence intervals for Ψ may be constructed with endpoints

$$\hat{\Psi} \pm t^*\sqrt{\left(\sum\limits_{k=1}^{K}\frac{c_k^2}{n_k}\right)MS_{error}}. \tag{9.17}$$

However, a confidence interval for the standardized contrast

$$\Psi_s = \sum\limits_{k=1}^{K}\frac{c_k\mu_k}{\sigma}, \tag{9.18}$$

is generally more informative, because it expresses how false the null hypothesis is in standardized units of measurement. Because

$$\Psi_s = \frac{\Psi}{\sigma} = \delta\sqrt{\sum\limits_{k=1}^{K}\frac{c_k^2}{n_k}}, \tag{9.19}$$

it is a trivial matter to convert a confidence interval for δ into one for Ψ_s, the standardized contrast.

Example 4. Contrasting the Mean Differences for Two Experiments. Suppose, for the sake of simplicity, that MS_{error} is equal to 100 in both experiments in Table 9.2. If we compare the mean differences for the two experiments, the contrast weights are

$$c_1 = 1,\ c_2 = -1,\ c_3 = -1,\ c_4 = 1.$$

The mean differences are 11.628 in Experiment 1 and 1.959 in Experiment 2. The t statistic comparing the two mean differences is 2.127. The noncentrality interval estimation technique may be applied to the data in Table 9.2 to obtain a .95 confidence interval estimate on the difference in standardized effects between Experiments 1 and 2. We find that this confidence interval has endpoints of .0739 and 1.859. Since the confidence interval does not include zero, the first ("less significant") experiment has a significantly higher standardized effect than the second ("more significant") experiment, although the size of the effect difference has not been established with much precision.

This confidence interval provides much more useful, and much more accurate information about the relative effects in the two experiments than a comparison of the p levels.

Exact Confidence Intervals for Root Mean Square Standardized Effect Size in the One-Way Fixed Effects Analysis of Variance.

The ideas we developed for a single contrast on means in the context of the t-statistic generalize readily to the case of several contrasts in the analysis of variance. In orthogonal analysis of variance designs with equal cell sizes, the F statistic has a noncentral F distribution that, in general, is a simple function of the *root mean square standardized effect.* Here we examine the simplest special case, the one-way fixed-effects analysis of variance with n observations per group. Consider the F statistic in a one-way, fixed-effects ANOVA with n observations per group, and K groups. Let α_k be the treatment effect associated with group k, and σ^2 be the error variance. The F statistic with $K - 1$ and $K(n - 1)$ degrees of freedom has noncentrality parameter

$$\delta = n \sum_{k=1}^{K} \left(\frac{\alpha_k}{\sigma} \right)^2 . \tag{9.20}$$

The quantity δ/n is thus the sum of squared standardized effects. Now, suppose we wish to "average" these standardized effects in order to obtain an overall measure of strength of effects in the design. One possibility is simply the arithmetic average of the K standardized effects, that is, $\delta/(nK)$. One problem with this measure is that it is the average *squared* effect, and so is not in the proper unit of measurement. A second problem is that because of the way effects are defined in the analysis of variance, there are only $K - 1$ mathematically independent effects, because there is one constraint imposed upon the effects for identifiability, that is, that the effects sum to zero. Because the definition of "effect" in the analysis of variance depends on a mathematical restriction that is arbitrary, there are in fact infinitely many ways we *could* choose to define an ANOVA effect. Often, the "effects" defined by the standard ANOVA restriction need not coincide with experimental effects the way we commonly think of them. Consider the very simple special case of a two-group experiment involving a treatment group and a placebo control. Suppose the population standard deviation is 1, and the control group has a population mean of 0, the experimental group has a population mean of 2. In this case, there is one standardized experimental effect, and it is 2 standard deviations in size. On the other hand, the analysis of variance defines two effects, and they are $\alpha_1 = -1$ and $\alpha_2 = +1$, respectively. So, if we average the sum of squared ANOVA effects, we come up with an average squared effect of 1. Clearly, this is misleading, an artifact of the way ANOVA effects are defined.

There is, in our opinion, no simple, universally acceptable solution to this problem. However, averaging with K appears to underestimate effect levels consistently. Consequently, we propose to average by the number of independent effects, that is, $K - 1$. With this stipulation, $\delta/[(K-1)n]$ is the average squared standardized effect, and the root mean square standardized effect is

$$RMSSE = \sqrt{\frac{\delta}{(K-1)n}}. \qquad (9.21)$$

With this definition, we find that, in the above numerical example, the RMSSE is 1.41.

In order to obtain a confidence interval for $RMSSE$, we proceed as follows. First, we obtain a confidence interval estimate for δ by iteration, using the noncentrality interval estimation approach. Next, we directly transform the endpoints by dividing by $(K-1)n$. Finally, we take the square root. The result is an exact confidence interval for the root mean square standardized effect in the analysis of variance.

Example 5. Confidence Intervals on the RMSSE. Suppose a one-way fixed-effects ANOVA is performed on 4 groups, each with an n of 20. An overall F statistic of 5.00 is obtained, with a p level of .0032. The F test is thus "highly significant" and the null hypothesis is rejected at the .01 level. In this case, the noncentrality interval estimate provides a somewhat less awe-inspiring account of what has been found. Specifically, the 95% confidence interval for δ ranges from 1.866 to 32.5631, and the corresponding confidence interval for the root mean square standardized effect ranges from .1764 to .7367. Effects are almost certainly "there," but they are on the order of half a standard deviation.

Example 6. Confidence Intervals on Hays' η^2. Fleishman (1980) described the calculation of confidence intervals on the noncentrality parameter of the noncentral F distribution to obtain, in a manner equivalent to that employed in the previous two examples, confidence intervals on Hays' η^2, which is defined as

$$\eta^2 = \frac{\sigma_a^2}{\sigma_t^2},$$ (9.22)

where σ_a^2 is the variance due to effects, and σ_t^2 is the total variance. Fleishman also discussed the "signal to noise ratio"

$$f^2 = \frac{\sigma_a^2}{\sigma_e^2}.$$ (9.23)

Fleishman (1980) defined the "effect variance" σ_a^2 in the fixed-effects case as

$$\sigma_a^2 = \frac{\sum_{k=1}^{K} \alpha_k^2}{K},$$ (9.24)

and so f^2 relates to δ in a one-way fixed-effects ANOVA via the equation

$$f^2 = \frac{\delta}{nK}.$$ (9.25)

Fleishman (1980) cites an example given by Venables (1975) of a 5-group ANOVA with $n = 11$ per cell, and an observed F of 11.221. In this case, the .90 confidence interval for the noncentrality parameter δ has endpoints 19.380 and 71.549, whereas the confidence interval for f^2 ranges from .352 to 1.301.

Exact Confidence Intervals for RMSSE in Fixed-Effect Factorial ANOVA

The method of the preceding section may be generalized to completely random-ized factorial designs in the analysis of variance. However, some modification is necessary, because the noncentrality parameter for factorial fixed-effects designs is a function of the number of cells in which an effect operates. Consider, for ex-ample, the two-way fixed-effects ANOVA, with J rows, K columns, and n ob-servations per cell. Consider the F statistic for row effects. This statistic is es-sentially the one-way analysis of variance computed on the row means collapsed across columns. Consequently, the statistic has a noncentral F distribution with noncentrality parameter

$$\delta_a = nK \sum_{j=1}^{J} \left(\frac{\alpha_j}{\sigma_e} \right)^2.$$ (9.26)

Each row effect operates on K columns, and naturally the noncentrality parameter of the F distribution reflects that fact. Similarly, the F statistic for column effects is essentially a one-way analysis of variance performed on the column means collapsed across rows, and the noncentrality parameter for the overall F statistic for column effects is

$$\delta_b = nJ \sum_{k=1}^{K} \left(\frac{\beta_k}{\sigma_e} \right)^2 . \tag{9.27}$$

In general, the RMSSE for a particular effect is of the form

$$RMSSE_{effect} = \sqrt{\frac{\delta_{effect}}{n_{effect} df_{effect}}} , \tag{9.28}$$

where δ_{effect} is the noncentrality parameter for the F statistic for the effect, and n_{effect} is the total number of observations in the collected cell means used to compute the effect. For example, in a two-way ANOVA, the row effects are estimated by summing across the K columns to reduce the ANOVA, in effect, to a one-way ANOVA on cell means based on nK observations per "cell." For the AB interaction, however, n_{effect} is n, because interactions are computed on individual cells, not on rows or columns that are summed across. In a three-way ANOVA, with J rows, K columns, and H levels of the third factor, n_{effect} for the row effect is nKH.

Example 7. RMSSE in a Two-way ANOVA. Suppose a two-way 2×7 ANOVA is performed with $n = 4$ observations per cell, and the source table is as in Table 9.3. In this source table, all 3 effects are significant. There is a significant main effect for factors A and B, and a significant AB interaction. Notice that the p level for the A main effect (.0186) is about half that for the interaction (.0369).

One might be tempted to declare the A main effect to be "more significant" than the interaction. However, the 90% RMSSE confidence intervals for the main effects and interaction would seem to dispute that. The low ends for the confidence intervals are virtually identical. The upper end of the confidence interval for the AB interaction effect is substantially higher for the AB interaction than for either main effect.

This suggests that there is less power (and precision of estimate) for detecting interaction effects than for detecting main effects in this design. It is wise to remember this when making decisions about the "additivity" of models in the analysis of variance. The table also dramatizes that, because of the different power curves, different numbers of cells, and different constraints on effects, it is

TABLE 9.3
A Two-Way (2×7) Fixed Effects ANOVA

Source	SS	df	MS	F	p level	RMSSE Lower	RMSSE Upper
A	14.40	1	14.40	6.00	.0186	.136	.782
B	38.16	6	6.36	2.65	.0285	.135	.754
AB	36.00	6	6.00	2.50	.0369	.139	1.038
Error	100.80	42	2.40				

very risky to characterize one result as "more significant" than another on the
basis of p levels in ANOVA.

Exact Confidence Intervals for the Squared Multiple Correlation

One very common statistical application that practically cries out for a confidence interval is multiple regression analysis. Publishing an observed R^2 together
with the result of a hypothesis test that the population squared multiple correlation, P^2, is zero, conveys little of the available statistical information. A confidence interval on P^2 is much more informative. *Exact* confidence intervals on
P^2 can be computed using the inversion interval estimation approach. Yet general purpose statistical packages do not calculate such a confidence interval, and
numerous well-known textbooks on multivariate analysis at both the theoretical
and applied levels (e.g., Anderson, 1984; Morrison, 1990) do not allude to the
possibility of calculating such an interval. The result is that numerous multiple
regression studies have published R^2 values (along with various "shrunken" estimators) with no indication of experimental precision.

Kramer (1963) and Lee (1972) described methods for calculating the cumulative distribution of the squared multiple correlation coefficient. Both authors
included tables in their articles. For a given observed R^2, fixed sample size, and
number of predictors, the distribution of R^2 can be expressed as a function of P^2.
(See, for example, Lee (1972), p. 178.) Consequently, the inversion confidence
interval principle can be employed. However, the tables of Kramer and Lee provide only the upper percentage points of the distribution. Consequently, only the
lower confidence limit, or "statistical lower bound" can be determined, and this
must be accomplished by tedious linear interpolation.

Steiger and Fouladi (1992) provided a computer program, R2, for calculating
exact confidence intervals on P^2. The program iterates an exact confidence in-

terval and confidence limit, using the noncentrality interval estimation approach. Such intervals can be quite revealing.

Example 8. Confidence Intervals for the Squared Multiple Correlation. Suppose a criterion is predicted from 45 independent observations on 5 variables and the observed squared multiple correlation is .40. In this case a 95% confidence interval for P^2 ranges from .095 to .562! A 95% lower confidence limit is at .129. On the other hand the R^2 value is significant "beyond the .001 level," because the p level is .0009, and the shrunken estimator is .327. Clearly, it is far more impressive to state that "the R^2 value is significant at the .001 level" than it is to state that "we are 95% confident that P^2 is between .095 and .562." But we believe the latter statement conveys the quality and meaning of the statistical result more accurately than the former.

Some writers, like Lee (1972), prefer a lower confidence limit, or "statistical lower bound" on the squared multiple correlation to a confidence interval. The rationale, apparently, is that one is primarily interested in assuring that the percentage of variance "accounted for" in the regression equation exceeds some value. Although we understand the motivation behind this view, we hesitate to accept it. *The confidence interval, in fact, contains a lower bound, but also includes an upper bound, and, in the interval width, a measure of precision of estimation.* It seems to us that adoption of a lower confidence limit can lead to a false sense of security, and reduces that amount of information available in the model assessment process.

We believe that confidence intervals always should be reported with a multiple correlation. However, we add a note of caution. Strictly speaking, such confidence intervals (as well as the significance test) will not be accurate unless distributional assumptions have been met, and the independent variables in the regression equation specified a priori. In many cases, the final regression equation has been determined by some kind of exploratory stepwise approach, and no attempt has been made at cross-validation. It is important to reemphasize that estimates of P^2 and confidence intervals are biased by this specification search. For the interval estimation approach discussed here to be valid, a cross-validation sample should be used.

Asymptotic Confidence Intervals for Goodness of Fit in the Analysis of Covariance Structures

A key area where noncentrality interval estimation has been applied with excellent results is in the analysis of covariance structures, sometimes referred to as "causal modeling." In this area, the statistical inference is usually of the accept-support (AS) variety. In this kind of situation, standard significance testing logic is badly strained.

Until approximately 1980, models were evaluated in the analysis of covariance structures by using the chi-square test of fit. The problem with the procedure is that it tests a hypothesis of perfect fit. Since this hypothesis is often false, the statistical decision rendered by the chi-square statistic often boiled down to a question of sample size. With small samples, poorly fitting models might be "accepted," while with large samples a model with excellent fit (in the practical sense) might be overwhelmingly rejected. The results were often embarrassing. Sometimes models which appeared to fit very well were rejected "beyond the .01 level." Awkward mental contortions were required to simultaneously praise the maximum likelihood chi-square statistic as a technical breakthrough, while ignoring its result.

Steiger and Lind (1980) demonstrated that performance of statistical tests in common factor analysis could be predicted from a noncentral chi-square approximation. The noncentrality parameter was n times the "population discrepancy function," which is the (maximum likelihood or generalized least squares) discrepancy function calculated on the population covariance matrix. Consequently, the population discrepancy function was an excellent candidate for a descriptive index of how badly a model fit in a particular population. Steiger and Lind suggested abandoning the tradition of hypothesis testing in favor of constructing a *confidence interval on the population discrepancy function* (or some particularly useful function of it). This approach offers two worthwhile pieces of information at the same time. It allows one, for a particular model and data set, to express (a) how bad fit is in the population, and (b) how precisely the *population* badness of fit has been determined from the *sample* data.

Steiger (1989, 1990b) implemented three noncentrality-based indices of fit in the computer program EzPATH, including the index originally proposed by Steiger and Lind (1980). All these indices can be computed with confidence intervals. One index, the RMSEA, divides the population fit function F^* by the degrees of freedom, then takes a square root to obtain a "Root Mean Square Error of Approximation," in a manner roughly analogous to the RMSSE we recommended for the fixed effects factorial ANOVA earlier in this article. Most current structural modeling programs (e.g., LISREL, EQS, SEPATH, CALIS, RAMONA) calculate the RMSEA, which Browne and Cudeck (1992) also recommend.

The other two noncentrality-based indices developed by Steiger were population analogs of the GFI and AGFI of Jöreskog and Sörbom (1984). Jöreskog and Sörbom recommended the finite sample equivalents of these as sample-based indices, but offered no population rationale for them. Steiger (1989) and Maiti and Mukherjee (1990) demonstrated that the sample-based GFI and AGFI could be viewed as biased estimators of Steiger's (1989) equivalent population quantities, and that both of these indices, under fairly general conditions, could be written as a simple monotonic function of the population noncentrality parameter. For example, for structural models (based on p observed variables) that are invariant under a constant scaling factor, Steiger's Γ_1, the population equivalent of the GFI (i.e., the GFI calculated on the population covariance matrix) can be written

$$\Gamma_1 = \frac{p}{2F^* + p}.$$ (9.29)

This simple monotonic relationship implies that, via the confidence interval transformation principle, a confidence interval on the noncentrality parameter of a noncentral chi-square distribution can be converted easily into a confidence interval on Γ_1.

In the documentation for the structural equation modeling program SEPATH, Steiger (1995) extended the noncentrality-based indices to multiple samples, and gave a simplified formula for estimating the bias in the Jöreskog and Sörbom (1984) indices.

There are several advantages to the noncentrality-based approach. First, when the RMSEA and adjusted gamma are employed, the index is automatically corrected for model parsimony. For example, as models become more complex, fit tends to improve, all other things being equal, whereas degrees of freedom decrease. The RMSEA, calculated in the population (for single-sample models) with the equation

$$R^* = \sqrt{\frac{F^*}{df}},$$ (9.30)

compensates for this by dividing by the degrees of freedom. Second, high sample size now works "for the experimenter" instead of against the experimenter, because larger sample sizes result in smaller confidence interval widths, reflecting greater precision of estimation. Third, the distinction between a "statistically significant" badness of fit and a "meaningful" badness of fit can now be made. The following example clarifies these advantages.

Example 9. Evaluating the fit of a circumplex model. A perfect, equally spaced circumplex correlation matrix (Guttman, 1954) has equal correlations on sub-diagonal strips. For example, a 6×6 correlation matrix would be of the form

TABLE 9.4
Correlation Pattern for a 6×6 Circumplex

1					
ρ_1	1				
ρ_2	ρ_1	1			
ρ_3	ρ_2	ρ_1	1		
ρ_2	ρ_3	ρ_2	ρ_1	1	
ρ_1	ρ_2	ρ_3	ρ_2	ρ_1	1

shown in Table 9.4. Guttman (1954) observed a correlation matrix that has been reprinted in a number of places, including Jöreskog (1978).

Suppose we were to test the null hypothesis that the Guttman (1954) correlation matrix is a perfect, equally spaced circumplex, using structural equation modeling software. The sample size ($n = 710$) is very large in this example. Hence, we would expect the precision of estimation to be very high. At the same time, we would have to keep in mind that the "accept-support" approach of the chi-square test commonly used in structural modeling would be of very limited usefulness in this situation. We recognize that a model with as many constraints as this one will almost certainly not fit perfectly in the population, and we have very high power to detect an imperfect fit.

The chi-square statistic yields, in this case, a value of 27.05 with 12 degrees of freedom. The probability level is .008, indicating that the null hypothesis of perfect fit must be rejected. However, a reasonable conclusion from confidence interval analysis is that, although it is highly probable that the data do not fit a circumplex *perfectly,* they do fit a circumplex well. The 90% confidence interval for the Steiger-Lind (1980) RMSEA index is between .021 and .064.

The corresponding confidence interval for the *adjusted* population *gamma* coefficient, the population equivalent of the Jöreskog-Sörbom (1984) AGFI, is between .972 and .997.

Both confidence intervals show excellent fit of the model was determined with high precision. A reasonable conclusion would seem to be that Guttman's data fit the model in Table 9.4 *very* well.

Statistical Bounds on Power.

Occasionally, in the aftermath of a failure to reject a statistical significance test, reviewers or authors speculate about the role of inadequate power in causing the failure to reject. Ironically, statistical inference about power itself is frequently absent from such discussions. Often it need not be. In many situations power is, all other factors held constant, a monotonic, strictly increasing function of a noncentrality parameter. Consequently, we can use the confidence interval transformation principle to construct post hoc statistical upper bounds on power, *after* a significance test has been performed.

Taylor and Muller (1995) have discussed such an approach in the general context of the multivariate linear model. The procedure is, in principle, quite straightforward. For example, consider the F test in the 1-way fixed-effects ANOVA. Suppose we obtain a 90% confidence interval on the noncentrality parameter. Since power and the noncentrality parameter are monotonically functionally related for a given sample size and α, we may use the confidence interval transformation principle to obtain a confidence interval, *after seeing the data*, for power.

To avoid misunderstanding, we emphasize that (a) we do not favor the significance testing approach for exploratory social science research, and that (b) in situations where significance tests are to be performed, it is better to analyze power before gathering one's data. However, situations arise where data have been gathered, a significance test has been performed, and then someone raises a question about power.

In such situations, a confidence interval on power provides, in its upper and lower limits, a "best case" and "worst case" scenario, respectively, for power in the test just performed. The upper bound of the confidence interval for power, can be considered a 95% *statistical upper bound on power*. This is a number below which the true power occurs 95% of the time over repeated samples. If the 95% statistical upper bound on power is below a reasonable target value, say .90, it means that the most optimistic reading of the available evidence suggests that power was inadequate to detect the effects present in your data with a significance test. The lower end of a 90% confidence interval is a 95% *statistical lower bound on power*. If this end of the confidence interval exceeds some reasonable value, it can confirm that power was almost certainly adequate in the experiment just performed. Post-hoc statistical bounds on power combine information about the precision of estimate in a study with information about the actual effects in the study. As such, it relies more on available information and less on speculation than posterior power analyses based on hypothetical effect sizes.

Example 10. A Confidence Bound on Power in a One-Way ANOVA. Suppose a 1-way ANOVA is performed on two independent groups, with sample sizes of 15 in each group, and an F value of 2.0 is obtained. In this case, the two-tailed p level is .1683, and the null hypothesis is, of course, not rejected. The 90% confidence interval on the noncentrality parameter ranges from 0 to 9.459. When the noncentrality parameter is zero, "power," strictly speaking, does not exist (i.e., the null hypothesis is true), but the rejection probability is alpha (i.e., .05). So, in a sense, the lower bound of the confidence interval for power is .05. The upper bound of the confidence interval on power is the power corresponding to a noncentrality parameter of 9.459. This value (which may be calculated as .843) is a 95% *upper confidence limit* on power. The 90% confidence interval on the RMSSE ranges from 0 to .794. This suggests that (a) effect size cannot be determined with high precision in this design, and (b) even if the effect size is assumed to be the maximum statistically reasonable value, power is .843. This suggests the sample size in this study is too low to afford the precision of estimation deemed desirable in many areas of social science.

CONCLUSIONS AND NOTES ON APPLICATIONS

In this chapter, we have discussed confidence interval methods that offer a superior alternative to significance testing in situations where confidence intervals are seldom applied, or applied in a suboptimal manner. These confidence intervals provide all the information inherent in a significance test. They are no longer computationally impractical, and should augment or replace the corresponding significance test procedures. We have, in the body of the chapter, given examples of how the procedures may be used in many common statistical testing situations.

Many users will find that these techniques serve as a superior replacement for significance testing in common situations. Others will consider this view too radical, and will use them to augment the more traditional approaches.

Several times in this article, we emphasized the value of using the width of the confidence interval as in index of precision of estimate of a parameter. It should be remembered that the width of a confidence interval is generally a random variable, subject to sampling fluctuations of its own, and may be too unreliable at small sample sizes to be useful for some purposes.

In this regard, there are two additional issues that arise in implementing the inversion approach to interval estimation. The first issue arises in some common situations when the parameter space (i.e., the set of all possible parameter values) is bounded. For example, suppose one is constructing a confidence interval for the squared multiple correlation, or for the RMSEA index of fit in structural modeling. Neither of these parameters takes on negative values, so the parameter space is bounded on the left at zero. The inversion approach to interval estimation requires one to find a values of a parameter θ that imply sampling distributions in which the observed statistic is at the $\alpha/2$ and $1-\alpha/2$ quantiles. These values are the endpoints of the confidence interval. In some cases, however, the value of the observed statistic is so low that it is not possible to find a nonnegative value of θ that places it at the required percentage point. Standard procedure in this case is to arbitrarily set the confidence limit at zero, since the parameter cannot be less than zero. This maintains the correct coverage probability for the confidence interval, but the width of the confidence interval may be suspect as an index of precision of measurement when either or both ends of the confidence interval are at zero. In such cases, one might consider obtaining alternative indications of precision of measurement, such as an estimate of the standard error of the statistic. Often such estimates are readily available. A more proactive solution is to assure, in advance, that sample size is adequate to provide reasonable precision of estimation across a typical range of parameter values. For example, MacCallum, Browne, and Sugawara (1996) provide guidelines for appropriate sample size when using the RMSEA as an index of fit in structural equation modeling. Steiger and Fouladi (1992) provide a computer program, *R2*, for calculating appropriate sample size in multiple regression. These guidelines (developed in the context of power calculation within a hypothesis testing approach) should be given careful attention during the design of structural modeling and multiple regression studies. If they are followed, confidence intervals should seldom intrude on the boundaries of the parameter space.

There is a second issue that is probably of less concern in practice. When the *true* parameter is on the boundary of the parameter space, the coverage probability for the confidence interval may be *higher* than the nominal value. For example, suppose the population squared multiple correlation is zero. In such a situation, it is not possible to obtain a confidence interval that "misses" the true parameter on the low side, and so the confidence interval is *conservative*, i.e., the actual coverage probability is $1 - \alpha / 2$, rather than $1 - \alpha$.

The fine details of programming computations were not discussed in this paper, but their importance should not be underestimated. Implementing the techniques is *much* more difficult than understanding them. Much of the development behind these methods is highly technical. In general, noncentral distribution routines present many more programming challenges than their central variants, and iterative routines used in the inversion approach must be programmed very cautiously to assure reliable performance.

Some of the methods discussed in this chapter already have been implemented in software whose availability is described on the website http://www.interchg.ubc.ca/steiger/homepage.htm. The program *R2*, available for computers running either the MSDOS or Windows operating system, computes confidence intervals, power, sample size required to achieve a given power, and other statistics on the squared multiple correlation. This program is available now. Other software will be announced as it becomes available. Interested readers may contact the senior author via email, at steiger@unixg.ubc.ca.

ACKNOWLEDGMENTS

We are very grateful to Michael W. Browne, John C. Loehlin, Stephen G. West, and to the editors of this volume, for their helpful comments, important theoretical insights, and encouragement provided during drafting and revision of this paper.

REFERENCES

Anderson, T. W. (1984). *Introduction to multivariate statistical analysis* (2nd ed.). New York: Wiley.

Browne, M. W., & Cudeck, R. (1992). Alternative ways of assessing model fit. In K. A. Bollen & J. S. Long (Eds.), *Testing structural equation models.* Beverly Hills, CA: Sage.

Cohen, J. (1994). The earth is round ($p < .05$). *American Psychologist, 49,* 997–1003.

Cox, D. R., & Hinckley, D. V. (1974). *Theoretical statistics.* New York: Chapman & Hall.

Fleishman, A. E. (1980). Confidence intervals for correlation ratios. *Educational and Psychological Measurement, 40,* 659–670.

Guttman, L. B. (1954). A new approach to factor analysis: The radex. In P. F. Lazarsfeld (Ed.), *Mathematical thinking in the social sciences.* New York: Columbia University Press.

Guttman, L. B. (1977). What is not what in statistics. *The Statistician, 26,* 81–107.

Hedges, L. V., & Olkin, I. (1985). *Statistical methods for meta-analysis.* New York: Academic Press.

Jöreskog, K. G. (1978). Structural analysis of covariance and correlation matrices. *Psychometrika, 43,* 443–477.

Jöreskog, K. G., & Sörbom, D. (1984). *Lisrel VI. Analysis of linear structural relationships by maximum likelihood, instrumental variables, and least squares methods.* Mooresville, IN: Scientific Software.

Kendall, M., & Stuart, A. (1979). *The advanced theory of statistics.* (Vol. 2). New York: MacMillan.

Kramer, K. H. (1963). Tables for constructing confidence limits on the multiple correlation coefficient. *Journal of the American Statistical Association, 58,* 1082–1085.

Lee, Y. S. (1972). Tables of upper percentage points of the multiple correlation coefficient. *Biometrika, 59,* 175–189.

MacCallum, R. C., Browne, M. W., & Sugawara, H. M. (1996). Power analysis and determination of sample size for covariance structure modeling. *Psychological Methods, 1,* 130–149.

Maiti, S. S., & Mukherjee, B. N. (1990). A note on the distributional properties of the Jöreskog–Sörbom fit indices. *Psychometrika, 55,* 721–726.

Meehl, P. E. (1978). Theoretical risks and tabular asterisks: Sir Karl, Sir Ronald, and the slow progress of soft psychology. *Journal of Consulting and Clinical Psychology, 46,* 806–834.

Morrison, D. F. (1990). *Multivariate statistical methods.* (3rd Ed.). New York: McGraw-Hill.

Rozeboom, W. W. (1960). The fallacy of the null hypothesis significance test. *Psychological Bulletin, 57,* 416–428.

Schmidt, F. L., & Hunter, J. E. (1997). Eight common but false objections to the discontinuation of significance testing in the analysis of research data. In L. Harlow, S. A. Mulaik, & J. H. Steiger (Eds.), *What if there were no significance tests?* Mahwah, NJ: Erlbaum.

Steiger, J. H. (1989). *EzPATH: A Supplementary Module for SYSTAT and SYGRAPH.* Evanston, IL: SYSTAT Inc.

Steiger, J. H. (1990). Structural model evaluation and modification: An interval estimation approach. *Multivariate Behavioral Research, 25,* 173–180.

Steiger, J. H. (1995). *Structural equation modeling (SEPATH).* In *Statistica/W 5.0.* Tulsa, OK: StatSoft, Inc.

Steiger, J. H., & Fouladi, R. T. (1992). *R2:* A Computer Program for Interval Estimation, Power Calculation, and Hypothesis Testing for the Squared Multiple Correlation. *Behavior Research Methods, Instruments, and Computers, 4,* 581–582.

Steiger, J. H., & Lind, J. C. (1980). *Statistically based tests for the number of common factors.* Paper presented at the May annual meeting of the Psychometric Society, Iowa City, IA.

Taylor, D. J., & Muller, K. E. (1995). Computing confidence bounds for power and sample size of the general linear univariate model. *The American Statistician, 49,* 43–47.

Venables, W. (1975). Calculation of confidence intervals for non-centrality parameters. *Journal of the Royal Statistical Society, Series B, 37,* 406–412.

Chapter 10

When Confidence Intervals Should Be Used Instead of Statistical Tests, and Vice Versa

Charles S. Reichardt
Harry F. Gollob

University of Denver

The inferences that can be drawn from confidence intervals and statistical tests depend on the researcher's definition of probability and on the researcher's prior knowledge of the parameter that is being estimated. For two definitions of probability and three types of prior knowledge, the relative advantages and disadvantages of confidence intervals and statistical tests are compared. Under conditions equally favorable to both statistical tests and confidence intervals, statistical tests are shown generally to be more informative than confidence intervals when assessing the probability that a parameter (a) equals a prespecified value, (b) falls above or below a prespecified value, or (c) falls inside or outside a prespecified range of values. In contrast, confidence intervals are shown generally to be more informative than statistical tests when assessing the size of a parameter (a) without reference to a prespecified value or range of values or (b) with reference to many prespecified values or ranges of values. In addition to discussing differences in informativeness, we also compare confidence intervals and significance tests in terms of their cognitive demands and their effects on bias in publication decisions. Finally, we discuss when confidence intervals should be used, describe obstacles to their use, and suggest how these obstacles can be overcome.

Probably the greatest ultimate importance among all types of statistical procedures we now know, belongs to confidence procedures. . ..   (Tukey, 1960)

Significance testing in general has been a greatly overworked procedure, and in many cases where significance statements have been made it would have been better to provide an interval within which the value of the parameter would be expected to lie.   (Box, Hunter, & Hunter, 1978)

Over the years, numerous articles have been published in the social science literature containing criticisms of statistical tests (e.g., Bakan, 1966; Carver, 1978; Cohen, 1994; Dar, 1987; Meehl, 1967, 1978; Morrison & Henkel, 1970; Rozeboom, 1960; Schmidt, 1996), and many defenses of statistical tests have been written in response (e.g., Chow, 1988, 1996; Hagen, 1997). Given its long and durable history, the debate over the utility of statistical tests is not likely to end soon. As the discussion of the strengths and weaknesses of statistical tests continues, it also would be useful to assess when statistical tests should be used in spite of their weaknesses and when they should be replaced by alternatives in spite of their strengths.

Confidence intervals are one of the most widely proposed alternatives to statistical tests (e.g., Blackwelder, 1982; Cohen, 1994; Gardner & Altman, 1986; Hauck & Anderson, 1986; Makuch & Johnson, 1986). The specific inferences that can be drawn from either confidence intervals or statistical tests depend both on how probability is defined and on the researcher's prior knowledge of the parameter that is being estimated. For two definitions of probability and three types of prior knowledge, the present chapter describes and compares inferences that can be drawn from confidence intervals and statistical tests. As summarized at the end of the chapter, our conclusions specify conditions and tasks for which confidence intervals both are and are not to be preferred to statistical tests.

The present chapter uses the Greek letter psi, ψ, to denote a population quantity about which inference is being drawn. The value of ψ can represent the value of a single population parameter or a function of more than one population parameter. For example, ψ could be a single population mean, the difference between two population means, or a linear combination of several population means, among many other possibilities.

For expository convenience, we follow current convention in the social sciences and ignore distinctions between Fisher's statistical significance test and Neyman–Pearson's hypothesis test. Therefore, we use the term *statistical test* to refer interchangeably to hypothesis tests and statistical significance tests. In addition, although the results can easily be generalized, the discussion explicitly considers only two-tailed statistical tests at significance level α and the corresponding two-sided $100(1 - \alpha)\%$ confidence interval. In the two-tailed statistical test, the null (H_0) and alternative hypotheses (H_1 and H_2) are denoted:

$$H_0: \ \psi = \psi_0$$

$$H_1: \ \psi > \psi_0$$

$$H_2: \ \psi < \psi_0$$

where ψ_0 is the null hypothesis value. Finally, we assume that the obtained probability value (which hereafter is called the obtained p value or simply p) is always included as part of the results of a statistical test.

DEFINITIONS OF PROBABILITY

The two most common interpretations of probability are given by the "frequentist" and the "subjectivist" definitions (Barnett, 1982). Most statistics texts in the social sciences present only the frequentist definition. Perhaps as a result, the frequentist definition is the one most widely held by social scientists. Nevertheless, many prominent social scientists and statisticians subscribe to the subjectivist view instead.

The Frequentist Definition of Probability

In discussing the frequentist definition of probability, it is important to distinguish between repeatable and unrepeatable (or unique) events. For example, the flipping of a coin is a repeatable event, but a specific flip of a coin is a unique event that can't be repeated. Note that a specific flip of a coin could be either a flip that has already occurred or a flip that has yet to occur.

For a frequentist, the probability of a particular outcome of a repeatable event is the asymptotic relative frequency with which the given outcome occurs when the event is repeated an unlimited number of times under circumstances that are identical except for random variation. For example, the probability that a fair coin lands heads when flipped randomly is 0.5 because that is the asymptotic relative frequency of a heads outcome when a fair coin is flipped randomly an unlimited number of times.

For unrepeatable (unique) events, the frequentist definition of probability specifies that the probability of a particular outcome is either 0 or 1 (i.e., a particular outcome is either impossible or certain) with no in between values being allowed. For example, for a frequentist, the probability that a specific coin flip produces a head is equal to either 0 or 1 depending, respectively, on whether the coin lands tails or heads on that particular flip, even if it is not known which of these two outcomes occurs.

A consequence of these specifications is that, for a frequentist, probability is defined as a state of nature that is independent of a person's cognitions. As a result, if two frequentists disagree about the value of a probability, at least one of them must be wrong.

The Subjectivist Definition of Probability

In agreement with frequentists, subjectivists believe that the probabilities of outcomes should be consistent with the mathematical axioms of probability. However, the subjectivist interpretation of probability differs from the frequentist interpretation in at least three ways. First, the subjectivist definition defines probability as a belief an observer has about nature rather than as a state of nature independent of an observer. Second, the subjectivist definition of probability need
not distinguish between repeatable and unique events.

Third, subjectivists' beliefs about probability may differ across individuals.
For example, consider three subjectivists' who have different information and
correspondingly different beliefs about the outcome of a specific toss of a fair
coin. Subjectivist A, who saw the specific flip of the coin come up heads, would
say the probability the coin landed heads is 1. Subjectivist B, who didn't see the
outcome of the specific coin flip, might say the probability the coin landed heads
is .5. Finally, subjectivist C, who didn't see the specific coin flip land but did see
the look on subjectivist A's face immediately following the specific coin flip,
might say the probability the specific coin flip landed heads is .75. Under the
subjectivist definition of probability, all three of these individuals would be
equally correct as long as their probability beliefs were consistent with the
axioms of probability.

The Frequentist's Definition of Confidence

In the example in the preceding paragraph, only the statement by subjectivist A
that the coin landed heads with probability 1 is correct according to the frequentist definition of probability. This is because, as noted earlier, the frequentist
definition specifies that the probability of a particular outcome of a specific
event must be equal to either 0 or 1. But though a frequentist can't say, as does
subjectivist B in the preceding, that the "probability" is 50% that a specific coin
flip landed heads, frequentists do allow themselves the option of saying they are
50% "confident" that a specific coin flip landed heads.

A frequentist's confidence that a particular outcome of a specific event did or
will occur is definitionally and numerically equal to the asymptotic relative frequency with which the particular outcome would occur if the corresponding
event were repeated an unlimited number of times under random variation. In
other words, the frequentist's confidence in a particular outcome of a specific
event is equal to the numerical value of the frequentist's probability of the same
outcome if the specific event could be repeated an unlimited number of times
under random variation. It follows that the axioms of probability hold for the
frequentist's notion of confidence as well as for the frequentist's notion of probability.

SPECIFIC INFERENCES FROM A CONFIDENCE INTERVAL

A $100(1 - \alpha)$% confidence interval for the value of ψ for a given data set is the range of scores that has the following property. If any score within the confidence interval were used as the null hypothesis value in an α–level statistical test of ψ on the given data set, the null hypothesis would not be rejected, whereas if any score outside the confidence interval were similarly used, the null hypothesis would be rejected. Of course, many confidence intervals in practice are approximations and therefore satisfy this definition only approximately.

As a result of the preceding definition of a confidence interval, if infinitely many independent random samples were drawn with replacement from the same population and if a $100(1 - \alpha)$% confidence interval for the value of ψ were constructed from each sample, $100(1 - \alpha)$% of these confidence intervals would contain the value of ψ and 100α% of these intervals would not contain the value of ψ. For example, if a 95% confidence interval for a population mean were created for each of an infinite number of random samples, 95% of these confidence intervals would contain the population mean and 5% would not contain the population mean.

Unfortunately, knowing that 95% of an infinite number of 95% confidence intervals would contain the population mean is not the inference that a researcher ordinarily desires. What usually is desired is not an inference about ψ based on an infinite number of confidence intervals but an inference about ψ based on the results of the specific confidence interval that is obtained in practice. The inference that can be drawn about ψ based on a specific confidence interval depends on one's definition of probability.

A Specific Probability Inference

Under conditions described later, a subjectivist can make the following statement. A specific $100(1 - \alpha)$% confidence interval for ψ contains the value of ψ with probability $100(1 - \alpha)$%. This statement is called the "specific probability inference from a confidence interval." For example, concluding that a specific 95% confidence interval for ψ contains the value of ψ with probability 95% is a specific probability inference from a confidence interval.

A frequentist can't draw a specific probability inference from a confidence interval because a frequentist must conclude that any particular outcome of a specific event has a probability of either 0 or 1. But a specific probability inference requires the conclusion that a particular outcome of a specific event has a probability equal to $100(1 - \alpha)$%, which is strictly between zero and one (except in the degenerate case where α equals either 0 or 1). As a result, a frequentist can obtain no useful information about the probability that a specific confidence interval contains ψ.

A Specific Confidence Inference

However, under conditions described later, a frequentist can make the following statement. I am $100(1 - \alpha)\%$ confident that a specific $100(1 - \alpha)\%$ confidence interval for ψ contains the value of ψ. This statement is called the "specific confidence inference from a confidence interval." For example, concluding that one is 95% confident that a specific 95% confidence interval for ψ contains the value of ψ is a specific confidence inference from a confidence interval.

SPECIFIC INFERENCES FROM A STATISTICAL TEST

As noted earlier, a $100(1 - \alpha)\%$ confidence interval for ψ reveals whether or not a statistical test for ψ at significance level α would reject the null hypothesis for any null hypothesis value. Thus, in terms of the decision to reject or not to reject a null hypothesis, an α-level statistical test contains no information that is not also contained in a $100(1 - \alpha)\%$ confidence interval. However, an α-level statistical test provides an obtained p value that is not readily obtainable from a $100(1 - \alpha)\%$ confidence interval, and therein lies a potential advantage of a statistical test compared to a confidence interval.

The obtained p value is the lowest value of α at which a statistical test would reject the null hypothesis for the given set of data. This is equivalent to saying that a p value less than or equal to the obtained p value would occur $100p\%$ of the time in an infinite number of random samples if the null hypothesis were true. For example, if the obtained p value were equal to, say, .043 and if ψ equals ψ_0, a p value less than or equal to .043 would occur 4.3% of the time in an infinite number of random samples.

However, a researcher wants to draw an inference about ψ given the obtained p value in a single sample, rather an inference about the p values that would occur in an infinite number of random samples given that ψ equals ψ_0. The kind of inference that can be drawn about ψ given the p value obtained from a single sample depends on one's definition of probability.

A Specific Probability Inference

Under conditions described later, a subjectivist can make the following statement given an obtained p value. The probability is $1 - .5p$ that ψ and its estimate lie on the same side of ψ_0 and the probability is $.5p$ that either ψ is equal to ψ_0 or ψ and its estimate lie on opposite sides of ψ_0 (Pratt, 1965; Rouanet, 1996). (As an aside, the two ".5"s would be omitted in the preceding statement if the p value from a one-tailed statistical test were used instead of the p value from a two-tailed test as we are assuming.) This statement is called the "specific probability inference from a p value." For example, if the obtained p value is .01 and the obtained estimate of ψ is greater than ψ_0, the conclusion that the probability ψ is greater than ψ_0 is .995 and that the probability ψ is smaller than or equal to ψ_0 is .005 is a specific probability inference from a p value. If the estimate of ψ is greater than ψ_0, for example, another way to state a specific probability inference from a p value is the following. The probability that H_1: $\psi > \psi_0$ is true is $1 - .5p$ and the probability that either H_0: $\psi = \psi_0$ or H_2: $\psi < \psi_0$ is true is $.5p$.

It is often reasonable to specify that there is a zero probability that the null hypothesis is true. In such cases, a specific probability inference from a p value becomes: The probability is $1 - .5p$ that the value of ψ and the value of the obtained estimate of ψ lie on the same side of ψ_0 and the probability is $.5p$ that ψ and its estimate lie on opposite sides of ψ_0.

In contrast to a subjectivist, a frequentist can't draw a specific probability inference from a p value. The reason is the following. A specific probability inference will result in the conclusion that the probabilities of two specific events are $1 - .5p$ and $.5p$, both of which are greater than 0 and less than 1 because an obtained p value can never be exactly 0. But frequentists must conclude that specific events have probabilities of exactly 0 or 1. As a result, a frequentist can obtain no useful information about the probability of the null or alternative hypotheses from an obtained p value.

A Specific Confidence Inference

However, under conditions described later, a frequentist can make the following statement given the obtained p value from a statistical test. I am $100(1 - .5p)\%$ confident that the value of ψ and the value of the obtained estimate of ψ lie on the same side of ψ_0 and I am $100(.5p)\%$ confident that either ψ is equal to ψ_0 or ψ and its estimate lie on opposite sides of ψ_0. This statement is called the "specific confidence inference from a p value."

WHEN SPECIFIC PROBABILITY AND CONFIDENCE INFERENCES CAN AND CANNOT BE DRAWN

A researcher's prior beliefs about the value of ψ determine when a subjectivist can and cannot make specific probability inferences and when a frequentist can and cannot make specific confidence inferences. The manner in which prior beliefs about the value of ψ are to be incorporated in statistical inference is prescribed by Bayes' theorem.

Bayes' Theorem

Bayes' theorem follows from the axioms of probability. Because both subjectivists and frequentists accept the axioms of probability, they both accept Bayes' theorem. For this reason, we don't follow the common practice of using the labels *Bayesian* and *subjectivist* interchangeably. We believe equating these two fosters the incorrect impression that only subjectivists believe in Bayes' theorem.

Applications of Bayes' theorem require that a "prior distribution" of the value of ψ be specified. If a prior distribution can't be specified, neither subjectivists nor frequentists have sufficient information to apply Bayes' theorem. On the other hand, if a prior distribution can be specified, both subjectivists and frequentists must apply Bayes' theorem, either implicitly or explicitly, or else their inferences will be inconsistent with the axioms of probability.

With regard to Bayes' theorem, the critical difference between subjectivists and frequentists has to do with how a prior distribution of ψ is specified. A prior distribution for subjectivists is determined by the researcher's beliefs about the probability distribution of ψ prior to assessing the value of ψ in the current research project. The prior distribution of ψ for frequentists is determined by the sample space from which units are sampled in the current research project. In showing how the prior distribution of ψ affects inferences, we will distinguish among uniform, nonuniform, and no usable prior distributions.

Uniform Prior Distribution

Uniform prior distributions also are called uninformative, flat, or diffuse prior distributions. In a uniform prior distribution, all logically possible values of ψ have equal probability. For example, a subjectivist would have a uniform prior distribution if a random sample were to be drawn from a population in which all logically possible values of ψ were thought to be equally likely. Analogously, a uniform prior distribution would arise from a frequentist's perspective if a random sample were drawn from a population that itself had been randomly drawn from a pool of populations across which all logically possible values of ψ occurred with equal probability.

Assume the prior distribution of ψ is uniform. Further, assume the shape of the sampling distribution of the test statistic is the same for all values of ψ_0. Such shape invariance in the sampling distribution occurs, for example, when using the t distribution to draw inferences about quantities such as means. Under these assumptions, a subjectivist can draw a specific probability inference from both a confidence interval and a p value, and a frequentist can draw a specific confidence inference from both a confidence interval and a p value.

Now assume the prior distribution of ψ is uniform but the shape of the sampling distribution of the test statistic varies with the value of ψ_0. Such variability in shape occurs, for example, when using the binomial distribution to draw inferences about proportions. Under these assumptions, specific probability inferences drawn by a subjectivist and specific confidence inferences drawn by a frequentist will be only approximately correct. However, good approximations tend to be obtained for large sample sizes. Alternatively, rather than using conventional confidence intervals and statistical tests that result in approximate inferences, exact inferences could be obtained using Bayesian statistical methods (Box & Tiao, 1973; Novick & Jackson, 1974; Pollard, 1986; Zellner, 1971). These methods are not widely used by social scientists, but the methods are well established and equally appropriate for subjectivists and frequentists

Nonuniform Prior Distribution

A nonuniform distribution is also called an informative distribution. As the label suggests, a nonuniform distribution is any distribution that is not uniform. For example, a subjectivist would have a nonuniform prior distribution if a random sample were to be drawn from a population in which the distribution of ψ were thought to be distributed normally rather than uniformly. Analogously, a frequentist would have a nonuniform prior distribution if the study sample was drawn at random from a population that itself was drawn at random from a pool of populations where the value of ψ across the populations was distributed normally rather than uniformly.

If the prior distribution is nonuniform, neither a specific probability inference drawn by a subjectivist nor a specific confidence inference drawn by a frequentist will be exactly correct. In addition, to the extent the prior distribution deviates from a uniform distribution, specific probability and specific confidence inferences will not necessarily be approximately correct, even for large sample sizes. For example, although a researcher could perform the calculations to create a conventional 95% confidence interval, the probability (or confidence) that this interval contains the value of ψ will tend to deviate from 95% to the extent the prior distribution is not uniform, and could deviate substantially even for large sample sizes. Nonetheless, an interval of scores that contains the value of ψ with $100(1 - \alpha)\%$ probability (or confidence) and the probabilities (or confidences) that the null and alternative hypotheses are true could be obtained using Bayesian statistical methods, but these intervals and probabilities (or confidences) would differ from those obtained with classical statistical methods.

No Usable Prior Distribution

The present section, which may be controversial, is self-contained. The results in the rest of the chapter hold whether or not one believes it possible to have no usable prior distribution.

A researcher will be said to have no usable prior distribution either when no information is available about the prior distribution of ψ or when a prior distribution of ψ is specified in insufficient detail to be able to apply Bayes' theorem. In either case, Bayes' theorem can't be used in drawing inferences.

A subjectivist would have no usable prior distribution, for example, if a uniform distribution were thought to be incorrect but the shape of the nonuniform distribution couldn't be completely specified. A frequentist would have no usable prior distribution, for example, if a random sample were drawn from a population that itself was drawn randomly from a larger set of populations across which the value of ψ has an unknown distribution. For example, a frequentist might believe that the prior distribution of ψ is a distribution in which only a single value has a nonzero probability but the location of that value is unknown.

When no usable prior distribution is available, a confidence interval can be used by a subjectivist to draw a specific probability inference and can be used by a frequentist to draw a specific confidence inference. That specific inferences can be drawn from a confidence interval follows because, by definition, a $100(1 - \alpha)\%$ confidence interval contains the value of ψ $100(1 - \alpha)\%$ of the time regardless of the prior distribution of ψ. Without a usable prior distribution, however, a subjectivist can't draw a specific probability inference from a p value and a frequentist can't draw a specific confidence inference from a p value. This follows because the correctness of a specific probability inference varies with the prior distribution of ψ. For example, a specific probability inference from a p value can be exactly correct if the prior distribution is uniform, as already noted. But if the prior distribution of ψ is, for example, a distribution with a nonzero value at only one point, the probability that either alternative hypothesis is true is a constant rather than a function of the p value as required by our definition of a specific probability inference from a p value. The same argument applies to a specific confidence inference from a p value.

COMPARING SPECIFIC INFERENCES DRAWN FROM A CONFIDENCE INTERVAL TO THOSE DRAWN FROM A P VALUE

The present section assumes that the prior distribution of ψ is uniform and the shape of the sampling distribution of the test statistic is invariant for all values of

ψ_0. Under these conditions, a researcher can draw either specific probability inferences or specific confidence inferences from both a confidence interval and a p value (and a researcher usually can draw approximately correct specific probability or confidence inferences when the shape of the sampling distribution varies with ψ_0 but the sample size is large). However, the specific inference that can be drawn from a confidence interval provides a different type and amount of information than the specific inference that can be drawn from a p value. To understand these differences, we examine the use of confidence intervals and p values for four purposes. Although these four purposes are not exhaustive, they cover a broad range of applications of statistical inference in practice.

To simplify the ensuing discussion, we explicitly compare confidence intervals and p values only in terms of a subjectivist's specific probability inferences and not in terms of a frequentist's specific confidence inferences. However, because specific probability inferences and specific confidence inferences have a parallel structure, parallel conclusions would be reached if we drew comparisons using a frequentist's specific confidence inferences instead. As a technical aside, when the sampling distribution of the test statistic is asymmetric, the two-tailed p value is set equal to twice the one-tailed p value for the alternative hypothesis which specifies that ψ is on the same side of ψ_0 as is the obtained estimate of ψ.

Task 1: Assessing Whether a Parameter is Equal to a Prespecified Value

Researchers often ask whether ψ is or is not equal to a prespecified value. For example, research reports often are written as if the main task of a study were to assess whether or not a null hypothesis is true. Questions about the probability that ψ equals a prespecified value are called questions of exact equality.

If, as we are assuming, the prior distribution of ψ is uniform, and if, in addition, ψ logically can be equal to any one of an infinite number of values, the probability that ψ equals any prespecified value is zero, regardless of the outcome of the data. Therefore, neither a statistical test nor a confidence interval provides any useful information about the probability that ψ equals a prespecified value under these conditions.

However, if ψ logically can be equal to any one of only a finite, rather than an infinite, number of values, the probability that ψ equals a prespecified value need not be zero when the prior distribution is uniform. Under these conditions, the probability that ψ equals a prespecified value can be obtained from the results of two statistical tests. Let p_A be the obtained p value from a statistical test with ψ_0 set equal to the prespecified value, ψ_A. And let p_B be the obtained p value from a statistical test with ψ_0 set equal to the next logically possible value

of ψ that is closest to ψ_A and on the side furthest away from the obtained estimate of ψ. Then the probability that ψ equals the prespecified value is
$.5(p_A - p_B)$. There is no correspondingly simple way to obtain this answer from
the results of confidence intervals.

Alternatively, rather than use two statistical tests to obtain the exact
probability that ψ equals ψ_A, the results of a single statistical test with $\psi_0 = \psi_A$
can be used to conclude that the probability ψ equals ψ_A is at most $.5p_A$. This
result follows because p_B is no greater than p_A, so $.5(p_A - p_B)$ is no greater than
$.5p_A$. Therefore, the smaller is the p_A value when ψ_0 is set equal to ψ_A, the
smaller is the maximum probability that ψ equals ψ_A.

Task 2: Assessing the Direction of a Parameter
Relative to a Prespecified Value

Another question that researchers often ask is whether ψ is greater than a prespecified value or whether ψ is less than the prespecified value. For example, a
researcher might want to assess the probability that the effect of a treatment is
greater than zero and the probability the effect is less than zero. Or a researcher
might want to assess whether an innovation has an effect that is greater than the
minimum size that must be achieved if the innovation is to be economically feasible. Questions such as these are called questions of direction.

By setting ψ_0 equal to the prespecified value, information about both the
probability that ψ is less than ψ_0 and the probability that ψ is greater than ψ_0 can
be derived from the p value from the statistical test. Specifically, if the obtained
estimate of ψ is less than ψ_0, the probability that ψ is itself less than ψ_0 is $1 - .5p$
and the probability that ψ is greater than ψ_0 is no greater than $.5p$. A directly
analogous result holds if the estimate of ψ is greater than ψ_0. Thus the smaller is
the p value, the greater is the probability of drawing a correct conclusion, based
on the obtained estimate of ψ, about the direction in which ψ lies relative to ψ_0.

A confidence interval also can be used to provide information about both the
probability that ψ is less than ψ_0 and the probability that ψ is greater than ψ_0.
But the information provided by the confidence interval is never more precise
and usually is less precise than the information provided by the statistical test.
For example, if the prespecified value, ψ_0, lies outside the $100(1 - \alpha)\%$
confidence interval, one can conclude that the probability ψ and its estimate lie
on opposite sides of ψ_0 is no greater than $.5\alpha$. But when ψ_0 lies outside the
confidence interval as is being assumed, the statistical test gives a more precise
answer than the confidence interval because $.5p$ is less than $.5\alpha$. For instance, if
$p = .01$ so ψ_0 lies outside a 95% confidence interval, the results of the statistical
test let one conclude that the probability ψ and its estimate are on opposite sides
of ψ_0 is no greater than $.005$ (i.e., $.5p$), but the confidence interval lets one

conclude that this probability is only no greater than .025 (i.e., .5α). An analogous result holds if ψ_0 lies inside the confidence interval.

Task 3: Assessing the Size of a Parameter Within a Prespecified Range

Researchers sometimes want to make the case that the value of ψ falls within a prespecified range of values. For example, a researcher might want to argue that ψ falls within a range of values that are all small enough to be ignored, such as when ψ represents either (a) the difference between the beneficial effects of an expensive and an inexpensive treatment, (b) an unpleasant side effect of a treatment, or (c) the degree of violation of an assumption of a statistical procedure (Reichardt & Gollob, 1989; Yeaton & Sechrest, 1986).

The probability that ψ lies within a prespecified range can be computed by using the results of two statistical tests. For expository convenience, we assume the null hypothesis is not exactly true in either of the statistical tests. Let ψ_A and ψ_B, respectively, denote the lower and upper bound of the prespecified range of values. Then use ψ_A and ψ_B as the null hypothesis values in two separate statistical tests that yield the corresponding p values, p_A and p_B. If the estimate of ψ lies between ψ_A and ψ_B, the probability that ψ itself lies inside this range is equal to $1 - .5(p_A + p_B)$ and the probability that ψ lies outside the range is $.5(p_A + p_B)$. If the estimate of ψ lies outside the prespecified range of values, the probability that ψ itself lies inside the range is equal to $.5|p_A - p_B|$ (which is half the absolute value of the difference between the two p values) and the probability that ψ lies outside the prespecified range is $1 - .5|p_A - p_B|$. Though they follow directly from the subjectivist definition of probability and the classic definition of p values, we have not previously seen the aforementioned results.

A confidence interval also can be used to obtain information about the probability that ψ lies inside a prespecified range of values (Bradstreet & Dobbins, 1996; Rogers, Howard, & Vessey, 1993), but the statistical test method just described usually provides a more informative answer and never provides a less informative answer. The two methods will give the same answers only in the unlikely event that the bounds of the confidence interval fall exactly on ψ_A and ψ_B.

We consider two cases to illustrate the advantage of the significance test method over the confidence interval method; namely when the confidence interval lies either completely inside or completely outside the prespecified range of values. Using the confidence interval, the most one can conclude in the first case is that the probability ψ lies inside the prespecified range is no less than $1 - \alpha$ and in the second case that this probability is no greater than to .5α. In contrast, the statistical test method gives the actual probability that ψ lies inside the prespecified range, rather than giving only a lower or an upper bound on this probability.

Task 4: Assessing the Size of a Parameter Without Using a Prespecified Range

Under the conditions that are being assumed, a $100(1 - \alpha)$% confidence interval for ψ contains the value of ψ with probability $100(1 - \alpha)$%. The range of scores that make up a confidence interval can be expressed as a point estimate, which is the single best estimate of ψ, and a margin of error, which quantifies the uncertainty that random sampling causes one to have about the value of ψ compared to the point estimate. For estimates of ψ that have symmetric sampling distributions, the margin of error is half the width of the confidence interval. For simplicity, we assume that the estimate of ψ has a symmetric sampling distribution, but the same arguments also apply to asymmetric cases.

Unlike a confidence interval, the results of a statistical test by itself provide neither a point estimate of ψ nor a margin of error. Therefore, a statistical test by itself doesn't provide as much information about the size of ψ and uncertainty about the size of ψ as does a confidence interval.

The difference between confidence intervals and statistical tests in the information provided about the size of ψ and uncertainty about the size of ψ is illustrated in Figure 10.1. The four lines in Figure 10.1 depict a $100(1 - \alpha)$% confidence interval that was obtained in four different studies estimating the values of four different parameters, using the same value of α. The points marked "(" and ")" on each number line are the edges of the confidence intervals. In each case, the null hypothesis for a statistical test was that the parameter equals 0 and this null hypothesis value, $\psi_0 = 0$, is also marked on each of the four number lines.

First consider cases A and B in Figure 10.1. Both confidence intervals in these cases lie completely above 0, so the null hypothesis that the parameter equals 0 would be rejected at significance level α in both cases. Moreover, the midpoint of each of the confidence intervals is six standard errors above 0, so the test statistics and p values would be the same in both cases. Yet, there are dramatic differences in what the confidence intervals reveal about the likely size of the parameter in these two cases. Because the confidence interval in case A only contains values that are close to zero, the value of the parameter is likely to be close to 0. In contrast, because the confidence interval in case B contains only values that are far from zero, the value of the parameter is likely to be far from 0. To reiterate, these differences in size are revealed by the confidence intervals but not by the results of the statistical tests.

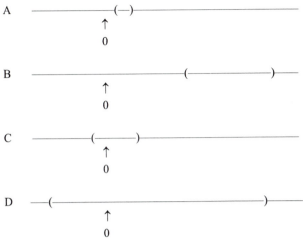

FIGURE 10.1   Four outcomes illustrating the different information provided by confidence intervals and statistical tests.

Now consider cases C and D. Both confidence intervals in these cases contain 0, so the null hypothesis would not be rejected in either case. Moreover, the midpoint of each of the confidence intervals is one standard error above 0, so the test statistics and the p values would be the same. Yet, as in cases A and B, there are dramatic differences in what the confidence intervals reveal about the likely size of the parameters in cases C and D. Because the confidence interval in case C contains only values close to 0, the parameter value is likely to be close to 0. In contrast, the confidence interval in case D includes a wide range of values that are far from 0. Therefore, it is much more likely in case D, than in case C, that the value of the parameter is far from 0. Again these differences in information about size are revealed by the confidence intervals but not by the statistical tests.

OTHER ISSUES IN CHOOSING BETWEEN CONFIDENCE INTERVALS AND P VALUES

Given the preceding results, choosing between confidence intervals and p values would appear to be straightforward. Determine the task that is to be performed and choose the method that provides the most information in fulfilling that task. However, both the choice among tasks and the choice between methods are not that simple in practice. Tasks rarely fall neatly into one of the four previously described categories and often more than one task will be of interest at any one time. In addition, other considerations besides informativeness are important in choosing between confidence intervals and p values, yet informativeness is the only criterion we have discussed so far. Examples of other criteria that could be considered are cognitive demand and publication bias. These sets of issues are discussed next.

The Importance of Assessing Size

Although theories in the social sciences tend to be concerned more with questions of either exact equality or direction than with questions of size, the ultimate goal in most, if not all, sciences is to develop theories that account for the size of parameters. Certainly sciences such as physics and chemistry are concerned with assessing size (e.g., estimating the strength of the earth's gravity) and not just direction (e.g., deciding whether objects fall up or down). In addition, reporting and focusing on estimates of size rather than merely on direction is likely to help foster the development of quantitative, rather than merely directional, theories (Oakes, 1986). Both Greenwald, Pratkanis, Leippe, and Baumgardner (1986) and Reichardt and Gollob (1987, 1989) explicated other disadvantages of focusing on exact equality or direction rather than on size.

Some critics of confidence intervals have suggested that estimates of the size of parameters are not useful without more meaningful units of measurement than are common in the social sciences. These critics are correct in noting that making substantive sense of the units of measurements of many social science variables can be difficult (though see Ware, Keller, Gandek, Brazier, & Sullivan, 1995). And certainly estimates of size are less useful to the extent the variables don't have substantively meaningful units of measurement. But researchers can provide at least some meaning by using standardized (i.e., standard deviation) measurement units as, for better or worse, is usually done when conducting meta-analyses or making power calculations (Becker, 1991). In addition, if more emphasis were placed on estimating the size of parameters, more emphasis likely would be placed on making sense of units of measurement and on developing measures that have meaningful units, which in turn would make estimates of size even more useful.

Problems Introduced by Differences of Opinion About Prespecified Values or Ranges of Values

One way to show that the value of ψ is small enough to be ignored is to specify a range of values that are considered small enough to be ignored, collect data, and determine the probability that ψ lies within this range as described in the discussion of Task 3 earlier. One difficulty with this approach is that differences of opinion can arise about the range of values that are considered small enough to be ignored. In addition, as is said to occur in judging pornography, perhaps it is difficult to set standards ahead of time for judging when ψ is small enough to be ignored, but "you can recognize it when you see it." Or an estimate of ψ might be so large that every reasonable criterion value would be obviously surpassed, so effort spent on deciding upon arbitrary cut points would be wasted.

Similarly, differences of opinion may arise over the prespecified value of ψ_0 to use in assessing the direction of ψ relative to ψ_0, as described in Task 2 earlier. For example, some research consumers may be interested primarily in knowing whether an effect is likely to be positive or negative; whereas other consumers may want to know whether the effect is larger or smaller than a nonzero value to determine either (a) whether the benefits of a treatment outweigh the costs of implementation, or (b) whether the treatment effect is likely to be larger than the size of a suspected bias in the estimate.

These considerations suggest that, in performing Tasks 2 or 3, a confidence interval used without reference to a prespecified value or range of values can be more useful than a method that uses statistical tests in conjunction with a prespecified value or range of values. Compared to the statistical test methods previously described in the discussion of Tasks 2 and 3, a confidence interval doesn't provide as precise an answer to a question of the direction or size of ψ relative to a single prespecified value or to a single prespecified range of values. But when assessing the direction or size of ψ relative to (a) a variety of prespecified values, (b) a variety of prespecified ranges of values, or (c) no prespecified value or range of values, a confidence interval can be more useful than the statistical test methods.

Cognitive Demands

Researchers often want to report or sift through estimates of a large number of parameters. In such cases, presenting a full confidence interval for the estimate of each parameter of interest can be unwieldy or even cognitively overwhelming. Consequently, it may be preferable to use point estimates and their associated p values (or asterisks that categorize p values into a few levels of statistical significance and nonsignificance) either to present a mass of data or to select a subset of estimates to study more fully later (though see Meeks & D'Agostino, 1983) than to use confidence intervals. In other words, p values may be preferred to confidence intervals precisely because p values, in some ways, present less information than confidence intervals.

Publication Bias and the File-Drawer Problem

At present, journal reviewers and editors are strongly predisposed to accept for publication only articles reporting results that are statistically significant at $p < .05$. Greenwald (1975) has labeled this the "publication bias." One of the negative consequences of the publication bias is that Type I errors tend to remain uncorrected in the published literature. Another negative consequence is that overestimates of effects are more likely to be published than underestimates, because overestimates are more likely to be statistically significant. As a result of this bias toward publishing overestimates and because published results are generally easier to locate than unpublished results, both qualitative and quantitative literature reviews will tend to overestimate the size of effects. Rosenthal (1979) has labeled the problem of locating unpublished studies, and the resulting bias when they are not found, the "file-drawer problem" based on the tendency for researchers to bury their statistically nonsignificant results in file drawers.

One way to reduce both publication bias and the file-drawer problem would be to publish results partly on the basis of the precision of the estimate of ψ (i.e., favor small margins of error) rather than solely on the basis of statistical significance. Such a change in publication criteria could have other salutary effects as well. For example, using present publication criteria, statistically nonsignificant results such as in case C in Figure 10.1 are unlikely to be published even though they reveal important information, namely that ψ is likely to be close to 0. The suggested change in publication criteria would increase the likelihood that the results in case C would be published because the estimate of ψ is relatively precise.

Although we recommend increasing the weight given to precision in making publication decisions, we believe it would not be wise to make high precision a necessary condition for publication. Otherwise one would have to forego publishing results such as those in case B in Figure 10.1 which are informative because they show that ψ is probably large even though they provide only a relatively imprecise estimate of just how large. Although we oppose requirements that remove human judgment, perhaps one criterion for publication should be that of attaining either statistical significance or high precision.

A shift in publication criteria as we recommend would be more likely to occur if the use of confidence intervals were increased relative to the use of statistical tests. This is because, compared to using statistical tests, confidence intervals (a) focus attention more on the precision of estimates while still allowing the statistical significance of the results to be easily assessed and (b) more readily reveal why publishing statistically insignificant but precise results (such as depicted in case C in Figure 10.1) might well be justified.

WHEN TO USE CONFIDENCE INTERVALS, *P* VALUES, OR BOTH

When they are both interpretable, a researcher need not necessarily choose between confidence intervals and statistical tests. Both can be calculated, examined, and reported. Indeed, if one presented both a confidence interval and the *p* value from a statistical test, one would be providing more complete information on exact equality, direction, and size than would be provided by presenting either a confidence interval or a p value alone. However, an important drawback to presenting both a confidence interval and a p value is that interpreting all that information would be more cognitively demanding than interpreting either a confidence interval or a p value alone.

To balance the advantages and disadvantages of having so much information on exact equality, direction, and size, researchers could report both a confidence interval and a p value only for the most important and central findings in a study. For less important results, a confidence interval by itself or—perhaps to reduce cognitive demands even further—the results of a statistical test by itself could be reported. If a large number of results were equally central and important, various compromises could be used.

One widely used compromise is to report a table of point estimates along with information about p values. In cases where the margins of error for tabled values are similar, the table could be made even more useful by reporting information about the margins of error (e.g., the standard errors) in a note to the table. In addition, both parameter estimates and uncertainties about their sizes could be addressed in further detail in the body of the text, a practice that is not presently commonplace.

Confidence intervals should probably replace statistical tests as the usual norm in reporting research results. But if such a change occurs, researchers still should be encouraged to add p values or even to report p values in place of confidence intervals when there is good reason for doing so.

POTENTIAL SOURCES OF RESISTANCE TO THE USE OF CONFIDENCE INTERVALS

We believe confidence intervals should be used more frequently and statistical tests less frequently than is currently the case. Unfortunately, urging this type of reform, as often has been done in the past, has not been sufficient to alter the present imbalance between the use of confidence intervals and statistical tests (e.g., Bakan, 1966; Blackwelder, 1982; Carver, 1978; Cohen, 1994; Dar, 1987; Gardner & Altman, 1986; Hauck & Anderson, 1986; Makuch & Johnson, 1986; Meehl, 1967, 1978; Morrison & Henkel, 1970; Rozeboom, 1960; Schmidt, 1996). Perhaps reform will come about only if engineered with an understanding of the obstacles that have stood in the way of the increased use of confidence intervals. Some of these probable obstacles are described next:

1. Convention so strongly favors statistical tests that other options, such as confidence intervals, often aren't even considered.

2. Conditions in which confidence intervals are preferable to statistical tests often aren't recognized. This is not surprising given that texts and other pedagogical material (including the American Psychological Association's publication manual, 1994) devote far more attention to statistical tests than to confidence intervals.

3. Computer programs often don't produce confidence intervals as readily as statistical tests, and formulas for confidence intervals often aren't as easy to find in texts as are formulas for statistical tests.

4. The size of parameter estimates are often disappointingly small and reporting confidence intervals, rather than the results of statistical tests, would tend to focus more attention on the small size. It often appears more impressive (to both journal reviewers and other readers) to report that a result is statistically significant than to report a confidence interval that shows the result, though statistically significant, is estimated to be trivially small.

5. Confidence intervals often are disappointingly wide. In such cases, researchers may believe it would reflect unfavorably on their research if they were to present confidence intervals and thereby focus attention on the large degree of uncertainty in their parameter estimates. As a result, reporting a confidence interval rather than a statistical test might lower the chance that a researcher's work would be accepted for publication.

6. When no uniquely defined parameter is associated with a statistical test, no unique confidence interval exists. The chi-square test of association in a 2×2 contingency table is an example. Different confidence intervals would result depending on whether the strength of association were indexed by a phi coefficient, an odds ratio, or any of the several other available measures for such data. Therefore, calculating a confidence interval in these cases requires an additional step of deciding which index to use and potentially being required to defend that choice. Although we believe this is an advantage, it nonetheless puts additional demands on researchers.

7. Many arguments in favor of confidence intervals focus more on criticizing statistical tests than on emphasizing the advantages of confidence intervals. Unfortunately, many of the criticisms of statistical tests are either false or exaggerated. As a consequence, readers who recognize these inaccuracies may tend to discount the accompanying recommendations that confidence intervals be used instead of statistical tests. For example, many critics state that statistical tests are uninformative because the null hy-

pothesis is always false, yet this criticism is misguided. Most important, even in cases where the null hypothesis is known to be false a priori, statistical tests can provide useful information about direction and size, and not only information about exact equality. In addition, tests of exact equality sometimes can reasonably be interpreted as providing information about approximate, rather than exact, equality. Finally, some substantively interesting null hypotheses, for example concerning the existence of extrasensory perception, may not be false (but only if either the prior distribution is not uniform or ψ can logically take on only one of a finite number of values). Similarly, many critics of the use of significance tests state that p values can't provide information about the probability that either the null or alternative hypotheses are true. But, as we have shown, the subjectivist approach does enable such probabilities to be easily computed from p values under many conditions.

8. Sometimes recommendations to use confidence intervals are accompanied by recommendations to abandon the use of statistical tests altogether. Some researchers have perhaps interpreted recommendations to abandon "hypothesis tests" as implying that they must thereby also abandon the "testing of hypotheses" altogether, which obviously is thought to be undesirable. Of course, such interpretations are not true. In fact, because of the way they focus on size, confidence intervals often can provide demanding and risky tests of substantive hypotheses more easily than can statistical tests (Meehl, 1967, 1978).

Given the obstacles just described, we believe a substantial increase in the use of confidence intervals is unlikely to occur unless substantial changes are made in the process by which submitted articles are accepted or rejected for publication. One step in this direction would be to adopt journal policies that place more emphasis on confidence intervals. Without such changes in publication policies, researchers are less likely to increase their use of confidence intervals if only because of the fear that using confidence intervals would make it more difficult to get their work published.

Of course, a change in journal policy to encourage greater use of confidence intervals also would likely require that guidelines be devised to deal with practical questions of detail such as the following. Should the 95% level of confidence be the convention in reporting confidence intervals and how should one report the level of confidence if one wanted to deviate from this convention? When is it best to report the end points of a confidence interval and when is it best to report a point estimate and the margin of error (or the standard error)? Should a different format be used for reporting confidence intervals that are symmetric versus asymmetric around the point estimate? When would it be beneficial to use standardized rather than unstandardized measurement units in confidence intervals?

SUMMARY AND PRACTICAL IMPLICATIONS

Frequentists define probability as an "objective" state of nature that is independent of the observer. In contrast, subjectivists define probability as a "subjective" belief about nature that is dependent on the observer. As a result of this and other differences, frequentists and subjectivists obtain different types of information from confidence intervals and statistical tests. The information that can be obtained from confidence intervals and statistical tests is also influenced by the researcher's prior distribution for the population parameter of interest.

With certain forms of prior distributions, subjectivists can draw specific probability inferences about the value of the population parameter, ψ, from both a confidence interval and the obtained p value from a statistical test of the null hypothesis that $\psi = \psi_0$. Specific probability inferences specify that (a) a $100(1 - \alpha)\%$ confidence interval for ψ has a $100(1 - \alpha)\%$ probability of containing the value of ψ, (b) the probability is $1 - .5p$ that the value of ψ and the value of the obtained estimate of ψ lie on the same side of ψ_0, and (c) the probability is $.5p$ that either ψ is equal to ψ_0 or ψ and its estimate lie on opposite sides of ψ_0.

In contrast to subjectivists, frequentists can never draw specific probability inferences from either confidence intervals or statistical tests. However, with certain forms of prior distributions frequentists can draw specific confidence inferences. Specific confidence inferences specify that a frequentist can be (a) $100(1 - \alpha)\%$ confident that a $100(1 - \alpha)\%$ confidence interval contains the value of ψ, (b) $100(1 - .5p)\%$ confident that the value of ψ and the value of the obtained estimate of ψ lie on the same side of ψ_0, and (c) $100(.5p)\%$ confident that either ψ is equal to ψ_0 or ψ and its estimate lie on opposite sides of ψ_0. Though specific probability and confidence inferences have different meanings, they are parallel in structure. In addition, the conditions under which specific probability inferences can and cannot be made by a subjectivist are the same as the conditions under which specific confidence inferences can and cannot be made by a frequentist.

There is an irony here. Probability is explicitly subjective for the subjectivist and explicitly objective for the frequentist. But a subjectivist's specific probability inference sounds more objective than a frequentist's specific confidence inference.

If the prior distribution for the population parameter of interest is nonuniform, neither specific probability inferences by a subjectivist nor specific confidence inferences by a frequentist can be drawn from either confidence intervals or statistical tests. Therefore, there is no reason to prefer a confidence interval to a statistical test, or vice versa, when the prior distribution is nonuniform. But although specific inferences as they are defined in the present chapter would be incorrect, correct inferences from either the subjectivist or frequentist perspective when the prior distribution is nonuniform could be derived using Bayesian statistical methods.

If insufficient information is available to specify a prior distribution for the population parameter of interest, specific probability inferences by a subjectivist and specific confidence inferences by a frequentist can be drawn from a confidence interval but not from a statistical test. Because of this difference in informativeness, confidence intervals are preferable to statistical tests when a usable prior distribution can't be specified.

The case in which the prior distribution for the population parameter of interest is uniform is of special interest for two reasons. First, this is the only case under which specific probability inferences by a subjectivist and specific confidence inferences by a frequentist can be drawn from both confidence intervals and statistical tests. Because it may be easier for a subjectivist than a frequentist to justify assuming a uniform prior distribution, subjectivists may have an advantage in this regard compared to frequentists. Second, results from Bayesian analyses that assume a uniform prior distribution often are reported even when the analyst's prior distribution is really nonuniform or when there is no usable prior distribution. The reason for using a uniform prior distribution when it is not correct is to provide a reference point for, and increase communication with, groups of people who are likely to hold a diverse array of prior distributions.

When the prior distribution is uniform, whether a confidence interval or a statistical test provides more useful information depends on the type of questions being asked. A statistical test generally provides more information than a confidence interval about the probability or confidence that (a) a parameter equals a prespecified value, (b) a parameter lies in one direction or another relative to a prespecified value, and (c) a parameter lies within a prespecified range of values. In contrast, relative to statistical tests, confidence intervals provide more useful information about the size of a parameter either (a) when no reference value or range of values is prespecified or (b) when many reference values or ranges of values are of interest. In the social sciences, the two tasks at which confidence intervals tend to excel generally arise more often than the three tasks at which statistical tests tend to excel. As a result, confidence intervals are usually, but not always, more informative than statistical tests.

To obtain relatively complete information about the equality, direction, and size of a population parameter when the prior distribution is uniform, the most important and central results in a study could be reported using both a confidence interval and the obtained p value from a statistical test. However, to reduce cognitive demands on both authors and readers, less important results could be reported using either confidence intervals or p values alone. In many cases, confidence intervals are to be preferred to p values from statistical tests. However, because of resistance to their use, confidence intervals are unlikely to be widely reported in the literature unless their use is encouraged, or at least not penalized, by the publication criteria of journals.

ACKNOWLEDGMENTS

We thank Michael Neale, Jenny Novotny, George Potts, Bob Pruzek, David Rindskopf, Frank Schmidt, Will Shadish, and an anonymous reviewer for helpful comments on earlier drafts.

REFERENCES

American Psychological Association (1994). *Publication manual of the American Psychological Association* (4th. ed.). Washington, DC: Author.

Bakan, D. (1966). The test of significance in psychological research. *Psychological Bulletin, 66,* 423–437.

Barnett, V. (1982). *Comparative statistical inference* (2nd. ed.). New York: Wiley.

Becker, G. (1991). Alternative methods of reporting research results. *American Psychologist, 46,* 654–655.

Blackwelder, W. C. (1982). Proving the null hypothesis in clinical trials. *Controlled Clinical Trials, 3,* 345–353.

Box, G. E. P., Hunter, W. G., & Hunter, J. S. (1978). *Statistics for experimenters.* New York: Wiley.

Box, G. E. P., & Tiao, G. C. (1973). *Bayesian inference in statistical analysis.* Reading, MA: Addison-Wesley.

Bradstreet, T., & Dobbins, T. (1996). When are two drug formulations interchangeable? *Teaching Statistics, 18,* 45–48.

Carver, R. P. (1978). The case against statistical significance testing. *Harvard Educational Review, 48,* 378–399.

Chow, S. L. (1988). Significance test or effect size? *Psychological Bulletin, 103,* 105–110.

Chow, S. L. (1996). *Statistical significance: Rationale, validity and utility.* Thousand Oaks, CA: Sage.

Cohen, J. (1994). The earth is round (*p* < .05). *American Psychologist, 49,* 997–1003.

Dar, R. (1987). Another look at Meehl, Lakatos, and the scientific practices of psychologists. *American Psychologist, 42,* 145–151.

Gardner, M. J., & Altman, D. G. (1986). Confidence intervals rather than *p* values: Estimation rather than hypothesis testing. *British Medical Journal, 292,* 746–750.

Greenwald, A. G. (1975). Consequences of prejudice against the null hypothesis. *Psychological Bulletin, 82,* 1–20.

Greenwald, A. G., Pratkanis, A. R., Leippe, M. R., & Baumgardner, M. H. (1986). Under what conditions does theory obstruct research progress? *Psychological Review, 93,* 216–229.

Hagen, R. L. (1997). In praise of the null hypothesis statistical test. *American Psychologist, 52,* 15–24.

Hauck, W. W., & Anderson, S. (1986). A proposal for interpreting and reporting negative studies. *Statistics in Medicine, 5,* 203–209.

Makuch, R. W., & Johnson, M. R. (1986). Some issues in the design and interpretation of "negative" clinical studies. *Archives of Internal Medicine, 146,* 986–989.

Meehl, P. E. (1967). Theory-testing in psychology and physics: A methodological paradox. *Philosophy of Science, 34,* 103–115.

Meehl, P. E. (1978). Theoretical risks and tabular asterisks: Sir Karl, Sir Ronald, and the slow progress in soft psychology. *Journal of Consulting and Clinical Psychology, 46,* 806–834.

Meeks, S. L., & D'Agostino, R. B. (1983). A note on the use of confidence limits following rejection of a null hypothesis. *The American Statistician, 37,* 134–136.

Morrison, D. E., & Henkel, R. E. (Eds.). (1970). *The significance test controversy-A reader.* Chicago: Aldine.

Novick, M. R., & Jackson, P. H. (1974). *Statistical methods for educational and psychological research.* New York: McGraw-Hill.

Oakes, M. (1986). *Statistical inference: A commentary for the social and behavioral sciences.* New York: Wiley.

Pollard, W. E. (1986). *Bayesian statistics for evaluation research: An introduction.* Newbury Park, CA: Sage.

Pratt, J. W. (1965). Bayesian interpretations of standard inference statements (with discussion). *Journal of the Royal Statistical Society*, Series B, *27*, 169–203.

Reichardt, C. S., & Gollob, H. F. (1987). Taking uncertainty into account when estimating effects. In M. M. Mark & R. L. Shotland (Eds.), *Multiple methods in program evaluation* (New Directions in Program Evaluation, No. 35, pp. 7–22). San Francisco: Jossey-Bass.

Reichardt, C. S., & Gollob, H. F. (1989). Ruling out threats to validity. *Evaluation Review*, *13*, 3–17.

Rogers, J. L., Howard, K. J., & Vessey, J. J. (1993). Using significance tests to evaluate equivalence between two experimental groups. *Psychological Bulletin*, *113*, 553–565.

Rosenthal, R. (1979). The "file-drawer problem" and tolerance for null results. *Psychological Bulletin*, *86*, 638–641.

Rouanet, H. (1996). Bayesian methods for assessing importance of effects. *Psychological Bulletin*, *119*, 149–158.

Rozeboom, W. W. (1960). The fallacy of the null-hypothesis significance test. *Psychological Bulletin*, *57*, 416–428.

Schmidt, F. L. (1996). Statistical significance testing and cumulative knowledge in psychology: Implications for the training of researchers. *Psychological Methods*, *1*, 115–129.

Tukey, J. W. (1960). Conclusions vs. decisions. *Technometrics*, *2*, 423–433.

Ware, J. E., Keller, S. D., Gandek, B., Brazier, J. E., & Sullivan, M. (1995). Evaluating translations of health status questionnaires: Methods from the IQOLA project. *International Journal of Technology Assessment in Health Care*, *11*, 525–551.

Yeaton, W. H., & Sechrest, L. (1986). Use and misuse of no-difference findings in eliminating threats to validity. *Evaluation Review*, *10*, 836–852.

Zellner, A. (1971). *An introduction to Bayesian inference in econometrics*. New York: Wiley.

A Bayesian Perspective
on
Hypothesis Testing

Chapter 11

An Introduction to Bayesian Inference and its Applications

Robert M. Pruzek
University at Albany
State University of New York

Students in the social and behavioral sciences tend generally to learn inferential statistics from texts and materials that emphasize significance tests or confidence intervals. Bayesian statistical methods support inferences without reference to either significance tests or confidence intervals. This chapter provides an introduction to Bayesian inference. It is shown that this class of methods entails use of prior information and empirical data to generate posterior distributions that in turn serve as the basis for statistical inferences. Two relatively simple examples are used to illustrate the essential concepts and methods of Bayesian analysis and to contrast inference statements made within this subjectivist framework with inference statements derived from classical methods. In particular, the role of posterior distributions in making formal inferences is described and compared with inferences based on classical methods. It also is argued that Bayesian thinking may help to improve definitions of inferential problems, especially in the behavioral and social sciences where the complex nature of applications often may require special strategies to make it realistic for investigators to attempt rigorous formal inferences. Sequentially articulated studies are seen as particularly desirable in some situations, and Bayesian methods are seen as having special virtue in using results from previous studies to inform inferences about later ones. Numerous references are briefly described to aid the reader who seeks to learn more about Bayesian inference and its applications.

Significance tests and confidence intervals constitute the central topics of most chapters in this volume, with the tacit suggestion that there are no other mechanisms with which to make inductive statistical inferences. It would be a pity for the reader to believe this, however, because one of the most respected of all modes of inductive statistical reasoning makes no reference whatsoever to either significance tests or confidence intervals. As can be seen from my title, I have in mind work done to advance *Bayesian* statistical methods. Bayesian and classical forms of statistical inference are fundamentally different from one another because these systems entail different assumptions at the outset. I first examine basic concepts associated with one of the simplest classical inferential problems and then go on to describe its Bayesian or subjectivist counterpart. Specifically, in the next three paragraphs when terms like *probability* and *parameter* are used, the context intended is that of classical or frequentist statistical inference; but for virtually all of the remainder of this chapter these and other related technical terms are used with reference to the Bayesian or subjectivist paradigm.

Consider a standard problem in inductive inference, that of estimating a population parameter for a single categorical variable. Suppose, for example, that one has sampled $n = 100$ prospective voters and wishes to use the resulting information, say 60 "yes" and 40 "no" answers to proposition A, as a basis for estimating the proportion (denoted as π) of people in the parent population who favor this proposition. Use of these data and standard techniques yields a 95% confidence interval for the parameter π with approximate limits .50 and .70. Consequently, on the basis of classical—also called frequentist—statistical reasoning, an investigator would be justified in saying that he or she had 95% *confidence* that the population parameter π is within these limits. Although this usage constitutes what has become an acceptable convention, at least among applied statisticians, it seems somewhat shrewd or artful to use the word *confidence* this way, and not to permit use of the term *probability*. Following are the essential elements of this logic.

Because any such numerical interval *either does or does not* include the parameter π, one is *not* justified to say "The probability is .95 that the population parameter π lies between the limits .50 and .70." It should be understood that the population π is a single value describing the proportion of the fixed population's members that endorse proposition A. The sample proportion, .60, is merely an observed result based on a single, arbitrary sample. The conception that the population is pre-specified, wholly fixed, even if unknown or unknowable, is fundamental to classical statistical reasoning. Although these data also might be used to test pre-specified hypotheses, such as the parameter $\pi = .50$, this objective is not pursued so that other issues can be explored in more detail.

Classical statistical reasoning does sanction use of the word *probability* in this context with reference to repeated sampling. Thus, it would be correct to say: "Were a large number of independent (random) samples of size n to be drawn from the same (fixed) population, and the proportions of "affirmatives" to the proposition recorded in each sample, then—supposing the same approved procedure for generating a confidence interval were to be used for each sample—the probability of any one such interval spanning or including the parameter π is .95." It is notable, however, that this conclusion leaves out reference to the specific numerical interval obtained with the extant sample. Frequentist reasoning allows that investigators may use the word *confidence* for the specific numerical interval, but they are explicitly forbidden to use the term *probability* when making inferences from the same interval. It is perhaps not surprising that students often have difficulty with this distinction. This semantic peculiarity is of special relevance here.

The first purpose of this chapter is to describe in some detail the Bayesian or subjectivist approach to this limited inferential problem and to contrast this with the standard inferential approach based on frequentist methods. By so doing, it is hoped that the essential logic and interpretive value of Bayesian inferential methods can be made clear, and can be distinguished from the classical mode of statistical inference. Certain more general Bayesian inferential problems also are summarized. Special virtues follow from focusing on a limited inferential problem: It brings into sharp relief some of the major ways in which problem statements or design strategies for studies may bear on prospects for both analysis and interpretation, and it helps to clarify the role of formal statistical induction in applications. This leads to a second but related purpose, which is to argue that *formal* inferences in the context of applied research, at least in the social and psychological sciences, often must have to be sufficiently qualified that they cannot be expected to lead to clear or straight-forward interpretations. Thus, a case is made for attending more carefully than may be common to issues of planning and study design, perhaps including sequential strategies, to enhance the prospects of being able to make formal inferences with respect to *sets* of what often may be rather specific or narrow questions. One approach to the development of sets of questions that may be amenable to inductive inferences is sketched in outline form, using subjectivist concepts for guidance. Given limitations of space, the chief target for such applications is intervention studies.

The Beta Distribution and Subjective Priors for a Single Parameter

The technical problem discussed next is that of pre-specifying a *prior* distribution for the parameter π. Then it will be shown how empirical data can be used through the vehicle of a *likelihood* to generate a *posterior* distribution for the parameter π from which one's ultimate inferences can be made explicit. In order to provide the desired explanation, however, some background on the *beta distribution* is required. The beta distribution has the virtue of being one of the easiest of distributions to describe whose use engages a wide range of Bayesian thinking in the context of a standard inferential problem. Many readers will recognize close connections between beta and the binomial distribution.

The beta distribution has two parameters, here labeled a and b, both greater than zero. The height of the curve associated with beta can be written as

$$y = \frac{(a+b-1)!}{(a-1)!(b-1)!} \pi^{a-1}(1-\pi)^{b-1} \qquad (11.1)$$

where π is taken to have the range 0 . . . 1 for any positive integer choices of a and b. To refresh your memory, note that for a whole number x,

$$x! = x(x-1)(x-2) \dots (2)(1) \,;$$

that is, $x!$ is just the product of x terms, each reduced by one after the first. Thus, for relatively small values of a and b it is easy, if a little tedious, to sketch this distribution by selecting a few values for π, say $\pi = .1, .2, \dots, .9$, computing y for each, and then outlining the curve that connects these values of y for the selected series of π values. (Recall that if a or b equal one or two, then the factorial terms, which then would be 0! or 1!, are by definition taken to be unity.) If $a = 3$, $b = 4$, and $\pi = .3$, the left-hand term is (6! / 2!3!) = 60, whereas the product on the right = $(.3^2)(.7^3)$ = .03087 so $y = 1.852$ in this case. Several examples of beta distributions are soon illustrated and discussed.

Suppose you aim to construct a beta distribution that describes *your particular beliefs or opinions about different values for* a particular parameter; that is, your distribution of subjective probabilities. Let the parameter π represent what for you is the (uncertain) probability of a "success" or perhaps "1" (where "failure" is denoted by "0") for any single, clearly defined binary event. For example, you might think of tossing a thumbtack in the air and letting it fall on a hard, flat surface. Consider the question, "What subjective prior distribution, $p(\pi)$, describes my particular beliefs about the probability that a certain tack will land point down (a "success") for an arbitrary toss?" One might imagine asking this question before making any toss. One strategy for generating your prior distribution, $p(\pi)$, would be to divide the π-scale up into, say, 10–12 intervals, and think carefully about how likely each subset of values for π seems to be in relation to the others. You might roughly sketch your distribution for these probabilities and then choose two beta parameters that yields a shape that comes close to reproducing your sketch. Taking such a problem seriously almost certainly will provide a range of guesses for your personal probability distribution for the parameter in question. Given that the relative heights of such a curve correspond to your personal beliefs concerning the likelihoods of different π values, the curve can be taken to constitute your prior distribution for this parameter. Although such a distribution is indeed subjective, Bayesian analysts counsel that its construction be taken seriously.

In a particular application, you might help ensure that the curve soundly represents your opinion by deciding what bets you would be willing to take for different conceivable values for π, with odds based on your distribution, $p(\pi)$, that is, those values of your personal probability associated with π in various narrowly spaced intervals. For the thumbtack problem you might decide that your prior has its maximum near $\pi = 1/3$, with prior probabilities, $p(\pi)$, about half as large for πs in the proximity of 1/6 and 1/2, and so forth. In this case, you should be equally willing to bet that the likelihood of the thumbtack landing point down is one out of two tosses, as that it is one out of six; but in relation to either of these outcomes your $p(\pi)$ distribution implies you would bet with doubled odds that the probability of the tack landing point down is one out of three. Ideally, all such prospective bets concerning different πs should be consistent with your subjective $p(\pi)$ distribution. It also can be useful to decide in advance how much data your opinion is worth, in the form of specifying the sum $a + b$, then identify a value for the ratio $a/(a + b)$. Modern computer software can facilitate such matters, as is shown later.

Before going on, pause to note that I have switched from what began as use of third-person pronouns in the initial paragraphs above, to the first- and second-person pronouns *I* and *you* now. This is a central point, fundamental to the Bayesian approach to inference, because the latter system is plainly a subjective or personalistic one. Rather than postulating some fixed, objectively defined "parent" population (such as zeros and ones), with a single value for π, the Bayesian statistician starts with the concept of a particular well-defined event, or class of events. Then he or she uses some symbol (e.g., π, a probability, for binary outcomes) to index a characteristic feature of this event, and proceeds to think about his or her beliefs about the feature associated with this symbol. As will be seen later, the operational system for making Bayesian inferences about the parameter in question generally entails three steps: (a) generate a *subjective* prior distribution (such as $p(\pi)$) for this parameter, (b) collect empirical data as a basis for constructing a likelihood distribution for this parameter, and (c) combine the prior and likelihood to form a final distribution, a posterior, that can be used to explicate one's formal inferences about the parameter in question. To the personalist, all three of these distributions are properly regarded as subjective and the entire inferential enterprise is regarded as a matter of refining subjective opinions about the parameter(s) in question. It is important in applications not to let technical complexities bearing on the inferential process interfere with the essence of personalistic logic.

Next I generalize the equation for beta, and use graphical methods to show how in practice one might choose values for the constants a and b to correspond with one's prior beliefs about the parameter π. Keep in mind that the idea is to choose these two constants so that they determine a beta distribution that *soundly reflects one's personal beliefs* about some parameter π, for some well-defined event. Given that π is continuous with range $0 \le \pi \le 1$, we write

$$p(\pi) = \frac{\Gamma(a+b)}{\Gamma(a)\Gamma(b)} \pi^{a-1}(1-\pi)^{b-1} \tag{11.2}$$

where the term $\Gamma(a)$, is called a gamma function, which can be interpreted as $(a-1)!$ if a is a positive integer value. That is, $\Gamma(\ )$ provides the generalization of the factorial needed to permit any positive, real numbered values for a (or b, or $a + b$). It is straightforward to use factorials to obtain terms like $\Gamma(a)$ for the case where a takes on integer values, then to use interpolation to estimate $\Gamma(a)$ for arguments such as $a = 3.5$ or 10.4. Bear in mind that the definition of the gamma function is such that for any integer argument such as a or $a + b$ in parentheses, you must subtract one before computing the factorial.

Technically, Equation 11.2 defines a continuous distribution, for which the total area under the beta curve is unity or one; the height of the curve is described as the *probability density* for the parameter π. One's personal probabilities, indexed by $p(\pi)$, are properly associated with *areas* under the curve between any two distinctive values for π.

Figure 11.1 shows six examples of beta distributions for various a,b combinations. Figure 11.1a, in the upper panel, shows three symmetric beta distributions; symmetry is a consequence of setting $a = b$ in each case. For larger values of a and b, the distributions for $p(\pi)$ are seen to have less spread or variance, and be relatively more peaked. Prior specification of distributions with relatively large a and b corresponds to having more information, or a more precise view initially, about the parameter in question than if a and b were small. As can be seen from examination of Equation 11.2, had the choices been $a = b = 1$, the distribution $p(\pi)$ would become flat, or uniform, corresponding to a prior state of ignorance about the parameter. The choices $a = b = 4$ correspond to a belief that the most probable π is near the value of .5, but could be reasonably far away from this value, perhaps as small as .1 or as large as .9. For $a = b = 10$, a similar opinion is implied, but prior beliefs in values for π below about .2 or above .8 are seen as most unlikely. The latter distribution is soon examined as part of an example.

Figure 11.1b, in the lower panel, depicts beta distributions corresponding to the prior belief that values of π near .3 are most likely; that is, that .3 is the modal value for the distribution. These three choices for this distribution imply different degrees of personal assurance about how near π may be to .3. To choose $a = 5/4$, $b = 8/5$, would be to say that considerable doubt is associated with the modal value, because a substantial part of the density for this curve is relatively far removed from the modal value. By contrast, the choices $a = 7$, $b = 15$ correspond to a moderately well defined prior opinion about π, to the effect that this parameter must not be far below .1, nor much above .6. The choices $a = 3$,

$b = 5.67$ correspond to an intermediate prior opinion about π, that is, a distribution between the other two distributions shown in Figure 11.1b. To have set $a <$ b has resulted in each distribution being positively skewed; were $a > b$, the mode would of course exceed .5 and the corresponding beta distribution would be negatively skewed.

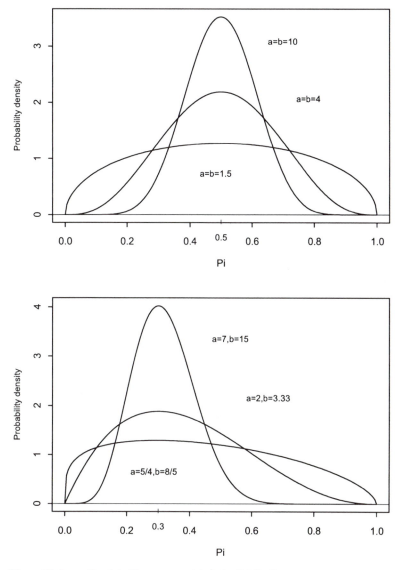

Figure 11.1   Top (a): Three symmetric beta distributions;
                     Bottom (b): Three beta distributions with mode = .3.

A beta distribution's mean = $a/(a + b)$, mode = $(a - 1)/(a + b - 2)$ and variance = $ab/(a + b)^2(a + b + 1)$. As can be seen from these examples, the beta family is fairly rich and is likely to include priors one would be apt to sketch using wholly subjective procedures. Note that none of these betas are irregular, nor multimodal; indeed, it seems that multimodal forms for $p(\pi)$ rarely could be construed as realistic. In what follows I do not consider any priors that cannot be chosen from the beta family.

An Example of Bayesian Inference Based on the Beta Distribution

My primary example entails an experiment in which each of a number of persons has taken *two* different drugs as remedies for backache. All individuals are assumed to have experienced this affliction often enough that some form of pain remedy is deemed appropriate; but to avoid complications in the argument let us assume that none of the participants has such severe backache that prolonging more serious treatment is likely to have untoward consequences. Because this is intended to be a fairly realistic example, sufficient contextual information is supplied to ensure that what eventuates is a reasonably well defined and realistic applied inferential problem, despite its fictitious nature.

Suppose each of $n = 100$ persons has used drug A as well as drug B, each for, say, 4 weeks. For half of the subjects, assume the drug A regimen has been given first; for the others, drug B will have preceded A; that is, this is a repeated measures experiment. Assume also that the ordering was randomly determined. To set aside further reproof, one might assume that the two drugs are sufficiently similar to permit a double-blind experimental protocol. For simplicity in this context, let us record only whether the participant judges A better than B (scored as "1"), or not (scored "0"), where each respondent must decide that drug A is better than B, or drug B is better than A; that is, equivocation is not allowed. Thus, the parameter π in this problem is defined as the probability that an arbitrarily chosen member of the *prospective universe of persons not unlike those who have agreed to participate in the experiment judges drug A to have benefited him* or *her more than drug B*. In this context, Bayesian inferential reasoning entails the notion that π indexes the (unknown) probability of a particular event, and that the prior distribution for π is initially to be the subject of introspective analysis. Hence, my first task is that of specifying a prior distribution, $p(\pi)$, by choosing two appropriate parameters from the beta family. Information contained in this prior is combined with information obtained from the ensuing sample of $n = 100$ cases to construct a posterior distribution for the parameter in question. This posterior provides a basis for inferences about the parameter.

Suppose my review of the development and previous laboratory tests of the two drugs, and the persons to whom they will be given, leads me to say that my prior distribution, $p(\pi)$, is centered near .5. That is, I really cannot decide whether I believe drug A is likely to outperform B, or vice versa. In addition, I do not believe that either drug will completely overwhelm the other in reducing back pain, so my opinion is that values of π rather far from .5 are not very credible. After comparison of several prospective priors, I conclude that the beta distribution with $a = b = 10$, realistically reflects my prior, $p(\pi)$. This choice also implies that I believe my prior opinion is worth about 20 data points, this being the sum $a + b$. One might say that a identifies the number of ones and b the number of zeros in a *hypothetical* sample, so that $a + b = n'$, say, constitutes the size of such a sample. Recall that Figure 11.1a displays a prior distribution for which $a = b = 10$.

Note that whereas the preceding information suggests uncertainty about π's prior distribution, beta(10, 10) is rather different from a flat or uniform prior. The reader may recall that setting a and b to one, a priori, yields a flat or uniform beta distribution; such a prior generally corresponds to a prior state of ignorance, which is what use of classical statistical methods typically implies. Because I have deliberated in selecting drugs A and B from several possible treatments, it is only reasonable to expect that I would have acquired enough information to be able to say something more specific about their relative effectiveness than that all values for π in the range (0.0 to 1.0) are, a priori, equally likely.

Since my prior distribution $p(\pi)$ has now been specified, let me vault ahead and assume that the experimental data concerning the drug comparison have been delivered. It can be reported that out of 100 participants, 60 declared drug A better than B in ameliorating backache, whereas 40 made the opposite judgment, saying that drug B did better. We now aim to generate a likelihood distribution based on these data, incorporate the information provided by the prior, and proceed to generate the posterior distribution for π. The beauty is that for this especially simple statistical problem, all three distributions, the prior, the likelihood, and the posterior, can be constructed as beta distributions. Consequently, all that is needed is to show how various beta constants are derived from the available information.

In view of the fact that there are three conceptually distinct distributions associated with the beta model, the notation for the two beta parameters must be elaborated so as to reflect the necessary distinctions. I use orthodox notation, where a', b' correspond to the prior; a^*, b^* correspond to the likelihood; and a'', b'' identify posterior beta parameters. The pleasing simplicity is that the posterior beta parameters are additive functions of the prior and likelihood constants, so that $a'' = a' + a^*$, and $b'' = b' + b^*$. Given that the sample of $n = 100$ observations has led to the finding that 60 persons favor drug A, and 40 favor B, this means that $a* = 60$ and $b* = 40$; that is, $a* + b* = n$ is the total number of ones and zeros. Consequently, the posterior beta constants are $a'' = 10 + 60 = 70$, and $b'' = 10 + 40 = 50$.

Figure 11.2a, the upper panel of Figure 11.2, depicts both the prior and the likelihood, the two distributions that combine to form the posterior from which inferences are made. Note that the prior and likelihood betas have different means as well as different variances or spreads. The distribution for likelihood is balanced on the observed sample mean $p = .6$ (the mode of beta(60,40) is .602, just above the mean), and the standard deviation of this distribution is .049. I have also noted on the plot the interval from .5 to .7 at the base of the beta likelihood distribution. Although these numerical limits were associated with a classical 95% confidence interval for π at the outset they can be shown to have a subjectivist interpretation, as is shown in due course.

Before going on, it may be helpful to comment on the likelihood itself, for this distribution has distinctive features that the reader should stop to appreciate. The likelihood derives wholly from one's sample data. In particular, the likelihood summarizes all information contained in the sample that is informative about the parameter in question. In the case of the parameter π, heights of the likelihood for different values of π describe the relative credibilities of different values of this parameter, based on the extant sample. Multiplication of the prior by the likelihood makes explicit how the data modify one's prior knowledge of the parameter. This effect, illustrated in Figure 11.2b, is discussed in the next paragraph. Note, however, that had one denied any prior knowledge of the parameter in question, such as having stated a uniform prior, then the posterior would reflect only the information in the sample data. In such a case, probabilities associated with the posterior distribution would be based exclusively on the likelihood, which is to say the likelihood and the posterior would coincide.

The lower panel, Figure 11.2b, shows the posterior distribution obtained by combining the prior and the posterior shown in Figure 11.2a. Note that the posterior beta(70, 50) has slightly less variance than beta(60, 40), the likelihood. The standard deviation (SD) of beta(70, 50) is .045, its mean is .583, and its mode is .585. That the posterior beta has been shifted slightly to the left in relation to the likelihood is, of course, a consequence of having combined information from the beta prior, which is centered on $\pi = .5$, with the likelihood, which is balanced on .6. The posterior distribution generally can be seen as a particular compromise between the prior and the likelihood. The conclusion here is that the observed data from the backache experiment have shifted my personal probability distribution for the parameter π to the right and sharpened my opinion. Most important, the relative heights of the posterior distribution provide information about the relative strengths of my current beliefs for different possible values of the parameter π. Of course, these results still leave room for doubt about whether

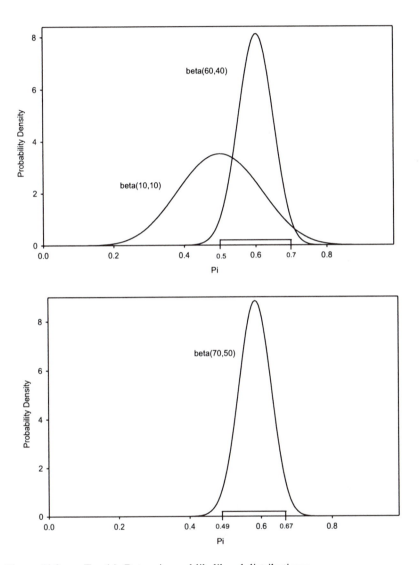

Figure 11.2   Top (a): Beta prior and likelihood distributions;
                   Bottom (b): Beta posterior distribution.

comparable backache patients in the future should ignore drug B, with preference to drug A. Further issues bearing on interpretation are discussed in some
detail later.

In the next section, I contrast Bayesian subjective interpretations with their counterpart frequentist interpretations of the same sample data. But first note that the Bayesian paradigm routinely provides a mechanism to incorporate prior information with empirical information; moreover, the prior information could come either from one's opinion or empirical data. In the case of the backache problem, if an investigator were to replicate this experiment with a *new* sample of data, it would be appropriate to use the preceding a'' and b'' as *prior* values, add these to the latest $a*$ and $b*$ derived from an independent sample, thus to get beta parameters for a new posterior distribution. For example, suppose fresh data come from a sample of, say, 80 patients not unlike the $n = 100$ who participated in this study. If it were found that the numbers favoring drugs A and B respectively, turn out to be $a* = 47$ and $b* = 33$, then the derived posterior beta would have parameters $a'' = 70 + 47 = 117$ and $b'' = 50 + 33 = 83$. These new a'', b'' values would yield a posterior with mean $= .585$, mode $= .583$, and $SD = .035$. This distribution corresponds to a somewhat more sharply defined and informative final opinion based on data from $n = 180$ empirical records as well as the initial subjective prior, viz., beta(10,10).

The more data one accumulates in such a fashion, founding each new study's results on those that came before it, the less the initial subjective prior information influences results. But if one's prior is fairly sharp over a particular value of π, then, supposing new data provided support this value, the posterior distribution will be more sharply defined than it would have been, had the prior been diffuse or flat. In the case of a relatively sharp prior, one's posterior inferences about the parameter generally will be stronger than they would have, had the prior been diffuse. Of course, in the event that the prior is tight and the data *contradict* the modal π, the posterior will tend to become more diffuse initially as empirical data are accumulated, but with more and more data should eventually become sharply defined over a different value for π. More often than not experience has shown that when investigators are honest in forming their priors, taking all relevant information into account at the outset, strong contradictions between subjectively based priors and data-based likelihoods tend to be rare. Still, this is always a possibility and when it happens discovery of the reasons for the conflict may itself be significant.

Comparing Subjectivist and Frequentist Inferences about π

Although the classical or frequentist model for inference is relatively well known, I quickly review this system for inference, so as to aid its comparison with the foregoing subjectivist model. In the classical paradigm, the central tool is that of a sampling distribution of a statistic, in this case a sample proportion, labeled p. In this context, one assumes the existence of a *fixed* parent population, meaning simply that there exists a (possibly finite) set of zeros and ones for which π indexes the mean, or proportion of ones. Here, the sampling distribution of the mean can be derived from the binomial expansion of $\{(1 - \pi) + \pi\}^n$, whose $n + 1$ terms give the respective sampling probabilities of x out of n one's, for $x = 0, 1, \ldots, n$, where each sample contains only zeros and ones. Each sample mean, a proportion, can be written as $p = x/n$, so the form of the sampling distribution of p coincides with that of the corresponding binomial. Alternatively, one can generate the sampling distribution of the mean by taking all possible samples of size n from a finite population consisting of π times N ones and $(1 - \pi)$ times N zeros (for N the population size), sampling with replacement, whence the mean can be computed for each sample. For example if $\pi = .5$, then we may set $N = 2$ (that is, the population is $\{0\ 1\}$) in which case one could identify $N^n = 2^n$ distinctive samples of size n. Recall that as sample size is increased the sampling distribution of the mean, which here has the *form* of a binomial, tends toward a *normal distribution*.

As is well known, the mean of any such a distribution of means necessarily equals the population mean π. Also the variance of the sampling distribution of p equals the population variance divided by n, which here is $\pi(1 - \pi)/n$, so the square root of the latter term gives the standard error of p. At least for relatively large n, this variance is usually soundly estimated as $p(1 - p)/n$. According to standard frequentist doctrine the only source of information one has about π is the sample mean p; from this value two relatively extreme estimates for π are constructed by adding and subtracting a multiple of the estimated standard error to the sample mean. For a 95% interval the limits are .6 ± 2 (.049)—because $\sqrt{(pq/n)} = \sqrt{(.6)(.4)/100} = .049$. I have taken the liberty of rounding to obtain limits of .5 and .7, respectively, although more exact limits, based on standard methods for the 95% interval, are .497 and .695. The two alternative sampling distributions of the mean in Figure 11.3 are both consistent with the observed sample mean, $p = .60$. Supposing that the left-hand distribution here described the true sampling distribution, then the sample mean will have come from near the .975 quantile; if the right-hand distribution in Figure 11.3 described the true distribution, then the sample mean would have come from the .025 quantile.

Because the data are binary the proper model for the sampling distribution of p is discrete, with the form of a binomial, meaning that in Figure 11.3 the vertical lines provide the actual picture of each postulated sampling distribution of the mean. I have overlaid each set of these vertical lines with a smooth distribution to emphasize the general shape of each distribution and to distinguish the 5% region in the center. Finally, a proper statement of inductive inference within the classical or frequentist framework is, "One can have 95% *confidence* that the population π is spanned by the limits .50 and .70; in the population, 95% of like

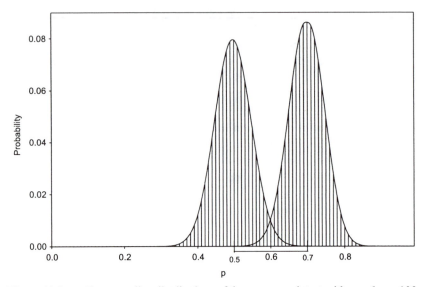

Figure 11.3.   Two sampling distributions of the mean consistent with p = .6, n = 100.

intervals should span the parameter π." Still, it is verboten to use the language of probability to describe such a derived numerical interval.

Now, consider a corresponding inferential statement in the subjectivist context. In this case, we recall that the parameter π corresponds *not* to a fixed population, but rather to a characteristic of a well-defined event. Assume that a posterior distribution has been constructed from a prior and a likelihood. A standard method for summarizing information in a Bayesian posterior distribution is to generate the shortest interval that encloses a given percentage of the area. This is called either a highest (posterior) density region (HDR), or a posterior credible interval (PCI), or just a credible interval, for some prespecified probability level or area. Such an interval is obtained by choosing two scale values on the abscissa that enclose a particular part of the area in question, two points as close together as possible with the same ordinate. By choosing the shortest interval, one obtains the greatest probability density for the parameter in the narrowest possible interval. Given this construction, it is generally true that PCIs will not be symmetric around their means or modal values. In the case of the posterior beta (70,50), in Figure 11.2b, the 95% PCI has the limits of approximately .49 and .67. This interval is noted on the baseline of the distribution. A proper conclusion within the subjectivist framework is, "My personal probability is .95 that the parameter π lies between the values .49 and .67." Although such an interval provides a particularly direct interpretation, note that it is the posterior distribution itself that contains *all* available inferential information following a Bayesian analysis, so any such interval derived from the posterior is incomplete by comparison.

I do not think there is any question that for most people the Bayesian interpretation is both simpler and more natural than its frequentist counterpart. Moreover, as noted, the Bayesian system provides a mechanism for incorporating prior data or opinions when they are available. The classical paradigm for inference makes no such provision. Although it may be pleasing to be able to report that the numerical values of conventional confidence intervals and posterior credible intervals are in virtual agreement when the prior distribution is uniform, it should equally be noted that the qualitative nature of the corresponding interpretations are wholly distinctive. It is also common to find that release from tacit belief in uniform priors results in quite different formal inferences.

Long, often protracted, debates have been published as to the merits and demerits of each system. Later, I provide references of relevance to both theory and prospective applications. But first I examine a fundamental complication with relevance to the preceding example in order to broach problems that are likely to arise in applications.

Some Elementary Complications Bearing on Inference

The key feature of the preceding inferential problem is its simplicity; indeed, in the classical context a single parameter π is sufficient to completely describe the corresponding parent population, including its shape, its variance, and so on. The thumbtack example is compelling because tossing a tack seems to present a well-defined event for which it is realistic to define or specify one's personal probability distribution to characterize the subjective likelihoods of different possible results when a particular tack is tossed above a hard, flat surface. Further, the mean of any random sample based on n replications is known to provide a sound or reasonable sample-based estimator of π, particularly when n is relatively large.

Nevertheless, one must admit that the analogy between tossing thumbtacks and the problem based on human experiences with drugs in a clinical trial is not strong. After all, what assurance is there that *different* people, with different back problems, different histories, and so forth, will have the *same underlying propensity* to judge drug A better than drug B? Surely it is more realistic to think that different people may have different propensities to favor one drug over the other, depending on their special needs and histories, and that it is some particular *mixture* of various groups of people that is at least partly responsible for the observed results. Indeed, groups could be of size one. The inferential problem here might better be identified *not* with tossing one unchanging thumbtack numerous times, but rather with tossing each of n *different* tacks just once, where the various tacks may differ physically from one another. Were n tacks to be physically different from one another, then presumably one's personal probability distributions associated with the event "landing point down" also would differ for the different tacks. This surely strengthens the analogy between tack tossing and the backache problem. However, it would be difficult to obtain several repeated, independent or "exchangeable" observations from each of several backache patients in a clinical trial. For this and other reasons the inferential problem thus becomes more complicated once it has been reconceptualized so as to become more authentic.

To be more specific in the context of the backache problem, it could have happened that persons with low back pain tended strongly to favor drug A, and others, with generalized or higher back pain, tended strongly to favor B. Such a finding, were it to be discovered, could hardly be omitted from the scientific report of the backache experiment because it would bear strongly on recommendations concerning use of these drugs in the future. When the data have not been collected to identify distinctive subgroups of backache respondents, such an explanation is only a post hoc possibility that requires further data collection and analysis to assess its veracity.

Another way to speak about this kind of complication is to say it represents a possible *interaction*, where the two treatments may have worked differently, depending on the group. That such an interaction may be relevant regardless of whether various groups have been identified in a particular study is especially problematic. What initially was seen as a relatively simple inductive inferential result could well be confounded or simply made irrelevant by the existence of subgroups such as low-backache sufferers and those with generalized backache. Naturally, such a prospect complicates prospects of making sound formal statistical inferences.

The preceding issue was introduced because, for persons who are interested in applied science it is too realistic to ignore. Had the problem not involved low backache versus generalized pain, it might have concerned two or more other groups. Moreover, such groups may or may not ever be identified, even after the experimental data have been collected. In applied science, it is generally difficult to satisfy oneself that various distinctive subgroups do not exist, because human and most other experimental units are sufficiently complex that such possibilities are real, not merely hypothetical.

Given that such interactions and related complications are often likely to occur, they cannot be dismissed as irrelevant. It follows that one's initial concept as to what constitutes the inferential problem, not just for the backache example, of course, but for a wide range of applied scientific inference problems, often may have to be revisited and perhaps redefined. It all depends on what is learned in collecting, analyzing, and interpreting empirical data relative to the phenomena to which they relate. Furthermore, there is nothing unique or distinctive about this kind of difficulty vis-à-vis the Bayesian paradigm. Neither mode of inferential reasoning, classical-objectivist nor Bayesian-subjectivist, has a notable advantage over the other in dealing with such difficulties.

The foregoing issues lie at the heart of the endless, open-ended system that modern statisticians typically associate with problems of *data analysis*, and not just statistical inference, when considered in the broad context of applied scientific practice (cf. Dempster, 1971; Mosteller & Tukey, 1977; Tukey, 1969). Note, however, that there is nothing about the prospect of such complications that either invalidates or weakens the general subjectivist logic. Rather, the caveat concerns the question of whether particular problems are sufficiently well defined so that simple forms of formal inductive inference can be viable possibilities in particular applications.

Although the backache problem is one of the simplest realistic scientific problems I could think of that did not entail careful preparation by way of theoretical analysis, careful thought about an applied study of backache has led to a more complicated picture than many authors of introductory statistics textbooks have been wont to consider. Next, I examine some basics concerning how the Bayesian system works when applied to analysis of data for one or more *quantitative* variables. I concentrate on a relatively simple version of Bayesian analysis in the context of comparing two or more treatments, but it should be clear that many of the concepts at issue generalize to a wide range of applications.

Bayesian Inference with a Quantitative Outcome Variable

As previously noted, a primary feature of the preceding formal inferential problem is that to identify a single value for the parameter π is to say all there is to say about the corresponding parent population. By contrast, most scientific applications concern more complicated problems—such as qualitative variables with more than two categories, or more commonly, one or more quantitative variables. Many, perhaps most, applied questions concern relationships among measures of central tendency, or relations among several variables.

One of the most basic and common problems in applied science concerns a comparison of two groups with respect to measures taken on a single quantitative response variable. I initially focus on an example with two experimental treatments, where the reader might imagine that persons have been randomly assigned to treatments. The outcome measure is taken to soundly reflect treatment differences, were they to exist. A principal goal might be to aid cause-and-effect inferences in comparing two treatments, perhaps a control versus an intervention.

A major issue that arises as soon as one focuses on a quantitative outcome measure is that of characterizing the shape or form of its distribution. In general, distribution shapes have infinite variation, and it is more than a little difficult to characterize their forms with just a few summary indices. To deal with this problem, what is usually done—as is the case here—is to *assume* relatively simple forms of conceived population distributions, in particular, normality. Although this assumption should not in a particular case be made blindly, it has the great virtue that only two parameters are needed to completely specify such a distribution: the mean and the variance. My focus here is on the difference between two distributions, specifically the difference between two population means.

The Bayesian approach to making an inference about the difference between two population means, written as $\delta = \mu_A - \mu_B$, entails complications not ordinarily seen in conventional statistics textbooks, but the central problem is analogous to that about inferences concerning π. Hence it would be reasonable for the reader to ponder his or her beliefs about the distribution of the parameter δ, perhaps in the fashion detailed earlier for the backache problem. However, to follow this line of reasoning would take more space than is available. In order to avoid undue complications in dealing with this inference problem, I make assumptions consistent with standard practice based on frequentist statistics, as well as some additional assumptions required to make Bayesian methods manageable. The first thing to recognize is that the parameter δ corresponds not to a fixed population, but to a subjectively defined "event," specifically, the difference $\mu_A - \mu_B$ where each μ is also subjectively defined. Similarly, the parameter σ^2, the variance that I take as common to the respective treatments, has a subjective interpretation. As noted, I assume a normal sampling process for each of the two sets of sample values, and I limit consideration to the case where the sample size n is the same in each group and stipulate that the observations $X_{11}, X_{12}, \ldots, X_{1n}$ and $X_{21}, X_{22}, \ldots, X_{2n}$ are mutually independent.

In this case, the prior distribution is a *joint* distribution for the three parameters μ_A, μ_B, and $\log(\sigma^2)$, the variance requiring transformation to deal with the fact that it can never be negative, whereas its logarithm can. Given that the joint prior distribution for these parameters is taken to be *uniform,* which is equivalent to saying the joint prior for the parameters is uninformative, it is possible to derive a relatively simple posterior distribution for the parameter δ, the difference between the population means. Specifically, with preceding assumptions, the posterior distribution for δ takes the form of a conventional t distribution with degrees of freedom $= 2(n - 1)$. The mean of this posterior is the observed difference between the two sample means, and the variance is equivalent to the conventional variance error of estimate associated with the classical model for inference.

Consider the following example: Suppose again that we have two drugs under study, once again labeled A and B, for treatment of persons who in this case suffer migraine headaches. Suppose the outcome variable is a quantitative measure reflecting a subject's assessment of his or her drug's effect on a ten point scale. Let $n = 50$, the number of persons assigned randomly to each drug for the duration of the experiment. Here, each person receives only one of the drugs, unlike the previous backache study where each person received both treatments. Following a period of several weeks of use of a particular drug, each participant, who might have been asked to monitor effectiveness following treatment of each headache, is to provide a rating on the designated scale: 1 = no effect, 2 = very minor effect, . . . , 9 = strong effect, and 10 = relieved head-ache completely. This is a what is usually called a two-independent-sample problem, assuming equal population variances, but it is now conceived within the Bayesian, subjectivist paradigm.

Suppose these drug trial data yielded: $\overline{X}_A = 5.2$ and $\overline{X}_B = 6$ with $s_p^2 = 4$, the pooled sample variance for the two groups. The results show that drug B seems to have worked better for these respondents than drug A. The next question is whether the evidence supports generalization beyond this sample. Since $n = 50$ for each group, the Bayesian analog of the variance error of the mean is $s_p^2(2/n)$, which leads to the standard deviation $\sqrt{4}\,(2/50) = .4$. Consequently, the posterior distribution is centered on the difference $\overline{d} = \overline{X}_A - \overline{X}_B = -.8$, with standard deviation equal to .4; the corresponding t distribution has 98 degrees of freedom, so that it is near to normal form.

Figure 11.4 exhibits this posterior with a 95% credible interval noted on the abscissa. This interval has approximate limits $-.8 \pm 2(.4)$, or -1.6 and 0.0. Because I had declared ignorance at the outset about all three parameters by stipulating a uniform joint prior, these data alone lead me to say that my personal probability is .95 that the parameter δ lies between -1.6 and 0.0. The posterior distribution in Figure 11.4 describes the relative merit I associate with different values for δ, given my particular assumptions as well as the data. Take special note that unlike classical confidence intervals, which tell nothing about the relative credibilities of different values of a parameter, such a posterior distribution quantifies empirical information precisely for different possible values of the parameter in question, within the subjectivist framework.

Although the foregoing analysis used an indifference or ignorance prior, it is of interest to ask how a Bayesian system could be used to accommodate meaningful prior information when it is available. A convenient way to examine this question is to see how current data could be used to inform subsequent study of the same phenomenon.

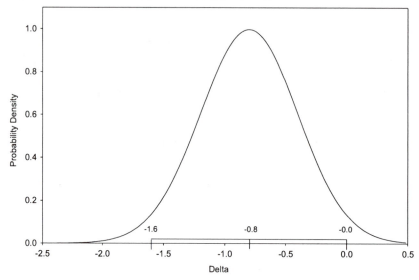

Figure 11.4   Posterior distribution for delta, $t(98)$.

Imagine new data are available for n_2 additional subjects in each of two groups of migraine patients, in contrast to the preceding n_1 which denotes *each* of the two earlier sample sizes. Suppose the new means, derived from groups that had initially been made comparable through random assignment, are $\overline{X}_{2A}$ and $\overline{X}_{2B}$, to distinguish them from the previous means, now written $\overline{X}_{1A}$ and $\overline{X}_{1B}$. Write the second mean difference as $\overline{d}_2 = \overline{X}_{2A} - \overline{X}_{2B}$ to contrast it with the preceding mean difference, now denoted $\overline{d}_1 = \overline{X}_{1A} - \overline{X}_{1B}$. The new pooled variance is s_{2p}^2 to distinguish it from the preceding pooled variance, written as s_{1p}^2. Note again that sample sizes are assumed equal in the treatment groups, so each pooled variance is just the simple average of two within sample variances.

A Bayesian posterior can be derived from the preceding information. This distribution can be shown to have the form of Student's $\underline{t}$ distribution with degrees of freedom = $2(n_1 + n_2 - 2)$ and mean = $(n_1 \overline{d}_1 + n_2 \overline{d}_2)/(n_1 + n_2)$; that is, the final mean difference is just the weighted average of the two observed mean differences. The variance of the derived posterior simply entails a pooling of the variances s_{1p}^2 and s_{2p}^2, accounting for the sizes of their respective samples. Consequently, based on the two sets of data, the variance of the posterior distribution is $2\{(n_1 - 1)\,s_{1p}^2 + (n_2 - 1)\,s_{2p}^2\,\}/\{(n_1 + n_2 - 2)(n_1 + n_2)\}$. It should be recognized that this posterior has the same t distribution, as would have been derived had the data from the two independent sets been pooled, that is, treated as one system with all the sample data combined. Novick and Jackson (1974) discussed details of related posteriors, including that associated with the two-dependent-sample problem; also see Lee (1989).

What I have associated with the first sample system, discussed previously, could be reconceived in terms of prior information, possibly using introspective analysis or subjective opinion. In such a case one must prespecify scalar values for the mean difference, $\overline{d}_1$, and variance, $s_{1_p}^2$, and proceed more or less as I have done; however, some small technical modifications are required. Insomuch as it is difficult explicitly in most applied situations to choose singularly compelling values for such quantities, a uniform or uninformative prior will often be quite reasonable in the two-sample context, within the Bayes paradigm.

As in the case of the earlier beta-binomial problem, it is pleasant to find that use of an uninformative prior in the Bayesian context yields, with what are often reasonable assumptions, the same numerical limits for credible intervals as those found using classical methods for confidence intervals. Because the latter methods are so commonly taught and found so abundantly in the literature of applied science this may give comfort. What this brief analysis fails to say, however, but what seems to be becoming clearer with each new stage of basic research on inference, is that frequentist methods generally are plagued by a catalog of inconsistencies and anomalies, whereas Bayesian (subjectivist) methods rarely are found to yield logical inconsistencies. Despite their virtues, however, Bayesian methods are often much harder to implement. Moreover, subjectivist techniques remain to be developed for practical implementation in many situations that are commonly seen as amenable to classical statistical analysis.

In the next section, I examine certain alternative approaches to study design and analysis that seem effectively to capitalize on available prior information, and to be consistent with standard tenets of experimental design. The aim is to broaden the conception of what constitutes relevant prior information to include matters relevant to study design and corresponding analysis.

Using Elements of the Subjectivist Paradigm in Study Design

The preceding problem was couched in terms that should be understandable to anyone who has studied the classical two-sample problem for so-called parametric inference. However, it often may be helpful to reflect more on what it means to incorporate relevant prior information when comparing treatments, such as interventions. The history of experimental design provides a rich variety of mechanisms to accommodate various kinds of prior information, so it is of interest to reflect on how subjectivist principles might inform planning of intervention studies analogous to what is commonly seen in various design contexts.

Needless to say, what follows represents no more than an introduction, perhaps to motivate applications.

It is commonly said that all science depends on careful observation and well-reasoned inference. Statistical methods most often concern inference. But particularly in the context of design, comprehensive observation often can inform allocation of units to treatments or interventions to strengthen inference and to enhance interpretations. Because I aim to focus only on basic issues common to intervention practice, I limit attention to how observation of experimental units can aid allocation to treatments and, briefly, to how certain strategies might play out in sequential designs. The role of subject-matter knowledge or theory is ignored, as are numerous logistical and contextual details, despite their central relevance.

Consider a basic statistical dilemma, which for convenience I frame in standard terms, viz., comparing two treatments, assuming random assignment, with respect to a quantitative outcome variable: If one samples initially so as to obtain a relatively homogeneous group of respondents—with respect to the response variable—one has a relatively good chance in statistical analysis of detecting treatment effects, when the treatments are indeed different. This is because the *within-sample* variance is likely to be relatively small and this will enhance sensitivity (think "power") for a given sample size. Notwithstanding its virtues, the liability of this approach is that it denies generalization beyond the narrowly defined universe of respondents assigned to the respective treatments.

In order to enhance generalizability, one can sample from a broadly defined or heterogeneous group of individuals, assign them randomly to treatment subgroups, and go on to compute statistics to aid inferences about treatment effects. This approach has the possible advantage of helping strengthen generalizability to a broadly defined population—except for a key weakness: That is, in its simplest form such a strategy generally yields a relatively large within-group variance that in turn reduces sensitivity of the statistical comparison. In classical terms, the inference is weakened when the estimated standard error is relatively large. Furthermore, recalling the discussion of problems associated with interpretations of the backache data, use of heterogeneous subject pools can lead to interpretive confounding when various subgroups respond differently to treatments.

Authors of standard books on experimental design often make reference to the foregoing dilemma—although not generally identifying it as such. It is well known that individual differences among experimental units can be accounted for in two principal ways. One is to use statistical adjustments based on antecedent information. The other is to use design strategies that identify multiple subgroups in advance of assignment to treatments, subgroups that ideally are relatively homogeneous in the sense that treatment effects are likely to be similar among individuals in such groups. The latter strategy is usually called blocking, or stratification, and it is a well-respected principle for accommodating relevant individual differences in design. I use the term *blocks* in the following discussion with reference to this precedent.

Suppose units are sampled broadly so as to represent a relatively diverse subject pool. The purpose of the interventions, and the nature of the intended outcome measure, will have a strong bearing on what is seen as a suitable sample. Except for the labor involved, there is little reason to discourage extensive—and when feasible, intensive—efforts to identify relevant individual differences among potential subjects in an experiment in advance of allocating units to treatments.

Supposing that relevant and comprehensive individual difference data are available, it may be possible to use this information to generate priors for parameters thought to characterize the outcome measure (for each treatment) for each of what are regarded as distinctive and homogeneous blocks. To simplify discussion, suppose for each block-treatment combination that such prior distributions differ principally in their means. Now the problem is to allocate persons, or experimental units, to treatments based on one's prior information, or "prevision," concerning outcome means in a fashion likely to aid inferences about treatment effects.

The key role of subjectivist analysis in this context is that of generating prior means of the anticipated response variable for what may be termed *distinctive* blocks. By distinctive blocks, I mean subgroups of experimental units for which treatment results are expected to be only mildly variable for all units if there are no treatment effects; but if the treatments do have differential effects then between treatment variance should dominate variance within groups for each block. Ideally, one should be able to make a persuasive argument that further decomposition of blocks would not be likely to yield notable differences in treatment effects, but that aggregation of designated blocks could obscure effects. Post-treatment responses frequently may be expected to vary minimally around the latter means, that is, to reflect little more than "noise."

It should be emphasized that all information used to inform prior means should come from data collected in advance of allocations of units to treatments. To the extent that post-treatment data show that scores associated with block-treatment combinations are in fact relatively homogeneous, pooled within-(treatment/block) variance often may serve as a standard for comparison of post-treatment means. Corresponding Bayesian posterior distributions for single degree of freedom (planned) contrasts would often appear to be especially well suited to such uses based on the preceding logic when the investigator has taken the additional step of deciding in advance of analysis which particular treatment comparisons are of interest for the respective blocks. Lewis (1993) provided a useful discussion of Bayesian analysis based on planned contrasts.

It would appear that whenever there exists a nonignorable high probability of distinctive subgroups in a particular intervention context the inductive inferences, and recommendations about future treatments, are likely to profit from explicit identification and analysis of results for blocks. Absent advance identification and analysis with respect to such blocks, the investigator risks that treatment effects for subgroups may be masked or ignored, or that the inferences will be confounded.

The foregoing conception is based on the premise that differential treatment results for distinctive blocks should be anticipated. That is, interactions should be viewed as commonplace, not exceptional. Despite the additional effort involved in such an approach, the payoffs in applications may be substantial. However, the cost of accounting for such subgroups may at times be relatively small in another sense, because when different blocks yield similar treatment effects, then aggregation may be justified, which in turn can simplify results and may well strengthen corresponding inferences.

The key difference between the proposed strategy and that ordinarily associated with comparing treatments in the context of standard blocking designs is the prospect of using a subjectivist mechanism to form blocks based on constructed priors, particularly prior response variable means. Such means should facilitate assignment to treatment groups as well as development of explicit questions for analysis (especially using planned contrasts) based on anticipated treatment differences for blocks. Note that blocking conventionally is based on using *individual* antecedent variables to form categories. When there are several so-called covariates, it can be problematic to combine category systems across covariates, especially when these variates are interdependent. Unfortunately, this feature tends to discourage use of several antecedent variables. The approach suggested here should not break down even when there are numerous interrelated covariates. When combined with use of derived single degree of freedom contrasts, derived posteriors may become especially compelling as a basis for multiple formal inferences.

Some authors with a Bayesian orientation, such as Lindley and Novick (1981), have argued that randomization should generally be a "last resort" for assignment of units to treatments, and the preceding considerations may help make their reasoning clear. But it seems difficult to argue against randomized assignments of units to treatments within what are seen as distinctive or homogeneous blocks. This is because the preceding logic can be construed as saying one should be indifferent, or exchangeable, about various different splittings of any block into treatment groups once distinctive blocks have been designated. A special virtue of within-block randomization is that it usually helps persuade consumers of research results that the deck had not been stacked in advance. This role of randomization seems especially significant when used in the context of subjectivist methods. The justification for using randomization alongside Bayesian reasoning seems also to be consistent with Rubin's (1978) thinking, among others.

The nature of extant knowledge about phenomena—especially in psychological and social sciences—is often such that one should anticipate a need for sequentially articulated studies. Framed by the foregoing argument, initial stages might entail comprehensive observation and development of what are deemed to be sound and relevant measurements on all covariates thought likely to be helpful for predicting response variables. Indeed, there often may be advantages in delaying interventions until it can be established that a sound predictor battery exists for what are seen as appropriate post-treatment outcome measures. Subsequent stages might entail articulation of expected treatment effects by blocks such that explicit prior distributions, or previsions, concerning group-treatment interactions can be soundly assessed, both descriptively and for inferences. The special virtue of Bayesian approaches to inference, that they provide mechanisms for incorporating relevant prior information when it exists, often will be most valuable in sequentially articulated studies. Indeed, it is conceivable that sequences of studies, each analyzed within a Bayesian framework, might sometimes obviate the need for what has come to be known as meta-analysis. By way of contrast, classical statistical methods generally regard each sample as completely new, and typically provide no mechanisms for incorporating prior information even when it may be readily available.

Some Perspectives on Uses of Subjectivist Concepts and a Guide to Related Literature

Experience suggests that typical problems in scientific practice involve identification of many parameters, so in Bayesian applications both priors and posteriors often will be multivariate in form. But even for the simpler statistical and design problems we have come to deem as standard, it is almost inevitable in practice that one's model for the situation will be less than fully formed. Consequently, applications generally entail backing and filling, revising models in the light of data, reconsidering questions of interest, perhaps over several cycles of data examination and statistical analysis. Choice of variables, including transformations, decisions about what are primary and secondary questions, how blocks should be formed, how to handle so-called missing data, and even what it means to have missing data, are all matters that can be expected to shape typical analyses. Dempster (1971), in an especially readable article, comprehensively discussed these and many other relevant matters.

It follows that models and corresponding interpretations should be expected to change, perhaps substantially, as data inform judgments about any particular problem or situation. Considerations like these suggest that in many, perhaps most, situations the chances for clear and relatively unqualified formal inferences often will be small. However important the prospect of formal inferences may be, this part of the research enterprise often may be expected to pale in relation to the larger issues about which data may have something to say.

Some of the most thoughtful students of this broad subject, notably Bruno deFinetti (1974), have argued that the whole enterprise of induction in applied science should be as natural as possible, as close to context and available information as practicable, with special efforts going into the choice of priors so as to reflect opinion accurately. DeFinetti argued that one should not expect to be able to produce formal inferences in many situations since much of what we do is best seen as "scientific guessing." Moreover, he noted that Bayesian techniques as such are just as easily misused or abused as frequentist methods, because it is only the issue of sound or reasoned use that matters.

Consistent with deFinetti's (1974) counsel, it seems wise not to sever too sharply the links between description and inference. Statistical models, including inferential ones, seem to offer special hopes for understanding phenomena, and for communicating what data have to say. Yet models, almost by definition, are imperfect representations of "reality," so they will virtually always be unsatisfactory in at least some respects. Nevertheless, as aids to understanding phenomena or testing scientific theories, models repeatedly have been shown to have distinctive value. Indeed, model-based communication seems sufficiently worthwhile that in the foreseeable future statisticians are unlikely to get along without models. Bayesian inference seems to many statisticians to offer distinctive advantages over frequentist-based inference, but the complications of real-world applications are often likely to overwhelm our skills in developing persuasive systems for formal Bayesian inferences.

Further reading of subjectivist and related literature should be rewarding. Two symposium volumes that contain numerous chapters of relevance are Godambe and Sprott (1971) and Harper and Hooker (1976). Many of the contributors to these volumes are well-known statisticians with long-standing interests in subjectivist methods, including Dempster, Good, Jaynes, and Lindley. Other articles of special relevance are Box (1980), Cornfield (1969), deFinetti (1974), as well as Efron (1986); the first and last of these include useful discussions, with multiple participants. Introductory books of special note are Phillips (1973) and Schmitt (1969), and at a somewhat higher level, Barnett (1982), Lee (1989), Lindley (1965), and Novick and Jackson (1974). Two other foundational books of note are those by Good (1983) and deFinetti (1971). The first of these is a compendium of philosophically oriented articles by the subjectivist I. J. Good, articles with lively coverage of a wide range of topics, both practical and abstract. DeFinetti (1971) is one of the most highly regarded of all books on probability and subjectivist thinking; this first of his two volumes is at least partially accessible to the nontechnical reader, even though some of the book is quite mathematical in form. Geertsma (1983) effectively summarized many issues bearing on the controversy between frequentist and subjectivist statistics. A recent book by Gelman, Carlin, Stern, and Rubin (1995) points the way to many practical applications of Bayesian data analysis.

Many of these authors discuss concepts such as objectivity in science, coherence in specifying priors, the role of careful use of language and a variety of problems bearing on applications. Rubin has been a strong defender of Bayesian methods and has carefully examined basic questions and methods in the context of comparative experiments; see especially, Rubin (1974, 1978). Tukey (1969, 1977), one of the giants of 20th-century statistics, has distinguished carefully between so-called exploratory and confirmatory modes of scientific activity and has argued persuasively that exploratory strategies and methods generally must be given more attention than often has been the case in practice. He has been a major proponent of *data analysis* as an essential and distinctive activity in statistical practice.

Of course, the foregoing references provide only an introduction to concepts and principles related to the focus of this article. It also should be made explicit that many scientists and philosophers do not accept the central concept of subjectivism in applied science. The inquiring reader no doubt will find many sources reflecting this view, but a useful and serious analysis of the pertinent issues can be found in Howson and Urbach (1993) as well as the chapter by Rozeboom in this volume.

Further information of particular relevance for psychologists can be found in the writings of Rozeboom (1961, 1972, 1977). The last of these is a good entry to many other writings by this author and provides valuable guidance for how language and concepts can effectively be sharpened or refined to aid data-based theory development. These works are likely to repay careful study for anyone concerned with foundations of methodology in psychological science. Also, see Meehl (1978), as well as his chapter in this volume.

Some Application Ideas

In this section, I briefly discuss a subjectivist approach to intervention that follows the preceding logic, with reference to comparing multiple interventions, assuming a quantitative outcome measure. For readers familiar with classical analysis of variance methods, my purpose can be described as that of showing how a priori comparisons based on linear contrasts can be simply constructed and interpreted within the Bayesian paradigm. I make various assumptions consistent with that well-known methodology, viz., a normal sampling process, as well as equal (but unknown) variances, and I briefly discuss reasoning associated with applications of subjectivist logic.

Suppose we wish to compare two newly devised treatments, perhaps interventions, with one another as well as with a standard or conventional treatment. For example, two new therapies may be theorized to have special virtues for alleviating pain, or for reducing stress, and so forth. The new therapies might be considered as interventions in a context where there is interest in comparing them with a standard or conventional therapy. In addition, in order to model a strategy that was advocated earlier, I assume that prior assessments led to the identification of two distinctive blocks of potential respondents or subjects. Blocks typically would be constructed to be relatively homogeneous with respect to the response variable. Sampling, and allocation to treatment groups, is assumed to have been done separately for each such block; each person gets only one therapy. I assume that a sound outcome measure is available, as well as appropriate, for post-treatment assessment of the two new therapies and the control. Finally, it is supposed that each therapy is administered to the same number of respondents within each distinctive or homogenous block, and for simplicity of notation, let each block be of the same size. Thus, each of the six groups is taken to be of size n.

Following a period of treatment using each therapy, we may suppose that for each block of respondents, measurements will be taken on some outcome variable X. In this case, there are two linear comparisons of interest: one that compares one new treatment with the other (A with B), the other that compares the two treatments with the control (C). In conventional notation, I denote the first sample linear contrast as $L_{1j} = \overline{X}_{Aj} - \overline{X}_{Bj}$ and the second as $L_{2j} = \overline{X}_{ABj} - \overline{X}_{Cj}$ where $\overline{X}_{ABj}$ denotes the average of $\overline{X}_{Aj}$ and $\overline{X}_{Bj}$. The subscript j indexes blocks, so $j = 1,2$. I have described four contrasts for these six groups, but there is one more, L_{Blocks}, that could be computed to compare the three means for Block 1 with those for Block 2.

In the context of the Bayesian paradigm, the basic inferential problem is to describe the posterior distribution of the parameter associated with each L-contrast. I focus on credible intervals, however, thereby gaining simplicity at the cost of ignoring some inferential information. Given the nature of the preceding contrasts, and equal n's for each therapy, the respective contrasts are mutually orthogonal. This means that interpretations for these respective posteriors can be done independently of one another. Nevertheless, account should be taken of the fact that five different inferential questions are being asked of the same data. Readers familiar with the logic of Bonferroni methods for controlling Type I error rates should recognize that the choice of α for each credible interval is best made to accommodate multiple contrasts; for example, if five contrasts are to be made, one might choose $\alpha = .01$ for each L-contrast in order that 95% credibility can be associated with the system of 5 contrasts.

Given the foregoing assumptions and specifications, each Bayesian credible interval is of the form $L \pm t_{\alpha/2}(s_L)$, for

$$k = \sum c_i^2,$$

with c_i the ith contrast coefficient, and

$$s_L = \sqrt{\frac{k}{n}(\text{AvgWithinSampleVariance})}.$$

So $k = 2$ in the case of each L_{1j}, $k = 3/2$ for each L_{2j}, and $k = 2/3$ for L_{Blocks}. $t_{\alpha/2}$ is an alpha-percent quantile from a t distribution with degrees of freedom $= 6(n-1)$ because there are six groups.

For example, if each of the three therapies were intended to alleviate stress and X represents a sound measure of the respondent's post-treatment stress, we might take our data for the six groups, each of size $n = 15$, as the following: Means: $\overline{X}_{A1} = 20$, $\overline{X}_{B1} = 25$, $\overline{X}_{C1} = 30$, $\overline{X}_{A2} = 40$, $\overline{X}_{B2} = 41$, and $\overline{X}_{C2} = 45$; with AvgWithinSampleVariance = 25. To generate 99% credible intervals for the contrasts, I use $t_{\alpha/2} = t_{.005}$ with 84 degrees of freedom, that is, $t_{.005(84)} = 2.64$. The data yield the following contrasts/intervals: L_{11} (-5 ± 4.82), L_{21} (-7.5 ± 4.17), L_{12} (-1 ± 4.82), L_{22} (-4.5 ± 4.17) and L_{blocks} (-17 ± 2.78).

For the reader aiming to understand exactly what is at issue here, I suggest it will repay the effort to sketch these five posterior distributions, each having roughly a normal form (t with 84 degrees of freedom), using L to index the mean, specifying the lower and upper (.005 and .995) quantiles to correspond with the numerical limits given above. For example the first such interval, for L_{11}, has essentially the same form as Figure 11.4 above, but is centered on -5; and virtually the entire posterior lies to the left of zero (since $-5 + 4.82 = -.18$, so that the .995 quantile is below zero).

Of most relevance is the personalistic interpretation for each interval. Specifically, with an "ignorance prior" at the outset, the investigator may say, "My personal probability is .99 that the first contrast parameter lies between -9.82 and $-.18$; further, my personal probability is .95 for all five such numerical intervals, simultaneously." Note that the probability level drops to accommodate the fact that there are five such intervals. As with classical statistical methods, the Bayesian also makes weaker inferential statements as more and more questions are asked of a given body of data. The reader again will want to compare such interpretations with those associated with the application of classical statistical methods.

It may also be worth noting that had there simply been six unstructured groups of outcome measures, then *any* system of five orthogonal contrasts could have been constructed, computing credible intervals for each, similar to what was done above. An analog of conducting a one-way ANOVA F test would then be to ask if any of the credible intervals failed to span zero; only if *none* did should the sample evidence lead one to conclude that the six population means being compared were not "statistically different" at the chosen level of credibility. Only by finding at least one credible interval in such a context that did not span zero would there be evidence the frequentist statistician would associate with a significant omnibus F statistic. Of course, like the Bayesian, the frequentist will ordinarily profit by using meaningful planned contrasts. However, because the Bayesian statistician gets a posterior distribution for each single degree of freedom contrast, he or she gets more information than their frequentist counterpart who analyzes the same data.

Notes on Software

For the reader interested in applying Bayesian methods, programs such as Minitab (currently, version 11 for Windows) and S-Plus (version 4.0 for Windows) provide straightforward mechanisms for generating beta distributions. Albert (1996) provides numerous macros for Minitab. All methods discussed above are relatively easy to implement with such software. But Bayesian methodology is undergoing dynamic development at this time, so new software systems can be anticipated to deal with increasingly complex problems being tackled in many areas of statistical practice. Of course, the Internet and World Wide Web also may provide access to information pertaining to applications.

ACKNOWLEDGMENTS

I wish to express my special appreciation to William Rozeboom, David Rindskopf and Thomas Knapp as well as Bruno Zumbo, B. Dale Bryant, and Michael Divak for helpful comments on earlier drafts.

REFERENCES

Albert, J. (1996). *Bayesian computation using Minitab.* Belmont, CA: Wadsworth.

Barnett, V. (1982). *Comparative statistical inference* (2nd ed.). New York: Wiley.

Box, G. E. P. (1980). Sampling and Bayes inference in scientific modeling and robustness (with discussion). *Journal of the Royal Statistical Society-A, 143,* 383–430.

Cornfield, J. (1969). The Bayesian outlook and its application. *Biometrics, 25,* 617–657.

deFinetti, B. (1971). *Theory of probability: A critical introductory treatment (Vol. 1),* New York: Wiley.

deFinetti, B. (1974). Bayesianism: Its unifying role for both the foundations and applications of statistics. *International Statistical Review, 42,* 117–130.

Dempster, A. P. (1971). An overview of multivariate data analysis. *Journal of Multivariate Analysis, 1,* 316–346.

Efron, B. (1986). Why isn't everyone a Bayesian? (with discussion). *American Statistician, 40,* 1–11.

Geertsma, J. C. (1983). Recent views on the foundational controversy in statistics. *South African Statistical Journal, 17,* 121–146.

Gelman, A., Carlin, J., Stern, H., & Rubin, D. B. (1995). *Bayesian data analysis.* London: Chapman and Hall.

Godambe, V. B., & Sprott, D. A. (Eds.). (1971). *Foundations of statistical inference.* Toronto: Holt, Rinehart and Winston of Canada.

Good, I. J. (1983). *Good thinking: The foundations of probability and its applications.* Minneapolis: University of Minnesota Press.

Harper, W. L., & Hooker, C. A. (Eds.). (1976). *Foundations of probability theory, statistical inference, and statistical theories of science:* Vol. II. *Foundations and philosophy of statistical inference.* Dordrecht, Netherlands: D. Reidel.

Howson, C. & Urbach, P. M. (1993). *Scientific reasoning: The Bayesian approach* (2nd ed.). LaSalle, IL: Open Court.

Lee, P. M. (1989). *Bayesian statistics: an introduction.* New York: Oxford University Press.

Lewis, C. (1993). Bayesian methods for the analysis of variance. In G. Keren & C. Lewis (Eds.) *A handbook for data analysis in the behavioral sciences—Statistical issues* (pp. 233–256). Hillsdale, NJ: Lawrence Erlbaum Associates.

Lindley, D. V. (1965). *Introduction to probability and statistics: From a Bayesian viewpoint:* Part I, *Probability;* Part 2, *Inference.* Cambridge, England: Cambridge University Press.

Lindley, D. V., & Novick, M. R. (1981). The role of exchangeability in inference. *Annals of Statistics, 9,* 45–48.

Meehl, P. E. (1978). Theoretical risks and tabular asterisks: Sir Karl, Sir Ronald, and the slow progress of soft psychology. *Journal of Consulting and Clinical Psychology, 46,* 806–834.

Mosteller, F., & Tukey, J. W. (1977). *Data analysis and regression.* Reading, MA: Addison-Wesley.

Novick, M. R., & Jackson, P. H. (1974). *Statistical methods for educational and psychological research.* New York: McGraw-Hill.

Phillips, L. D. (1973). *Bayesian statistics for social scientists.* New York: Crowell.

Rozeboom, W. W. (1961). Ontological induction and the logical typology of scientific variables. *Philosophy of Science, 28,* 337–377.

Rozeboom, W. W. (1972). Scientific inference: The myth and the reality. In S. R. Brown & D. J. Brenner (Eds.). *Science, psychology, and communication: Essays honoring William Stephenson* (pp. 95–118). New York: Columbia University Press.

Rozeboom, W. W. (1977). Metathink–a radical alternative. *Canadian Psychological Review, 18,* 197–203.

Rubin, D. B. (1974). Estimating the causal effects of treatments in randomized and non-randomized studies. *Journal of Educational Psychology, 66,* 688–701.

Rubin, D. B. (1978). Bayesian inference for causal effects: The role of randomization. *Annals of Statistics, 6,* 34–58.

Schmitt, S. A. (1969). *Measuring uncertainty: An elementary introduction to Bayesian statistics.* Reading, MA: Addison-Wesley.

Tukey, J. W. (1969). Analyzing data: Sanctification or detective work? *American Psychologist, 24,* 83–91.

Tukey, J. W. (1977). *Exploratory data analysis.* Reading, MA: Addison-Wesley.

Chapter 12

Testing "Small," Not Null, Hypotheses: Classical and Bayesian Approaches

David M. Rindskopf
CUNY Graduate Center

> "Reports of my death have been greatly exaggerated."
>
> — attributed to Mark Twain[1]

Critical attacks on null hypothesis testing over the years have not greatly diminished its use in the social sciences. This chapter tells why the continued use of hypothesis tests is not merely due to ignorance on the part of data analysts. In fact, a null hypothesis that an effect is exactly zero should be rejected in most circumstances; what investigators really want to test is whether an effect is nearly zero, or whether it is large enough to care about. Although relatively small sample sizes typically used in psychology result in modest power, they also result in approximate tests that an effect is small (not just exactly zero), so researchers are doing approximately the right thing (most of the time) when testing null hypotheses. Bayesian methods are even better, offering direct opportunities to make statements such as "the probability that the effect is large and negative is .01; the probability that the effect is near zero is .10; and the probability that there is a large positive effect is .89."

Given the many attacks on it, null hypothesis testing should be dead. The brief argument is as follows: The null hypothesis is that some parameter (usually a difference between groups on some outcome variable) is exactly equal to zero. This is never true. Therefore, we can always reject a null hypothesis without collecting any data, let alone doing any statistical analyses. If we insist on col-

---

[1] This is the usual citation; the actual quotation is "The report of my death was an exaggeration." (*New York Journal*, June 2, 1897).

lecting data, we will either (correctly) reject the null hypothesis, or (incorrectly, due to lack of power) fail to reject the null hypothesis.

If this argument is right, why is null hypothesis testing still so widely used and taught? Why hasn't it been replaced by alternatives such as confidence intervals or Bayesian methods? In this chapter, I show why the continued use of hypothesis tests is not simply irrational behavior, but can be justified by changing the interpretation of such tests. In addition, I show how Bayesian methods can give additional insights not available using classical techniques.

POINT VERSUS COMPOSITE NULL HYPOTHESES

The usual null hypothesis-testing rationale arises from a test that a parameter is exactly zero (or some other value). This is a point (or simple) hypothesis; that is, a hypothesis that the parameter is exactly equal to some point (single value) in the space of possible parameter values. But, in fact, most researchers probably don't really want to test this hypothesis. Instead, they probably want to test the hypothesis that an effect is so small that it is unimportant, versus the alternative hypothesis that the effect is large enough to be considered important. In statistical terms, both the null and alternative hypothesis would be *composite hypotheses;* that is, they each consist of ranges of possible values, rather than single values. For example, rather than testing the null hypothesis that "The mean difference in IQ scores between two groups is exactly equal to 0," the researcher might really want to test the "small" hypothesis that "The mean difference in IQ scores between the two groups is less than 2 IQ points." The alternative hypothesis would be that the mean difference is at least 2 IQ points. This viewpoint is not new (see, e.g., Bakan, 1966; Binder, 1963; Browne & Cudeck, 1993; Edwards, 1950; Hodges & Lehmann, 1954; Rouanet, 1996; Serlin & Lapsley, 1985, 1993; Walster & Cleary, 1970); however, it is not widely known and even less widely practiced.

If this is what researchers want to test, why don't they test this hypothesis directly? Because in the classical framework for statistics it is much simpler mathematically to test a point null hypothesis than it is to test a composite "nearly null" hypothesis. Some attention is now being devoted to discussing practical procedures for such tests (see, e.g., Serlin & Lapsley, 1985, 1993). These procedures, like power tests, involve noncentral distributions, and (also like power tests) are not found in most standard statistical packages. (The usual hypothesis-testing procedure involves the use of central distributions, which describe the distribution of a statistic, such as t or F, when the null hypothesis is true. For testing composite hypotheses we must use noncentral distributions, which describe the distribution of a statistic when the null hypothesis is false.)

But even without these methods for testing composite "nearly null" (or "small") hypotheses, all is not lost: If the sample size in a study is not too large, the usual hypothesis-testing procedure is a good approximation to what would be needed to test the "small" hypothesis that the researcher would really like to test. Therefore, unless the sample size is large, the power to declare a "small" effect significant will be near .05. If so, then the usual (point) null hypothesis test is also an approximately correct test of the composite hypothesis that "the effect is small." This is why null hypothesis tests are still used: They are testing approximately the right thing under many real circumstances, even though most researchers do not know the rationale. (Berger & Delampady, 1987, made a similar point in the context of Bayesian approaches to testing exact null hypotheses.)

One question that immediately arises is how to define "small." Of course this is subjective, just as the definition of small, medium, and large effect sizes in power analysis is subjective. And the definitions probably will change as progress is made in studying any particular content area; as more progress is made, what once was considered a small effect may become a medium-size effect. In a practical sense, a researcher has implied that an effect is small if the power of a study to detect that size effect is near .05. If the power is appreciably greater than .05 (or whatever alpha level is chosen), then the hypothesis test has a greater significance level than desired; that is, the study is too likely to declare a very small effect significant, just because the power is high.

In practice, with large sample sizes one simple adjustment cures this problem: If the observed effect size is small, do not reject the null hypothesis. In other words, we end up with the usual advice found in textbooks: To be declared significant, an effect must be large enough to be both statistically significant and of practical importance.

We conclude that null hypothesis testing still is used because it actually approximates what we usually want. Furthermore, most studies (especially experimental studies) have small enough sample sizes that the approximation is probably very good, even without considering the question of practical importance. But researchers who believe strictly in null hypothesis testing, without considering the practical importance of the effect size, must do a balancing act when choosing the sample size for a study: The sample size must be (a) small enough that the power to detect a "very small" effect is still near their alpha level, yet (b) large enough to have a high power to detect a "big" effect.

As an example, consider a two-group study in which a t test is done to compare the means of the groups. If there are 50 subjects in each group, then the power to detect a very small effect (.1 standard deviations) is .07; the power to detect a medium-size effect (.5 standard deviations) is .71. There is little likelihood of rejecting the null hypothesis if the effect is truly small, but a very high likelihood of rejecting the null hypothesis if the effect is at least medium-sized.

With fewer subjects, the power to detect reasonably large effects gets too small. With more subjects, the probability of rejecting the null hypothesis for a very small effect gets large, and one must in addition consider the question of practical importance of the effect size.

Of course, one may ask why we still test hypotheses at all, rather than just giving a point or interval estimate of parameters. The reason is that we still have to make decisions. As an example, even if I know the interval estimate for the difference in effectiveness of two drugs, I still have to make a decision about which drug to use (or a decision that they are so similar that either drug can be used). In psychological studies, I want to decide whether the effect of some variable, such as teacher expectancy, is large enough so that I should keep doing studies of it or not, and whether attempts to change such expectancies are worth the effort. In essence, we want to decide which effects are large enough to worry about and which are not. As a field develops, the definition of what is "large enough to worry about" may change, but this decision process is always operating.

BAYESIAN METHODS

The Bayesian approach is especially useful for such decision making. This section assumes a basic knowledge of Bayesian methods. A short summary is be given here; more details can be found in the chapter by Pruzek (chapter 11 of this volume) and the references therein. I italicize the first use of each technical term.

Bayesians view *probability* as degree of belief about unknown quantities (parameters). They usually begin by assessing their beliefs prior to collecting data in a study; these beliefs are summarized in their *prior distribution*. In situations like those considered in this chapter, Bayesians combine their prior beliefs with the information provided by the data in a study to produce a *posterior distribution*. The posterior distribution frequently looks just like a classical sampling distribution, centered around a parameter estimate, that is used to calculate confidence intervals. However, the interpretation given to this distribution is much different for Bayesians: The area under the posterior distribution, between two points on the horizontal axis, is the Bayesian's probability that the true value of the parameter lies between those two points.

A *credible interval* is calculated like a classical statistician's confidence interval, but again the interpretation is different: The area under the curve is the probability that the parameter lies within the credible interval. This is the interpretation given to classical confidence intervals by almost all beginning statistics students; although it is incorrect within the classical framework, it is viewed as correct (and perfectly natural) within the Bayesian framework. Bayesians who calculate a 95% credible interval would say that there is a 95% probability that the parameter lies within the interval.

A full Bayesian approach to decision-making involves assigning costs and benefits, called *utilities*, to each possible action and outcome. I do not demonstrate this, because of the complications that arise, but instead discuss some useful analogues in Bayesian statistics of classical hypothesis-testing procedures. Related Bayesian approaches were given by Zellner (1987) and Brophy and Joseph (1995).

Consider a situation in which two treatments are compared, and the parameter of interest is the difference δ in response to the two treatments. A value of zero for δ means that the two treatments are equal, and values different from zero mean that one treatment is more effective than the other. The Bayesian posterior distribution shows the beliefs of the experimenter about how plausible different values of this difference are, after collecting data from a study.

Suppose that in such a study, each group has 10 subjects. The first group has a mean of 10, the second group has a mean of 7, and each group has a standard deviation of 3.18. The posterior distribution for the mean difference between groups for such a study is shown in Figure 12.1.

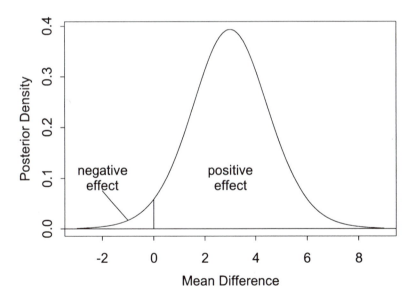

FIGURE 12.1 Posterior distribution for the mean difference from a hypothetical study with 10 subjects per group. The observed mean difference of 3 is also the mode of the posterior distribution; the scaling factor of the posterior distribution (spread relative to a t distribution) is 1.5.

This distribution has the same general shape as a t distribution, with $n_1 + n_2 - 2$ degrees of freedom (here, $10 + 10 - 2 = 18$ degrees of freedom), centered at the observed mean difference (3), and with a scale factor equal to the standard error of the mean difference (1.5).

The most plausible values of δ are those where the curve is highest; these points are not particularly close to zero. In fact, we can calculate the proportion of the area under the curve for values of δ greater than zero. In the Bayesian context, this gives the probability that δ is greater than 0. (Conversely, the area under the curve to the left of zero gives the probability that δ is less than zero.) These numbers—the probabilities that an effect is positive or negative—sound much more like what we would like to know than we can get from classical statistics. They are related to calculations in classical statistics (if the Bayesian uses a *uniform* or *noninformative prior distribution*), but have a much more intuitively pleasing interpretation. In classical statistics, the smaller of these two probabilities would be the one-tailed significance level for a null hypothesis test.

Because of the analogy between these probabilities and usual hypothesis tests, Bayesians sometimes report these values to help non-Bayesians understand their results. But these numbers by themselves are insufficient, and may even be misleading. Consider Figure 12.2, which shows two posterior distributions, one with a small variance, the other with a large variance. In both of these distributions, the probability that δ is greater than zero is the same. However, it is obvi-

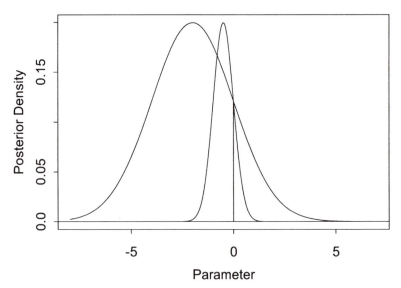

FIGURE 12.2 Posterior distributions for hypothetical studies with small and large variances, but same probability that the effect size is greater than zero.

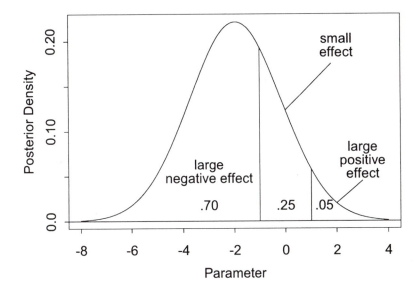

FIGURE 12.3   Posterior distribution divided into three parts, corresponding to large negative, small, and large positive effect sizes. Here, "small" is defined as "less than 1 in absolute value." The numbers within the areas represent the posterior probabilities that the effect is large negative, small, or large positive, respectively.

ous that the estimate of δ is much more accurate in one case than in the other: With a small variance, one is very certain of the value of δ, whereas with a large variance, one is very uncertain about the exact value of δ. How can we convey our results more informatively?

Our previous discussion of "small" hypothesis tests may lead us to reason as follows: We may not be interested in making one of two choices ("treatment A is better" or "treatment B is better"), but rather one of three choices: "treatment A is appreciably better," "treatment B is appreciably better," or "treatments A and B are about the same." Again, the choice of a dividing line is subjective. We now divide the posterior distribution into three areas, as demonstrated in Figure 12.3 for data from a hypothetical study. The three areas correspond to the probabilities of each of the three outcomes. This figure illustrates what happens when the estimated effect size is not small, but there is relatively little evidence, so the posterior distribution has a fairly large variance. Here, the area on the left, indicating the probability that δ is "very negative", is large (about .70); the area in the middle, indicating the probability that δ is so small that we are indifferent between the treatments, is moderately large (about .25); and the area on the right, indicating the probability that δ is "very positive", is very small (about .05).

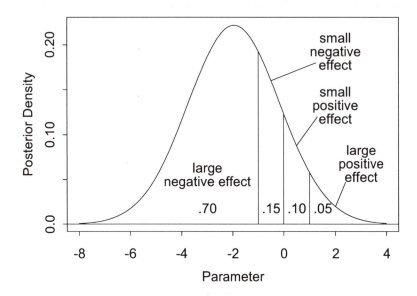

FIGURE 12.4 Posterior distribution, divided in four parts, corresponding to large negative, small negative, small positive, and large positive effect sizes. Here, "small negative" means between -1 and 0, and "small positive" means between 0 and 1. The numbers within each area are the probabilities that the effect sizes are large negative, small negative, small positive, and large positive, respectively.

This approach would lead us to state our conclusions as "The probability of a large negative effect is .70; of a small effect, .25, and the probability of a large positive effect is .05." Although not leading directly to a decision, this statement may be very useful in the decision-making process (including a decision about whether more data are needed).

One could follow this strategy further, dividing the "small effect" area into two parts: a small negative effect, and a small positive effect (see Figure 12.4). One then would make conclusions such as "The probability of a large negative effect is .70; of a small negative effect, .15; of a small positive effect, .10; and of a large positive effect, .05."

In principle, of course, one could also further subdivide the "large" effect size areas. Each additional subdivision makes the procedure somewhat more complicated. Whether the additional information would be useful depends on the types of decisions that might be made as a result of the study.

EXAMPLE: IS T-PA SUPERIOR TO STREPTOKINASE
IN TREATING HEART ATTACK?

We illustrate these possibilities by using a real data set (see Brophy & Joseph, 1995), from a study to compare two methods of treating heart attacks. Both treatment methods involve the administration of medicines that dissolve blood clots. One (t-PA) is much more expensive than the other (streptokinase), and if the results are at least as good for the cheaper medicine, there would be no need to use the more expensive medicine. (In this example, as in the rest of this chapter, no explicit consideration is made of costs or benefits. Technically, we are just discussing statistics, not decision theory. But implicitly, by defining the various possible decisions and effect sizes, we must be using ideas of costs and benefits of various decisions.)

The parameter of interest in this study is the difference in the fatality rates of the two drugs, t-PA and streptokinase. The observed fatality rates (proportion of patients dying) in this study[2] were .063 for t-PA, and .073 for streptokinase. Relatively simple calculations from the original data show that, using a uniform prior distribution, the posterior distribution of the difference in mortality rates should be approximately normal, with a mean of .01 (that is, a 1% difference favoring t-PA), and a standard deviation of .0031. The calculations used by a Bayesian to arrive at the value .0031 are the same as a classical statistician would use to derive the standard error of a difference in proportions. This small standard deviation of the posterior distribution is a result of a very large sample size: just over 20,000 for the streptokinase group, and just over 10,000 for the t-PA group.

Figure 12.5 shows the posterior distribution. This same distribution would be used by a statistician using classical methods to obtain a point estimate of the difference (.01), confidence intervals (e.g., a 95% confidence interval goes from .004 to .016), and to do hypothesis tests (here, we reject the hypothesis that δ is zero).

Note that in this case, the sample size is so large that the usual null hypothesis test tells us very little. And yet, even in this case the null hypothesis test is not completely worthless. The power to detect a difference in fatality rates of .001, or one tenth of 1%, is .052, which is close to the alpha value of .05 that would be used. Therefore, the rejection of the exact null hypothesis also allows us to reject the "very small" null hypothesis. This leads us to conclude that the effect is not "very small," if "very small" is defined as less than .001.

---

[2] Here only the data from the GUSTO study are used. Additional issues arise if data from several studies are combined.

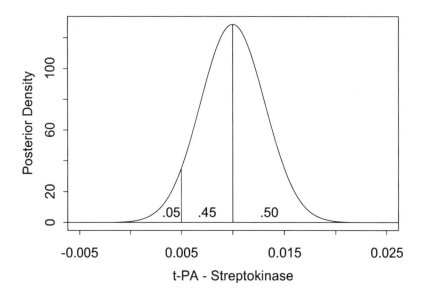

FIGURE 12.5 Posterior distribution of difference in mortality between streptokinase
(SK) and t-PA. Values greater than 0 indicate that t-PA has lower mortality; numbers less than 0 indicate that SK has lower mortality. The
points corresponding to effect sizes of .005 and .010, and the posterior
probabilities corresponding to areas below .005, between .005 and .010,
and above .010, are displayed. Almost all of the area under the curve is
between 0 and .02, indicating that t-PA has lower mortality.

A Bayesian who wanted to do something comparable to a classical hypothesis
test would compute the probability that the difference was less than zero. This
probability is represented by the area under the curve to the left of zero; this
probability is very nearly zero. This is the same probability that a classical statistician would derive for a one-tailed test (it would be doubled for a two-tailed
test). The Bayesian conclusion from this calculation is that there is little chance
that streptokinase is superior to t-PA.

As discussed previously, more informative Bayesian results can be presented
by choosing an effect size that is large enough to be clinically significant. For
these data, the general consensus among the doctors conducting the study was
that the difference in mortality between methods would have to be greater than
1% (.01) in order for them to have a clear preference of one drug over the other.
That is, the death rate would have to be at least .01 higher for one group than for
the other group. We use this value to calculate Bayesian results. (We determine

the importance of this choice by doing a sensitivity analysis, in which we recalculate using other values, such as .02 and .005.)

The probability that the effect is a large one favoring t-PA is represented by the area to the right of the value .01; it is easy to see in this case that this probability is .50. The probability that the effect is a large one favoring streptokinase is represented by the area to the left of the value -.01 (a value so unlikely that it does not even appear in the figure). This corresponds to a standard normal deviate (z-score) of $\{(-.01) - .01\}/.0031 = -.02/.0031$, or about -6.4. As expected from examining Figure 12.5, the probability that a standard normal deviate is less than -6.4 is very near zero. Therefore, by subtraction we calculate that the probability that the effect is "small," in the sense of being less than .01 in absolute value (i.e., between $-.01$ and $.01$), is about .50.

We can further refine our method by dividing the area of "small" effect into "small difference in favor of t-PA," and "small difference in favor of streptokinase." These probabilities are nearly .50, and nearly zero, respectively. (For example, the probability that the effect is less than zero can be calculated from the z-score $(0 - .01)/.031 = -3.2$. The desired probabilities then can be calculated by subtraction.) One can conclude, therefore, that streptokinase is not only extremely unlikely to be highly superior to t-PA, it is quite unlikely to be even slightly superior to t-PA.

How sensitive are these results to the choice of .01 as a clinically significant effect? First, suppose that we had used .005 instead of .01. Figure 12.5 shows that we would calculate the probability of a small effect as, approximately, the probability of finding a standard normal deviate z less than $(.005 - .010)/.0031 = -1.67$; this probability is about .05. The probability that the effect is clinically significant in favor of t-PA is about .95. We are reasonably certain in this case that the effect is clinically significant. Next, suppose that we had used a criterion of .02 for clinical significance. We see from the figure that the probability is near 1 that the effect is a small one in favor of t-PA, and near zero that it is "large" in favor of t-PA. From this example, we see that when the mode (peak) of the posterior distribution is near the dividing line between "small" and "large," the location of the dividing line can have an effect on the interpretation. The Bayesian lesson is that we may need to look at the whole posterior distribution.

APPLICATION IDEAS

The Bayesian calculations in many instances can be found by simple modifications of calculations used in classical statistics. When this is true, the only additional tools required are those used to calculate areas under probability distributions. For normal curves, tables of the standard normal distribution function are found in nearly every textbook, although using a computer can be faster and more accurate. For other distributions, such as the t-distribution, additional aids are needed. I used the program Mathcad to do the calculations and S-Plus to produce the figures in this chapter; many other mathematical and statistical programs have similar capabilities. Mathcad and S-Plus have built-in functions to evaluate needed quantities for many common statistical distributions. As an example, to find the probability that a random value from a t-distribution with 18 degrees of freedom would be less than $-.5$, you merely type the expression

$$pt(-.5, 18) =$$

and Mathcad will immediately list the result. As in any programming environment, you can give these quantities names and then use them in further calculations.

CONCLUSIONS

This chapter has two main conclusions. First, null hypothesis testing is not as irrational as it is sometimes made to seem. One must merely understand that it does approximately the right thing most of the time, especially in many social science studies, where small to medium sample sizes are typical. If we follow the usual advice to declare an effect significant only if it is both statistically significant and large enough to matter, then our methods may be roughly right. Exact methods of testing "small" null hypotheses are preferable and available, but not yet as part of popular statistical packages. In any case, null hypothesis tests serve a useful purpose in decision making, from the viewpoint of classical statistics.

Second, the Bayesian method offers more gratifying interpretations than classical methods. One can easily present probabilities that the effect size is small, or is large in either direction. These probabilities can be extremely helpful in making decisions. Further, in many situations the Bayesian only needs to use central distributions, which are widely found in tables and computer programs, rather than noncentral distributions, which are not.

In some situations, of course, confidence intervals (for a classical statistician) or credible intervals (for a Bayesian) are more useful than explicit hypothesis tests.

Finally, note that in all null hypothesis tests, there is a bias against rejecting the null hypothesis. To see an extreme example of this, consider what result is necessary to reject a null hypothesis with a one-tailed test at the .05 level. From a Bayesian perspective, this means that there is a greater than 95% probability that the parameter in question is greater than zero (or less than zero, depending on the direction). So the odds must be at least 19 to 1 that the parameter is on one side of zero before the null hypothesis is rejected. In classical inference, the implication is that a Type I error is much more serious than a Type II error.

Why should this be so? The reason lies in an ancient tradition in philosophy, based on Occam's razor, which states (in terms relevant to social science theory) that one should not postulate the existence of effects unless necessary. The simplest "theory" is that no treatment makes a difference, and nothing is related to anything else (i.e., the null hypothesis is always true). We keep that theory until some treatment effect or relationship is demonstrated to exist ("beyond a reasonable doubt", to use the legal analogy). This keeps our theory as simple as possible. Occam's razor provides the implicit scientific basis for the central role of null hypothesis testing in statistical inference. Other aspects of science lead us to other goals, such as estimating a parameter (e.g., the gravitational constant, g, or speed of light, c) whose value may not be known from theory. In these cases, null hypothesis testing may be inappropriate, whereas estimation and confidence intervals (or Bayesian credible intervals) would be more useful tools.

ACKNOWLEGEMENTS

Thanks to Robert Cudeck, Robert Pruzek, and Charles Reichardt for comments and discussions that improved this paper.

REFERENCES

Bakan, D. (1966). The test of significance in psychological research. *Psychological Bulletin, 66,* 423–437.

Berger, J. O., & Delampady, M. (1987). Testing precise hypotheses. *Statistical Science, 2,* 317–352.

Binder, A. (1963). Further considerations on testing the null hypothesis and the strategy and tactics of investigating theoretical models. *Psychological Review, 70,* 101–109.

Brophy, J. M., & Joseph, L. (1995). Placing trials in context using Bayesian analysis: GUSTO revisited by Reverend Bayes. *Journal of the American Medical Association, 273,* 871–875.

Browne, M. W., & Cudeck, R. (1993). Alternative ways of assessing model fit. In K. A. Bollen & J. S. Long (Eds.), *Testing structural equation models* (pp. 136–162). Newbury Park, CA: Sage.

Edwards, A. L. (1950). *Experimental design in psychological research.* New York: Holt, Rinehart & Winston.

Hodges, J. L., & Lehmann, E. L. (1954). Testing the approximate validity of statistical hypotheses. *Journal of the Royal Statistical Society (B), 16,* 261–268.

Rouanet, H. (1996). Bayesian methods for assessing importance of effects. *Psychological Bulletin, 119,* 149–158.

Serlin, R. C., & Lapsley, D. K. (1985). Rationality in psychological theory: The good-enough principle. *American Psychologist, 40,* 73–83.

Serlin, R. C., & Lapsley, D. K. (1993). Rational appraisal of psychological research and the good-enough principle. In G. Keren & C. Lewis (Eds.), *A handbook for data analysis in the behavioral sciences: Statistical issues* (pp. 199–228). Hillsdale, NJ: Lawrence Erlbaum Associates.

Walster, G., & Cleary, T. (1970). Statistical significance as a decision rule. In E. Borgatta & G. Bohrnstedt (Eds.), *Sociological methodology* (pp. 246–254). San Francisco: Jossey-Bass.

Zellner, A. (1987). Comment. *Statistical Science, 2,* 339–341.

Philosophy of Science Issues

Chapter 13

Good Science is Abductive, Not Hypothetico-Deductive

William W. Rozeboom
University of Alberta

Statistics and their sampling uncertainties remain a large concern in our design of research and interpretation of results. But these matter only as instruments of deeper research strategies; and the sharpest of scalpels can only create a mess if misdirected by the hand that drives it. With strategic intent, this essay meditates on the conceptual foundations of scientific inference through overview of three major outlooks on the nature of rational belief change—hypothetico-deductive, Bayesian, abductive—and the still challengingly obscure character of conditionality and lawfulness. Most of these considerations have no direct bearing on what statistical techniques you should prefer. But their indirect relevance is greater than you have probably had occasion to appreciate, and at summary time some practical advice will be drawn from them.

PHILOSOPHIES OF SCIENTIFIC INFERENCE

Null-hypothesis significance testing is surely the most bone-headedly misguided procedure ever institutionalized in the rote training of science students. But you don't need me to tell you that. Ever since its inception, thoughtful statisticians and data analysts have decried this doctrine's more unsightly flaws (see Cohen, 1994, for a recent review); and although it is a sociology-of-science wonderment that this statistical practice has remained so unresponsive to criticism, recognition that confidence intervals, when feasible, are a much superior way to exploit our standard models of sampling noise finally appears to be growing with sufficient vigor that with luck, research reports in our professional journals will soon no longer be required to feign preoccupation with H_0.

However, significance testing is just the statistical excrescence of a deeper malaise that has pervaded our discipline's education in research design and data analysis, namely, the hypothetico-deductive (HD) model of scientific method.

When this modern orthodoxy, that natural science is best advanced by empirical tests of theoretical speculations, is construed loosely as just advice to continue improving our provisional generalizations and explanations of observed phenomena in light of performance evaluations, it is a tolerably benign way to apprise outsiders that the epistemic management of statements we honor as "scientific" differs considerably from that of religious scriptures. But it is worse than useless as an operational guide for the conduct of research. The HD program's failure to advise on which hypotheses are worth testing becomes an evasion of educational responsibilities when science students are admonished that design of their research projects must begin with choice of a hypothesis to test. And far more damaging than this mild sin of omission are the HD outlook's commissional sins in misdirecting the interpretation of experimental[1] results.

Why Hypothetico-Deductivism is Pernicious

When H is some uncertain prospect that would much influence our conduct of important affairs were we to feel sure of it, and we realize that one implication of H is a proposition C whose truth can with tolerable effort be settled here and now, it is only commonsense prudence to determine whether C is in fact the case and adjust our confidence in H accordingly if the anticipated gain of knowledge from this appraisal is worth its cost. But clumsy use of power tools can do much damage; and what research practice has to gain from the simplistic models of HD procedure imported into psychology's method canons from Popperian[2] philosophy of science is akin to the benefits of purging computer viruses with defibrillation paddles.

---

[1] I here understand "experiments" to comprise all interpretation-oriented compilings of empirical data regardless of whether subjects are observed under manipulated input conditions.

[2] When psychology students are advised that hypothetico-deductivism is the philosophically approved way to conduct science, Karl Popper is the authority whose name is usually invoked. Popper himself described his account of scientific inference as "deductivism," and many philosophers of science (e.g. Salmon, 1966, p. 21) have held that Popper rejected hypothetico-deductivism because it allows theories to be *confirmed* by the data they entail, which Popper denied is possible. But Popper disowned confirmation on grounds that 'confirm' has the connotations of "establish firmly", "put beyond doubt", and "verify" (Popper, 1959, p. 251 fn. 1). He did, however, allow theories to be "corroborated" by data; and the corroboration formulas in Popper (1959, Appendix *ix) imply that evidence e corroborates hypothesis h just in case, after e has been deduced from h, learning that e is true increases the logical probability of h. And if "logical probability" is interpreted as "credibility" (though Popper disallowed construing that as subjective), this is an acceptable English reading of 'confirm' that moreover is the sense in which hypothetico-deductivism understands it.

Described as a normative epistemic process, the standard model of hypo-thetico-deductive reasoning is:

1. We determine that uncertain proposition C (a possible experimental out-come or other data prospect) is logically entailed by uncertain hypothesis H;
2. We ascertain that C is (a) true, or (b) false;
3. We conclude that H has been respectively (a) confirmed, or (b) disconfirmed;

wherein *confirmed/disconfirmed* means that it is rational for the confidence we give H to increase in response to event (2a) or decrease in response to (2b). Commonsensically, inference pattern (1)–(3) seems entirely reasonable even when *disconfirmed* in (3b) is strengthened to *refuted*; and there is little chance that any theory of rational belief will ever successfully impugn it, or want to. The problem with (1)–(3) is that it doesn't imply what folk who extol hypo-thetico-deductive reasoning take it to imply. Insomuch as the payoff we expect from testing H is an appropriate shift of confidence in additional implications of H that are still uncertain given the test result but will not forever remain so (e.g. in light of our sample results, will it be safely beneficial to market this new medication or designer gene?), procedure (1)–(3) may well seem pointless unless it further includes

4. Any other uncertain logical consequence D of H is thereby also respective-ly (a) confirmed or (b) disconfirmed.

But although (4) is true for *some* consequences of H (notably, when D is H in its entirety), it is flagrantly *not* true of all. One counter-instance in all cases is H's logical consequence *Either not-C or H*, whose plausibility is decreased by learning C and increased by learning *not-C*. Or for a less obviously artificial ex-ample, suppose that when wagering on a coin-toss sequence, you entertain the hypothesis H_{ht}: *The next two tosses of this coin will come up first heads and then tails.* One consequence of H_{ht} is C: *The next toss will be a head*, whose truth will be revealed by the next coin toss. But H_{ht} also entails D: *At least one of the next two tosses will be tails.* So if you are a holistic Popperian, your initial confidence in D should be increased by observing the first toss to be a head and noting that this confirms H_{ht}, whereas ordinary odds advises that observing C should de-crease your initial confidence in D.

No great skill in logic is needed to appreciate how grotesque is conclusion (4)'s fallacy: Any hypothesis is equivalent to the conjunction of all its logical consequences, and any logically consistent conjunction of propositions conversely qualifies as a hypothesis amenable to *HD* appraisal regardless of how confirmationally cohesive that collection may be. There are arbitrarily many uncertain hypotheses that entail a given test result *C*, and for any one *H* of these having an additional uncertain consequence *D*, not equivalent to *H* or *C*, that we are tempted to view as supported by *C* through the confirmational mediation of *H* there are others of which *not-D* is a consequence and by parity of *HD* reasoning should mediate disconfirmation of *D* by evidence *C*. In short, *the bare deducibility of both C and D from some hypothesis H has no intrinsic relevance to whether learning C makes D more plausible.*

Yet in research practice we *do* consider repeatedly successful tests of particular hypotheses to enhance our trust in their still-unverified observational consequences. Is this just institutionalized foolishness? To some extent Yes; but in the main, surely not. Expert scientific intuition says that some theories do indeed mediate confirmation from some of their verifiable consequences to others. But these intuitions are far from infallible, and we have yet to identify, or even acknowledge our ignorance of, whatever may be the special conceptual relations that establish channels of credibility transmission among the constituents of a confirmationally cohesive hypothesis or theory.

Thinking out the empirical consequences of imaginative speculations is an excellent way to come up with provocative experiments. But interpreting the resultant data by holistic *HD* reasoning is intellectually at par with a dictator's executing all his senior advisors in response to evidence that one of them is a traitor. Verifying consequence *C* of hypothesis or theory *H* tells us that *something* in *H* beyond *C* may well be more belief-worthy than we thought previously. But *HD* inference pattern (1)–(3) gives us no clue how to separate the wheat in *H* from its *C*-wise chaff and contaminants (i.e. components of *H* to which *C* is confirmationally indifferent or even hostile). Rather, the *HD* model of scientific inference becomes not merely unhelpful but actively pernicious when students are trained to appraise hypotheses or theories in holistic accord with schema (1)–(3) with no binding of ears against the rationality shipwreck to which siren (4) is lure. Even more potentially destructive in applications is its urging researchers to disregard any surprising feature of their experimental results whose possible occurrence was not envisioned in the *H*-testing prediction their study has been designed to ascertain. (Competent researchers ignore this admonition, of course, but that is another demonstration of the gulf between *HD* metatheory and expert scientific practice.)

There are, however, other models of scientific inference with literatures to which our students deserve some exposure, not merely to loose their *HD* shackles but also because these spin off operational directives that under congenial circumstances can be genuinely beneficial.

Bayesian Confirmation Theory

Though seldom brought to our students' attention, this has been a major player in the philosophy of inference ever since the advent of probability theory, and has accrued considerable technical development by mathematicians and philosophers of science. (See Howson & Urbach, 1993, for an easy-access partisan overview that is exceptionally comprehensive albeit vulnerable to criticism such as Chihara, 1994.) It comprises models of rational belief whose most classical version posits that the distribution of credences (belief strengths, degrees of confidence) assigned by an ideally coherent believer having background knowledge K to the assorted propositions expressed by declarative sentences in his language can be scaled by a function $Cr_K(\ )$ over these sentences (or propositions) whose value ranges from 1 (complete certainty) down to 0 (utter disbelief) and whose mathematical behavior over logically compound sentences mirrors that of statistical probability over logical compounds of properties. (This parallel between subjective credibility and objective probability is by stipulation ideal "coherence." Bayesian background "knowledge" comprises beliefs held at strength near certainty regardless of their truth.[3]) Among the basic principles of Bayesian credibility theory are that for any propositions p and q, $Cr_K(p) = 1$ and $Cr_K(\sim p) = 0$ if p is logically true, and $Cr_K(p \vee q) = Cr_K(p) + Cr_K(q)$ if $Cr_K(p \cdot q) = 0$. ('$\sim$', '$\vee$', and '$\cdot$' abbreviate '*not*,' '*or*,' and '*and*' respectively).

> This posited Cr-scale of belief strength is in theory computable from odds the believer is willing to accept in wagers on the truth of the propositions at issue. And linkage of quantified confidence to betting behavior also enables a case to be made for the ideality of coherence through "Dutch book" arguments that an inveterate bettor who believes payoff propositions incoherently is sure to lose money even in the short run. (See van Fraassen, 1989, p. 159f. for an elegantly simple version.) However, insomuch as bets are settled only when their participants reach consensual certainty on the target propositions, this doesn't show how arguments based on betting payoffs can support the ideality of coherence for beliefs resistant to conclusive verification, such as conjectures about the origins of the universe. Moreover, it is far from clear that idealizing belief strength as a point value on a Cr scale is benign: Arguably, the *diffusion* of our confidence in a proposition p plays an important role in how our p belief participates in our reasoning, especially in its resistance to change and its effect on other beliefs.

---

[3]This contrasts both with the commonsense construal of propositional knowledge, which takes "knowing" that p to be *having good reason to be highly confident that p*, and its philosophical ideal that requires p to be true, for its knower to be totally confident of this, and further for that confidence to be completely justified in some normative sense never adequately clarified (see, e.g., Chisholm & Swartz, 1973). In this essay, "know" is to be understood commonsensically.

It is further posited that rational belief systems contain *conditional* belief-strengths $Cr_K(q \mid p)$—read "the credibility of q given p"—that interlace with unconditional $Cr_K(\ )$ through principle

$$Cr_K(q \mid p) = Cr_K(p \cdot q) / Cr(p) \tag{13.1}$$

or, equivalently,

$$Cr_K(p \cdot q) = Cr_K(p) \times Cr_K(q \mid p) . \tag{13.2}$$

This allows conditional credibility to subsume unconditional credibility $Cr_K(q)$ as the special case $Cr_K(q \mid p)$ wherein p is logically true and, as a direct consequence of Equations 13.1–13.2, yields Inverse Credibility principles

$$Cr_K(p|q) = \frac{Cr_K(p)}{Cr_K(q)} \times Cr_K(q|p) \tag{13.3}$$

$$Cr_K(p|q \cdot c) = \frac{Cr_K(p|c)}{Cr_K(q|c)} \times Cr_K(q|p \cdot c) \tag{13.4}$$

wherein c is any background conjecture. (Equation 13.3 is the special case of (13.4) wherein c is logically true.) Moreover, whereas satisfaction by $Cr_K(\ )$ of classical probability postulates demarks only *synchronic* (simultaneous) coherence of an ideal belief system, this quantification of rationality becomes Bayesian confirmation theory when it further posits the *diachronic* principle that if K is an ideal believer's background knowledge at a time just prior to his acquiring evidence e, it is ideally rational for this knowledge enrichment to change the strength of his belief in a hypothesis h, conditional on any possibly-empty conjecture c, from $Cr_K(h \mid c)$ to

$$Cr_{K,e}(h \mid c) = Cr_K(h \mid e \cdot c). \tag{13.5}$$

Hence synchronic coherence principle (13.4), and similarly for (13.3), has a diachronic counterpart in rational belief change, namely, Bayesian *inference* ideal

$$Cr_{K,e}(h|c) = \frac{Cr_K(e|h \cdot c)}{Cr_K(e|c)} \times Cr_K(h|c). \tag{13.6}$$

Most practical applications of Bayesian reasoning (mainly, in statistical data modeling) use an elaboration of Equation 13.6 that is important to put on record even though you needn't sweat its details. Almost always a scientific hypothesis h that interests us is just one in a set $\mathbf{h} = \{h_1, ..., h_n\}$ of alternatives that we want to appraise simultaneously. (Finite n here is not really necessary, but it can always be contrived with no significant loss of generality and keeps the mathematics simple.) Then for any conjunction c of background conjectures, it is an easy consequence of Equation 13.3 that

$$\frac{Cr_{K,e}(h_i \mid c)}{Cr_{K,e}(h_j \mid c)} = \frac{Cr_K(e \mid h_i \cdot c)}{Cr_K(e \mid h_j \cdot c)} \times \frac{Cr_K(h_i \cdot c)}{Cr_K(h_j \cdot c)} \quad (i, j = 1, ..., n). \quad (13.7)$$

This tells how the comparative plausibilities of the **h**-alternatives conditional on c should be affected by learning e. Equation 13.7 is the standard Bayesian model for inference based on "likelihood ratios" and holds for any arbitrary collection of hypotheses **h** and auxiliary conjectures c. In applications, however, hypothesis set **h** is usually a "partition" of c in the sense that each h_i in **h** entails c (i.e., c comprises presumptions common to all the h_i) while c entails that exactly one h in **h** is true. (Notably, c may be a statistical "model" with open parameters of which each h_i is a specification.) In this case each h_i is equivalent to $h_i \cdot c$, whence for each h_i in **h**,

$$Cr_K(h_i \mid c) = \frac{Cr_K(h_i)}{Cr_K(c)}$$

$$Cr_K(h_i \mid c) \times Cr_K(e \mid h_i \cdot c) = \frac{Cr_K(e \mid h_i) \times Cr_K(h_i)}{Cr_K(c)}$$

and, since **h** partitions c,

$$Cr_K(e \mid c) = \sum_{j=1}^{n} Cr_K(h_j \mid c) \times Cr_K(e \mid h_j \cdot c) = \frac{\sum_{j=1}^{n} Cr_K(e \mid h_j) \times Cr_K(h_j)}{Cr_K(c)}$$

Substituting into Equation 13.6 for $h = h_i$ then yields, for any partition **h** of any c,

$$Cr_{K,e}(h_i \,|\, c) = \frac{Cr_K(e|h_i) \times Cr_K(h_i)}{\displaystyle\sum_{j=1}^{n} Cr_K(e|h_j) Cr_K(h_j)} \qquad (13.8)$$

From there, the distribution of unconditional plausibility over the **h**-alternatives in light of evidence e is simply

$$Cr_{K,e}(h_i) = Cr_{K,e}(c) \times Cr_{K,e}(h_i|c) \quad (i = 1,\ldots,n) \qquad (13.9)$$

This is just Equation 13.8 shrunk by whatever doubt may persist in c, though to bring out e's full impact on the credibility of h_i, $Cr_{K,e}(c)$ therein needs a form-(13.5) analysis of its own. If mathematical data modeling lies in your future, you may well become intimate with the details of (13.7) and (13.8–13.9). But for now, the salient point is simply that uncertainty about e is no longer the foreground input concern in (13.8–13.9) that it is in (13.6). $Cr_K(e)$ still appears with diminished import in analysis of $Cr_{K,e}(c)$, and neglect of the latter (notably, in failure to appreciate when our data undermine our model's background presumptions) is too frequently an incompetence in applied data analysis. Nevertheless, if **h** is given enough breadth to make $Cr_K(c)$ large, most aggressively by extending a model's natural **h**-set to include

$$\tilde{h} = \sim(h_1 \vee \ldots \vee h_n),$$

(13.8–13.9) allows Bayesian reasoning to interpret evidence e without explicit concern for $Cr_K(e)$ as a problematic input factor. (Insomuch as $Cr_K(\tilde{h})$ and $Cr_K(e|\tilde{h})$ will seldom be more than a wild guess, that is not without risk of self-deception.)

Henceforth, I follow the common notational practice of omitting subscripts for background knowledge K in contexts where that is not an issue. But when Bayesian discussions refer, as they often do, to the "prior" vs. "posterior" credibilities of a hypothesis h, it is important to be clear that prior $Cr(h)$ is the h-plausibility on the right in a belief-change equation like (13.6) or more elaborately (13.8–13.9), whereas posterior $Cr(h)$ is its counterpart on the left.

Confirmation principle (13.6) with empty c implies that new evidence e increases the credibility of h by multiplier $1/Cr(e)$ if h logically entails e, and drops it to zero if h entails $\sim e$, in complete agreement with HD model (1)–(3) (see page 337). But unlike (1)–(3), (13.6) does not require strict entailment relations for evidence to confirm or disconfirm hypotheses; intermediate levels of $Cr(e \,|\, h)$ also yield Bayesian adjudication of h by e. Specifically, learning e confirms h at least a little so long as $Cr(e|h) > Cr(e)$, and disconfirms it at least a little if $Cr(e|h) < Cr(e)$. Moreover, even when e is contained in results from a hypothesis-testing experiment, there is no presumption much less requirement that e or its negation was predicted for these results or even that h is the hypothesis this experiment was designed to test.

However, there are many reasons why Bayesian inference is still a shaky foundation for real-life belief revisions. One need that has received considerable cutting-edge attention since its introduction by Jeffrey (1965) is relaxing the simplistic classical view of background "knowledge" as a totality of propositional information believed with unshakable conviction. We want a broader notion of a rational person o's "epistemic base" (my term for this, not one that is standard), which at any particular time t comprises whatever cognition-determining attributes K of o are the immanent source of o's believings $\{Cr_K(p_i)\}$ at t. Change from $Cr_K(p_i)$ at t to $Cr_{K'}(p_i)$ at $t' = t + \Delta t$ is then allowed to derive in part from sensory input that elicits perceptual judgments in which o has less than total confidence at t', yet which ramify into other belief changes by a generalization of (13.6) that posits, in effect, that credences conditional on the beliefs most directly altered by input are unaffected thereby. However, the logic of this development is still problematic. (For an instructive overview, see Howson & Franklin, 1994.)

Second, it remains obscure what is the basis for confirmation theory's posit that some facets of human believings deserve idealized representation by formalism $Cr(q \mid p)$. Foremostly, conditional credibilities are postulated because modeling rational belief by the probability calculus demands them; and if we can find no better way to cash these out we can stipulate that $Cr(q \mid p)$, by definition, is nothing more than the ratio of $Cr(p \cdot q)$ to $Cr(p)$. Later, I will discuss a more cogent candidate for the conditional-credibility role; however, the operational character of that is still importantly mysterious both in philosophic theory and scientific practice.

Further, even though no sensible Bayesian takes synchronic coherence to be more than a normative ideal to which real-world believings can conform at best only roughly, it is far from clear that classical coherence defined by the probability axioms *is* ideal for rational belief systems. For *metabeliefs*—beliefs about believings and more broadly about practical epistemology—have a major role to play in intelligent thinking (see Rozeboom, 1972a, pp. 81ff.) for which classical coherence makes inadequate provision. Most evident are tensions arising from beliefs about logic and confirmation. For example, if proposition τ is logically true, ideal coherence requires $Cr(\tau \mid p) = Cr(\tau) = 1$ for every proposition p whose Cr-value is not zero.[4] This implies that under no circumstance is it ideal to have

---

[4]Conditional credibilities $Cr_K(p \mid q)$ with $Cr_K(q) = 0$ are an awkward singularity for technical confirmation theory. When such a q is one of infinitely many disjoint al-

any doubt about logical truth τ, much less to allow any possibility that τ may be logically false, even when we are not sure that τ *is* logically true. But this seems passing strange as a model for ideal management of mathematical beliefs. Here is a typical instance in point:

> Many years ago, when exploring the algebra of some new ideas in multivariate correlation, I was struck by a possible theorem τ so pretty that I couldn't quite convince myself that it was invalid despite having apparently disproved it by constructing a counterexample. Careful study of the latter enabled me to find a flaw in that; and with τ once again a live possibility I was able to work out a proof of it.[5]

How could it have been irrational of me to have been unsure of τ before hard proof of this was in hand, or to suspect that it was invalid when I had apparently disproved it? Sometimes credibilistic coherence seems foolish.

More generally, metabeliefs that urge norms for the conduct of our practical reasoning—opinions about what patterns of argument confer evidential support under what circumstances; how reliable are our perceptions and memories of particular kinds under particular conditions of evocation; when and how strongly we can trust verbal communications from others or even from our own written records, etc.—are of large operational concern to scientists, jurists, and other epistemic engineers who seek to optimize the professional quality of their propositional output. The extent to which these can be conjoined with the believings they help monitor in a unified belief system that is ideally Bayesian is far from clear.

There are many other facets of human reason for whose management Bayesian confirmation models are not particularly helpful, such as coping with the vaguenesses, ellipticalities, and other varieties of semantic obscurity that always afflict our utterances and the thoughts behind them to one degree or another. (A major quality-control endeavor of any science is to eliminate such flaws from the sentences it considers worthy of refined plausibility appraisals.[6]) And how

---

ternatives, this can generally be handled by appeal to credence "density" comparable to the probability densities long domesticated by the statistics of continuous distributions. But less graceful tactics are needed when q is logically false.

[5]Published as Theorem 8 in Rozeboom (1965). Strictly speaking, it is not τ that is logically true but $\tau \vee \sim\alpha$ where α comprises axioms of linear algebra.

[6]Vagueness and imprecision in our thoughts and their verbalizations certainly do not defeat our attaching fuzzy credences to these and acting rationally on them. Thus if I like to wager on the games of our local sports team and hear its coach grumble at a private gathering, "There's been a lot of dissing among our guys recently", I may well infer with moderate confidence the covertly verbalized thought, "Our team will play badly this weekend", and adjust my bets accordingly. But as Bayesian confirmation theorists, would we really consider a system of credenced propositions built upon concepts with semantic

should Bayesian coherence reckon with statements incorporating theoretical constructs of the sort whose semantics/ontology was foreground in philosophy of science throughout the first half of this century? Thus given the epistemic base of an ideally rational chemist during the early development of combustion theory, should strict coherence require $Cr(All\ burning\ objects\ emit\ phlogiston)$ + $Cr(Not\ all\ burning\ objects\ emit\ phlogiston)$ = 1?[7] Or can room be found for nonzero $Cr(Phlogiston\ does\ not\ exist)$ and, if so, how can a belief system be classically coherent if the plausibility of its sentences can be undermined by doubting the existence of the entities these purport to name?

By further belaboring the operational difficulties of Bayesian inference, I could surely convince you that this outlook on rational inference has little practicality. But that is not my intent. Although human thought can seldom proceed in close accord with the Bayesian quantitative model, we can still profitably allow our thinking to be influenced by metabelieving that our opinions should generally *try* to approximate Bayesian ideals. In fact, that converts the most notorious infirmity of Bayesian reasoning into a heuristic strength. In order to implement a Bayesian reappraisal of hypothesis h in light of new evidence e, we have to specify how plausible h and e seemed just prior to learning e as well as how conditionally credible h would have become with e adopted as a supposition for conjecture. But with one large qualification, Bayesian theory leaves these prior conditional/unconditional credibilities purely a matter of personal whim so long as they are coherent. The qualification is that as dutiful Bayesians we should have derived these most recently prior beliefs from ones less recently prior by conditionalization on more recent evidence, and so on for increasingly earlier stages of a Bayesian learning sequence. But on pain of infinite regress, this process must have a non-Bayesian origin. And there is no coherent credibility distribution assigning certainty to evidence e that cannot be reached by conditionalization on e from some other coherent credibility distribution. So if a theory of rational belief can advocate no normative standards beyond Bayesian ideals, neither has it any grounds for preferring one coherent allocation of posterior belief strengths compatible with our accumulated data to another. By no means does this defeat the Bayesian perspective. But it does urge that an operational theory of scientific reasoning—one that spins off how-to-do-it advice worth inclusion in our methods education and the standards of merit by which we appraise our own research publications—needs to flesh out its Bayesian

---

quality akin to that of "a lot", "dissing", "recently", and "badly" capable of ideal synchronic coherence? Arguably, credences and their synchronic/diachronic relations can generally be no more precise than the propositions to which they apply.

[7]A simpler example: Should coherence require $Cr(Pegasus\ was\ a\ clumsy\ flier)$ + $Cr(Pegasus\ was\ not\ a\ clumsy\ flier)$ = 1?

skeleton (insofar as we metabelieve that) by additional principles of justified belief acquisition.

And what would the Bayesian frame contribute to such an account? If nothing else, a goad to thinking out how to get a Bayesian argument going. Your posterior confidence in conjecture h resulting from evidence e cannot knowingly conform to principle (13.6) even crudely unless you have first made some rough identification of your prior $Cr(h)$, $Cr(e)$, and, most pivotally, $Cr(e|h)$. And contrary to the impression that abstract formulations of synchronic belief coherence may suggest, you do *not* carry in your head a replete library of confidence-rated propositions from which any subset of current interest can be errorlessly retrieved on demand into your active mental workspace. How you can activate the wanted beliefs depends greatly on local circumstances. (Consider, e.g., the difference between working out your prior confidences in (a) certain competing theories well-established in your field's literature that you plan to evaluate by a forthcoming experiment, and (b) various ad hoc hypotheses such as *My fan belt is loose?* elicited by your observing an elevated positioning of your car's temperature gauge.) But presumably your prior $Cr(h)$ will arise as some blend of confidence contributions from assorted origins such as:

Evoked (Intuitive) Confidence. When a propositional thought is activated or reactivated in your awareness, the modality features ("propositional attitude") with which it is delivered perforce includes some degree of belief. If you have contemplated this proposition before, that presumably reflects to some extent the strength of activated belief it attained for you most recently. But it surely has other, poorly understood, determinants as well, in particular preconscious inference mechanisms that also influence a proposition's intuitive plausibility even when first contemplated.

Remembered Confidence. When proposition h becomes reactivated in your thinking, your belief in it may well be affected by remembering how plausible h seemed previously. (You don't recall a precise quantified belief-strength, of course, but you can recover qualitative levels such as verbalized by phrases like "seemed unlikely," "felt pretty sure," and "hadn't a clue.") Remembered confidence isn't the same as evoked confidence: You may recall having previously trusted an h about which you now feel intuitively uneasy.

Communicated Confidence. Verbal communications that you encounter either fortuitously (when reading a news release, attending a lecture, participating in a discussion, suffering a TV commercial, etc.) or by intent (as when reviewing the established literature or your private data files on a selected topic) generally are accompanied by credibility claims, implicit[8] if not explicit, that influence how plausible you take the communicated propositions to be. This influence comes on strong when the communication is flagged as authoritative, especially when its topic is one on which you have no strong opinions; and an important facet of intellectual maturity is learning how to discount the plausibility allegations in received messages even while also becoming discriminatingly aware of elite conditions under which these merit trust.

Reconstructed Reasoning. Remembered or communicated evocation of $Cr(h)$ often is accompanied by some restoration of the reasoning that grounded h's appraisal at source; and those arguments may now have force for your present $Cr(h)$ independent of how they influenced the previous believing. (Thus you may consider a received argument to be even stronger, though more likely weaker, than it seemed originally.) Reconsidering arguments for or against a proposition h can be edifying on two levels. Up front, a received argument may present you with evidence bearing on h, or a model of how that is relevant, which would not otherwise have occurred to you just now. But it also provides a metabelief-educational occasion to test whether you *can* reconstruct this argument for h and, if you can, whether the h-plausibility you take from it decently agrees with the plausibility your source alleges it to confer. Repeated failure of an argument style to pass such reconstructed-plausibility tests casts doubt for you on the reliability of arguments so styled.

Metabeliefs. When you think that your currently active h-belief has arisen from memory, or communication, or reconstructed reasoning, or some other typable source, it is clearly appropriate for the force of these influences on your $Cr(h)$ to be modulated by whatever metabeliefs you also activate about the reliability of beliefs so evoked. Not so clear, however is whether the manner in which metabeliefs are influential is amenable to Bayesian treatment. Beyond that, my present posit that prior $Cr(h)$ in a Bayesian argument arises as some amalgam of belief potentials from a multiplicity of contributors is distinctly non-Bayesian in outlook. This is no threat to the cogency of Bayesian inferences when these can be mounted; but it does urge that as a normative theory of belief, the Bayesian account is importantly incomplete.

Comment. In light of the multifaceted complexities just sketched in assembling your current $Cr(h)$, shouldn't you just dismiss the Bayesian perspective as hopelessly impractical? Perhaps so, but that would waste its heuristic benefits. How strongly you believe various propositions in your research area—hypotheses, prospective evidence, and conditionalities among these (more on that

---

[8]For example, a message identifying h as a theorem, or as someone's observation, urges presumption that h is veridical. And spoken communication is rich with intonations conveying various shades of belief/disbelief.

shortly)—is obviously important for your work regardless of your views on rational belief management. And equally important for you to feel justified in that allocation of your convictions is some awareness of their metabelief-appraisable sources. Serious effort to initiate a Bayesian argument around these propositions compels you to think out rather carefully *why* you believe them as you do even if slogging through to a quantitative Bayesian conclusion is not feasible.

To execute Bayesian revision of your h-belief in light of evidence e, you also need activation of your $Cr(e)$ and $Cr(e \mid h)$ or, exploiting principle (13.8)–(13.9), a set of $Cr(e \mid h_i)$. Contributions to these evoked believings should be broadly of the same kinds that prompt $Cr(h)$. But $Cr(e \mid h)$ raises additional issues whose importance transcends partiality to Bayesian argument. Presuming that human cognition really does involve conditional credences that ideally should satisfy Equations 13.1–13.6, a fundamental question is where these $Cr(q \mid p)$ are positioned in the *becausal* structure of a belief system, especially in relation to $p \cdot q$. By "becausal" I refer to the asymmetric relations we envision (not as clearly as we might wish) when, for two states of affairs s_1 and s_2, we conjecture that s_1 accounts for or explains or is responsible for or is a source of or is why s_2, or that s_2 is due to or derives from or is because s_1. (These locutions allow that s_2 may not be due solely to s_1, and include causation as just a special case albeit a major one.) In terms of explanatory derivation, is $Cr(q \mid p)$ just an abstraction from $Cr(p \cdot q)$ and $Cr(p)$ defined by their ratio as in (13.1), or might $Cr(p \cdot q)$ instead derive from $Cr(q \mid p)$ and $Cr(p)$ in accord with (13.2)? In the first case, $Cr(q \mid p)$ *supervenes*[9] on $Cr(p \cdot q)$ and is no part of *why* the latter has whatever value it may have in particular instances; in the second, derivation of $Cr(p \cdot q)$ from $Cr(q \mid p)$ would most plausibly be causal. Whether Bayesian theory has ever taken an explicit stand on this matter I do not know; however, the easy symmetry it posits between $Cr(q \mid p)$ and $Cr(p \mid q)$ is tenable only if each is held to derive in accord with (13.1) from the joint and marginal Cr-distributions on $\{p, \sim p\}$ crossed with $\{q, \sim q\}$. But it is hard to design a plausible model of how input disturbances—perceptions, communications, recovered memories, or whatever—could result in coherent change in a coherent $\{Cr(p \cdot q), Cr(p \cdot \sim q), Cr(p \cdot \sim q), Cr(\sim p \cdot q), Cr(\sim p \cdot \sim q)\}$, in particular achieving $Cr(p) = 1$ by decrease of $Cr(\sim p \cdot q) + Cr(\sim p \cdot \sim q)$ to zero, while scarcely ever changing the ratio of $Cr(p \cdot q)$ to $Cr(p \cdot q) + Cr(p \cdot \sim q)$ unless $Cr(q \mid p)$ or some belief condition measured by it guides this belief process. Details on feasible dynamics for a belief system under input disturbances and coherence constraints are too intri-

---

[9]"Supervenience," a useful concept that has become prominent in the recent philosophy-of-mind literature (see especially Kim, 1993), refers to dependencies wherein some properties derive noncausally from others, and has much in common with older notions of "epiphenomenal" dependency.

cately technical to pursue here. Let it suffice to claim that any such model for believing the propositions in a set $\{p_i\}$ closed under conjunction and negation needs to include adjustable parameters governing how altered strengths of belief in some of these p_i derive from that of others. Such parameters would reflect Cr-dependency features of the belief system whose function is similar to what Bayesian theory intuits for conditional-Cr except for sharing responsibility for some of these $Cr(p_i)$ rather than supervening upon them and, in all likelihood, not satisfying exact counterparts of the Bayesian conditional-Cr equations except in special circumstances still to be worked out.

Conditionality

Have we any reason to think that belief dependencies are genuine forces operative in our thinking, something demanding recognition by any theory of rational belief regardless of Bayesian sympathies? Yes indeed. From the prevalence of claims having form *If p then (probably) q* (indicative conditional), *Were p then (probably) would q* (subjunctive conditional), and *Had p then (probably) would have q* (counterfactual conditional)[10] in the discourse of our practical affairs at all levels of intellectual sophistication, it is evident that *conditionality* concepts play a vital role in human reason. It is debatable whether such *If/then* locutions should be clarified as declarative statements or as elliptical arguments.[11] Quite possibly we should view their cognitive function as dually to summarize an argument while simultaneously serving as cryptic assertion of something distinctive in this context that enables the explicitly stated antecedent to make plausible the explicitly stated conclusion. You have every right to be puzzled by this suggestion; and chasing *If*-ness into its technical literature would only deepen your mystification: The work is formalistically advanced without having yet created any exportable tools of benefit to empirical science. Even so, commonsense

---

[10]The last two formulations are compact at some cost of idiomacy; their sense is more clearly expressed by *If p were to be the case then probably so would be q* and *If q had been the case (even though it wasn't), then q would probably also have been the case.* These three standardized forms by no means exhaust the reach of conditionality notions, as instructively demonstrated by *Even had not p then still would have q.* What is not a genuine conditional, however, is the "material implication" that logicians define as *either not-p or q*, symbolize $p \supset q$ or sometimes $p \rightarrow q$, and often verbalize as *If p then q* because it is the weakest and best understood condition α such that $\alpha \cdot p$ entails q.

[11]Thus, *p, therefore q* expresses an argument from premise p to conclusion q, albeit one that usually makes implicit appeal to context-dependent background conditions under which proposition p finishes the job of making q plausible. But analysis of *p, therefore q* urges that this is equivalent to the conjunction of p and *If p then q*, whence *If p then q* would also appear to be an elliptic argument—a hypothetical, not declarative one—with the same suppressed auxiliary premises as *p, therefore q.* I expand upon this prospect shortly.

conditionality talk makes abundantly clear that a great deal of human reason involves drawing hypothetical conclusions—sometimes firm, more often tentative—from premises that are in part hypothetical and generally include inarticulate presumptions which may well resist verbalization. Arguably, a hypothetical inference's cognitive role is to establish a channel of belief transmission from its premise to its conclusion through which adjustments of unconditional confidence in those premises modify the unconditional plausibility of its conclusion. If so, the best candidates for what Bayesian confirmation theory seeks to denote by '$Cr(q \mid p)$' may well be an idealization of something closely related to what ordinary language addresses by 'If p, then probably q'.

Because conditionality is so pivotal in human reasoning, I attempted in an earlier draft of this chapter to explore in some depth the logic of commonsense expressions of form 'If p then probably* q', or more broadly 'Since s, if p then probably* q', where 'probably*' goes proxy for a phrase apparently expressing some degree of confidence ('almost surely', 'with 75% chance', 'likely not', etc.) that we can idealize as numerically exact even though in real life it is most often broadly imprecise. Unhappily, this matter is so darkly complex that a well-argued account of it is not feasible here. Nevertheless, I can sketch my major conclusions and invite you to take them under consideration. To mobilize your intuitions in this matter, I begin with a commonplace example:

As we start to leave the diner where we have had lunch, you approach its window to get a look outside, notice how ominous the sky has become, and suggest that we wait awhile because

If we leave now, it's very likely that we'll get wet. (13.10)

And when I ask *why*, you explain

The sky looks really black and I hear thunder. (13.11)

At this point I understand you perfectly well, and normally would either agree to wait if I believe your (13.11) report or would check out the sky myself if for some reason I mistrust that. But since we have just been discussing the psychology of inference, I ask you to explain what relevance (13.11) has for (13.10). This query seems silly to you, but knowing my penchant for challenging the obvious you decide to take it seriously and, after some reflection, reply

Whenever the daytime sky turns black and thunder is audible it usually rains soon in that vicinity. And when we are rained on we almost always get wet. (13.12)

I suggest that this, and many other instances that you can readily find in your personal coping with the world urge conclusions to which the following are passable first approximations:

First: Probabilistic *if/then* locutions such as (13.10) are basically hypothetical *arguments*, not propositions. Their primary cognitive function is to establish a *probably**-damped conduit for flow of belief-strength from their antecedents (*if*-clauses) to their consequents (*then*-clauses), though they also channel flow of other propositional attitudes as well, notably desirability from consequents to antecedents with resultant effects on volitional behavior. (That is why, when I accept (13.10), I try to falsify its *if*-clause.) An *if/then* argument is "hypothetical" in the sense that it is putatively indifferent to the truth of its *If*-clauses, though neither does it preclude strong belief or disbelief in those as an appendage to the argument. *If/then*s often include *since*-clauses, such as your (13.11) (which in real life you would probably have mentioned without my needing to prompt you for it), that are additional premises presumed to be true. However, *since* can always(?) be downgraded to *if* without affecting the argument's *probably** strength. Almost always, an *if/then*'s verbalization is truncated by omission of some or all of its *since*-premises, especially ones that in this context are presumed uncontroversial. Moreover, when contemplating a proposed *if/then* we are generally less aware of its suppressed premises than of its foreground clauses; rather, those seem to function like Bayesian "background knowledge" by influencing our cognitions in the manner of active beliefs even when, like the generalities in (13.12) before you made effort to uncover them, they remain unconscious. (Clarifying the nature and functioning of such silent background beliefs remains a major challenge for theories of conditionality or indeed for all accounts of rational inference.)

> *Note*: A conditional's *since*-clauses are not generally as distinct from its *if*-clauses as I have just imputed. In practice, *since* is often appreciably uncertain and might just as well be treated as an *if* except, perhaps, in that its current credibility level is expected to persist. And a conditional's secondary *if*-clauses, too, are apt to be suppressed. (For example, (13.10)'s antecedent implicitly continues, "and we don't dash back inside.") But such refinements don't much matter here.

Second: Insofar as *if/then*s are arguments rather than propositions, we do not believe/disbelieve these but accept/reject them or, with less categorical extremity, are *persuaded* by them to some degree. Even so, we often assert or dispute conditionals as though they are statements that are factually true or false and should have a determinate *Cr*-value in an ideal belief system. Insomuch as real-life utterances often manage to transmit multiple messages simultaneously, it would scarcely be without precedent to allow that in a suitable context, assertion of 'If p then probably* q' may also convey one or more propositions distinctively associated with this argument. For one, it might be construed to imply that the speaker's $Cr(q \mid p)$ is *probably**, or that his channel of belief transmission from p to q has damping parameter *probably**. Or it might be understood as the claim that *If p then probably* q is a sound argument once its suppressed *since*-clauses are made explicit. But such metabelief sophistication is probably uncommon in practice. More prevalently—or so I venture—asserting *If p then probably* q when the argument remains unpersuasive when truncated so severely, like (13.10) before you back it with (13.11) and eventually (13.12), is a programmatic way to avow suppressed premises that make it more forceful. In itself that does not much illuminate what those are, but it urges us to make them more verbally articulate in foreground attention. To put the point more briskly, if you find *If p then probably* q intuitively persuasive but aren't altogether clear why, you can treat this locution as an assertion that goes proxy for the missing reasons until you can think those out and state them less cryptically.

Third: Unlike the strict (absolute, all-or-none) *If p then q* conditionals classically studied by philosophers (most extensively in accounts of logical necessity), the ordinary-language *if/thens* operative in your real-life thinking embody *probably** qualifiers that are plainly related in some fashion to belief-strengths. But precisely how so is not so clear, nor is even the logical form of qualified conditionals. Regarding the latter, it might be proposed that these are absolute at core. For 'If p then probably* q' can be read in three quite different ways, namely (*i*) *Probably**, *if-p-then-q*, (*ii*) *If p, then-probably* q, and (*iii*) *If p then probably*-q*, in two of which the conditionality is classically strict. However, neither (*i*) nor (*iii*) agrees with our ordinary use of qualified *if/thens*. The first fails because strict *If p then q* is incompatible with $p \cdot {\sim} q$, which is untrue of qualified conditionals. (Thus in scenario (13.10–13.12) were we to leave anyway in full expectation of getting wet, failure of the rain to materialize would lead us to conclude only that we had lucked out rather than that (13.10) was in error.) And (*iii*) takes the conditional's consequent to be an unconditional probability of q, with the generally-unacceptable implication that a conjunction of two conditionals with different antecedents but the same consequent, say *If p_1 then probably*$_1^*$ q* and *If p_2 then probably*$_2^*$ q*, entails that if $p_1 \cdot p_2$ then q's unconditional probability is both *probably*$_1^*$* and *probably*$_2^*$*. Accordingly I submit that (*ii*), which puts gradation into the connection between antecedent and consequent, is the proper way to understand qualified conditionals.[12] From there, it is an easy

---

[12]This and my preceding contention, that qualified *if/thens* are basically arguments, are somewhat at odds with the outlooks on conditionality most prominent in its recent philosophical literature. (See Eells & Skyrms, 1994, for a rather formidable smorgasbord of these.) These have largely focused on the thesis that when locution 'If p then q' carries

step to propose (as I have already suggested) that *probably** scales a parameter of belief flow from *if* to *then* installed by acceptance of the conditional it qualifies. In the simplest model of this, *probably** is the belief strength that, under ideal conditions in a believer who actively accepts *If p then probably* q*, is transmitted to *q* from becoming sure of *p*. (In addition to maximal persuasion by this conditional and confidence in its antecedent, the ideal preconditions here include absence of input to *Cr(q)* from other persuasively active conditionals whose antecedents have also become plausible. But a precise *probably** needn't be stipulated by the idealized model unless the resultant *Cr(q)* is required to be ideally precise.) But how our *Cr(q)* is or should be affected when we become rather confident but far from certain of *p* while being persuaded less than totally of *If p then probably* q*, or when our *Cr(q)* arises from a confluence of several different *if/then*s with plausible antecedents and *q* as common consequent, together with other sources of *q*-belief such as reviewed earlier, is considerably more problematic. The challenge of such complications is less to create tidy models of how an ideally precise and coherent belief system might manage them in principle than to work out vetted guidelines for what to do in real-life situations wherein our inferential intuition falters.

Fourth: Most if not all of the qualified *if/then*s we find persuasive in practice are grounded on probabilistic *laws*, most commonly in background *since*-clauses. (For convenience, I shall use 'law', 'generality', 'regularity' and, with somewhat different focus, 'data' to denote either propositions having certain special conceptual characters or the states of affairs these signify if true, trusting context to resolve ambiguity.) The nature of lawfulness is so obscurely and deeply intricate that I can say little about it here that does not verge on travesty. For now, it suffices to note that the simplest conception of these, standard in the philosophical literature though far too primitive for technical science, is expressed by statements of form

$$\text{In occurrences of property } A, \text{ property } B \text{ occurs with probability } r. \qquad (13.13)$$

or assorted paraphrases thereof, most tersely

$$\text{The probability of } B \text{ given } A \text{ is } r \text{ (in symbols, } \Pr(B \mid A) = r). \qquad (13.14)$$

---

subjunctive/counterfactual force, it asserts a proposition whose unconditional credibility equals the conditional credibility of *q* given *p*, or at least that something like this equivalence is largely correct. My take on this approach is that even if some strict *if/then*s warrant such an idealization (which I doubt), they are not the qualified conditionals that govern our reasoning in science and everyday life.

It is important *not* to read this as "Each A has probability r of having B," because under that misconstrual of (13.14), $\Pr(B \mid A) = r$ and $\Pr(B \mid A') = r'$ for two compatibly different properties A and A' would entail that anything having both A and A' has both probability r and probability r' of having B. Neither should $\Pr(B \mid A)$ be confused either with the relative frequency of B in the population of all As, or with the limit of B's relative frequency in an infinite sequence of As.[13] And especially do not confuse $\Pr(B \mid A) = r$ with $Cr(q \mid p) = r$ for any propositions p and q, first of all because the A and B terms in $\Pr(B \mid A)$ are only predicates or common nouns, not complete sentences constructed from those, and second because $\Pr(B \mid A) = r$ is a statement not about beliefs or their conceptual constituents but about the extralinguistic attributes signified by Pr's arguments.[14] Although it is not yet time to argue the point, I put it to you that a probability statement of form (13.14) is a venture about how the world works, one that professes to tell us something about *why*, in a large group of As, the proportion that are B should be rather close to r.

Be all that as it may, the distinctions and interpretations I have just urged upon you become issues for us only when we try to clarify and perfect the cognitive force of our beliefs of form (13.14) or its more colloquial variants. Long before we become that analytically sophisticated, and for the most part even afterward, we use such notions uncritically in whatever ways seem intuitively sensible even though, like much of everyday language, that usage is generally vague and ambiguous.[15] Or rather—since you have probably understood r in (13.14) as

---

[13]Introductions to sampling statistics often give the former impression, but it is shot down by the very real prospect that property A has no instantiations. (For example, we may ban use on humans of a proposed new medical treatment because animal studies convince us that the probability of its having disastrous side effects in human applications is high.) And the latter is obviated by failure of infinite sequences for most As to exist in reality, especially when the class of As is empty.

[14]This is demonstrated by a standard philosophy-of-language test of "extensionality": The truth of $\Pr(B \mid A) = r$ is intuitively unaffected if its A term (or similarly B) is replaced by a another predicate signifying the same property as A but differing from it in meaning (e.g., 'red' vs. 'the color of ripe tomatoes'), whereas this truth-invariance would not generally obtain were $\Pr(B \mid A) = r$ a claim about meanings. This test is not conclusive in applications, however, because the ontology of properties is still so problematic that we can seldom decide with confidence when two coextensive predicates (i.e., ones with the same satisfiers) signify—that is, are semantically *about*—the very same property.

[15]These adjectives are not intended pejoratively: Vagueness and ambiguity should not be scorned unconditionally as cognitive defects; rather, they are powerful dexterities essential for us to maneuver through the minefields of imperfect knowledge about that of which we speak. They become objectionable only when we get so comfortable with them that we shun responsibility for their refinement when greater precision becomes needed.

I intended, namely, as placeholder for a precise number between 0 and 1—your commonsense versions of (13.14) are generally more like

As are mostly* Bs,   (13.15)

As tend to be Bs,   (13.16)

An A is likely* to be a B,   (13.17)

Anything that is an A is probably* also a B,   (13.18)

If something is an A, then probably* it is also a B,   (13.19)

wherein *mostly**, *likely**, and *probably** are imprecise qualifiers such as 'commonly', 'often', 'seldom', and 'rarely', sometimes modified by 'very', 'fairly', 'not', etc., and 'tend' can be shaded by the likes of 'strongly', 'moderately', 'weakly', and 'not'. These variants are not perfectly synonymous and some, notably (13.15), encourage one or another of (13.14)'s misreadings against which I have just cautioned. But we use them more or less interchangeably while (13.16) shows most cleanly the underlying theme they share with precision upgrade (13.14).

Considering (13.12)'s contribution to example (13.10–13.12), and version (13.19) of (13.14)'s ordinary-language precursors, it should be plain why I suggest that most if not all the *if/thens* we find persuasive include imperfectly-reliable generalities in their *since*-clauses. You will surely agree it inheres in the meaning of (13.19) that if you are quite sure of this for some predicate concepts A and B, and your nominal concept c of some particular thing is neutral on its referent's B-status (as for example *the largest B* is not), you then find

In light of (13.19), if c has property A then probably* c has property B

persuasive, perhaps even when generality (13.19) remains silent in your taken-for-granted background knowledge. (Persuasion by this hypothetical argument when you are further confident that c is indeed an A pushes the strength of your *c-has-B* belief toward level *probably**. However, additional influences on $Cr(c \text{ has } B)$ at work in your thinking may countervail against it becoming exactly or even close to that.) And example (13.10–13.12) illustrates how efforts to justify the intuitive persuasiveness of a truncated *if/then* can retrieve from muted background knowledge one or more probabilistic generalities that set the foreground *if/then*'s *probably** level.

Indeed, when you accept *Since S(c), if P(c) then probably* Q(c)*, wherein each *X(c)* (*X* = *S,P,Q*) is a proposition asserting that the referent of nominal-concept *c* has the property signified by predicate-concept *X*, you should in principle be able to convince yourself that for any other nominal *c'* within a certain range *R* of substitutions for *c*, *If S(c') and P(c'), then probably* Q(c')* is just as convincing a hypothetical argument as the original even when your confidence in *S(c)* doesn't transfer to *S(c')*. In this way you can discover, if you weren't aware of it already, that you believe probabilistic generality, *R-things that have properties S and P probably* have Q as well.* In practice, you would likely need considerable analysis and reconstruction to bring that off, and even if you succeeded it would not follow that your acceptance of the original particularized *if/then* derived from your background-believing precisely this generality. Nevertheless, if we ever achieve articulate understanding of the "unconscious beliefs" and "background knowledge" that precondition the flow of our active thinking,[16] we may want to argue that accepting a particularized *if/then* manifests a cognitive underlay tantamount to conscious or more likely unconscious belief in some generality of form (13.19) or its ilk. Even if unrealistically idealized, this model has considerable heuristic value for theories of inference by mapping questions and answers about the circumstances under which we rationally should or in fact do accept *if/then*s into questions/answers about the circumstances under which we should or do believe imperfectly reliable generalities.

Fifth: The generic logic of *if/then*s is considerably more complex and problematic than I have so far let on. Here are a few of the more salient questions these raise:

> When I contemplate both whether *p* and whether *q*, should I usually find *If p then probably* q* convincing at some reasonably tight *probably**? (13.20)

> If I am convinced both of *If p_1 then probably$_1^*$ q* and of *If p_2 then probably$_2^*$ q*, how convincing should I find *If $p_1 \odot p_2$ then probably** q*, where $\odot$ is either *and* or *or*, at what level of *probably***? (13.21)

> If I am convinced both of *If p_1 then probably$_1^*$ p_2* and of *If p_2 then probably$_2^*$ p_3*, how convincing should I find *If p_1 then probably** p_3* at what level of *probably***? (13.22)

> If I am convinced of *If p then probably* q*, how convincing should I find *If not-q then probably** not-p* at what level of *probably***? (13.23)

---

[16]The double quotes here acknowledge that when we talk this way we are largely faking it.

Question (13.20) frames the issue of what it takes to install an *if/then* connection and whether every Bayesian conditional credence has an *if/then* counterpart; the others probe the force of accepted *if/thens* beyond simple transmission of credence from their premises to their conclusions. When the *probably**s in (13.21)–(13.23) are certainty, commonsense insists that *probably*** should also be certainty. So it is reasonable to presume further that if the *probably**s are very close to certainty, *probably*** should usually be so as well, and more broadly that some answers to (13.21)–(13.23) for the less reliable *if/thens* we live by should also prove eventually to be within our reach, at least when the basic *probably**s are precise. That time has not yet arrived, however; and translation of (13.21)–(13.23) into corresponding questions about belief in probabilistic generalities presumed to underlie particularized conditionals clarifies why these answers remain elusive. But that is a story for another occasion, as is also the complication of how our thinking is affected by tentative acceptance of the *if/thens* we find less than totally persuasive.

Why am I trying your patience by agonizing over these conditionality obscurities instead of getting on with your practical needs on how to do statistics? Because these are serious problems not just at the level of abstract metatheory but also in many specific real-life instances wherein our inferential intuitions speak to us only hesitantly. In particular, questions of form (13.21)–(13.23) frequently arise in applied statistics, and when you encounter these it is of some importance to appreciate just how limited is the reliable advice you should expect to find on them. Even so, human competence in non-deductive reasoning is still actively evolving in the crucible of our tougher intellectual disciplines; and what seems inferentially perplexing today may become rather less so tomorrow. Stay tuned. Or better, aspire to help improve the broadcast's quality.

Conclusions. The global Bayesian ideal of rational inference as an orderly sequence of form-(13.5) conditionalizations on accumulating evidence launched from some initial coherent Cr-distribution over all the propositions conceivable by the believer is hopelessly unrealistic. (Note that I am scoffing only at the *global* outlook on this that professes an ideal history for the totality of one's unconditional beliefs. *Local* Bayesian models (13.5)–(13.9) for special *given*-clauses c, in particular ones featuring probabilistic generalities, are still very much worth respect in applications.) A better model might be that our unconditional $Cr(q)$ at any given moment is the consensus of a transient committee whose current members (diverse determinants of our q-belief) submit with varied insistence their individual q-appraisals. (This is not unlike a Bayesian composite

$$Cr(q) = Cr(p_1)\,Cr(q \mid p_1) + ... + Cr(p_n)\,Cr(q \mid p_n)$$

with $Cr(p_i)$ interpreted as the suitably normed insistence of the participant whose q-appraisal corresponds to $Cr(q \mid p_i)$, except that the compositing of such opinions needn't be this algebraically simple.) But such consensus is as unstable as the flux of its contributors, and shouldn't be the primary focus of applied confirmation theory. Rather, we want practical advice on how best to manage the *conditionals* under which we extract the inferential import of whatever data we momentarily believe strongly enough to act upon. Bayesian theory takes these conditionals to be its $Cr(p \cdot q)/Cr(p)$ ratios, which are as common as dirt—we have two of them for every pair of propositions in our belief system—with nothing recognized by Bayesians to demark some as inferentially special. And it has nothing to say about how we get these, or whether that may have a logic more distinctive than iterations of dynamic (13.5) applied to an arbitrary initial prior. In contrast, I have argued that genuine conditionalities, the backbone of human reasoning and expressed in ordinary language by *if/then* locutions, are *sources* of our belief strengths that guide how some of these change in response to change in others. And although my thesis that *if/then*s are primarily arguments precludes my describing them as additional propositions we consider plausible—see Lewis Carroll (1898) on the folly of taking an argument's persuasive form to be one of its premises—I have also contended that these arguments are grounded on *since*-clauses, sometimes explicit but more often covert, such that an *if/then*'s persuasiveness for us is largely (though perhaps not entirely) equivalent to the strength of our belief in its *since*-foundation. And as a rule, the most important components of that foundation are propositions that tell *why* it is rational for us to infer the conditional's *then*-clause from its *if*-clause. That is, though I have not yet made a forceful case for this, analysis of the conditionals we accept lays bare our commitment to explanatory sources of the transient surface events most directly accessible to our experience.

Where do we get our explanatory beliefs, and what can possibly justify our believing them so strongly as we often do? Hypothetico-deductivism holds that we let our imagination create a riot of conjectures and then winnow out losers by testing their consequences without concern for whether some survivors may be considerably more plausible than others. And as already noted, Bayesian confirmation theory has nothing to say about how any beliefs originate, explanatory or otherwise, beyond acknowledging that some—notably, perceptions—are imposed upon us. But Popper notwithstanding, there does indeed exist a "logic of discovery." Though still unrecognized in our standard texts on research design and data interpretation, the lore is out there and in plain sight too.

Lawfulness

Explanatory discoveries are of two basic sorts, or rather take place on two levels insomuch as one builds upon the other. The first of these, probabilistic generality, has been debated for centuries by scientists, statisticians, and philosophers; the second has been a well-kept secret about common practices whose outing has scarcely begun. The main intent of this essay is to proselytize for the latter; but prefatory to that I must say more about the former than its mention circa formalism (13.14) above.

The claim to be put is that probabilistic generalities, unlike the statistical frequencies with which they cohabit, are genuinely explanatory, though I can barely touch on this here beyond voicing some key issues. These are most nakedly evident in the strongly idealized regularities of which philosophers have been fond. In their classic philosophical treatment, "laws" are universally quantified generalities whose most primitive form is expressed by 'All *A*s are *B*s' (with variants such as 'Every *A* is a *B*' and 'Anything having property *A* also has property *B*'), wherein '*A*' and '*B*' are predicates or common nouns. But many philosophers have argued further, and commonsense agrees, that an important distinction needs to be drawn between generalities that are "nomic"—that is, genuinely lawful—and ones that are merely "accidental." For example, suppose that Roger Smythe has five children. Then even if it is true that

All children of Roger Smythe are male, (13.24)

we can easily dismiss this gender imbalance as a chance occurrence to be expected in more than 3% of families this large. However, suppose also that the progeny of Roger Smythe's great-great-great-grandfather, Adam Smythe, totals 326 to date with a well-documented genealogy showing that

All descendants of Adam Smythe have been male. (13.25)

It would surely be irrational for us not to infer that the universality of maleness among Adam Smythe's descendants is strongly lawful in some fashion that we initially refused to suspect of generality (13.24) even though we now realize that it probably underlies Roger's progenation as well.[17]

---

[17]Plainly this lawfulness must be heritable. And from principles of gender determination in bisexual species, it is straightforward to infer an explanation for local regularity (13.25) that is no less genetically lawful than that all offspring of parents who are both albino are also albino. But we induce from (13.25) that there must be some such mechanism before we begin to tease out its nature.

But what is this "lawfulness" that we concede to (13.25) but withhold from (13.24) before learning (13.25)? The simplest answer, or at least the framework of one, is that some men have an enduring feature $Q(\ )$ such that if $M(\ )$ is the property of being Male while $F(x,\ )$ is the relational property of being Fathered by x, then occurrence of $Q(x) \cdot R(x,y)$ for any parent x of an infant y brings about, or causes, or makes it happen that $M(y) \cdot Q(y)$. What the nature of bringing about, or causing, or making happen may be is still egregiously obscure. But we manifest our belief in some such forceful connection of *Is a descendent of Adam Smythe* to *Is male* in the strength of our expectation that all of Adam's future descendants will also be male, whereas our initial disinclination to take (13.24) as support for *If Roger Smythe has any more children they too will be male* reveals our reluctance to infer just from Roger's having five sons but no daughters that being sired by Roger has any influence on his children's gender.

Let's switch to a more flexible scenario. (Please don't let the whimsy of this distract you from taking it seriously. It differs only in exaggerated detail from localized medical mysteries reported not infrequently in the news media, and even its specific content is reality based—see Brackman, 1976, chapter 21, or Hoving, 1978, chapter 24.) Suppose that when ancient king TutTut's pristine tomb was discovered some decades ago by an archeological team that we will call the "Finders," 19 Finders entered TutTut's sarcophagus chamber in defiance of a posted warning that this would incur a lethal curse. Within three months, all were dead; 12 in a plane crash when leaving the site, five by a hitherto unknown disease similar to smallpox, and two by unexplained heart failure. Meanwhile, although the tomb was guarded against subsequent entries, local extremists managed to blast it into rubble shortly thereafter to prevent further desecration. So generality

> Everyone who enters TutTut's sarcophagus chamber after its curse
> was laid [in brief, every Transgressor] dies within three months of   (13.26)
> this entry [in brief, gets Quashed]

appears to be true. But is it *lawful*? Modern sensibilities are strongly inclined to dismiss limited regularities like this as "coincidence," "happenstance," or "chance." Even so, (13.26) *could* be more than fluke, even if the curse was only shaman bluster. (See *Illustration 2*, later.) And because (13.26) as worded is noncommittal to nomic vs. accidental, we are challenged to say what enhancement thereof would claim it to be lawful rather than accidental, and how that would matter for its participation in our thinking.

One ordinary-language enrichment that adds explicit lawfulness to (13.26) is

Transgressors are certain to get Quashed.   (13.27)

(A more traditional wording, 'Transgressors are necessarily Quashed', is best passed by to avoid entanglement in modern philosophy's currently bizarre treatments of *possible/necessary*.) But what is this *certain* to which (13.27) appeals? Attempts to construe it as confident belief founder on questions of whose beliefs under what circumstances. There are many possible variants on interpreting *certain* in (13.27) as a Cr extremity, but no reconstruction in terms of believings can capture (13.27)'s intent to express a state of nature independent of anyone's opinion thereof. Enrichment (13.27) of (13.26) envisions some compulsive connection between attributes T and Q importantly stronger than the "constant conjunction" immortalized for philosophers of science by David Hume[18]. Many skeptics since Hume have questioned whether such production forces ever exist in nature; and during the hegemony of logical positivism earlier this century, these were scorned as neither directly observable nor explicitly definable out of observables, a view held by some eminent philosophers even today (notably van Fraassen, 1989). Even so, modern philosophy has increasingly come to recognize that in science and everyday life we frequently develop semantically respectable concepts of the world's less perceptible furnishings through our use of the words that express them in contexts with other antecedently meaningful expressions.[19] The *certain* invoked in (13.27) is a "theoretical" notion of this sort, though its meaning lies more in how we reason than in what we say.

Presume that the deaths of all Finders who Transgressed and the tomb's subsequent destruction before anyone else entered it—call these background data B—have been documented to your provisional satisfaction. Then so long as you remain confident of B you have no qualms about accepting (13.26), whereas you would surely consider (13.27) absurd. This shows merely that the latter does indeed claim more than (13.26), though it is also strong evidence against any belief-strength construal of (13.27)'s *certain*. But suppose you hear of efforts underway to learn the fate of several Blasters (tomb destroyers) who are now thought to have Transgressed. With possibility (13.26) and its strengthening

---

[18]In Hume's seminal essay, "Of the idea of power, or necessary connection", first published in his collection entitled *Philosophical essays concerning human understanding* (1748) and later retitled "Of the idea of necessary connection" in his 1758 collection, *An inquiry concerning human understanding".*

[19]For more on this mode of meaning acquisition, which has been variously called functional definition, implicit definition, theoretic definition, and definition by conceptual role or context, and differs substantially from textbook explicit definition, see Rozeboom (1984, p. 211 ff.).

(13.27) both in mind, how do you get from your revised evidence *B* to some inferred degree of belief that any Blasters who Transgressed were also Quashed? If you reason from *B* first to rather high confidence in (13.27) (never mind how rational that might be) and from there to consequently high confidence that any Blaster who Transgressed has also been Quashed, you have implicitly interpreted (13.26) as (13.27) or something close to that voiced below. In contrast, if learning that a few Blasters also Transgressed leaves you with considerable doubt, despite your knowing the demise of all other Transgressors, that any much less all of these were Quashed, the disbelief in (13.26) you derive from that manifests your interpreting (13.26) as

Everyone who Transgresses is coincidentally Quashed.   (13.28)

And in that case, even when you are later informed that all Blasters who Transgressed were killed in the explosion, your concession that (13.26) is indeed apparently true needn't discomfort your continuing to understood that as (13.28).

Of course, your real-life reasoning in a situation like this would be more complicated than either of the two paths just described, and we cannot properly fathom the logic of *all*-statements without subsuming them under the broader class of generalities to be considered next. Even so, an important thesis has resurfaced: We display faith that generality *All As are Bs* is in some fashion lawful when our learning that it has a fair number of positive instances (cases wherein a particular *A* is also a *B*) with no known exceptions (*As* that aren't *Bs*) substantially increases our confidence that additional *As* we encounter will also turn out to be *Bs*. Whereas if this accumulation of *As* that are without exception *Bs* does not appreciably increase our confidence that *As* not yet examined are also *Bs*, we are judging *All observed As are Bs* and hence also *All As are Bs* to be accidental even when we are sure the latter too is true because production of *As* has been discontinued. In brief, we view lawful regularities as becausally antecedent to particular occurrences of the attributes they connect, whereas accidental generalities *derive* from their instances.

However, classically exceptionless *all*-statements are just limiting extremes in scientific conceptions of natural regularity. To exercise your intuitions about weaker regularities, suppose you now learn that the TutTut site is still intact. Its regional authority (*Rega*) publicly claimed otherwise to forestall public outcry over this site's scheduled razing by a forthcoming construction project, but has been quietly inviting distinguished archeologists such as yourself and, for a considerable fee, wealthy adventure seekers to Transgress while that remains possible. The invitation includes warning that Transgression is suspected by some to be risky, and mentions that periodic reports are available on the longevities of Transgressors whom *Rega* is able to track for at least three months thereafter.

You receive these reports and with each increase in the number of tracked Transgressors you update your opinion on

> *Q1*. What proportion of all Transgressors get Quashed?

> *Q2*. Considering how much your research on TutTut's era would profit from first-hand inspection of his tomb not to mention bragging rights, should you accept *Rega*'s invitation to Transgress?

At first you are confident that the unhappy endings of Transgressing Finders were merely bad luck. But suppose that after some time has passed and razing of the TutTut site is imminent, *Rega*'s latest report says that of the accumulated total of 206 tracked Transgressors, every single one has been Quashed. It also mentions that only 15 Transgressors remain untracked and that at most 40 more Transgressions will be feasible before the site is razed. So with confidence that this information is reliable, you conclude in approximate answer to *Q1* that the proportion $fr(Q|T)$ of *T*s that get *Q*d is at least .79, insomuch as the number of *Q*s is known to be at least 206 and the total population of *T*s should be no larger than 206 + 15+ 40. Were you to conclude no more than that you could continue believing, despite your knowledge that most *T*s get *Q*d, that the bad luck of past *T*s shouldn't much matter for the longevity of future ones. So shouldn't you hasten to *T* before your window of opportunity to do so closes? Of course not. No matter how you try to explain these data you cannot resist the persuasiveness of conditional, *If I Transgress I will almost certainly get Quashed*. And the major *since*-clause backing that is your recently acquired conviction that *Transgressors are almost certain to get Quashed*–not quite so strong as classical (13.27) but about as close to that as a skeptical temperament can allow. Given such evidence it would be perversely irrational not to conclude with high confidence that *something* about Transgressing is at present exceedingly jeopardous to a person's survival.

However, your *almost* qualifier here reminds us of our frequent need to cope with regularities whose reliability seems less than perfect. Because the "almost certain" in your conclusions from sample data so unequivocal as posited so far could be classically strict certainty about which you're not quite sure, let's change the data stipulation to say that only 49 of the 206 tracked *T*s have been *Q*d, that just four *T*s have not been tracked, and that just 10 more *T*s will be allowed before the site is razed. Then regarding *Q1*, you can infer with assurance that $fr(Q \mid T)$ is between .22 and .29. But how does that help you with *Q2*? In itself, not at all; and that would be just as true if you had learned instead that there were no past *T*s other than the 206 tracked and only one more *T* will be allowed, entailing that population statistic $fr(Q \mid T)$ differs from exact value .24 by at most .004. Only if your native intelligence has been numbed by platitudes of introductory sampling theory would you derive your *Q2* decision by reasoning that if you *T*, you will be a size-1 random sample from the population of *T*s wherein you know the relative frequency of *Q* is approximately .24. What matters for *Q2* is not your estimate of $fr(Q \mid T)$ but what the data on which that estimate is based induce you to believe about the tendency of *T*ing to influence longevity in instances still forthcoming, your own case in particular should you choose to *T*. Your verbalization of that particularized tendency in ordinary English would take the form of an accepted conditional something like *If I Transgress, there's an appreciable risk that I'll get Quashed.* But fluency in more advanced statistics enables you to conclude with greater precision and generality that

The probability of a *T*'s getting *Q*d is approximately .24, (13.29)

which persuades you that *If I do it, there's roughly a 24% chance that I'll get Quashed.*

It is scarcely news to you that we frequently center the spread of our uncertain belief about the total proportion of *A*s that are *B*s on the relative frequency of *B*s we think has been found in observed *A*s, and that our confidence concerning *B*'s prevalence among *A*s not yet encountered is distributed similarly. This is the one articulate form of non-deductive inference that has been widely recognized, now standardly known as *induction*, or better, since that is sometimes understood more broadly, *statistical induction.* But I am contending—a view far from original though often only mumbled—that our inferences in such cases reach deeper than mere statistical inductions about the relative frequency of *B*-ness in the real totality of *A*s or even in subpopulations thereof not yet observed. Such *fr*-conclusions are parasitical on our coming to accept generalized probabilistic conditionals roughly of form *If something is an A then with approximate probably r it is a B*; and that in turn manifests our provisional commitment to the existence of production forces that bring about this incidence of *B*-ness in the presence of *A*-hood. In brief, we are inferring from the known sample data a primitive theory of *why* this patterning of events occurs.

Mini-theories of form (13.29) are "primitive" in two major respects. In the first place, our $Pr(B \mid A) \approx r$ conclusions are usually provisional, not just benignly in that skimpy data may not support much confidence in the approximation's accuracy, but from risk of catastrophic revision that radically shifts our opinion of $Pr(B \mid A)$ or supersedes it altogether with probabilities on more finely conceived attributes while perhaps calling into question the scientific meaningfulness of probability hypotheses about *A* or *B*.

Illustration 1. After becoming confident of (13.29) from recorded data, you realize that almost all tracked *T*s have been adult humans who are either highly educated or wealthy. Unless you append these attributes to *T* in (13.29), your distribution of credence over the possibilities for Pr(*Q* | *T*) should abruptly undergo a strong increase in spread that is no longer centered near .24, especially if it occurs to you that sarcophagus-chamber visits by infants and perhaps lesser creatures should also count as Transgressions. (Clarifications or other meaning adjustments of the predicates in Pr(*B* | *A*) ≈ *r* is one though by no means the only reason why this mini-theory is apt to be ephemeral.)

Illustration 2. Suppose that after concluding (13.29), you learn further that *Rega*'s project manager, acting on suspicion aroused by the incidence of Nearpox among the Finders, installed a policy of advising all persons about to enter the sarcophagus chamber to breathe its air only through a proffered air-scrubbing device. And analysis of detailed health records on the tracked *T*s shows that apart from Finders in the plane crash, nearly all the *T*s who got *Q*d were Nearpox fatalities while *T*s who later contracted Nearpox, most of whom died, had all declined to breathe scrubbed air while *T*ing. This finding urges you to supersede interest in Pr (*Q* | *T*) with concern for Pr(*Q'*|*T'*), where *T'* is the property of breathing unscrubbed air from TutTut's sarcophagus chamber (which can be done with bottled chamber air without actually Transgressing) and *Q'* is contracting Nearpox, though that does not preclude continuing concern with Pr(*Q''*|*T''*) for other modifications *Q''* and *T''* of *Q* and *T* as well.

And second, the *probability* concept itself is still so loosely delimited by the contexts of usage that establish its meaning (the mathematical probability axioms are just a fragment thereof) that proposition Pr(*B* | *A*) ≈ *r* isn't nearly as informative about the nature of *B*'s connection with *A* as we can hope will be conveyed by future enrichments of the Pr-concept. In particular, the relation between probabilities and production forces is still deeply troublesome, one flagrant manifestation of which is probability theory's postulation that if Pr(*B*|*A*) exists then so does Pr(*A*|*B*), even though at most one of properties *A* and *B* can be a source of the other[20] and their Pr-connection may well derive instead from other sources they have in common.

The idea that natural events are governed by quantifiably indeterminate regularities in compliance with a rigorous mathematical framework is an astonishing

---

[20]If there is anything we can take to be axiomatically true of *becausal* relations, it is their antisymmetry, that is, that whenever *q* because *p* then never *p* because *q*. Applied to attributes *A* and *B*, this principle implies that it is never true of any object *x* that *B*(*x*) because *A*(*x*) while also *A*(*x*) because *B*(*x*) (That becausal relations prevailingly if not always connect events occurring at *different* locations, an important technicality that orthodox formulations of generality and lawfulness have never adequately recognized, cannot be addressed here.)

intellectual achievement that seems to have originated only a few centuries ago (see Hacking, 1975). So we have no reason for surprise that its development is still far from complete. Meanwhile, until such time as the foundations of applied probability theory become rather less mysterious, we should exercise prudence in how unconditionally we trust the statistical models through which we filter our empirical research findings. Meanwhile, it remains a brute fact of human reason that we respond to *fr*-distributions in sample data with nascent theories accounting for these data patterns that we don't just conjecture but provisionally *believe* with often-considerable conviction, even though these tentative prob-abilistic conclusions are only proto-explanatory in leaving still unspecified even the directionality of the inferred production forces much less their nature.

Are such inferences justified, as some philosophers still profess to doubt? Perhaps not—but I challenge the coherence of denying this unless one can de-scribe some rather different pattern of cognitive reaction to relative-frequency input, say why that seems more rational than standard statistical/probabilistic in-duction, and demonstrate some ability to live by it.

Abduction

A century ago, Charles Peirce (1839–1914) introduced the term *abduction* to de-note a type of practical inference that he viewed—rightly—as importantly dis-tinct from classically conceived deduction (logical entailment) and statistical in-duction.[21] This is our creation of *explanations* for observed phenomena, a mode of reasoning that not merely expands upon the information at hand ("ampliative" inference), as statistical generalization to relative frequencies in populations also does, but hypothesizes *why* these observations have their distinctive character. And these explanations invoke concepts other than the ones used to describe the observations explained. Thus from the Hartshorne and Weiss (1934) collection of Peirce's papers:

> Abduction consists in studying facts and devising a theory to explain them. (1903; Vol. 5, p. 90).

> Abduction is the process of forming an exploratory hypothesis. (1903; Vol. 5, p. 106).

---

[21]Peirce attributed this term to a latin translation of Aristotle's *Prior Analytica*, lib. 2, cap. 25 (Moore, 1984, p. 108). Peirce also refers to abduction as reasoning by "hypothesis" and, less often, "retroduction."

> Abduction must cover all the operations by which theories and conceptions are engendered. (1903, Vol. 5, p. 414).

And most provocatively,

> The great difference between induction and hypothesis [that is, abduction] is, that the former infers the existence of phenomena, such as we have observed in cases which are similar, while hypothesis supposes something of a different kind from which we have directly observed, and frequently something which it would be impossible for us to observe directly. (1857; Vol. 2, p. 388.)

Peirce returned repeatedly to this theme without, however, developing details on how to do it. And he urged that abduced hypotheses be appraised by follow-up tests of their additional implications insomuch as they generally remain far from a sure thing given just the observations that originally invoke them.[22] So it might be argued that Peircian abduction was but a softer, more tolerant precursor of Popper's fiercely astringent hypothetico-deductivism, which insisted both that there is no such thing as a "logic of discovery" (i.e., that hypothesis creation is purely a psychological phenomenon governed by no principles of rationality) and that hypotheses never gain credibility save through verification of their deductive consequences. But unlike Popper, Peirce would have welcomed the prospect that some abductions have determinate forms which transmit conviction. I shall argue that such inferences are the machinery of knowledge acquisition in both technical science and everyday life.

Be that as it may, the notion of "abduction" remained quietly where Peirce left it for the first half of this century during which our discipline's method orthodoxies were codified. But the massive mid-century swing of philosophic *zeitgeist* rejecting positivistic epistemology included an awakening of philosophers' desire to acknowledge abduction somehow. Hanson's *Patterns of Discovery* (1958) was warmly received as something of a breakout despite its arguing merely that our observations are impregnated with theory from the outset while endorsing a view of abduction as the intuitive onset of not wholly implausible conjectures, without concern for any identifiable principles that might govern these. And philosophers have also become increasingly inclined to speak sagely of "inference to the best explanation" since Harman (1965) introduced this phrase as a new take on Peircian abduction, even though neither Harman nor, until quite recently, anyone else had much to say about which hypotheses are explanatory or what conjectured explanations qualify as decent much less best.

---

[22]Thus in the 1903 lectures: "[Abduction's] only justification is that from its suggestion deduction can draw a prediction which can be tested by induction." (Hartshorne & Weiss, Vol. 5, p. 106.)

However, artificial intelligence (AI) work on problem solving expressly identified as Abduction (see especially Josephson & Josephson, 1994) has begun to put algorithmic muscle into the "best explanation" slogan. Meanwhile, Simon (1973) argued in explicit opposition to Popper that there does indeed exist a logic of scientific discovery, and has since developed programmable details within his own AI framework for problem solving (Langley, Simon, Bradshaw, & Zytkow, 1987). And in Rozeboom (1961), following my personal epiphany on deriving theory from data during graduate work on the behaviorist *What is learned?* problem,[23] I pointed out specific logical forms by which discerned data regularities are intuitively transformed into explanations thereof. Originally, I called this "ontological induction" because it creates concepts of entities (attributes and events) distinct from the ones described by the data statements. But later, in a user-friendlier and more mature statement of the position (Rozeboom, 1972b), I renamed it "explanatory induction" to stake out the seminal role I claim for it in real-life knowledge acquisition.[24] Although differing considerably in detail, all these revisionist views of scientific inference fit nicely within the broad tent of Peircian abduction. Even so, the version I have called explanatory induction has a tightly operational focus warranting recognition as a distinct species within Peirce's genus.

'Abduction' is at risk of becoming a buzzword in AI circles; and the extent to which psychology's research methods can profit from study of AI data-processing algorithms claimed to be abductive is problematic. A salient case in point is the sector of AI problem solving covered by Josephson and Josephson (1994), which has a considerable history of papers with 'abduc' in their titles. This has focused on deriving from a plurality of observations on a single individual— notably, medical symptoms and lab workups in the studies published, but also potentially data clusters such as features of a crime scene, or of a handwriting sample, or of style in artwork of uncertain authorship, etc.—the best diagnosis of that individual's configuration of underlying conditions responsible for those

---

[23]What came as revelation to me was realization that although non-mentalistic S-R mediation mechanisms could in principle account for a certain prospective transfer-of-training phenomenon that commonsense would take to manifest a mentalistic "idea" mediating between external stimuli and behavior, this phenomenon would demand explanation by a certain structure of mediation with indifference to whether that structure has a mentalistic, S-R mechanistic, or some other embodiment. (See Rozeboom, 1970, pp. 120-122).

[24]My original label proves to be the superior version in that I now want to emphasize that statistical induction, too, verges upon explanation when it reaches beyond population frequencies to underlying probabilities. However, I also submit that probabilities, though undeniably theoretical entities, are not themselves explanatory mechanisms but only supervene upon those.

symptoms. But the extant AI algorithms that accomplish this are preprogrammed with "domain knowledge" containing all the explanatory *if/then* laws posited to produce symptoms of the sort to be interpreted in particular cases. Algorithms that can do this effectively in difficult cases may well have applied value as expert systems; but they tell us nothing about how to conceive and acquire confidence in the explanatory laws they presume. (Elsewhere in the AI literature, programs can be found that profess to abduce laws as well; but the versions I have seen use a production logic more suited to fantasizing than to scientific inquiry.) In contrast, Simon and colleagues have said nothing in print about "abduction" or "inference to best explanation"; but their induction modeling has attempted to reconstruct discovery of laws and concepts that were historically important achievements in physical science. These prestigious scientific successes are paradigm examples of the inferences I have called explanatory induction; and I welcome Langley et al's (1987) progress in simulating these as support for my still-minority thesis that interpreting observations in this fashion is the engine of advance in epistemically praiseworthy scientific belief.

Explanatory induction, or "EI" for short (not to be confused with the "AI" of artificial intelligence), has two special epistemic merits typical neither of abduction in Peirce's broadly inclusive sense nor of output from the artificial intelligence programs that have been labeled abductive by their creators: Not merely do explanatory inductions call explanations for observations to mind in the first place by decently determinate inference forms, they also yield confidence in their conclusions that in favorable circumstances can approach the vivid strength of perceptual beliefs. So why has this essay's title paid explicit homage generically to abduction rather than specifically to EI when the latter is its real focus? Three reasons: First, good science does indeed profit from broadly abductive (imaginative) speculations so long as results from innovative research provoked by these are not interpreted by blue-sky HD reasoning. Second, 'abduction' is a word that for better or worse is bound to become increasingly prominent in discussions of scientific method; so you may as well get familiar with it. And third, it is clumsy style to use an eight-syllable phrase in slogans or titles when three syllables will do.

Explanatory Induction (EI): Examples

Suppose your hand calculator—call it CP for "this calculator at present"—is acting strangely: Whenever you enter numeral 8, its rightmost display cell responds with 6, and the same occurs when the result of a calculation should show 8 in that display position. Your conclusion is immediate and assured: *Something is wrong with* CP. Were you to observe further that CP responds to entry of any digit other than 5, 6, or 8 with a non-numeric shape in its rightmost display cell never containing an upper-right vertical stroke, you would probably conclude more specifically that *the upper-right pixel at end of* CP*'s display isn't working*. But even if no digit other than 8 manifests a problem in this display position and you know nothing about CP's display mechanism, you are still confident that some feature of CP has changed for the worse even though all you yet know about this altered condition is that it makes CP show 6 in its rightmost display cell under input circumstances that formerly would have put '8' there. In either case, you have committed an act of explanatory induction on these observations from which you would have been incapable of abstaining. You have inferred that CP is in some state that degrades the desirable input/output relations it sustained previously. And you do *not* take this state to be an ephemeral manifest property that CP has just at moments when depression of a key co-occurs with a display inappropriate to that key, but which vanishes when no key is pressed or when key entry and consequent display are in agreement (e.g., when entry and right-most display digit are both 5). Rather, you feel sure that it is an *enduring* property, one that is *responsible* for some key presses eliciting incorrect responses and persists in CP even when this is resting or giving correct responses.

What you know about a properly working CP is even more richly endowed by EI. First, even if you had never received instruction in how to use CP beyond its *on/off* switch and advice that pressing CP's keys (which we will describe as "entries" corresponding to the keys' assorted labels) generally alters CP's display, you could still have become confident, through observations on CP's display changes following key entries, of many generalities having form

> Whenever CP is in condition C and then receives sequence K of key entries, its display at end of this input sequence is R, $\qquad$ (13.30)

wherein C specifies, among other observable preconditions, CP's display at start of entry sequence K and some information about CP's recently prior entries. In practice (and you really have acquired such beliefs about hand calculators), these generalities would for the most part accrete silently in your "background knowledge" while entering your conscious judgment as particularized anticipations of how CP's display should respond to a possible key-entry sequence initiated here and now. And the salient point to take from this is what you thereby believe about CP at various stages in a sequence of its key entries:

To become aware of beliefs that in your normal use of CP are too fleetingly transient to reach foreground attention, suppose that your execution of some calculation with CP is interrupted by a phone call. On return, you observe that CP's current display is 5 and, instead of hitting CP's *clear-all* key to start afresh, you wonder what its display would become were you to enter a few more digits, say 9, 3, 9, followed by a function key such as the one labeled '='. You realize that you can't predict CP's future display just from the present one and your choice of input starting now, but can do so if you remember enough of your transaction with CP just prior to breaking for the call. And if you are fairly sure that your last function-key entry was × while CP's display then was 1.2, you can anticipate with some confidence that were sequence 939= now to be entered, CP's display immediately following the = entry would be the product of numbers 1.2 and 5939 or, more precisely, a digital representation of that which after some paper-and-pencil scratching you can identify in advance as digit string 7126.8. But your success in predicting CP's displays in this situation isn't the point here. What matters are your beliefs (a) that CP's display R at times t' later than the present t will be lawfully determined in part by its sequence of key entries between t and t'; (b) that the present *state* of CP at t also makes a large difference for R at t'; and (c) that although this state of CP so crucial to its subsequent display is ephemeral and not directly observable, its functional character—that is, its distinctive role in production of CP's behavior—can be inferred from past input to CP and described by the conditional

> If the symbol string that starts with CP's current display excluding terminal dot and thereafter describes the next sequence K of CP's key entries represents a number r, and entry of K is immediately followed by one of function keys +, -, ×, ÷, or =, then CP's resulting display will be standard notation for the number that equals 1.2-times-r,   (13.31)

to which in afterthought you append some auxiliary *if*-clauses constraining the size of r and how roughly CP is handled. Idiom urges that (13.31) be simplified to

> CP is currently disposed to respond to any input number with the product of that with 1.2,   (13.32)

and may even tempt you to say, more metaphorically than EI approves, that CP remembers 1.2 and is in the mood to multiply. Metaphor aside, the idiom of (13.32) makes it easy for you to acknowledge that when CP is working properly, it is capable of passing through many transitory states, each describable by a covert conditional—"covert" in that it is an *if/then* only implicitly—of form

> CP is disposed at time t to respond to input of any number r with $s \odot r$,   (13.33)

where s is a real number and $\odot$ is one of binary operators +, −, ×, ÷. Since at most one completion of schema (13.33) is true of CP at any particular time t, (13.33) in effect identifies a two-dimensional array of attribute alternatives which we might call CP's "*op*(eration)-states." From there, your theory of how the s and $\odot$ facets of CP's op-state at any given time have been brought about by input is a straightforward inference from your generalizations of form (13.30).

In resurrection of the positivist program early this century for clarifying science's theoretical concepts, one might argue that CP's op-state at any time t is nothing more than some logical construction out of CP's key entries prior to t. But your intuitive EI leap from observations on CP to beliefs such as (13.33) about CP's op-states insists that its property described by (13.33) is a contemporary event which, though due to and predictable from input/output events in CP's past, is distinct from those and mediates whatever causal influence those may have on CP's next response.[25] Of course, this interpretation of (13.33) could be wrong. But for better or worse it is the conclusion that EI delivers here.

The op-states of CP inferred by EI in this example are atypical of EI discovery both in their extreme ephemerality and in the accuracy with which CP's op-state at any given time can be predicted from its prior input history. But they usefully demonstrate the compulsive power with which explanatory inductions can occur. Given enough observations on CP to convince you that the form-(13.30) generalizations you have taken from these will continue to fit future observations on CP, it is psychologically impossible for you not to advance from there to indicative and counterfactual conditionals like (13.31) that in turn are arguably equivalent in meaning, or nearly so, to dispositional claims of form (13.32). These moves are far from epistemically unproblematic; but insomuch as they are as natural as breathing and nearly as indispensable, prudence advises us not to disown them but to develop expertise in their technical management.

I have taken pains to describe CP's op-states as "dispositions" because that is the established label for an enormous variety of qualities ascribed to things in everyday life: the sourness of lemons vs. sweetness of sugar, your uncle's stinginess vs. the generosity of your aunt, the fragility of chalk vs. the durability of wood, the stickiness of honey and adhesives vs. the slipperiness of teflon and wet ice, and so on for thousands of adjectives in ordinary language. Whatever may be the nature of what we attribute to the individuals said to be that way, it is deeply ingrained in our language that these are *dispositions*, or "tendencies" if you prefer; and over many decades of philosophers' efforts to reduce their aura

---

[25]To be sure, if you had the flu on this date last year, then it is a property of you-today that you had the flu a year ago. But we view such temporal displacements of natural events as linguistically contrived epiphenomena that supervene on the world's causal unfolding. (If you have persisting health problems today, this may well be due in part to your bout of flu a year ago through the iterated dynamics of certain body changes initiated at that time; but it is surely not brought about by your having today the property of having had flu a year ago.) This may only exhibit the naivete of our causality intuitions; but it's still the way to go until the error of those becomes more apparent.

of mystery (see Tuomela, 1977, for a collection of modern views) it has been more or less agreed that these are essentially the same as what we attribute by claims of form

$$\text{If } S(x), \text{ then (probably) } R(x), \tag{13.34}$$

or variations and elaborations (e.g. conjunctions) thereof. In this, 'x' is place-holder for names of whatever entities we may wish to characterize this way, '$S(x)$' describes an input condition that can be imposed on x, and '$R(x)$' de-scribes a response of x that may, though need not, be some display by another object to which x is coupled in some fashion specified in '$S(x)$'. (That is, $R(x)$ can be a meter reading.) Also, the conditionality expressed in (13.34) is under-stood to tolerate occasional failure of response R given input S. That is, whatever we mean by (13.34) in its disposition-demarking sense, not only does truth of '$R(x)$' not suffice for (13.34) to be correct, it is also allowed that (13.34) might hold in some instances even when '$S(x)$' is true while '$R(x)$' is false. In particu-lar, when x belongs to a set X of entities that we think are alike in respect to (13.34)—notably, when X comprises a succession of an enduring thing's tempo-ral stages over some limited time interval, or stages of different things that ap-pear be interchangeably similar in many ways—we are disposed to accept (13.34) if, among the members of X whose S and R conditions have been ob-served, R is considerably more prevalent among Xs that have been Sd than among those that have not. Indeed, in such cases we find ourselves talking about different degrees of the *If-S-then-R* disposition (which is thereby converted from an inferred state to a dimension of inferred states) such that the strength of this common to the members of an X presumably homogeneous in this respect is measured by the contrast of R's relative frequency among X-members who have been observed in condition S to its relative frequency observed among X-mem-bers lacking S.

Ordinary-language versions of such dispositional concepts usually specify their input/output conditions so vaguely and so categorically (that is, treating S and R as sloppy condition-present/condition-absent dichotomies) as to be nearly useless for scientific research save as targets of replacement by more precisely defined and more finely graded input/output alternatives. Sometimes such im-provements can be viewed as more accurate diagnoses of roughly the same un-derlying attribute dimensions detected crudely by their ordinary-language pre-cursors. But more often, invention of new measuring instruments—devices or special environments whose carefully controlled coupling with objects that in-terest us scarcely ever occurs naturally—afford display of precisely defined di-mensions of quantifiably graded response alternatives that initially provide conception, and thereafter finely discriminating detection, of our studied objects' underlying properties beyond the ken of everyday experience. These previously hidden properties have now become virtually observable even if not quite so manifest as the input/output conditions from which we infer them. And data on patterns of co-occurrence among these newly discernible attributes may—or may not—lead us through iterated explanatory inductions to understanding of even deeper levels of inner mechanisms responsible for these subjects' overt behavior.

Psychology has had its full share of instrument-grounded disposition concepts, though apart from physiological psychology the "instruments" have largely been special stimulus settings with constraints on subjects' movements therein rather than the meters, gauges, chemical reagents, and other sensor devices familiar in everyday life through spillover from the physical and biological sciences. Indeed, much of educational psychology and personality assessment has been grounded on subjects' reactions to numerous brief test items—paradigmatically, choice among a small number of alternative answers to a written or sometimes spoken question—that are collected into "scales" on which the subject receives a numerical score summarizing responses to the items comprising that scale. Much has been written and still more remains to be said about the technology of such questionnaires, especially about the rationale of item grouping which in practice often illustrates EI at work on a deeper level with techniques of factor analysis. But we cannot address that here. The point to be taken is that educational and psychological measurements of this sort are classic illustrations of explanatory-inductive concept formation accompanied by collection of data on the variables so inferred, even though their attendant circumstances seldom warrant trust at the higher confidence levels of which EI is capable, such as when these same subjects' body weight is measured by a balance or torsion scale, or their temperature by a thermometer. Each item's definition (standardized manner of stimulation and method of scoring) creates conception of a mini-tendency to get one score rather than another if so stimulated. High EI confidence that mini-dispositions so conceived genuinely exist requires subjects to show consistent differences in their responses to each item over repeated testings, which in practice is seldom demonstrated firmly. But there also exist other patterns of manifest intrasubject consistency in response to a battery of test items that urge inference to relatively enduring "traits" of tested subjects. These are measured, though with less-than-perfect accuracy, by subjects' composite scores over selected subsets of the test items and are inferred to dispose not merely subject-distinctive patterns of response to these particular test items but also—which may or may not be later confirmed—to other input conditions as well. (See McCrae & Costa, 1995.)

In practice, we seldom have much interest in dispositions identified by just one dimension of response to just one specific stimulus setting. But EI kicks in hard when we have observed a cluster of dispositions expressible in ideally simple cases by a plurality of sentences having form 'When a thing of sort B is disposed to R_i when S_id, then almost always it is also disposed to R_j when S_jd.' (The S_i envisioned here are a considerable diversity of conditions that can be imposed on B-things, each R_i is a response made possible by input condition S_i, and B is some background condition—often conceived only vaguely by reference to a few paradigm examples—under which this consilience of mini-dispositions seems dependable.) In such cases, EI waives the mini-dispositions in favor of a single theoretical property τ whose presence/absence in a thing of kind B can be diagnosed in diverse known ways (whether the thing does R_i in response to S_i for several different S_i-tests) and is moreover expected to partake in yet-to-be-discovered lawful relations with other observable and EI-inferable variables as well. Actually, finer details of these S_i/R_i tests (notably, when some of the R_i are graded response alternatives) usually yield conception of this τ as a theoretical variable taking a considerable range of alternative values over things of kind B.

Such "cluster concepts" (as some philosophers have called them) of classic simplicity abound in chemistry, mineralogy, and medicine wherein the "natural kind" of a chemical or mineral or, in medicine, the presence/absence of a particular disease condition is diagnosed by a battery of such tests. A powerful case in point is the chemical contrast originally conceived as *acid* vs. *alkali* vs. *salt*. Partington's (1935/1965) history of chemistry lists dozens of different tests described by Robert Boyle (a 17th Century founder of modern chemistry) wherein a sample x of some to-be-appraised material X is brought into contact with a sample s of some test material S_i. For suitably chosen S_i, changes in the appearance of s resulting from this contact reliably forecasts, for many other identified materials S_j, what changes in samples of S_j will result from their contact with samples of material X. (Many though by no means all of these test outcomes are changes in s's color that depend in part on the chosen S_j. Another especially important response in some tests is s's dissolution in liquid x.) Early chemists did not learn about acids and alkalis by first speculating that such theoretical properties might exist, next deducing observable consequences of this hypothesis, and finally confirming those predictions as a triumph of hypothetico-deductive science. Rather, the alkali/salt/acid notions and their eventual refinement into a continuum of *pH* levels were an explanatory induction from observed patterns of reaction such as collated by Boyle. Or so I submit.

Another good example from everyday life is your learning in childhood about *hot*. When in the kitchen, or near a fireplace, or perhaps in a family workshop, you had repeated experiences wherein touching a certain object resulted in your immediately feeling acute discomfort followed a little later, if your touch was firm or prolonged, by blistering of your skin at the point of contact. You easily convinced yourself that an object which so affected you when touched would do so every time you touched it for a short duration thereafter, though usually not after some longer lapse of time. So you concluded—not by deliberated reasoning but by wired-in cognitive compulsion—that some things at certain times have an *If-I-touch-it-I'll-get-hurt* property. And additional fooling around or watching others deal with such objects also taught you that a thing having this *touching-it-hurts-me* property is also featured by *If it is touched by a plastic object the plastic will melt*, and by *If fat is spilled on it the fat will sizzle and likely catch fire*, and by *If a scrap of paper is held against it the paper will turn curly brown and maybe burn*, and by *If a pan of water is put on it and it stays able-to-hurt-me long enough, the water will boil*. Indeed, you learned that any one of these if/thens holding for an *it-now* pretty well guaranteed that the others were true of *it-now* as well, whence you concluded—again by innate urge though not quite so compulsively as before—that all these simultaneous if/thens probably manifest a single underlying condition that you came to think of as "hot" because you also learned that a nearby grown-up's shouting 'hot' when you were reaching for something also dependably indicated that your target was in this danger state. From there, you went on to discover that a thing's glowing red often signaled that it was *hot*, that devices your folks called "thermometers" can finely discriminate differences in *hot* that you could previously distinguish only coarsely, and so on for a large repertoire of beliefs about gradations of *hot* so securely rooted in your direct observations that even today you may have trouble recognizing that these beliefs constitute a *theory* about a nonphenomenal Heat variable (degrees of *hot*ness) known to you, via explanatory induction, only through its causes and effects. Indeed, commonsense is inclined to hold that heat *is* observable, just not quite so directly as some attributes we perceive.

There is one more real-science example of explanatory induction that I consider especially luminous, namely, the discovery and measurement of electrical voltage and resistance. I have cited this briefly in Rozeboom (1984, p. 220f.), but its prominence in Langley et al. (1987) encourages a more articulate review here as well. To highlight the EI essence of this achievement uninhibited by strict historical accuracy,[26] I talk about a 19th Century German physicist named Fohm, who is a mildly fictionalized version of the real George Ohm (1789–1854).

Fohm's definitive studies of electrical circuits emerged from the then-novel inventions of electric batteries and galvanometers. We know galvanometers today as magnetized needles whose rotation around a mounting pivot diagnoses the strength of a magnetic field induced by a nearby flow of electrons. But Fohm

---

[26]Partly because the source material I have been able to consult is rather sketchy, but also because real Ohm's first report republished in Magie (1965) does not exhibit the EI nature of his research quite so cleanly as certain modifications of his procedure allow.

conceived of these just as detectors of a "strength of magnetic action" variable.[27] Batteries, or better, battery setups, were for Fohm special temperature-controlled assemblages of physical materials having two poles designed for attachment to wires, metal bars, or other physical objects which we shall call "loads," and were such that when a load bridged the gap between a battery's poles (circuit completion), the needle of a galvanometer held near the load showed some deflection from its resting position. Let us augment the "load" notion to include stipulation of two specific points (terminals) on the object to which a battery's poles are to be attached, so that different terminal placements on the same wire/bar/whatever define different loads, just as different temperature distributions over the same battery assemblage count as different battery setups.[28] Fohm found that when each of several different loads L_i completed the circuit separately with several different battery setups S_j, holding a particular prepared galvanometer G standardly close to L_i during its attachment to S_j rotated G's needle a consistently distinctive distance d_{ij} from its resting position.[29] And when studying his collection of d_{ij} readings, he discerned that a positive real number r_i could be assigned to each load L_i, and a pair of non-negative real numbers v_j, s_j to each battery setup S_j, such that for a constant of proportionality g which could be set equal to 1 by choice of G's scale unit, the errors of approximation

$$d_{ij} \approx g \times \frac{v_i}{r_i + s_j} \quad (g = 1) \tag{13.35}$$

over all L_i / S_j combinations were negligible. (Henceforth, we will treat (13.35) as an exact equality.) These v, r, s assignments are not unique, insomuch as multiplying all the r_i and s_j by an arbitrary constant and all the v_j by another can be compensated for by a corresponding change in G's scale unit. (Tinkering with G's calibration is fair play in any case, because G's responsiveness is affected by its construction and positioning in the circuit's vicinity, and is best construed to measure current strength only up to a constant of proportionality.) But the ratios among the r_i and s_j, and separately among the v_j, are fixed by Equation 13.35; so by choosing a particular load L_1, battery setup S_1, and galvanometric procedure

---

[27]See Magie (1965, p. 470). Ohm and his contemporaries had already begun also to think of this observational procedure more theoretically as measuring a "current" of flowing electric fluid.

[28]The "thermo-electric" battery setups favored by real Ohm comprised a bar of uniform metallic composition with its poles maintained at different temperatures by iced vs. heated water. This temperature disparity was an important determinant of current production.

[29]Real Ohm's galvanometric response measure was Coulomb's more sophisticated amount of torque required to counterbalance the current-induced disturbance.

G as reference standards, Fohm was able to stipulate a unique, reproducible assignment of the v,r,s numbers in circuit experiments like this.

It is instructive to note that when Equations 13.35 are error-free, their right-hand terms can be determined from the data as follows: First stipulate reference-standard values for r_1 and v_1, say 1 for both. Then s_1 is computable directly from d_{11} as $s_1 = v_1/d_{11} - r_1 = 1/d_{11} - 1$ from which, for every other load L_i, we can compute $r_i = 1/d_{i1} - s_1$. Now choose an offset load L_2 whose now-identified resistance r_2 differs from r_1. Then for every other battery S_j, $d_{2j}/d_{1j} = (r_1 + s_j)/(r_2 + s_j)$ so $s_j = (d_{1j}r_1 - d_{2j}r_2)/(d_{2j} - d_{1j})$ and hence $v_j = d_{1j}(s_j + r_1)$. Thus the d_{i1} for all loads L_i alternatively in circuit with reference battery S_1, together with the d_{1j} and d_{2j} over all batteries alternatively in circuit separately with reference load L_1 and its offset L_2, collectively suffice to compute all the v_j, r_i, s_j and, from there, to reproduce all the other d_{ij}. (The v,r,s assignments so identified are relative not only to choice of L_1 and S_1 but to galvanometer setup G as well. Dealing with variation in G is an additional facet of EI-grounded circuit theory that we needn't pursue here. Neither does it matter that modern data analysis would fit the $v,r,$ s assignments by more advanced methods designed to minimize approximation errors.)

Fohm described r_i and s_j as measures of the "resistance" of circuit components L_i and S_j, respectively,[30] while v_j measured S_j's "excitatory force" (later called "voltage"). Fohm further observed that the d_{ij} readings for particular load/battery pairs were essentially constant over repeated test occasions except for some initial variation that might have been due to exceptionally cold weather on two deviant days. From there, Fohm and his successors were able to work out deeper laws governing voltage and resistance. Thus when load L_i is a metal wire or other elongated object of homogeneous material with terminals at ends of its long axis and constant cross-section perpendicular to that axis, L_i's resistance equals its length divided by its cross-section area times a constant, specific to L_i's type of material though also influenced by the load's temperature, which may be called the "conductivity" of that material. Eventually, it was possible to assemble electric circuits comprising one or more current drivers and multiple loads joined by weblike interconnections and, using detectors of current flow (amperage), voltage drop, and resistance calibrated from these instruments' re-

---

[30]Initially, real Ohm took the r_i in equations (8) to be lengths of the copper wires he first used for loads in this experiment. But he also reported that when brass wire was substituted for copper, one inch of brass was current-wise equivalent to 20.5 inches of copper, showing that what plays the r-role in Ohm's law is not length of load but some other variable that is a function mainly of length among loads sufficiently alike in other respects. How soon thereafter the r-term in (8) became explicitly recognized as load resistance I do not know.

sponses to standardizing circuits, to confirm empirically the final theoretically polished version of Ohm's law, namely, that current flow through any load in an arbitrarily complex circuit equals the voltage drop across the load's terminals divided by its resistance. Also confirmed was that a load's resistance is a property that, within limits, persists throughout its participation in a variety of circuits.

You will observe that Ohm's law and its extensions are replete with implied dispositional concepts that are not simple surface-level *if/then*s. Intensity of electric current was initially disposition to affect devices having an identified disposition to respond to magnets, but later became more richly theoretical than that. And voltages and resistances are dispositions to affect current only interactively, so that initially some of these required simultaneous diagnosis in the fashion of Fohm's experiment even though once that was accomplished it became possible to construct standardized meters able to diagnose new voltages and resistances just by a direct meter reaction. From there, a material's conductivity is uncovered as a parameter in how the resistances of loads composed of that material vary as a function of their shape, size, and terminal placement; while in all likelihood (though I have no knowledge of this) the influence of temperature on conductivity has material-specific parameters diagnostic of still deeper attributes of materials.

Three major features of EI-driven theory development are prominent in this example. First, the numbers inferred to measure dispositions affecting observed performance protrude in frugal description of provocative patterning discovered in data collected under systematically varied conditions of observation. Pairing each of n_S battery setups with each of n_L loads repetitively on m occasions yields $n_S \times n_L \times m$ galvanometer readings that are reproducible under (13.35), with scarcely any error, just from $2n_S$ numbers $\{v_j\}$ and $\{s_j\}$ assigned to the batteries plus n_L numbers $\{r_i\}$ assigned to the loads. To appreciate the sense in which these v,r,s parameters characterize a *pattern* in Fohm's $n_S \times n_L$ data points $\{d_{ij}\}$ (whose constancy over repetitions is an additional facet of the pattern that we shall ignore), observe that the method of computing these assignments described previously defines an algebraic function f of five arguments such that, for any fixed choice of reference battery S_1, reference load L_1, and offset load L_2, data points d_{i1} over all the n_L loads in circuit just with S_1, together with d_{1j} and d_{2j} over all the n_S batteries in circuit just with L_1 and L_2, yield prediction of all remaining $(n_L - 2) \times (n_S - 1)$ data points by formula $d_{ij} = f(d_{i1}, d_{1j}, d_{2j}, d_{21}, d_{11})$. Although this function f is easy enough to program for computer computation, it looks like gibberish if written out as a single algebraic formula. Nevertheless, it makes precise a pattern of interpredictive redundancy within data array $\{d_{ij}\}$ that when we comprehend its strength overwhelms us with conviction that these observations have common sources which plainly cannot consist in some of the G-

readings being causes of others.[31]   And once we appreciate the lucid elegance
with which Equation 13.35 describes this data pattern by decomposing the surface-level f-interrelations into components associated with separable circuit
parts, with the directionality in this decomposition portraying all the observations d_{ij} as similarly dependent on variables over these circuit parts whose values
are estimated by the v,r,s parameters, this parsing of the data pattern demands as
much a realist interpretation as do the patterns other scientists see on the output
screens of telescopes, bubble chambers, and electron microscopes.

Second, the new variables defined by EI-provocative decomposition of a data
pattern generally project generalizations broader than orthodox statistical generalization. The loads (and similarly the batteries) in Fohm's experiment were
temporal continuuants (enduring things) from which only occasional time slices
(temporal stages) were in circuit with a battery. So the r_i value computed for load
L_i in its temporally extended entirety actually assigned the same resistance rating
to each of L_i's time slices that were in a circuit from which a galvanometer
reading was taken. The empirical within-load constancy of this rating under repeated assessments urges provisional inference that within limits not yet clear, r_i
is L_i's resistance (a) at every moment t at which L_i completes a galvanometer-
monitored electric circuit even with battery setups not used previously, and (b)
also at moments when L_i is not in a circuit at all. (Projection (a) is an empirical
prediction; (b) is an instance of believing that dispositions persist even when not
manifest.) And the force of projection (a) for anticipating future observations is
not prediction that the past relative frequency of some observed attribute will
tend to recur, but a set of conditional predictions about the behavior of new circuits containing L_i in which the conditionals' antecedents hypothesize information about the other circuit components.

Third, once data obtained under tightly controlled conditions have made such
a pattern evident, it can generally be found, by systematic variation of conditions
previously held constant, that this pattern's local parameters covary with other
features identified (often as dispositions) in more elaborate patterns whose additional parameters disclose still more source variables. Thus had Fohm's experiment suffered large temperature fluctuations from one circuit reading to another,
or (contrary to physical possibility as we know it) his loads asynchronously
changed their metallic composition every few hours, it would have been nearly
impossible for him to discern any lawfulness in his data. But once pattern
(13.35) was perceived under tight constraints and confirmed by replications, it
become straightforward to study how resistance varied as a function of condi-

---

[31]A thought problem for you: *Why* don't you consider it even remotely plausible that
some of these G-readings, or the current strengths that dispose them, could cause the
others?

tions previously held constant and discover conductivity in the parameters thereof associated with a load's material.

Explanatory Induction: Overview Principles

The generic character of explanatory induction can be summarized as follows:

1. For a scientific data collection to have any interpretive significance, it must exhibit some regularity that cries, or at least softly pleads, for generalization to other events.

2. When a generalizable regularity observed in local data is described with quantitative precision (generally an idealized pattern qualified by goodness-of-fit ratings), its description includes certain parameters that we suspect depend in part on local conditions that will change when the form of this regularity recurs for data of this sort in other situations.

3. When parameters of a local-data pattern are found to vary with changes in local background constraints that have been selectively relaxed with some care, that dependency will likely manifest a pattern having parameters of its own, and so on for an iteration of parameters disclosed by constraint relaxations.

4. When working observed pattern parameters into stories about what seems to be responsible for what, stories that we need to guide our predictions of new events from our accumulated experience with these phenomena, we are often compelled—willingly—to treat those parameters as estimated values of hidden variables[32] that we know only through the data regularities they dispose. However, data patterns are often not so clear as we would like; even when strong they may be frugally parameterizable in more ways than one; and systematically controlling or passively observing additional factors ignored previously may change the pattern's gestalt.

To illustrate this last point, which is important, consider the research of Rohm, an alter ego of Fohm whose experiments more closely resemble those of real Ohm. Initially, Rohm used a single battery setup S_1 and, repeatedly over sev-

---

[32]Source variables inferred from covariations have become commonly known in the factor-analytic/structural-modeling literature as "latent variables" or "latent factors." This label is somewhat misleading, insomuch as "latent" ordinarily connotes inactivity, whereas were hidden variables inactive we could not detect them. But once we do detect them, they are not really hidden anymore either. What we need here, but have not yet found, is a deft adjective connoting "observed only indirectly." (All observations are indirect to some degree, but some rather more so than others.)

eral days, took the G-readings of S_1's circuit completions with eight copper wires $\{L_i\}$ having the same rectangular cross-section but large differences in length. Each load's G-ratings were averaged over repetitions of L_i's circuit with S_1 to define mean datum d_i for this load. And when each d_i was inverted to $y_i = 1/d_i$ and plotted against wire length x_i over all these loads, it was plain that y was a linear function of x with a positive slope b and additive constant a. Rohm next observed G-readings on circuits of S_1 with four brass strips with the same cross-section but differing in length, and found the dependence of y on x in this set of brass loads to be again linear with the same additive constant but a different slope. Next, he changed the battery setup to S_2 and found the same linear data pattern as before within each same-metal group of loads, but with the pattern's a and b parameters both altered by the battery shift. However, the proportionate change in b under shift in load-metal with the same battery was constant across batteries; so Rohm was able (the algebra is simple though not entirely obvious) to summarize all these results by a law just like Equation 13.35 except that Fohm's r was replaced in Rohm's version by $m \times x$ for a numerical constant m specific to the load's metal. Rohm could have viewed m at this point as measuring a conductivity property of metals. But he aborted that conception when his study of varying the cross-sectional areas w of his loads showed that $m \times x$ equaled cx/w for a deeper numerical parameter c that differed across load metals. Rohm's c is the same conductivity coefficient that Fohm discovered when, after identifying load resistance, he looked for determinants of r. But Rohm's pattern parameters did not explicitly exhibit r at this stage of his research. Only later, when he varied loads over irregular shapes and odd terminal positionings did Rohm perceive that it was most insightful and computationally universal to characterize loads by their r-terms in pattern parameterization (13.35). That a load's resistance could also be estimated from its physical dimensions and the conductivity of its metal in the restrictive case of cylindrical loads with terminals at their ends had importance for practicalities of electrical transmission but mattered little for basic circuit theory.

Explanatory inductions are thus provisional conclusions that may well become revised, expanded, or superseded altogether by more intricate configurations of factors, hidden or manifest, as more of the total pattern enters our ken. But that does not mean that explanatory inductions are usually *wrong*, anymore than it is wrong to say that John weighs 150 lbs. when his exact weight is 153.2 lbs. Human cognitions seldom if ever match reality exactly. But not all cognitive inaccuracies are equally fallacious. Getting things roughly right is often all we need for the purpose at hand; and assertions that are somewhat vague or not entirely correct can still be vaguely or approximately true.[33] Just like material technologies, our conceptual resources and the beliefs these enable are constantly evolving, due in no small part though by no means entirely to science's explanatory inductions. But modern replacement of slide rules by electronic calculators doesn't show that slide rules didn't do good work in their day; and neither does the likelihood, that much in our contemporary repertoire of EI-driven theoretical constructs will eventually grow obsolete, at all impugn their value in affording the truest account of natural reality currently available to us.

EPILOG ON PRACTICALITIES

As you have observed, this essay has not attempted to advise you on specific statistical techniques to favor when personally analyzing and interpreting data. Rather, it has surveyed three major contrastive outlooks on the logic of scientific reasoning with intent to promote certain attitudes that should make a difference for what you do in research practice. In broadest outline, I encourage:

1. Feel free to draw upon imaginative speculations when planning a research study or soliciting support for its execution, but resist with all your might, so far as supervisors, grant appraisers, and journal editors allow, actually interpreting your resultant data as a binary pro/con vote on some hypothesis proclaimed in advance. As a corollary, shun null-hypothesis tests while appreciating that the statistical models these exploit readily avail you of conclusions vastly more informative than pass/fail grading of H_0.

2. Sniff at Bayesian confirmation models with cautious welcome, like a guard dog appraising strangers in the company of his master. You will seldom be positioned to revise any of your unconditional beliefs in accord with its quantitative ideal, nor would trust in the outcome be wise if you could. But when working toward a deliberated conclusion of some importance to you, the quality of your reasoning may well profit from a dry-run attempt to simulate Bayesian derivation of this conclusion from beliefs in which you feel considerable conditional/unconditional confidence, so long as you translate Bayesian conditional-Crs into probabilistic *if/thens* that you can verbalize. And although I have not developed the point, there are special contexts of data interpretation, notably ones involving inference to

---

[33]Failure to develop accounts of truth and reference that allow semantic *aboutness* relations to be matters of degree rather than all-or-none remains a large blemish on modern philosophy of language.

and from probabilistic generalities, where the Bayesian model offers guidelines through the fog in which commonsense intuition abandons us.

3. When analyzing data, try to summarize these as conforming to some predictive regularity describable by a small number of parameters within an orderly form such as exemplified by algebraic equations of modest complexity. (By "predictive" I mean that under this regularity, appreciable parts of the data array can be reproduced with decent accuracy from its remainder.) When circumstances permit, it is desirable to perceive this local data pattern as a fragment of patterning more strongly evident, and perhaps more intricate, in the collation of your results with findings by other studies varied in their conditions of observation. And when interpreting that pattern, view these parameters at least provisionally as measuring features of your data's underlying sources. Moreover, when seeking to replicate this pattern—an exceedingly important phase of research practice—under variation in the background constraints whose local constancy has enabled this pattern to become detectable, expect these parameters to emerge as variables that are predictively interrelated with other variables whose local constancy has also been relaxed.

Unpersuaded? Then let me offer another triplet of recommendations, not particularly rooted in what has gone before but focused on how to choose statistics for analysis of sample data.

THE STATISTICAL RELEVANCE PRECEPT: *Make sampling statistics your servant, not your master.* When designing an experiment, or analyzing data already in hand, first of all ask yourself what summary features of these results you would most desire to learn, or would like to see replicated if you have noticed them already, were this data array's sample size so large that any statistics you choose to take from it have essentially zero sampling error. Next, compute the values of these statistics for your sample data and think on how you would provisionally interpret them, either in cognitive inferences or in decisions to act, were you confident that they were population values. Finally, work out some conception of how this putative knowledge of your target population is degraded by the sampling error that statistical theory warns must in fact contaminate your sample statistics to some degree, and think through how that should attenuate your interpretation of these results.

Comments. This precept is neutral on conflicting philosophies of inference. It is your right to highlight a statistic because its value is predicted by a hypothesis this experiment is designed to test, or even, if you insist, to collapse its continuum of metrical alternatives into two or three categories. But if your primary interest shifts adventitiously to a feature of your results not anticipated by any statistical model you had intended to apply (e.g., when a bivariate relation's trend that your preplanned model describes by a linear correlation coefficient appears strongly curved in the data), that too is your right. The precept is also neutral on what may be meant by your statistics' "population values," in particular whether these (a) are abstractions from your data variables' joint frequency distribution in a larger totality of real individuals sampled by your subjects, or (b) are features of a probability distribution over these variables, conditional on a complex P of background properties common to your subjects, that is indifferent to how often P is realized. (These construals of "population" don't really need airing just yet; but your elementary statistics training has so often encouraged you to presume the first view that a caution against complacency in your understanding of this notion seems warranted.)

The precept's second admonition is more devious. It doesn't urge you to draft the journal article or lab report you would produce were your sample size truly enormous, but invites you to try on a frame of mind that frees your statistical thinking from enchantment by the sampling-theoretic tail that far too often wags the data-interpretive dog. Your struggles to master the technicalities of textbook statistics may well have depleted your zeal to question which outputs of their procedures are what you want to learn from your data, especially if you rely on data-analytic computer programs that squeeze numbers out of your raw input by routines whose documentation of algorithm or motivation you do not fully comprehend. Someone has judged these outputs relevant to questions they considered worth asking. But which of them matter for *your* questions? (How long should you treasure the t statistic computed for a mean difference in your data, or search for meaning in the numerical values of ANOVA's F ratios for a sample trend's main and interaction components in preference, say, to graphic comparisons of group means?) You have nothing to gain from concern for a statistic's sampling uncertainty (save to oblige colleagues who want it) if you have little idea of what to do with its population value were you to know that. Beyond that, if the statistics you have selected do indeed seem right for your intended interpretation, how precise a determination of their population values would your interpretation be able to exploit? (Might information just that they lie in one broad region of possible values rather than another be all the detail that you can use?) The point of asking is not to justify a needlessly sloppy report, nor even to take comfort in current tolerances for imperfect accuracy, but to think on this experiment's position in the larger scheme of work underway on its topic. If you don't know how interpretation of your chosen statistics could profit from learning their precise population values, shouldn't you be trying to develop a conception of your inquiry's target that does?

The precept's third admonition prompts two closing considerations, one tactical and the other strategic. Tactically, left to your own devices you would undoubtedly be at a loss to put much precision into your spread of subjective uncertainty about the population values of statistics you have sample-estimated. But through the logic of deriving particularized *if/thens* and consequent *Since/therefores* from probabilistic generalities, sampling-theoretic *confidence intervals* for your sample-statistics' population values give you near-unconditional posterior credibilities which, after some fine-tuning for which you may feel need,[34] may well be about as good as your rationally disciplined uncertainty about population statistics can get. To be sure, such posterior statistical confidences are conditional on the idealized premises of the statistical model under which they have been computed. And my fine-tuning qualification acknowledges the broader point, about inference to particulars from probabilistic generalities, that the strength of your *c-is-B* belief channeled from your *c-is-A* conviction through the *if/then* conduit set up by your confidence that $\Pr(B \mid A) \approx r$ may well be modulated by other things you also believe about object *c*. (Thus when you as fictional archeologist became convinced of generality (13.29), and at first provisionally concluded that your chance of getting *Q*d were you to *T* was near .24, you downshifted this to lower risk when you came to suspect that air contaminants were the main source of this statistic and planned to *T* only briefly while holding your breath.) Alternatively, if fine-tuned confidence intervals are not to your taste, you can estimate Bayesian posterior credibilities for your statistics' population values by computational procedures detailed in the technical literature. Except when confirming results from previous samples from what you are confident is the same population, this should seldom differ enough from your spread of uncertainty framed by confidence intervals to make any practical difference.

Strategically, however, efforts to be precise in our uncertainty about a sample statistic's population value are often pointless. The reason is a dirty little secret: We seldom have much clue to the identity of this population or for that matter any good reason to think of it as unique. According to statistical theory, probabilities in a mathematically structured system thereof are always conditional on one or another configuration *P* of population-defining properties variously described as preconditions, background constraints, local constancies, or other phrases similarly connoting limitation. In principle any simple or complex property can play this role: Whenever we envision a probability distribution $\{\Pr(A_i)\}$ over an array $A = \{A_i\}$ of attributes, we can always think of some con-

---

[34]Notably, when the interiors of some confidence intervals include regions of the real-number continuum wherein the statistic at issue cannot lie, for example, negative values for variance ratios.

straint P such that each $Pr(A_i)$ is really $Pr(A_i \mid P)$, whereas for any A in $\mathbf{A}$ the restriction of $Pr(\ )$ to $Pr_A = Pr(\ \mid A)$ defines what can be treated as an ostensively unconditional probability distribution over the more restricted population $P \cdot A$. When the probability calculus is applied to sample data comprising an array of attributes distributed over a set $\mathbf{s}$ of subjects, its "population" provision is interpreted as some conjunction P of properties, common to all the members of $\mathbf{s}$,[35] which statistics jargon treats as a population from which $\mathbf{s}$ is a "sample." But enormously many different populations are sampled by $\mathbf{s}$: In addition to common properties $\{P_i\}$ expressible by various logical compounds of the predicates used to describe subjects in our data records, the members of $\mathbf{s}$ share numerous additional properties $\{P_j'\}$ that we could have put on record but didn't, and uncountably many more $\{P_k''\}$ that we couldn't have ascertained at all, especially the ones of which we currently have no conception; and every conjunction $P_i \cdot P_j' \cdot P_k''$ of these is also a population sampled by $\mathbf{s}$. So when we talk about population values of statistics computed from the $\mathbf{s}$-data, which population do we have in mind? This wouldn't matter if our sample statistics at issue had the same population value in each of these, but of course that is wildly untrue. Is there something sufficiently distinctive about one of these to qualify it as *the* population relative to which $\mathbf{s}$-sample statistics have population values? The most logical candidate, the conjunction of all $\mathbf{s}$-shared properties, is a non-starter; for that includes being a member of $\mathbf{s}$, leaving no room to generalize. Another contender, motivated by sampling theory's yen for "random" sampling, is the P from which $\mathbf{s}$'s sampling is most nearly random. But even if we had a concept of random sampling that is not largely vacuous,[36] it would not define an

---

[35]"Common to all" doesn't preclude fine differences in what is said to be in common: For example, the members of a group of preschool children all share the property of being younger than six years (or some other upper bound) even when their exact ages are all different.

[36]The problem with this notion is not so much *random* as its coupling with *sample*. A random *variable* is just a scientific variable (dimension of attribute alternatives) over whose values we have posited a probability distribution conditional on some background condition. And in its original conception, a "random sample" is a set of things picked from a larger set S of real objects by a procedure under which each subset of S of given size has the same probability of selection. But what could it mean to sample randomly from a population-defining *property* that is indifferent to the prevalence or identities of its instances? The best prospect for extending the original selection-from-S sense of this to an open population P is to say that a set $\mathbf{s}$ of P-things is a "random" sample from P if the procedure by which $\mathbf{s}$ has been picked imposes an additional constraint C such that the probability distribution in $P \cdot C$ of certain distinguished variables has special stipulated features (e.g., equiprobability of all their values). But this prospect is highly programmatic: It would at best yield many different types of random sampling whose motivation remains obscure; and in any case, to my knowledge neither this nor any other approach to

effective criterion by which we can plausibly judge, from all we know about some other individual *i* not in **s**, whether *i* too is in this population most randomly sampled by **s**.

Note: For simplicity, I have put the population problem in terms of properties common to all individuals in a data collection's subject sample **s**. But preconditions of generalization also come in more complicated versions that incur correspondingly more complicated indeterminacies of population identity, especially when distributions of independent variables and statistics conditional on particular values thereof are at issue. To a large extent these can with some artifice be treated as special cases of the simple version. For example, each value of an independent variable is a property common to a subset of **s** that samples a subpopulation of any population sampled by **s**. And by viewing **s** as a single entity of which our individual sample subjects are parts, we can include holistic properties of **s**, such as the frequency distribution of an independent variable, in the defining features of a population of sets from which **s** is a sample of size 1. Even so, these more elaborate sample features contributing to population indeterminacy warrant explicit recognition because they underlie important operational issues of research design, notably an experiment's "controls."

Let's approach this problem from another direction. Given our sample statistics and an inventory of all the properties we know to be shared by our sample subjects **s**, how do we judge whether a statistic's value computed from the **s**-data should well-approximate the value of that same statistic in another group **s′** of individuals whose scores on the relevant variables are still unknown? In practice, we base such judgments on the similarity of properties shared in **s′** to the ones shared in **s**. But we don't include all the latter in this appraisal because in the first place we don't know most of them, and secondly don't think that all the ones we do know are relevant. We believe—never mind why, though there is much to say—that some **s**-shared properties made a difference for the **s**-data's statistics whereas others didn't matter, and that if **s′** too shares all the former then, regardless of what happens in **s′** on the latter, the statistics observed in **s** should well-approximate the corresponding statistics in **s′** so long as sample sizes are respectable. But we are also pretty sure that relevant/irrelevant here does not coincide with known/unknown. So even if most of the known **s**-shared properties are also common to **s′**, statistics from **s** may not generalize to **s′** very well if **s′** lacks some of the **s**-shared properties relevant to those statistics, whereas these statistics may generalize nicely to an **s′** lacking some **s**-shared

---

defining random samples from open populations has been advocated in the statistical literature. Old-style random sampling from extant totalities continues to have applications value—for example, in demographic surveys, quality-control batch testing, and assigning research subjects to treatment groups—but its scope is quite limited.

properties if those happen to be irrelevant. How we manage to learn which features of our data's background constancies make a difference, and what differences they make, are matters for a treatise on experimental design, not closing thoughts. The closing point to be taken here is simply that it makes little sense to fret over how closely our sample statistics approach their population values until we have made an honest effort to say *what* population, and to identify that in terms of properties we have reason to believe really matter. Meanwhile, you can't go wrong by heeding *Steiger's Maxim*:

> An ounce of replication is worth a ton of inferential statistics.
>
> (Steiger, 1990, p. 176).

REFERENCES

Brackman, A. C. (1976). *The search for the gold of Tutankhamen*. New York: Mason/Charter.

Carroll, L. (1898). What the tortoise said to Achilles. *Mind, 4,* 278–280.

Chihara, C. S. (1994). The Howson-Urback proofs of Bayesian principles. In E. Eells, & B. Skyrms (Eds.), *Probability and conditionals* (pp. 161–178). London: Cambridge University Press.

Chisholm, R. M., & Swartz, R. J. (Eds.) (1973). *Empirical knowledge*. Englewood Cliffs, N.J.: Prentice-Hall.

Cohen, J. (1994). The earth is round (*p* < .05). *American Psychologist, 49,* 997–1003.

Eells, E., & Skyrms, B. (Eds.). (1994). *Probability and conditionals*. London: Cambridge University Press.

Hacking, I. (1975). *The emergence of probability*. London: Cambridge University Press.

Hanson, N. R. (1958). *Patterns of discovery*. London: Cambridge University Press.

Harman, G. (1965). The inference to the best explanation. *Philosophical Review, 74,* 88–95.

Hartshorne, C., & Weiss, P. (Eds.). (1934). *Collected papers of Charles Sanders Peirce* (Vols. 1–5). Cambridge, MS.: Harvard University Press.

Hoving, T. (1978). *Tutankhamun the untold story*. New York: Simon & Schuster.

Howson, C., & Franklin, A. (1994). Bayesian conditionalization and probability kinematics. *British Journal for the Philosophy of Science, 45,* 451–466.

Howson, C., & Urbach, P. M. (1993). *Scientific reasoning: The Bayesian approach* (2nd ed.). La Salle, IL: Open Court.

Jeffrey, R. C. (1965). *The logic of decision.* New York: McGraw-Hill.

Josephson, J. R., & Josephson, S. G. (1994). *Abductive inference.* Cambridge, England: Cambridge University Press.

Kim, J. (1993). *Supervenience and mind.* Cambridge, England: Cambridge University Press.

Langley, P., Simon, H. A., Bradshaw, G. L., & Zytkow, J. M. (1987). *Scientific Discovery.* Cambridge, MS.: MIT Press.

Magie, W. E. (1965). *A source book in physics.* Cambridge, MS.: Harvard University Press.

McCrae, R. R., & Costa, P. T. Jr. (1995). Trait explanations in personality theory. *European Journal of Personality, 9,* 231–252.

Moore, E. C. (ed.) (1984). *Writings of Charles S. Peirce* (Vol. 2). Bloomington: Indiana University Press.

Partington, J. R. (1965). *A history of chemistry* (Vol. 2). London: Macmillan. (Originally published 1935)

Popper, K. R. (1959). *The logic of scientific discovery* (2nd ed.). London: Hutchinson & Co.

Rozeboom, W. W. (1961). Ontological induction and the logical typology of scientific variables. *Philosophy of Science, 28,* 337–377.

Rozeboom, W. W. (1965). Linear correlations between sets of variables. *Psychometrika, 30,* 57–71.

Rozeboom, W. W. (1970). The art of metascience; or, what should a psychological theory be? In J. R. Royce (Ed.), *Toward unification in psychology* (pp. 54–160). Toronto: Toronto University Press.

Rozeboom, W. W. (1972a). Problems in the psycho-philosophy of knowledge. In J. R. Royce & W. W. Rozeboom (Eds.), *The psychology of knowing* (pp. 25–93). New York: Gordon & Breach.

Rozeboom, W. W. (1972b). Scientific inference: The myth and the reality. In S. R. Brown, & D. J. Brenner (Eds.), *Science, psychology, and communication: Essays honoring William Stephenson* (pp. 95–118). New York: Columbia University Press.

Rozeboom, W. W. (1984). Dispositions do explain; or, picking up the pieces after Hurricane Walter. In *Annals of theoretical psychology* (Vol. 1, pp. 205–223). New York: Plenum.

Salmon, W. C. (1966). *The foundations of scientific inference.* Pittsburgh: University of Pittsburgh Press.

Simon, H. A. (1973). Does scientific discovery have a logic? *Philosophy of Science, 40*, 471–480.

Steiger, J. H. (1990). Structural model evaluation and modification: an interval estimation approach. *Multivariate Behavioral Research, 25,* 173–180.

Tuomela, R. (Ed.). (1977). *Dispositions.* Dordrecht, Netherlands: D. Reidel Publishing Co.

van Fraassen, B. C. (1989). *Laws and symmetry.* Oxford, England: Clarendon.

Chapter 14

The Problem Is Epistemology, Not Statistics: Replace Significance Tests by Confidence Intervals and Quantify Accuracy of Risky Numerical Predictions

Paul E. Meehl

University of Minnesota

Significance tests have a role to play in social science research but their current widespread use in appraising theories is often harmful. The reason for this lies not in the mathematics but in social scientists' poor understanding of the logical relation between theory and fact, that is, a methodological or epistemological unclarity. Theories entail observations, not conversely. Although a theory's success in deriving a fact tends to corroborate it, this corroboration is weak unless the fact has a very low prior probability and there are few possible alternative theories. The fact of a nonzero difference or correlation, such as we infer by refuting the null hypothesis, does not have such a low probability because in social science everything correlates with almost everything else, theory aside. In the "strong" use of significance tests, the theory predicts a numerical point value, or narrow range, so the hypothesis test subjects the theory to a grave risk of being falsified if it is objectively incorrect. In general, setting up a confidence interval is preferable, being more informative and entailing null hypothesis refutation if a difference falls outside the interval. Significance tests are usually more defensible in technological contexts (e.g., evaluating an intervention) than for theory appraisal. It would be helpful to have a quantitative index of how closely a theory comes to correctly predicting a risky fact, and one such index is proposed. Unlike widespread current practice, statistics texts and lecturers should clarify and emphasize the large semantic (logical) gap between a substantive (causal, compositional) theory and a statistical hypothesis about a population parameter that is derivable from the theory but does not derive it.

Any rational evaluation of the significance test controversy must begin by clarifying the *aim* of inferential statistics. The mathematics is usually quite rigorous or can be made so if desired; hence, dispute between "schools of statistics," or between critics and defenders of the conventional significance test procedure, is unlikely to concern the formalism, but instead involves some question of concept formation, epistemology, or context. This chapter considers (without claiming to settle) when it is and is not appropriate to use null hypothesis tests, examines some complexities we face when doing research in the social and life sciences, and suggests a corroboration index that may be useful in appraising theories. I emphasize the methodological and epistemological questions as being more important than the purely "statistical" ones that are conventionally stressed.

TECHNOLOGICAL VERSUS THEORETICAL CONTEXTS

The first distinction to make is that between the use of significance tests (or proposed alternatives) in a *technological* versus a *theoretical* context. Making this initial distinction does not presuppose that the succeeding analysis will reveal an important difference. It merely follows the sociologists' methodological principle that one should initially disaggregate, leaving open the possibility of reaggregation if the subdivision turns out not to matter; whereas, if one begins by aggregation, one may be throwing away important information that is not recapturable. It is a defect of statistics texts and classroom teachers of statistics that the division between technological and theoretical tasks is almost never made explicitly and, if made, is not examined in detail.

Beginning with technology, we have two broad kinds of questions: those dealing with purely *predictive* tasks (e.g., can the Minnesota Multiphasic Personality Inventory [MMPI] predict suicide risk better than the Rorschach?) and *intervention* problems (e.g., does a certain psychotropic drug help depressed patients more than cognitive psychotherapy?). Discerning no relevant difference between these two pragmatic tasks, I consider only intervention. (The predictive task is always a component of the intervention-appraisal task, because the latter compares outcome probabilities associated with interventions, including "doing nothing.") Depending on the utilities and disutilities (e.g., probability of death from an illness), it may be that inferring *any* influence, however small, from a certain intervention is so important that we would want to know about it. For example, I recently came down with *subacute bacterial endocarditis*, an infective lesion of the heart valve leaflets, which has around a 15% mortality rate (100% prior to antibiotics). Because the infective organism in my case was *Streptococcus viridans*, the antibiotics used were gentamicin and ceftriaxone. Doubtless the choice of antibiotics was based on comparative research, and the superiority of these two drugs in treating this grave illness may have been slight, although statistically significant. But when I am the patient, I care about even small differences in therapeutic efficacy among the antibiotics that might be used. However, if there were powerful counterconsiderations such as side effects, amount of discomfort, danger, time required, or even cost, then the size of a therapeutic difference might matter to the patient, the insurance company, and the physician. Even an alteration in life and death probabilities, if minuscule but involving a hundred times more expensive procedure, might affect some persons' willingness to accept a slightly higher risk.

What is the role of conventional significance testing in this technological context? One easy and obvious answer (which may be the right one, for all I know) is that the proper statistical procedure is to set up a confidence interval. Its protagonists argue that, if this interval is known with a specified probability, the null hypothesis H_0: $\delta = (\mu_1 - \mu_2) = 0$ either falls inside the confidence interval or falls outside of it; thus any practical question answered by a significance test also is answered by establishing a confidence belt, and the latter is more quantitatively informative. Everyone agrees that the formalism is identical for the two procedures, it being just a question of moving the denominator $SE_{\bar{d}}$ of a t test to the other side of the inequality for a confidence interval. When the difference in utilities of the two kinds of errors is sufficiently large, it has been cogently argued (e.g., by Simon, 1945) that it may be rational simply to look for the existence of an observed difference as to direction, because the observed difference between two means is an unbiased and maximum likelihood estimator of the true difference. Whatever may be the values of the two kinds of errors in a significance test, the best bet is that δ has the same algebraic sign as the observed $\bar{d}$. (I should mention here that I am not a subjectivist Bayesian, and my discussion throughout postulates the existence of objective probabilities, whether they are physical frequencies or "rational, inductive logic" epistemic supports. Quantifiable or not, some claims of strong evidentiary support are wrong, e.g., astrology. That vexed issue is beyond the scope of this chapter.)

We all learned from Fisher that you cannot prove H_0 but you can (almost!) refute it. Although this is correct as a mathematical truth, the unelaborated assertion can be misleading. In practical contexts, when we have sufficient power $(1 - \beta)$ so that there is not too big an asymmetry in the values of error rates α and β, we do want to make the "quasi-null" inference, not that H_0 as a precise point value is literally true, but that something close to it is. If we were to scrupulously refrain from saying anything like that, why would we be doing a significance test in the pragmatic context? The clinician's conclusion from a failure to refute H_0 (given high power) is: "These drugs do not differ (at all, or appreciably, or enough to matter), so I can use either—selected randomly or by other considerations (e.g., cost)." This point holds for both technological and theoretical uses of the significance test.

If we consider all of the statistical inferences or pragmatic "decisions" that an investigator makes in the course of a research career, conclusions that a parameter θ lies within a confidence interval $[l_1, l_2]$ based on $(1 - \alpha)$ will err in α

proportion of the occasions. Unless I am mistaken, this statement is correct regardless of where one stands on the controversy between Bayesians, Fisherians, Neyman–Pearsonites, and pure-likelihood people. I have heard statisticians explain patiently to psychologists that "δ has the value it has, so no 'probability' applies." Common as this remark is and plausible as it sounds, I think it is a mistake. Any application of a probability number involves, one way or another, what Reichenbach (1938) called a *posit*, employing that number to decide how we should think or act about the instant case. If there is *no* intelligible sense in which a *p* value "applies" to a particular instance, on the philosophical or metaphysical ground that the parameter we are interested in has objectively a certain definite value (although unknown to us), it is unclear why anybody would engage in significance testing or confidence belt estimation. Suppose I am asked to wager whether a thrown pair of dice will turn up a deuce. If the dice are not loaded and the shaking is thorough and fair, any statistician—of whatever "school"—would say it is reasonable to accept a bet on a deuce with odds of 1:6, and it would surely be advantageous to accept a wager if the house offered me, say, 7:1 odds. Assume I am a betting person, happy with those benevolent odds, and believe the house is honest. Would it matter whether I am to bet (a) before the dice are shaken, (b) while the shaking is going on, or (c) after the shaking is concluded but the cup is still inverted so we cannot see how the dice have in fact come up? I do not think any reasonable person would care to distinguish among these three cases as concerns personal betting.

Depending on whether you are a strict determinist at the macro level (cf. Earman, 1986), you could say that it was already determined how the dice would land before the shaking begins; but whether you are a determinist or not is irrelevant here. As long as I have not looked at the dice, what odds it is reasonable for me to take are unaltered by the meta-comment, "It doesn't make sense to talk about the *probability* of a deuce, because we have stopped shaking the dice and either there is a deuce under the cup or there isn't." Furthermore, the argument that if something is objectively the case (although unknown to us), therefore, it is meaningless to talk about probabilities would apply equally strongly whether we are dealing with a problem of estimation or a problem of significance.

I think the confusion here comes from failure to make Carnap's (1945) distinction between the two kinds of probability. Probability$_1$ is *epistemic*, the assertion of it takes place in the metalanguage, its subject matter is "inductive logic," and it is about someone's state of knowledge, about the relation of evidence to a probandum. Probability$_2$ is a relative frequency; the assertion of it occurs in the object language (e.g., of physics, genetics, psychometrics). There is usually no practicable algorithm for computing probability$_1$. That is why scientific judgments or judgments in courts of law or in ordinary life allow a certain leeway within the domain of the rational. Whether an algorithm for inductive inference in complex cases (such as the evidence that Jones committed the murder) can ever be formulated is in doubt, but most logicians and philosophers of science think not, and I tend to agree.

It is tempting to conflate the inference relation between statistics and parameters with the relation between accepted parameter values and the substantive theory; and because the former is numerified (e.g., a Bayesian posterior, a confidence belt, a significance level), one tends to think the latter is numerified also, or (somehow) *should* be. For example, evolutionary theorists cite evidence from the facts of geographical distribution (Darwin's original basis), embryology, comparative anatomy, paleontology, and so on. Some of these fact domains are analyzed statistically, and recently available DNA comparisons are intrinsically statistical. Each of these diverse databases is capable of yielding *numbers*, quantifying various probability$_2$ values concerning their respective concepts. But suppose one then asks, "What is the scientific probability of the neo-Darwinian theory based on this heterogeneous body of empirical evidence?" Nobody has the faintest idea how to calculate a *numerical value* of $p_1(T \mid p_{2i}, p_{2j}, p_{2k} \ldots)$, an epistemic probability, not a physical relative frequency. The only probability number some might write for $p_1(T \mid e)$ is a human knower's strength of belief in T given evidence e, a "subjective probability" expressing that individual's betting odds.

However, in dealing with empirical investigations that permit specification of a physical model (events, persons, fruit flies, attributes) to which the formalism applies, although usually somewhat idealized and hence numerically only approximate, these two probabilities—one epistemic and one physical, one about the state of the human knower and one about the state of the external world—may be the same or very close. If I say that the objective statistical frequency of throwing a deuce is approximately .028, and I accept the proposition that unbiased dice are being thoroughly shaken and fairly thrown, then that same probability$_2$ number can be reasonably used to refer to my state of knowledge of the external world and, further, to warrant my accepting the corresponding betting odds. So it is quite appropriate in the pragmatic context to talk about probabilities despite one's belief—sometimes near certainty—that there is such and such an objective state of affairs that is at the time of betting (or choosing a treatment, or whatever) not directly known to us.

Significance tests are appropriate in technological contexts, such as evaluating the efficacy of interventions, but setting up confidence intervals is preferable. In scientific communication, authors should always present confidence intervals, so that readers who prefer them will have the information they desire without depriving the significance testers of what they want to know. I consider it atrocious malcommunication for psychologists to publish tables that do not even give the value of t or F, let alone the means and standard deviations for their data, and who only state whether or not significance was achieved at a given level (hence the "tabular asterisks" in Meehl, 1978). It forces the reader who wants to know, for example, the approximate overlap or the mean separation in relation to the standard deviations to do computations that the author should have done and the editor should have required.

THEORY APPRAISAL

Theory "appraisal" is preferable to theory "testing" because the latter phrase is too specifically tied to Sir Karl Popper's philosophy of science. The arguments I make here do not depend on the reader's sharing my neo-Popperian sympathies. Before getting to the role of statistics, we have to be clear about the sheer logic of appraising a scientific theory. It is always more complicated than most college professors make it sound. Adopting the following convenient notation (Meehl, 1978, 1990a):

T: Main substantive theory of interest;

A_x: Auxiliary theories relied on in the experiment;

C_p: *Ceteris paribus* clause ("other things being equal");

A_i: Instrumental auxiliaries (devices relied on for control and observation);

C_n: Realized particulars (conditions were as the experimenter reported);

O_1,   Observations or statistical summaries of observations;
O_2:

then the logical structure of a test of a theory is the conceptual formula:

$$(T \cdot A_x \cdot C_p \cdot A_i \cdot C_n) \vdash (O_1 \supset O_2)$$

where dots " · " are conjunctions ("and"), turnstile " $\vdash$ " is deductive derivability (entailment, "follows that . . ."), and the horseshoe " $\supset$ " is the material conditional ("If . . . then . . .").

The first thing to be clear about is that, given this structure, a "successful outcome" of the experiment obviously cannot clinch the truth of the theory T, even if all of the other components are granted, because the argument is in the logical form: "If p, then q; q; therefore, p." In deductive logic, there are four possible inference patterns when we say "If p, then q," and these are shown in Table 14.1. Treated as if it were a deductive inference, the theory appraisal formula is in the third figure of the mixed hypothetical syllogism, which is formally invalid, the

TABLE 14.1

Deductive Inference Possibilities for the Hypothetical Argument: If p, then q

Figure	Form	Name	Conclusion
I	If p then q p $\therefore q$	Modus ponens ("Establishing mode")	Valid
II	If p then q $\sim p$ $\therefore \sim q$	Denying the antecedent	Invalid
III	If p then q q $\therefore p$	Affirming the consequent	Invalid
IV	If p then q $\sim q$ $\therefore \sim p$	Modus tollens ("Destroying mode")	Valid

formal fallacy called "affirming the consequent." It affirms the consequent (q) and concludes that the antecedent (p) is true. Unfortunately, it is the form of all scientific inference aimed at supporting a theory by verifying its observational consequences. (This is what led to the famous witticism by eminent philosopher of science Morris R. Cohen, "All logic texts are divided into two parts. In the first half, on deductive logic, the fallacies are explained. In the second half, on inductive logic, they are committed.")

Notice that this occurs at two levels in the appraisal formula: It holds for the term on the right-hand side of the formula ($O_1 \supset O_2$); and it is a problem when we consider the formula as a whole, where the conjunction on the left entails the argument on the right. The difference is that the material conditional ($O_1 \supset O_2$) is *truth-functional*; it depends solely on the pattern of truth and falsity of the propositions and has nothing to do with their semantic content; "If Nixon is honest, I'll eat my hat," is a common-discourse example of the material conditional. Deductive entailment, symbolized by the turnstile ("$\vdash$"), hinges on the meaning and structure of the theoretical system we are investigating; if there were no theory, there would be no *reason* for expecting the O_1, O_2 conditional on the right.

It is this irksome truth of formal logic that gives rise to what philosophers call Hume's problem, or the problem of induction. Likewise, it was this "scandal" that led Sir Karl Popper to say that we can never *justify* scientific theories, we can only make efforts to *refute* them. The conceptual formula for appraising a theory says: From the *conjunction* of the theory of interest *and* auxiliary theories that we rely on *and* all other things being equal *and* auxiliaries with respect to the instruments we use *and* conditions having been correctly reported, it follows that *if* we do (or observe) O_1, *then* O_2 will be observed. If O_1 and O_2 are observed, the right-hand conditional $(O_1 \supset O_2)$ is satisfied, so the experiment "came out right" (i.e., as the theory predicted). If O_1 is observed but O_2 is not, we have $(O_1 \cdot {\sim}O_2)$ factually, falsifying the conditional $(O_1 \supset O_2)$, and thereby falsifying the left-hand conjunction. This inference is in the fourth figure of the syllogism; it is a valid logical form, the medieval logicians' *modus tollens* ("destroying mode"), made a byword of metatheory by Popper's emphasis on it as the basic testing process of science (O'Hear, 1980; Popper, 1934/1959, 1962, 1983; Schilpp, 1974). When strong efforts to refute a theory continue to fail so that the theory is not killed, we should not say it is confirmed or supported, but simply that it has, so far, survived tests. For the survival of tests, Popper used the word *corroborated*. Whether his is a thoroughly adequate analysis is beyond the scope of this chapter, so I confine myself to saying that the Popperian analysis in a pure form has, as yet, not seemed persuasive to the majority of philosophers of science, and I feel confident in saying it has not been accepted by most working scientists, although of course neither of these two failures to convert shows that Popper is wrong. The important point is that this state of affairs is not a matter of one's preferred philosophy of science, but it is a matter of formal logic.

In addition to that formal fallacy, the structure of the appraisal formula has regrettable methodological consequences that are not matters of taste or philosophy of science (such as whether one is a realist or an instrumentalist or a fictionist, or whether one is a Popperian or an inductivist, or any of these interesting disputes), but also are a matter of formal logic. The negation of a conjunction is formally equivalent to the disjunction of the negations. Thus, having observed O_1, when we observe the falsification of O_2, then the falsified truth functional relation represented by the horseshoe in $(O_1 \supset O_2)$ falsifies the conjunction on the left. But,

$$\sim(T \cdot A_x \cdot C_p \cdot A_i \cdot C_n) \equiv \sim T \vee \sim A_x \vee \sim C_p \vee \sim A_i \vee \sim C_n$$

where " $\vee$ " means "or." Thus, although we intended to appraise only the main substantive theory T, what we have done is to falsify the *conjunction*; so all we can say "for sure" is that *either* the theory is false, *or* the auxiliary theory is false, *or* the instrumental auxiliary is false, *or* the *ceteris paribus* clause is false, *or* the particulars alleged by the experimenter are false. How confident we can be about the falsification of the theory of interest hinges upon our confidence in the truth of the other components of the conjunction.

To think clearly about this, one must recognize the distinction between the *substantive theory* T (causal, or compositional, or both) being appraised and some *statistical hypothesis* H^* that supposedly flows from it. Hardly any statistics textbooks and, so far as I have been able to find out, hardly any statistics or psychology professors lecturing on this process bother to make that distinction, let alone emphasize it. A substantive causal theory, such as Festinger's theory of cognitive dissonance or Meehl's theory of schizotaxia, consists of a set of statements about theoretical entities that are causally connected in certain ways, and these statements are *never* equivalent to a mere assertion about such and such a population parameter. Despite this obvious conceptual difference between T and H^*, there is an almost irresistible temptation to move from a small p value in a significance test, via a high confidence that H^*: $\delta > 0$, to a (similarly high) confidence that the substantive theory T (which entailed that nonzero directional δ) is true, or at least has high verisimilitude. The trouble is that the directional nonzero δ can be derived from other theories than T, and in the "soft" areas of psychology a sizable number of those competing theories have plausibility.

An Example of Theory Appraisal. How would the theory appraisal formula apply in a research situation? To illustrate briefly, suppose we wish to test Meehl's theory that schizophrenia is the decompensated form of schizotaxia, a neurological disorder due to an autosomal dominant gene (see, e.g., Meehl, 1990d). Examining clinically normal parent pairs of carefully diagnosed schizophrenic probands, we predict that the parent showing "soft" neurological signs (e.g., SPEM eye-tracking anomaly, adiadochokinesia) will have a higher MMPI schizotypy score than the neurologically normal parent. The logical structure, much abbreviated here, reads:

T (theory of interest):	Meehl's schizotaxia dominant gene theory.
A_x (auxiliary theory):	For example, most schizotypes are not decompensated, they appear "normal."
C_p (*ceteris paribus*):	No other factor (e.g., test anxiety in parents worried about their own mental health) exerts an appreciable influence to obfuscate the main effect.
A_i (instrumental auxiliary):	For example, the MMPI is valid for psychological schizotypy; the soft signs are valid for schizotaxia.
C_n (realized particulars):	For example, the probands were correctly diagnosed in accordance with *Diagnostic and Statistical Manual* (*DSM*) criteria, as alleged.

O_1 (first observation):   Subset S_1 of parents have soft neurology pattern and spouses do not.

O_2 (second observation):   Subset S_1 of parents each have MMPI score > spouse.

If we had no theory (Meehl's or some other, competing one) there would be *no reason* for expecting that the higher MMPI-scoring spouse would have difficulty tracking a moving visual target (the SPEM eye-tracking anomaly). If the conditional $(O_1 \supset O_2)$ is empirically verified as predicted, we have corroborated T. If not, if we find factually that $(O_1 \cdot \sim O_2)$, T has been discorroborated. How strongly, either way, depends on how much confidence we have in the left-hand conjuncts other than T. Corroboration and discorroboration are matters of degree.

THE CRUD FACTOR

The causal and compositional structure of mind and society (including biological matters like genetics) being what they are, almost all of the variables that we measure are correlated to some extent. In the behavioral sciences, the saying "everything correlates with everything," gives rise to what David Lykken has termed the *crud factor* (Meehl, 1990e). Some readers have taken Lykken and me to be referring to the crud factor as a source of random sampling error, and therefore somehow connected with the values α, β or their ratio, hence correctable by refining the statistics, converting to Bayesianism, or some other statistical ploy. This is a complete misunderstanding of our position. *The term "crud factor" does not refer to statistical error, whether of the first or the second kind.* The crud factor consists of the objectively real causal connections and resulting statistical correlations that we would know with numerical precision if we always had large enough samples (e.g., a billion cases) or if we had measured all of the members of the specified population so that no sampling errors (but only errors of measurement) remained. In purely correlational studies, the crud factor is ubiquitous. In experimental studies, where we randomly impose a manipulation, the true $\delta = \mu_1 - \mu_2$ or ρ may be zero. If so, the class of explanatory theories usually will be smaller; but the non-null relation is still not semantically equivalent to the substantive theory that entails it. (Lykken and I disagree about the pervasity of crud factor in controlled experiments.)

The ubiquitous crud factor in social science is what *empirically* corresponds to the *formal* invalidity of the third figure of the implicative syllogism (see Table 14.1). The whole class of theories that could explain an experimental finding is what makes it impossible to deduce T from the "successful" observational outcome. This is a logician's or an epistemologist's problem; it is not a statistician's problem in the sense of something answerable by proving theorems in the formalism. Thinking of the class of substantive theories T, T', T'', . . . that could occur on the left of our appraisal formula as, say, a set of subject populations from which our sample could have been drawn, or a set of frequency distributions having various parameters μ, μ', μ'', . . . , σ, σ', σ'', . . ., is a totally wrong-headed notion. These hypothetical populations are what the *statistical hypotheses H, H', H'', . . .* are about. These *H*s are numerical consequences of the substantive *T*s, not their semantic equivalents. This is most clearly seen if we suppose the sign of δ to be known for sure, that is, as if $\alpha = \beta = 0$. In that epistemically delightful circumstance, *what does the investigator know* about the truth of *T*? The investigator clearly does not know for sure that *T* is correct, and this would be the case even if all of the other conjuncts on the left hand of the theory appraisal formula were known for certain. Critiques of null hypothesis testing (e.g., Bakan, 1966; Carver, 1978; Cohen, 1994; Hogben, 1968; Lykken, 1968; Meehl, 1967, 1978, 1990a; Morrison & Henkel, 1970; Rozeboom, 1960; Schmidt, 1996) are not primarily aimed at the two kinds of errors discussed in statistics books, and their criticisms cannot be rebutted by manipulation of the formalism.

I said that the crud factor principle is the concrete empirical form, realized in the sciences, of the logician's formal point that the third figure of the implicative (mixed hypothetical) syllogism is invalid, the error in purported deductive reasoning termed affirming the consequent. Speaking methodologically, in the language of working scientists, what it comes to is that there are quite a few alternative theories T', T'', T''', . . . (in addition to the theory of interest T) that are each capable of deriving as a consequence the statistical counternull hypothesis H^*: $\delta = (\mu_1 - \mu_2) > 0$, or, if we are correlating quantitative variables, that $\rho > 0$. We might imagine (Meehl, 1990e) a big pot of variables and another (not so big but still sizable) pot of substantive causal theories in a specified research domain (e.g., schizophrenia, social perception, maze learning in the rat). We fantasize an experimenter choosing elements from these two pots randomly in picking something to study to get a publication. (We might impose a restriction that the variables have some conceivable relation to the domain being investigated, but such a constraint should be interpreted very broadly. We cannot, e.g., take it for granted that eye color will be unrelated to liking introspective psychological novels, because there is evidence that Swedes tend to be more introverted than Irish or Italians.) Our experimenter picks a pair of variables randomly out of the first pot, and a substantive causal theory randomly out of the second pot, and then randomly assigns an algebraic sign to the variables' relation, saying, "H^*: $\rho > 0$, if theory T is true." In this crazy example there is no semantic-logical-mathematical relation deriving H^* from T, but we pretend there is. Because H_0 is quasi-always false, the counternull hypothesis $\sim H_0$ is quasi-always true. Assume perfect statistical power, so that when H_0 is false we shall be sure of refuting it. Given the arbitrary assignment of direction, the directional counternull H^* will be proved half the time; that is, our experiment will "come out right" (i.e., as pseudo-predicted from theory T) half the time. This means we will be getting what purports to be a "confirmation" of T 10 times as often as the significance level $\alpha = .05$ would suggest. This does *not* mean there is anything wrong with the significance test mathematics; it merely means that the odds of getting a confirmatory result (absent our theory) cannot be equated with the odds given by the t table, because those odds are based on the assumption of a true zero difference. There is nothing mathematically complicated about this, and it is a mistake to focus one's attention on the mathematics of t, F, chi-square, or whatever statistic is being employed. The population from which we are drawing is specified by variables chosen from the first pot, and one can think of that population as an element of a superpopulation of variable pairs that is gigantic in size but finite, just as the population, however large, of theories defined as those that human beings will be able to construct before the sun burns out is finite. The methodological point is that T has not passed a severe test (speaking Popperian), the "successful" experimental outcome does not constitute what philosopher Wesley Salmon called a "strange coincidence" (Meehl, 1990a, 1990b; Nye, 1972; Salmon, 1984), because with high power T has almost an even chance of doing that, *absent any logical connection whatever between the variables and the theory.*

Some have objected that the crud factor is not ubiquitous, or that it is usually negligible in size, so that H_0 is "almost true" in most psychological research. If the latter line of reasoning is adopted, one is now asking not whether $\delta = 0$, but what is δ's numerical nonzero value; and one should either restate the nonzero *numerical value* of the counternull H^* that "should rationally count" as a corroborator of the theory or use a confidence interval. I have been surprised to find psychologists seriously maintaining that H_0 is likely to be literally true in correlational studies in the "soft" areas of psychology (clinical, counseling, developmental, personality, and social psychology). It seems obvious on theoretical as well as common-sense grounds that the point value $\delta = 0$ can hardly ever be literally correct. Consider, for example, an experiment in which we draw the dichotomous variable *gender* and the continuous variables *speed* and *accuracy* of color naming from one pot and any arbitrary substantive personality theory T from the other pot. (If the reader objects to this absurdity, well and good, because that preposterous scenario is the one most unfavorable to the case Lykken and I are making.) Omniscient Jones knows the regression equation (in this instance also the causal equation, though they are not usually identical!) for males' color-naming score y to be

$$y = \beta_1 x_1 + \beta_2 x_2 + \beta_3 x_3 + \ldots + \beta_n x_n$$

so that the mean color-naming score of males is

$$\mu_m = \beta_1 \mu_{m_1} + \beta_2 \mu_{m_2} + \beta_3 \mu_{m_3} + \ldots + \beta_n \mu_{m_n}$$

The corresponding equation for females' means will be

$$\mu_f = \gamma_1 \mu_{f_1} + \gamma_2 \mu_{f_2} + \gamma_3 \mu_{f_3} + \ldots + \gamma_n \mu_{f_n}$$

In order for the parameter $\mu_m = \mu_f$, so that $H_0 : \delta = 0$ is a literally correct point value, either the β and γ weights and the means μ_{ij} of all of the determining variables (color vision, verbal fluency, aesthetic interest, number of conversations with mother about clothing, religiosity interest in seasonal changes in liturgical vestments, etc.—a long list) must be identical for boys and girls or, if not, differences in the μs must be delicately balanced with appropriate differences in the βs and γs so as to yield the same output means. I cannot imagine any social or biological scientist thinking that this could happen in the real world.

It would probably be worthwhile to know the average size of the crud factor, whether expressed as a correlation coefficient or a standardized mean difference, in various research domains in psychology; but researching this would be a rather thankless task. One easier study that should be done would be a large-scale archival sample in a couple of "soft" fields such as clinical and social psychology, in which the proportion of studies reaching a preassigned significance level α is plotted as a function of sample size, and a mathematically appropriate function fitted to those points. One could then answer the question, "What is the asymptote?" I record my confident prediction that the asymptote of this "significant result" function will be extremely close to $p = 1.00$. We do have some empirical evidence on this matter in a study by Lykken and myself (Meehl, 1990e); all of 105 pair-wise relationships between a hodgepodge of variables for high school students reached the .05 level of significance and 96% of them were significant at the 10^{-6} level. They involve, for example, such curious relations as between whether or not a teenager plays a musical instrument and to which of several Lutheran synods he belongs! With a sufficiently large sample, almost all of the 550 items of the MMPI are significant correlates of gender. In the early days of factor analysis employing orthogonal solutions, tests constructed with the aim of being factorially "pure" never turned out to be so. See other numerical examples in Meehl (1990a).

It has been suggested by defenders of null hypothesis testing that, although the crud factor may lead to a strong antecedent expectation of the falsity of H_0 for any given test, if tests are performed in several studies and each one yields significance in the predicted direction at some level α, we can combine these probabilities (the simplest way would be to merely multiply them, but I do not here enter the highly technical controversy about how best to put them together) and get a minuscule probability. There is something to this argument, but not very much. First, it still focuses attention upon the p value, that is, the improbability of getting a deviation if $\delta = 0$, and that is not the main point of the H_0-testing critics' objections. However, taking it as shown *in each individual experiment* that H_0 is false, we formulate the defender's argument thus: Assuming that everything is somewhat correlated with everything in the life sciences, the theorist has been making directional bets on the whole series of studies; if the atheoretical chance of guessing right, with the gigantic pots of theories and of observational variables that Meehl fantasizes, is one half for each guess (and neglecting imperfect power), then we should be allowed to use something like $.5^{10}$ when we look at 10 experiments that all "came out right." That is not a silly idea, and I readily concede that a big batch of H_0 refutations all going in the same direction must be deemed to provide considerable support for a theory that predicted them. However, I would not accept applying the multiplication principle of the probability calculus here, for two reasons.

First, it is an empirical fact over many domains of psychological research that we deal with a largely positive manifold. For example, in the case of intelligence and achievement, replicable negative correlations of subtests of an intelligence test, or of even "totally unrelated" achievement tests (e.g., spelling and art appreciation), almost never occur. Thorndike's dictum, which my undergraduate advisor Donald G. Paterson was fond of repeating, was that, "In psychology and sociology, all good things tend to go together." It is not, for instance, surprising to find a negative correlation between IQ and the incidence of tooth decay, although the explanation offered by dental hygienists in the 1920s was erroneous, because the true cause of this relationship is social class. So the chance of guessing the correct direction of a non-null difference is rarely only even, for a given empirical domain.

Second, most "interesting" psychological theories involve several "layers" or "levels" of theoretical constructs, and the layer that is closest in the causal chain to several observations may look pretty much the same in different theories. Taking my theory of schizotaxia as an example, one can easily come up with several plausible theories of why we might find a soft neurological sign (e.g., subclinical intention tremor) in the siblings of schizophrenes, theories that have no overlap in their "hard core" (Lakatos, 1970, 1974; Meehl, 1990a) with my schizotaxia conjecture, but that are eminently reasonable alternatives. There is no way to properly evaluate this point about accumulating successful directional predictions except to conduct large-scale archival studies as proposed by Faust and Meehl (1992).

The strongest rebuttal to this as a pro-H_0 argument is the well-known empirical finding in the research literature that you do not get highly consistent directional predictions for theories in most areas of soft psychology. You are lucky if your theory gives you successful directional predictions two thirds of the time. Here is where Sir Karl Popper enters the fray, in a way that does not depend on one's acceptance of his whole theory, but simply his emphasis upon the asymmetry between corroboration and falsification. It is incorrect to reason that if a substantive theory predicts a directional H_0 refutation correctly 7 times in 10 experiments and gets it wrong 3 times, then we have a "pretty good batting average for the theory." Given the crud factor, the seven correct predictions are weakly to moderately corroborative; but the three falsifications are—if accepted—*fatal*. It is not legitimate for the defender of H_0 testing to appeal to the problematic character of the other conjuncts in our corroboration formula to explain away the *modus tollens* falsifiers, meanwhile taking them for granted as unproblematic in considering the seven favorable outcomes. I repeat, this is not primarily a matter of α and β error rates; it goes through for any reasonable setting of the two kinds of errors.

STRONG VERSUS WEAK USE OF SIGNIFICANCE TESTS

In theory appraisal, significance tests may be used in a *strong* or a *weak* way, a distinction made by Meehl (1967; labeled as such in Meehl, 1990a, p. 116). This terminology is not a reference to the power function $(1 - \beta)$ or the size of α. It is not a question concerning the probability, confidence, confirmation, or corroboration of H at all. Rather, it asks what is the statistical hypothesis H that is being tested in order to appraise a substantive theory T, and how well can H serve to appraise T? The strong use of significance tests requires a strong theory, one capable of entailing a numerical value of the parameter, or a narrow range of theoretically tolerated values, or a specific function form (e.g., parabola) relating observables. Statistically significant deviation from the predicted point value, narrow interval, or curve type acts as a falsifier of the substantive theory. Hence, trying to refute the statistical hypothesis can function as a risky Popperian test or, for one who does not care for Popper but is an inductivist, as a Salmonian coincidence. The narrower the tolerated range of observable values, the riskier the test, and if the test is passed, the stronger the corroboration of the substantive theory. In the weak use, the theory is not powerful enough to make a point prediction or a narrow range prediction; it can say only that there is some nonzero correlation or some nonzero difference and, in almost all cases, to specify its algebraic direction. What makes this use weak, again, has nothing to do with the ratio $\alpha{:}\beta$, but involves the epistemic relation *between* the inference $H^*{:}\delta > 0$ and the alleged consequent confirmation of T.

The use of chi-square in social science provides a nice example of the difference between strong and weak uses. Pearson's (1900) classic article deriving what is often seen as his most important single contribution to biostatistics, the statistic chi-square, is titled: "On the Criterion That a Given System of Deviations From the Probable in the Case of a Correlated System of Variables Is Such That It Can Be Reasonably Supposed to Have Arisen From Random Sampling." Suppose some theory specifies a certain distribution of frequencies for various outcomes of throws of dice or colors of garden peas. The (strong) chi-square test is of whether the observed frequencies deviate from what the theory predicted. It was not until 4 years later that this same statistic was used in deriving the contingency coefficient, a statistic typically employed when the theory is not capable of predicting the tallies in various cells. The numerical prediction is based on multiplying marginals on the assumption of independence, but predicting (from a theory) that the two sets of categories being studied (such as eye color of siblings) are *not* statistically independent. In the strong use, the theory entails a set of numerical values, with a significant chi-square (indicating *departure* from the theoretically predicted values) functioning as a falsifier of the theory. In the weak use, the theory merely predicts "some (nonchance) relation," so a significant chi-square, falsifying statistical independence, tends to confirm the theory. What makes the weak use of a significance test weak is, of course, the crud factor, that there are numerous different theoretical ways that could account for some correlation or difference being nonzero; given the crud factor, a theory tested in this way takes only a small risk of being refuted if it is false. (Of course, the contingency coefficient could also be used strongly, if the substantive theory were strong enough to derive its numerical value, the *size* of a correlation of attributes. But in psychology that is almost never possible.)

There are special cases in the theory appraisal context in which refuting H_0 seems the appropriate statistical move rather than being merely a feeble substitute for something powerful (see Meehl, 1990a). The important one is the case of a strong theory according to which certain operations should yield a null effect. Here we have the strong use of a significance test that might be confused with the weak use. But here the point value predicted is $\delta = 0$, which the test attempts to refute, and *failing which refutation* the theory that predicts $\delta = 0$ is strongly corroborated. Recently, a radical theory in physics was proposed to the effect that gravitational force depended on something other than mass (the kind of elementary particle involved), or perhaps that there was a fifth force to be added to the received list (electromagnetic, gravitational, the strong and weak intranuclear forces). An experimental test involved lowering a plumbline into a deep mine shaft, for which the geological mineral surround was thoroughly known, and predicting its deflection, depending on the target element in the plumb. Result: A null effect. A good example in experimental psychology is latent learning, a disputed phenomenon with which my early research (with Kenneth MacCorquodale) was concerned. "Noncognitive" conditioning theories (Guthrie, Hull, Skinner) do not predict the latent learning phenomenon and cannot deal with it, although the Hullians attempted to do so by ingenious *ad-hoc*ery. If, during the "latent" (unreinforced) phase of such an experiment, rats show no increment in the strength of turning one way or the other in a T maze, but they show a preference when differential motivation or incentive is introduced, Tolman's cognitive theory predicts evidence of something having been learned that did not manifest itself previously, whereas the three SR theories predict a null result. Although Tolman's theory was too weak to predict a numerical point value, it did predict a deviation from the point $\delta = 0$, whereas that latter value was predicted by the three noncognitive competitor theories. Another example is telepathy, where the received theory—one might better say the received world view or metaphysic—predicts no transmission of information other than by photons, electrons, or sound waves. Thus, if a statistically significant amount of information is transmitted from one brain to another, absent any possibility of these kinds of physical pathways, we have evidence for a new kind of entity, force, or influence (which it is tempting to call "mental," because there is a *cognitive content*; and, following Brentano, we take *intentionality* as the earmark of the "mental").

The other helpful use of significant tests in the theoretical context is for a scientist deciding whether a certain line of research is worth pursuing. Suppose one of my graduate students has done an exploratory mini-experiment and tells me that in such and such a design 7 out of 12 rats made the predicted response. I agree that a description of a scientific experiment should be thought of rather like a recipe for baking cake (I believe it was B. F. Skinner who expressed this notion in conversation), so that what we ask is whether the recipe is described adequately enough that other competent cooks can make the cake by following it. If the experimental result replicates, we do not need a significance test. If it fails to replicate, the fact that it gave statistical significance when first reported is either dismissed as an improbable but always possible chance deviation, or simply left on the shelf as what the physicists call an "occult effect." The reproducibility, smoothness, and highly characteristic features of cumulative records (drawn by the rat!) in Skinner's 1938 classic are better science than any statistical significance tests, which is why the book contains none. But in some contexts matters are not so clear (e.g., maze learning—which is one of Skinner's reasons for rejecting the maze as a research instrument). In the discovery phase, what I as a research scientist want to know to help make up my mind whether I should attempt to replicate a pilot study with a larger sample involves what degree of credence I give to it as a genuine effect on the basis of the 12 subjects run by the student. It seems rational to do a sign test on the 7:5 tally and to conclude that this is such weak evidence of a departure from "chance" as not to be worthwhile pursuing when I have other more plausible effects to explore. A 12:0 split ($p < .01$) might make it rational to try for a replication. This kind of decision, which is not rare in scientific work, would be impaired as to rationality if we did not have significance tests in our tool kit.

Both the strong and the weak uses have their characteristic dangers. The weak use, wrongly using significance tests as if refuting the null hypothesis gives powerful support to a weak theory, is obviously dangerous. In the strong use, refutation of the statistical hypothesis is a potential falsifier of the substantive theory that entailed it, and the degree of threat to the theory corresponds to the statistical power. However, falsification of the theory in practice always means falsification of the conjunction on the left of the conceptual formula for theory appraisal; and so one must be careful not to pessimistically apply one's confidence in the falsification of the conjunction to an equal confidence in the falsification of the theory, as explained earlier. (Saying T is false neglects 31 other ways the left side of the theory appraisal formula can be false.) But a second danger lurks here also, about which the statistician has nothing useful to tell us from the formalism. Having concluded that the theory T is literally false as it stands, and that this is correctly inferred (which we can be confident about depending on the smallness of α and the degree of certainty we attach to the other components of the appraisal formula), it might be reasoned that, therefore, the theory should be wholly discarded. Popper has been misread as saying this, but of course it does not directly follow from his position, especially once he began to emphasize the verisimilitude ("truthlikeness") concept. A theory can be literally false, meaning that the conjunction of all of its postulates is false, which means that at least one of them is false; so that the same argument about conjunctions and disjunctions that we applied previously to the appraisal formula applies also to the conjunction of postulates that make up the theory. Whether all scientific theories are literally false as commonly alleged I do not discuss, although I think it is erroneous; but assuming that were true, we still would want to appraise theories as to their verisimilitude. Unfortunately, the verisimilitude concept has thus far resisted rigorous explication. I agree with Popper that (pending such rigorous explication, which may not be possible in mathematical terms) we simply cannot dispense with it. Consider, for example, a question such as the accuracy of a certain newspaper story: The answer could vary from a minor and unimportant slip (such as getting somebody's middle initial wrong) to its being a totally fabricated account in a state-controlled propaganda sheet (such as

Dr. Goebbels' fraudulent story of the Polish attack on the Gleiwitz radio transmitter, used as an excuse to invade Poland). I have made some tentative, rough-hewn steps toward formulating a metatheory of verisimilitude that takes a different approach from that of the logicians, but there is not space to discuss its merits and defects here (Meehl, 1990b, 1992a).

All theories in psychology, even in the most theoretically advanced "hard science" research domains, are at least incomplete, and in most domains, they are positively false as to what they do assert. Clarifying one's ideas about the strong and weak uses of significance tests is not as helpful as I had hoped when I first addressed this topic (Meehl, 1967). Answering a question about the point value or narrow interval of a statistical parameter does not tell us quite what we wanted to know in appraising the merits of a substantive theory. Even when the theory is so strong as to permit point predictions (as it is in special fields such as behavior genetics where, e.g., Meehl's dominant gene theory of schizotaxia leads to a point prediction about sibling concordance), the uncertainty of the auxiliaries, the doubtfulness of the *ceteris paribus* clause, the unreliability of measuring instruments, and so on, leave us wondering just what we should say when what appears to be a strong Popperian test is successfully passed or—even more so—is failed. "Error" here is a complicated mixture of conceptual error in the theory taken literally, along with conceptual error in the other conjuncts in the appraisal formula; the conceptual idealization leads to a numerical fuzziness, *even if* there were no errors of statistical inference of the kind conventionally addressed in statistics books. The history of science shows that—even for the most powerful of the exact sciences—numerical closeness to a theoretically predicted observational value is commonly taken as corroborative of a strong theory even if, strictly speaking, it is a falsifier because the observed value deviates "significantly" from the value predicted. That epistemological consideration greatly reduces the importance of the so-called "exact tests" or even "exact confidence intervals" dear to the hearts of statisticians and psychometricians.

A CORROBORATION INDEX FOR THEORY APPRAISAL

History of the advanced sciences shows that among the dozen or so properties and relations of theories that working scientists give weight to in theory appraisal, one of the most powerful is a theory's ability to derive numerical point predictions concerning the outcome of experimental measurements. Even when the numerical observation was known prior to a theory's formulation, if the derivation is "precise" (in a special sense I explain momentarily), it sometimes carries as much weight as the prediction of a numerically looser but novel or "surprising" observational finding. How often this happens, and under what social-cognitive circumstances, cannot be said until statistical studies of archival material in the history of science are conducted (Faust, 1984; Faust & Meehl, 1992; Meehl, 1992a, 1992b). In the meantime, one can only rely on anecdotal evidence as a working scientist, together with case studies by science historians. Brush (1989; see also Brush, 1995) has shown, for example, that the community of physicists was more impressed by general relativity's derivation of the anomalous Mercury perihelion—which had been known and puzzled over for a half-century before Einstein's 1916 exposition of general relativity—than they were by the allegedly "clinching" eclipse observations of 1919, so much emphasized by Eddington. I do not assert this ought to be the case; I merely point it out as the kind of historical episode that one must take into account in rational reconstruction of how scientists go about theory appraisal.

Independent convergence upon a theoretical number by qualitatively diverse experiments or statistical studies seems to exert an overwhelming influence on the convictions of the scientific community. A classic example is Perrin's (1916; see also Nye, 1972; Salmon, 1984) table showing the agreement of 13 independent observational methods for estimating Avagadro's number (the number of molecules in one gram molecular weight of a substance).

Perhaps the most powerful kind of theory corroboration occurs when a scientific theorist is able to combine *novelty* and *precision* as a derivation from theory, so that a new phenomenon or kind of qualitative observation is forecast from the new theory (an observation that had no rational expectation from background knowledge, from competing theories, or especially from the received theory), and the theory makes a numerically precise forecast that is confirmed. A theory's prediction of an observational numerical value—or if it is too weak to do that, its prediction that two or more different observational paths lead to a nearly identical inferred value—increases our strength of belief in the theory's verisimilitude, because if the theory had no truthlikeness, such a numerical agreement would be a Salmonian "strange coincidence." If one is a Popperian and disbelieves in induction (that is not my position, although I have strong Popperian sympathies in other respects), we say that the theory "surmounted a very risky hurdle"; it "took a big chance" in predicting with some exactitude something unknown. Failure to falsify an empirically dangerous test is what Popper meant by his term *corroboration*, as distinguished from the term *confirmation* employed by Carnap and other believers in induction. Fortunately, the dispute between inductivists and those philosophers of science who side with Popper in being skeptical about inductive logic need not concern us, because in this respect both lines of reasoning lead to the same methodological result.

But remember the fly in the ointment, arising from the logical structure of the corroboration formula presented earlier: the problematic character of the other conjuncts on the left side of the theory appraisal formula. It is often true in psychology that auxiliary theories A_x, instrumental theories A_i, or the *ceteris paribus* clause C_p are as problematic as the main theory T of interest. In addition to that problem, no psychologist believes that a theory is complete, although one may hope that none of the statements it makes are positively false. Also, in many areas of psychology it is usually pretentious to formulate strong theories that one cannot sincerely take literally. For these several reasons, precise predictions of numerical point values are difficult to come by. In rare cases (e.g., a dominant gene theory in behavior genetics) when we can make a numerical prediction, we cannot have much confidence that it will be exactly found in our observations because of the other components in the testing formula. This epistemologically loose situation leads us at times to count a "near miss" as almost as good as a numerical "hit," a practice that is also found in exact sciences such as astronomy, physics, and chemistry. Thus, what taken literally is a falsification is frequently an encouraging sign, especially in the early stages of theory construction, because "close enough" is a good reason for thinking that the theory has some merit (verisimilitude), despite not being exactly correct.

This reasoning leads us to seek a numerical index that will do justice to the methodological practice of giving positive weight to a "near miss" provided the prediction was sufficiently risky, given only background knowledge and absent our theory. The index I have proposed (Meehl, 1990a; 1990e) attempts to assess the riskiness of the observational prediction and the closeness to which it came. But I do not appraise closeness in terms of the conventional standard errors. What we mean by "closeness," as well as what we mean by "riskiness," depends on our background knowledge of the antecedently available range of numerical values, setting our theory (or competing theories) aside. I call that antecedent range of numerical values the *Spielraum*, following the 19th-century philosopher and statistician von Kries. The question of setting up a Spielraum and its rationale are discussed in Meehl (1990a), but the basic notion that risk and closeness should each be relativized to the Spielraum may be easily grasped in a commonsense, intuitive way:

> If I tell you that Meehl's theory of climate predicts that it will rain sometime next April, and this turns out to be the case, you will not be much impressed with my "predictive success." Nor will you be impressed if I predict more rain in April than in May, even showing three asterisks (for $p < .001$) in my *t*-test table! If I predict from my theory that it will rain on 7 of the 30 days in April, and it rains on exactly 7, you might perk up your ears a bit, but still you would be inclined to think of this as a "lucky coincidence." But suppose that I specify *which* 7 days in April it will rain and ring the bell; then you will start getting seriously interested in Meehl's meteorological conjectures. Finally, if I tell you that on April 4th it will rain 1.7 inches . . . and on April 9th 2.3 inches . . . and so forth, and get seven of these correct within reasonable tolerance, you will begin to think that Meehl's theory must

have a lot going for it. You may believe that Meehl's theory of the weather, like all theories, is, when taken literally, false, since probably all theories are false in the eyes of God, but you will at least say, to use Popper's language, that it is beginning to look as if Meehl's theory has considerable *verisimilitude*, that is, "truth-like-ness." (Meehl, 1978, pp. 817–818)

Or suppose I propound a genetic theory of mammalian embryology in reliance on which I claim to be able to predict the lengths of neonatal elephants' trunks with an average absolute error of .8 cm. You would not know whether to be impressed with my theory unless you knew the mean and (more important) the standard deviation of baby elephant trunks. Thus, if their mean length were 3 cm and the standard deviation 1 cm, my predictions average a 26% error and—worse—I could do just as well by simply guessing the mean each time.

To illustrate how a Spielraum might be specified when testing a theory in psychopathology, suppose I conjecture that 80%–90% of carefully diagnosed schizophrenes have become so on the basis of a schizotaxic brain, the latter due to an autosomal mutation completely penetrant for the integrative neural deficit. From this we infer that half of the siblings are schizotaxic. Reliability studies show that the *DSM* nosological label *schizophrenia* is about 90% correctly applied by skilled interviewers employing a quantified structured interview (e.g., SADS). Half the siblings should carry the dominant schizogene. Multiplying upper and lower bounds, we predict that from .360 to .405 of the sibs will be schizotaxic. This is the expected base rate range for a sibling schizotaxon estimated taxometrically (Meehl, 1995; Meehl & Yonce, 1994, 1996)—it does not assume perfect accuracy in classifying individuals—and it is the interval allowed by the theory, I in the index described shortly. If there were nothing heritable about schizophrenia, or the alleged schizotaxic soft neurology had nothing to do with it, the lower bound of a plausible Spielraum could be set at zero. An upper bound, as for DZ twins, would be .50, so here the Spielraum S is $.50 - .00 = .50$; hence the intolerance of the theory, In in the index, is $1 - I/S = 1 - (.405 - .360)/.50 = .91$, a pretty strong value for the "riskiness" component.

The same reasoning applies when a scientist appraises the accuracy of a measuring instrument or procedure. The standard error is the least informative in this respect, except in the strong use of a significance test. A percentage error is better, and it is commonly used among applied scientists (e.g., engineers). *Error in relation to an antecedently plausible range is often the most informative.* A numerical estimate with a 100-mile error is unacceptable in geography, mediocre in the solar system, brilliantly precise with respect to Alpha Centauri. In order to evaluate the bearing of an error (complement = "closeness," "accuracy," "precision"), what we most need to know is the range of values the physical world serves up to us, theory aside.

If this Spielraum reference is so important in powerful science appraisal, why do chemists and physicists not mention it? In those disciplines the notion is so universally understood and applied that they need no technical metatheoretical term for it. Everyone knows and daily applies the principle that a risky numerical prediction that turns out correct, or nearly correct, is a strong corroborator of the theory that accomplished this nice feat. Typically, it is in the late stages of refining and strongly challenging the limits of a well-entrenched theory that researchers in the exact sciences focus on the Popperian falsifiers, and at that point "close, but no cigar" becomes the ruling principle. Most of psychology is nowhere near that "ideal Popperian" stage of theory testing yet. Hence my former advocacy (Meehl, 1967, 1990a, 1990e) of the strong use of significance testing in psychology must be tempered.

Ideally, the theory is strong enough to derive a numerical observational value, such as the correlation of children's IQs with foster midparent IQs, or the incidence of a neurological sign in the siblings of schizophrenic patients on a dominant gene theory of schizotaxia (Meehl, 1962, 1989, 1990c, 1990d). In the life sciences, even a fairly strong theory cannot generate a numerical point value, but it may be strong enough to specify a numerical interval considerably narrower than the Spielraum. (Even a theoretical point value will be surrounded by a *measurement*-error interval, but I prefer to keep the *sampling* error dispersion out of my index.) The numerical interval that the theory allows being labeled I and the Spielraum S, we think of the ratio I/S as the theory's "relative tolerance" and the latter's complement $(1 - I/S)$ as the theory's intolerance, In. This functions as a crude measure of risk. Analogously, we measure the observed "closeness" as the complement of a relative error. If D is the deviation observed from the predicted point value, or the deviation from the edge of the interval predicted, then $(1 - D/S)$ is the experimental "closeness," Cl. Because I assume riskiness and closeness potentiate each other (i.e., they would, in a statistical study of the long-term history of successful and unsuccessful theories, display a Fisherian interaction effect), I multiply the two to get my confirmation index C_i provided by a particular experimental or statistical study. Thus, we have:

S: Spielraum;

I: interval tolerated by T;

I/S: relative tolerance of T;

In: $1 - (I/S)$ = intolerance of T;

D: deviation of observed value x_0 from edge of tolerated interval (= error);

D/S: relative error;

Cl: $1 - (D/S)$ = closeness.

Then the corroboration index C_i for the particular experiment is defined as:

$$C_i = (CI)(In)$$

Considering the best and worst cases, I standardize this index as C^*, which gives values lying in the familiar [0, 1] interval (Meehl, 1990a). I claim that the mean C^* value computed over a batch of empirical studies in which the theory is strong enough to make some sort of numerical prediction would be a more illuminating number to contemplate than a batch of significance tests refuting the null hypothesis.

One must resist the temptation to treat C^* as a probability merely because it lies in the interval [0, 1] as do its components. Even were they properly so interpretable, which is doubtful, no justification could be given for multiplying them in reliance on the independence assumption, clearly false. If the term *probable* is licit here, it is only in a loose epistemic (nonfrequentist, nonphysical) sense, that high values of C^* are not "likely" to arise in experiments whose numerical predictions flow from theories of low verisimilitude. I conceive this assumption as warranted mainly by history of science and scientific practice, although plausibility arguments can be offered in its favor from metatheoretical considerations. The (nonalgorithmic) epistemic move from a significance test or confidence interval—despite their being numerified—to a claim that the substantive theory T is thereby supported relies on exactly the same metatheoretical principle. But doesn't a quasi-Bayesian worry arise about the unknown distribution of values over the Spielraum, despite our eschewing a probability interpretation of C^*? (That we usually do not know this distribution is a further objection to writing $C^* = p$.) Suppose a crooked scientist routinely "predicts" numerical values at the middle of the Spielraum, setting a low-tolerance I, pretending these predictions are theoretically derived. Will this shady practice, relying on a sort of "least squares hopefulness," tend to produce a phony successful run of C^*s? No, it will not, for several reasons. First, most real-world experiments on interesting theories do not yield numerical values close to the Spielraum midpoint; if our pseudo-theorist sets the tolerance interval I low enough to be capable of generating an impressive C^* when the closeness component is good, the closeness component will not usually be good. Second, verisimilar competing theories that differentiate predicted locations will do better, as an algebraic necessity. Third, as the research data accumulate, it will become apparent that the mean and dispersion of our faker's errors are readily attributable to the average empirical bias of the midpoint prediction and the observed dispersion, a suspicious fact. (In the generalized correlation index, if the residual variance equals the predictand's total variance, C.I. = 0.) Fourth—the best safeguard—one does not treat a theorist's track record as if it arose from a black box predicting device. We require of any set of predictions to know how the *theory*, not the theorist, derives them. Guessing the center, even on the rare occasions when the center closely approximates the empirical mean, does not qualify conceptually as theory-derived. A mindless, automatic use of C^* as a truth-litmus test is, of course, unacceptable. *Rational interpretation of any statistic or index is subject to Carnap's Total Evidence Rule.*

Why propose an index of this sort, for which no exact "probabilifying" tables, such as those for F, chi-square, and t, exist or are likely to be constructed in the foreseeable future? Even assuming that those table values were precise for an actual life science situation (which they are not), their numbers denote conditional probabilities on the null hypothesis, and that is not the *kind* of probability that we seek in appraising a substantive scientific theory. I hope this has become clear from what has been explained here. I take the position (which I believe to be that of most philosophers of science and at least a sizable minority of applied statisticians and psychometricians) that it is better to have an index that appraises theory performance (corroboration, confirmation, degree of support) than it is to have a pseudo-exact number that only represents the first step in that chain of inference, namely, "something other than chance seems to be going on here." Accepting the view that no algorithm is capable of delivering a genuine probability$_1$ number for literal theoretical truth or quantifying a false theory's verisimilitude, we settle for less. My C^* is, of course, not a probability; it is an index of one aspect of empirical performance.

Second, I submit that the formula to some degree "speaks for itself," once its terms are understood. We have a standardized number lying in the familiar interval $[0, 1]$ whose upper and lower bounds are approached when certain extreme epistemic situations have arisen. That is, if our substantive causal theory is so weak that it tolerates almost all of the antecedently possible numerical range (i.e., it takes a negligible risk), a "successful" observational outcome provides only weak support. If, on the other hand, the theory tolerates a moderate numerical range, or even a fairly small one, but the observations come nowhere near the predicted interval, then the theory surely receives no support from this experiment. Finally, if the theory is strong enough to prescribe a very narrow range of the antecedently conceivable Spielraum, and our experimental result falls within that range, we will get a corroboration index at the high end of the interval close to 1, which is obviously what we would want. That there are not precise confidence meanings attached to regions of this index should not bother anybody who understands the difference between falsification of the statistical hypothesis H_0 and resulting empirical corroboration of a substantive causal theory T, because nobody has ever proposed a useable algorithm for that important last step either.

Third, it is presently feasible to conduct Monte Carlo studies employing postulated theoretical structures with varying parameters. One can degrade the true theory T by increasingly severe deletions, additions, or amendments of its theoretical postulates, supplementing this impairment by throwing random measurement and sampling error on top of the increasingly deviant conceptual structures. In this way one can investigate the rough metrical properties of such an index.

Finally, there are plenty of scientific theories whose rise and fall is traceable in detail in the archives so that, given willingness to expend the effort, the empirical properties of the index in various research domains can be ascertained. It can be argued (Faust & Meehl, 1992) that calibration of such indexes on the basis of large-scale archival research in the history of science would be well worth the trouble, perhaps as valuable as the astronomers' gigantic catalog of stars or the recent mapping of the human genome. To develop this line of thought would require a long excursion into current controversies in metatheory (a preferable term to "philosophy of science," for reasons given in Meehl, 1992a, p. 340, fn. 2), but that is beyond the scope of this chapter. However, I urge the reader to recognize that the problem of null hypothesis testing as well as other problems of applied statistics depend at least as much on the resolution of controversies in metatheory as they do on clarifying our conceptual interpretations of the formalism. As I stated at the outset, hardly any of the controversies in the applications of mathematical statistics arise from strictly mathematical disagreements.

Why is meta-analysis—a powerful tool in social science research—not suitable for this purpose?

> Meta-analysis was developed to study outcomes of interventions (e.g., influence of class size, efficacy of psychotherapy or psychotropic drugs) rather than as a method of appraising the verisimilitude of substantive theories. We do not normally assume *theoretical corroboration* to be a monotone function, even stochastically, of *effect size*; and in developed sciences an observed value can, of course, be "too large" as often as "too small." . . . [Further, a] representative ("typical") effect size, whether of aggregated or disaggregated studies, is interpreted or qualified in meta-analysis via estimates of its standard error, emphasizing its trustworthiness as a numerical value. This statistical stability (under the laws of chance) is a very different question from how closely the effect approximates a theoretically predicted value. More importantly, it does not ask how "risky" the latter was in terms of the theoretically tolerated interval, in relation to the *a priori* range of possibilities. These two questions, taken jointly as the basis of all theoretical appraisal, require a different approach from that of evaluating technological outcomes in a pragmatic context. (Meehl, 1990e, p. 242)

The C^* index taps the interaction effect between risk and closeness, potentiating each by the other as a multiplier.

An objection to the proposed corroboration index C^* is an element of arbitrariness in specifying the Spielraum. I readily concede that this presents a problem, but I think not a serious one, for several nonexclusive reasons that tend cumulatively to minimize the problem while recognizing its existence, qualitatively speaking. First, in the "soft" areas of psychology, where refuting H_0 is most widely abused under the misconception that it provides a strong test of weak theories, the great preponderance of studies express their empirical findings with a dimensionless "pure" number, such as a probability or base rate lying in the interval [0, 1], or some form of correlation index (Pearson's r, biserial, tetrachoric, ϕ-coefficient, η, κ, and so on). These indexes of association are mathematically constructed so as to fall in the correlation interval [0, 1], although one must sometimes pay attention to additional constraints imposed by the data (e.g., the upper bound on a ϕ-coefficient set by disparity between the marginals). Factor loadings, standardized regression weights, and path coefficients (which are merely standardized regression weights for the subset of variables conjectured to be "causally upstream" from the predictand) are also pure numbers lying within the familiar [0, 1] interval. In noncorrelational studies employing randomized *experimental* treatments analyzed by Fisher's powerful method, the total sum of squares is decomposable into components associated with treatments and their interactions, with a residual that is a composite of sampling and measurement errors. The ratios of all these quantities to the total sum of squares lie in that standard interval [0, 1]. Although in a late stage of cliometric research it may be found that some fancier way of specifying the Spielraum is more informative, an obvious way to avoid arbitrariness in the present primitive state of actuarial metatheory is to define the Spielraum in terms of these pure number indexes—probabilities, correlations, loadings, β-weights, proportions of variance accounted for, and the like.

Second, in research domains where physical units of performance are the measure, one usually will have upper and lower bounds set by known dispositions of the organism (e.g., thresholds, physiological limits) or by the definition of the task. Thus in a maze-learning experiment, the worst score a rat can get is to enter every cul and the best is error-free performance. In the operant conditioning chamber, an animal may press the lever zero times in an hour or at a very high limiting rate (such as found in lean fixed-ratio schedules). These kinds of limits come not from the algebra of a correlation index, but from definitions, physical facts, and our "background knowledge" as the philosophers call it.

Third, complaining as I do against the atrocious practice of reporting significance tests without giving means and standard deviations, I, of course, would insist that presentation of C^* values be associated with statements of the tolerance interval derived from the theory and the Spielraum specified, permitting the reader to recompute a C^* using a Spielraum that seems more appropriate. That the probative weight of various values of C^* remains a matter of scholarly judgment is unavoidable, but it is no different from the present situation in which, having inferred from a refutation of H_0 that H^* holds (i.e., a directional difference $\delta > 0$ predicted by a weak theory T exists), one then uses one's (more or less rational) "scientific judgment" in appraising how much corroboration of the theory this statistical trend provides. I record my prediction that nothing short of a Faust–Meehl cliometric research program will do better than that.

That the values of C^* computed on the basis of two different Spielraum values are not linear transformations of one another over a range of experiments is regrettable. But I see no way to solve that; and here again, that is not very different from the familiar nonlinearity of different measures of association applied to a data set that is legitimately analyzable in more than one way. We do not ordinarily have occasion to compare corroboration of theories across domains. The working scientist's problem of appraisal is comparing two theories to explain the facts of a given domain of interest, or, if there is only one theory available, to ask whether it is well or weakly corroborated on the evidence to date. There are two important exceptions to this, however: the fund-granting agency deciding where to place its bets and the individual researcher planning the next few years of a research career. Significance tests obviously provide no decision algorithm for those cases either!

A researcher might adopt an inflated value of S to make it look good for a favored theory, or a very small one to make it look bad for a competing theory. Unfortunately, both components of the C^* index work in the same direction for such cases, but the reader can deflate the Spielraum if editors insist upon an adequate presentation of the data that go into the index. It is, of course, no objection to say that editors or referees *may* be careless in this respect, inasmuch as they are today routinely negligent in not requiring an adequate presentation of the data that enter into significance tests, or even confidence belts.

The tolerance I is less subject to this worry. Even a weak theory cannot plausibly be employed to derive a tolerance unless it is at least strong enough to justify the value of I employed, and here an inflated or deflated I works oppositely in the two components of the formula for C^*. If the investigator favors the theory and sets an inflated tolerance (so that the observed value is very likely to fall within the allowed range, which is itself therefore a large proportion of S), then the riskiness embodied in the other multiplier component is correspondingly reduced. In this respect, the assignment of a tolerance is analogous to the usual problem in significance testing of the trade-off between α and β errors.

CONCLUSIONS

Null-hypothesis testing has a proper place in social science research, but it has been criticized because of its widespread mindless abuse. Some have even proposed that H_0-testing be banned from American Psychological Association journals; such an editorial policy would constitute illegitimate censorship. Competent scholars persist in strong disagreement, ranging from some who think H_0-testing is pretty much all right as practiced, to others who think it is never appropriate. Most critics fall somewhere between these extremes, and they differ among themselves as to their main *reasons* for complaint. Under such circumstances, the proposed proscription of all H_0 testing would be a form of thought control, as foreign to the spirit of science as political correctness or religious orthodoxy. No such draconian measure should be contemplated when a few simple editorial rules would largely cure the disease, rules that editors should have been applying all along, given what is known. When null hypothesis testing is appropriate for the task:

1. Confidence intervals should be stated before H_0-tests are even mentioned.

2. Having stated a confidence interval, it would be permissible to add, "Because $\delta = \mu_1 - \mu_2 = 0$ falls outside the confidence belt, it is unplausible to explain the observed difference as arising from random sampling error." The misleading term *significant* is thus avoided; but it would be bizarre to require that a scientist state the confidence belt but forbid mention of a deductive consequence of it! I might be willing to forbid use of this cancerous term, if stating its legitimate *content* (nonmisleadingly) is allowed.

3. If inferences are made by contrasting significant and nonsignificant differences, the statistical powers must be stated.

4. A suitable measure of overlap must be computed (e.g., the percent of the experimental group exceeding the 10th, 25th, 50th, 75th, and 90th percentiles of the control group).

5. In the discussion section it must be explicitly stated that because the semantic contents of the counter-null hypothesis H^*: $\delta > 0$ and the substantive theory T are not equivalent—T implying H^*, but not conversely—proving H^* by refuting H_0 provides only weak corroboration of the theory. (This last is not imposing Meehl's philosophy of science on others; it is merely stating a truism found in any freshman logic text.)

Most important, researchers should distinguish statistical from epistemic questions, that is, when they are making an inference concerning a parameter (point value, range, slope, sign) from a statistic versus when they are appraising the verisimilitude of a substantive theory (causal, compositional, or historical) on the basis of the inferred parameters. The important distinction between these completely different kinds of inference should be clarified and emphasized in statistical texts and lectures. Failure to see this distinction engenders the tendency to think that, because α is chosen to be small ($p < .05$ or $< .01$), refuting H_0 somehow subjects the substantive theory T to a strong, "risky" test, so that passing this test provides strong evidentiary support for the theory, which it usually does not.

In general, the use of null hypothesis testing is more defensible in technological contexts than in theoretical contexts. Technological evaluation always involves at least an implicit weighting of utilities and disutilities of the two kinds of inferential errors. Sometimes the rational decision policy is betting on the reality of an observed algebraic sign whether statistically significant or not.

In correlational studies of (usually weak) theories in "soft" psychology, very few empirical variables are literally independent (i.e., H_0 is quasi-always false, theory aside), hence a theory-mediated prediction of H_0 being false usually can provide only weak theory corroboration. The crud factor ("everything tends to correlate with everything") corresponds in empirical research to the logician's warning that the third figure of the implicative syllogism is formally invalid. Given $p \supset q$ and q, inferring p is the formal fallacy of affirming the consequent. The substantive empirical meaning of this logical truism is the existence of numerous alternative theories capable of deriving a mere non-null difference.

The distinction between the strong and the weak use of significance tests is logical or epistemological; it is not a statistical issue. The weak use of significance tests asks merely whether the observations are attributable to "chance" (i.e., no relation exists) when a weak theory can only predict some sort of relation, but not what or how much. The strong use of significance tests asks whether observations differ significantly from the numerical values that a strong theory predicts, and it leads to the fourth figure of the syllogism—$p \supset q$, $\sim q$, infer $\sim p$—which is formally valid, the logician's *modus tollens* ("destroying mode"). Psychologists should work hard to formulate theories that, even if somewhat weak, permit derivation of numerical point values or narrow ranges, yielding the possibility of *modus tollens* refutations.

All psychological theories are imperfect, either incomplete or positively false as they are stated. Hence one expects confidence intervals (and H_0 testing as part of them) to falsify meritorious theories that possess enough verisimilitude to deserve continued amendment, testing, and expansion. In the early stages of a good theory's life, a "near-miss" of prediction is an encouraging finding despite being a literal falsification of the theory and associated conjectures involved in the observational test. It is therefore desirable to have a quantitative index of how risky the test was and how close the prediction came, and for this purpose I have proposed a corroboration index C^* that potentiates closeness by risk.

Finally, the most important property of an empirical finding is intersubjective replicability, that other investigators, relying on the description of what was done, will (almost always) make the same (or closely similar) observations.

REFERENCES

Bakan, D. (1966). The test of significance in psychological research. *Psychological Bulletin, 66,* 423–437.

Brush, S. G. (1989). Prediction and theory evaluation: the case of light bending. *Science, 246,* 1124–1129.

Brush, S. G. (1995). Dynamics of theory change: The role of predictions. *PSA 1994, 2,* 133–145.

Carnap, R. (1945). The two concepts of probability. *Philosophy and Phenomenological Research, 5,* 513–532. Reprinted in H. Feigl & W. Sellars (Eds.), *Readings in philosophical analysis* (pp. 330–348). New York: Appleton–Century–Crofts, 1949. Reprinted in H. Feigl & M. Broadbeck (Eds.), *Readings in the philosophy of science* (pp. 438–455). New York: Appleton–Century–Crofts, 1953.

Carver, R. P. (1978). The case against statistical significance testing. *Harvard Educational Review, 48,* 378–399.

Cohen, J. (1994). The earth is round ($p < .05$). *American Psychologist, 49,* 997–1003.

Earman, J. (1986). *A primer on determinism.* Boston: D. Reidel.

Faust, D. (1984). *The limits of scientific reasoning.* Minneapolis: University of Minnesota Press.

Faust, D., & Meehl, P. E. (1992). Using scientific methods to resolve enduring questions within the history and philosophy of science: Some illustrations. *Behavior Therapy, 23,* 195–211.

Hogben, L. (1968). *Statistical theory.* New York: Norton.

Lakatos, I. (1970). Falsification and the methodology of scientific research programmes, In I. Lakatos & A. Musgrave (Eds.), *Criticism and the growth of knowledge* (pp. 91–195). Cambridge, England: Cambridge University Press. Reprinted in J. Worrall & G. Currie (Eds.), *Imre Lakatos: Philosophical papers: Vol. I. The methodology of scientific research programmes* (pp. 8–101). New York: Cambridge University Press, 1978.

Lakatos, I. (1974). The role of crucial experiments in science *Studies in the History and Philosophy of Science, 4,* 309–325.

Lykken, D. E. (1968). Statistical significance in psychological research. *Psychological Bulletin, 70,* 151–159.

Meehl, P. E. (1962). Schizotaxia, schizotypy, schizophrenia *American Psychologist, 17,* 827–838. Reprinted in Meehl, *Psychodiagnosis: Selected papers* (pp. 135–155). Minneapolis: University of Minnesota Press, 1973.

Meehl, P. E. (1967). Theory-testing in psychology and physics: A methodological paradox. *Philosophy of Science, 34,* 103–115. Reprinted in D. E. Morrison & R. E. Henkel (Eds.), *The significance test controversy* (pp. 252–266). Chicago: Aldine, 1970.

Meehl, P. E. (1978). Theoretical risks and tabular asterisks: Sir Karl, Sir Ronald, and the slow progress of soft psychology. *Journal of Consulting and Clinical Psychology, 46,* 806–834.

Meehl, P. E. (1989). Schizotaxia revisited. *Archives of General Psychiatry, 46,* 935–944.

Meehl, P. E. (1990a). Appraising and amending theories: The strategy of Lakatosian defense and two principles that warrant using it. *Psychological Inquiry, 1,* 108–141, 173–180.

Meehl, P. E. (1990b). *Corroboration and verisimilitude: Against Lakatos'"sheer leap of faith"* (Working Paper No. MCPS–90–01). Minneapolis: University of Minnesota, Center for Philosophy of Science.

Meehl, P. E. (1990c). Schizotaxia as an open concept. In A. I. Rabin, R. Zucker, R. Emmons, & S. Frank (Eds.), *Studying persons and lives* (pp. 248–303). New York: Springer.

Meehl, P. E. (1990d). Toward an integrated theory of schizotaxia, schizotypy, and schizophrenia. *Journal of Personality Disorders, 4,* 1–99.

Meehl, P. E. (1990e). Why summaries of research on psychological theories are often uninterpretable. *Psychological Reports, 66,* 195–244. Also in R. E. Snow & D. Wiley (Eds.), *Improving inquiry in social science: A volume in honor of Lee J. Cronbach* (pp. 13–59). Hillsdale, NJ: Erlbaum, 1991.

Meehl, P. E. (1992a). Cliometric metatheory: The actuarial approach to empirical, history-based philosophy of science. *Psychological Reports, 71,* 339–467.

Meehl, P. E. (1992b). The Miracle Argument for realism: An important lesson to be learned by generalizing from Carrier's counter-examples. *Studies in History and Philosophy of Science, 23,* 267–282.

Meehl, P. E. (1995). Bootstraps taxometrics: Solving the classification problem in psychopathology. *American Psychologist, 50,* 266–275.

Meehl, P. E., & Yonce, L. J. (1994). Taxometric analysis: I. Detecting taxonicity with two quantitative indicators using means above and below a sliding cut (MAMBAC procedure). *Psychological Reports, 74,* 1059–1274.

Meehl, P. E., & Yonce, L. J. (1996). Taxometric analysis: II. Detecting taxonicity using covariance of two quantitative indicators in successive intervals of a third indicator (MAXCOV procedure). *Psychological Reports, 78,* 1091–1227.

Morrison, D. E., & Henkel, R. E. (Eds.). (1970). *The significance test controversy.* Chicago: Aldine.

Nye, M. J. (1972). *Molecular reality.* London, England: Macdonald.

O'Hear, A. (1980). *Karl Popper.* Boston: Routledge & Kegan Paul.

Pearson, K. (1900). On the criterion that a given system of deviations from the probable in the case of a correlated system of variables is such that it can be reasonably supposed to have arisen from random sampling. *Philosophical Magazine, Series V.1,* 157–175.

Perrin, J. B. (1916). *Atoms* (D. L. Hammick, Trans.). New York: Van Nostrand.

Popper, K. R. (1959). *The logic of scientific discovery.* New York: Basic Books. (Original work published 1934)

Popper, K. R. (1962). *Conjectures and refutations.* New York: Basic Books.

Popper, K. R. (1983). *Postscript to the logic of scientific discovery: Vol. I. Realism and the aim of science.* Totowa, NJ: Rowman and Littlefield.

Reichenbach, H. (1938). *Experience and prediction.* Chicago: University of Chicago Press.

Rozeboom, W. W. (1960). The fallacy of the null hypothesis significance test. *Psychological Bulletin, 57,* 416–428.

Salmon, W. C. (1984). *Scientific explanation and the causal structure of the world.* Princeton, NJ: Princeton University Press.

Schilpp, P. A. (Ed.). (1974). *The philosophy of Karl Popper.* LaSalle, IL: Open Court.

Schmidt, F. L. (1996). Statistical significance testing and cumulative knowledge in psychology: Implications for training of researchers. *Psychological Methods, 1,* 115–129.

Simon, H. A. (1945). Statistical tests as a basis for "yes-no" choices. *Journal of the American Statistical Association, 40,* 80–84.

Skinner, B. F. (1938). *The behavior of organisms: An experimental analysis.* New York: Appleton–Century.

Author Index

Subject Index